T0224494

Communications
in Computer and Information Science 939

Commenced Publication in 2007
Founding and Former Series Editors:
Phoebe Chen, Alfredo Cuzzocrea, Xiaoyong Du, Orhun Kara, Ting Liu,
Krishna M. Sivalingam, Dominik Ślęzak, and Xiaokang Yang

More information about this series at http://www.springer.com/series/7899

Sukumar Nandi · Devesh Jinwala ·
Virendra Singh · Vijay Laxmi ·
Manoj Singh Gaur · Parvez Faruki (Eds.)

Security and Privacy

Second ISEA International Conference, ISEA-ISAP 2018
Jaipur, India, January, 9–11, 2019
Revised Selected Papers

 Springer

Editors
Sukumar Nandi
Indian Institute of Technology Guwahati
Guwahati, India

Virendra Singh
Indian Institute of Technology Bombay
Mumbai, India

Manoj Singh Gaur
Indian Institute of Technology Jammu
Jammu, Jammu and Kashmir, India

Devesh Jinwala
Indian Institute of Technology Jammu
Jammu, India

Vijay Laxmi
Malaviya National Institute of Technology
Jaipur, India

Parvez Faruki
Department of Technical Education
Government of Gujarat
Rajkot, India

ISSN 1865-0929   ISSN 1865-0937   (electronic)
Communications in Computer and Information Science
ISBN 978-981-13-7560-6   ISBN 978-981-13-7561-3   (eBook)
https://doi.org/10.1007/978-981-13-7561-3

This Springer imprint is published by the registered company Springer Nature Singapore Pte Ltd.
The registered company address is: 152 Beach Road, #21-01/04 Gateway East, Singapore 189721, Singapore

Preface

This volume contains the proceedings of the Second ISEA Conference on Security and Privacy (ISEA-ISAP 2018) held at Malaviya National Institute of Technology Jaipur during January 9–11, 2019. The conference was funded by phase II of ISEA (Information Security Education Awareness) project, an initiative of Ministry of Electronics and Information Technology, Govt, of India. The conference was organized by the Department of Computer Science and Engineering, MNIT Jaipur. This event was also co-hosted by the Indian Institute of Technology Jammu (IIT Jammu), the Center for Development of Advanced Computing (CDAC), and the Indian Institute of Information Technology Kota (IIIT Kota).

Six technical sessions were held wherein 21 papers were presented. These papers were selected from a total of 87 submissions through a rigourous double-blind review process. Any paper (1) revealing the authors' identity directly or indirectly and/or (2) exhibiting more than 5% match with any single source and/or overall match exceeding 20% was rejected. Each paper was assigned at least three reviewers. A paper was selected only after it received at least three favorable reviews. A team of 60+ reviewers from India and abroad helped in selecting quality papers for the conference. The selected papers were related to the domains of authentication and access control, malware analysis, network security, privacy preservation, secure software systems, and social network analytics.

This year, the conference comprised five invited keynotes, two invited tutorials, and two industry talks. The details are as follows:

Keynotes

1. "Generating Software Tests," Prof. Andreas Zeller, CISPA Helmholtz Center for Information Security, University of Saarland, Germany.
2. "Secure e-Voting," Bimal Roy, Indian Statistical Institute, Kolkata, India.
3. "From Gutenberg to Smartphones: Inferring Keypress from Side Channels," Mauro Conti, University of Padua, Italy.
4. "Correctness-by-Construction for Safe and Secure Systems," Dominique Méry, Telecom Nancy, Université de Lorraine, France.
5. "An 18th Century Mathematician, a $336 Million Patent, and Software Verifiability," Suresh C. Kothari, Richardson Professor (Department of Electrical and Computer Engineering, Iowa State University), President and Founder (EnSoft Corp)

Tutorials

1. "Secure System Engineering," Chester Rebario, IIT Madras
2. "Certification of Cryptographic Products," MR Muralidharan, IISc Bangalore

Industry Talks

1. "Digitalization Changing Paradigm of Cyber Security," Ms. Rama Vedashree, CEO, Data Security Council of India
2. "Massively Scalable Secure Wi-Fi Networks," Pravin Bhagwat, Arista Networks

The event was attended by 60+ delegates from academic institutions, CDAC, and MEITY. The third edition of the conference will be organized at IIT Guwahati, India during December 9–11, 2019.

January 2019

Sukumar Nandi
Devesh Jinwala
Virendra Singh
Vijay Laxmi
Manoj Singh Gaur
Parvez Faruki

Organization

Steering Committee

N. Balakrishnan	Indian Institute of Science, Bangalore, India
C. E. Veni Madhavan	Indian Institute of Science, Bangalore, India
R. K. Shyamasundar	Indian Institute of Technology Bombay, India
V. Kamakoti	Indian Institute of Technology Madras, India
Bimal Roy	Indian Statistical Institute, Kolkata, India
B. K. Murty	Ministry of Electronics and Information Technology, Government of India, India
Sh. Sanjay Kumar Vyas	Ministry of Electronics and Information Technology, Government of India, India

Reviewers

Sukumar Nandi (TPC Chair)	Indian Institute of Technology Guwahati, India
Virendra Singh (TPC Chair)	Indian Institute of Technology Bombay, India
Devesh Jinwala (TPC Chair)	Indian Institute of Technology Jammu, India
Alwyn Roshan Pais	National Institute of Technology Surathkal, India
Anil Saini	CSIR-Central Electronics Engineering Research Institute, Pilani, India
Anish Mathuria	Dhirubhai Ambani Institute of Information and Communication Technology, Gandhinagar, India
Ashok Singh Sairam	Indian Institute of Technology Guwahati, India
Atilla Elci	Aksaray University, Turkey
Ayan Mahalanobis	Indian Institute of Science Education and Research Pune, India
Badri Narayan Subudhi	Indian Institute of Technology Jammu, India
Bela Genge	Petru Maior University of Tirgu Mures, Romania
Chirag Navinchandra Modi	National Institute of Technology Goa, India
Chandra Sekaran	National Institute of Technology Surathkal, India
Debdeep Mukhopadhyay	Indian Institute of Technology Kharagpur, India
Dipanwita Roychowdhury	Indian Institute of Technology Kharagpur, India
Emmanuel S. Pilli	Malaviya National Institute of Technology Jaipur, India
Ferdous Ahmed	Indian Institute of Information Technology Guwahati, India
Gaurav Bansod	Symbiosis Institute of Technology, Pune, India

Gaurav Sharma	Université libre de Bruxelles, Belgium
Gaurav Somani	Central University of Rajasthan, India
Jaidhar C. D.	National Institute of Technology Surathkal, India
Jie Wang	University of Massachusetts Lowell, USA
Justin Cappos	New York University, USA
Kaushal Shah	Sardar Vallabhbhai National Institute of Technology Surat, India
Keshavamurthy B. N.	National Institute of Technology Goa, India
Keyur Parmar	Sardar Vallabhbhai National Institute of Technology Surat, India
Manik Lal Das	Dhirubhai Ambani Institute of Information and Communication Technology, Gandhinagar, India
Manoj Singh Gaur	Indian Institute of Technology Jammu, India
Mark Zwolinski	University of Southampton, UK
Mazdak Zamani	Felician University, USA
Mauro Conti	University of Padua, Italy
Mayank Dave	National Institute of Technology Kurukshetra, India
Meenakshi Tripathi	Malaviya National Institute of Technology Jaipur, India
Mikhail Gofman	California State University Fullerton, USA
M. P. Singh	National Institute of Technology Patna, India
Neminath Hubballi	Indian Institute of Technology Indore, India
Nishant Doshi	Pandit Deendayal Petroleum University, Gandhinagar, India
P. Santhi Thilagam	National Institute of Technology Surathkal, India
P. Sateesh Kumar	Indian Institute of Technology Roorkee, India
Parvez K. Faruki	AVPTI, Rajkot, India
Prabhat Kumar	National Institute of Technology Patna, India
Prabhat Kushwaha	Indian Institute of Technology Kharagpur, India
Priyadarshi Nanda	University of Technology Sydney, Australia
Rajat Subhra Chakraborty	Indian Institute of Technology Kharagpur, India
Rashmi Ranjan Rout	Indian Institute of Technology Kharagpur, India
Ramesh Babu Battula	Malaviya National Institute of Technology Jaipur, India
Sankita Patel	Sardar Vallabhbhai National Institute of Technology Surat, India
Sangram Ray	National Institute of Technology Sikkim, India
Santanu Sarkar	Indian Institute of Technology Madras, India
Santosh K. Vipparthi	Malaviya National Institute of Technology Jaipur, India
Shailesh Sathe	Visvesvaraya National Institute of Technology, Nagpur, India
Shweta Bhandari	Malaviya National Institute of Technology Jaipur, India

Shweta Saharan	Malaviya National Institute of Technology Jaipur, India
Smita Naval	National Institute of Technology Warangal, India
Spiridon Bakiras	City University of New York, USA
Subhasish Dhal	Indian Institute of Information Technology Guwahati, India
Sushmita Ruj	Indian Statistical Institute, Kolkata, India
Suvrojit Das	National Institute of Technology Durgapur, India
Syed Taqi Ali	Visvesvaraya National Institute of Technology, Nagpur, India
Subrata Acharya	Towson University, USA
Suman Bala	Université libre de Bruxelles, Belgium
Umesh Deshpande	Visvesvaraya National Institute of Technology, Nagpur, India
Venkatesan S.	Indian Institute of Information Technology Allahabad, India
Vijay Laxmi	Malaviya National Institute of Technology Jaipur, India
Vineeta Jain	Malaviya National Institute of Technology Jaipur, India
Vinit Jakhetiya	Indian Institute of Technology Jammu, India
Vinod P.	SCMS School of Engineering and Technology, Ernakulam, India
Zahra Pooranian	University of Padua, Italy

Organizing Committee

Manoj Singh Gaur (General Chair)	Indian Institute of Technology Jammu, India
Sukumar Nandi (Technical Program Chair)	Indian Institute of Technology Guwahati, India
Devesh Jinwala (Technical Program Chair)	Indian Institute of Technology Jammu, India
Virendra Singh (Technical Program Chair)	Indian Institute of Technology, Mumbai, India
Vijay Laxmi (Organizing Chair)	Malaviya National Institute of Technology Jaipur, India
Parvez Faruki (Publication Chair)	AVPTI, Rajkot, India

Contents

Authentication and Access Control

Secure Opportunistic Data Exchange Using Smart Devices in 5G/LTE-A Networks

Sumit Kumar Tetarave[(✉)] and Somanath Tripathy[(✉)]

Department of Computer Science and Engineering,
Indian Institute of Technology Patna, Patna 801103, India
{sktetarave,som}@iitp.ac.in

Abstract. Popularity of smart phones is increasing rapidly with the facility of Internet through 5G/LTE-A networks. Internet helps to share contents and brings about digital activities through smart devices. Meanwhile, it is a challenging task to communicate or access data in absence of the primary network signal. For members of such a disconnected network, the opportunity of data exchange through a visiting smart phone user, would be a prominent solution. However, security in such a scenario would be the major concern due to the possibility of mishandling of users' data and therefore, data to be exchanged only to authentic users. In this work, we propose a security framework for opportunistic data exchange in cellular networks. We analyze and evaluate the performance of our protocol with existing schemes providing secure data exchange through device-to-device (D2D) communication. Results show that our proposed framework achieves desired security while consuming significantly less communication overhead. Further, the security of our scheme is verified through AVISPA simulator.

Keywords: 5G/LTE-A networks · DHT overlay ·
D2D communication · Opportunistic data exchange · Smart devices

1 Introduction

Content sharing has become a common phenomenon in today's digital life to share and distribute data through various smart devices or user equipments (UEs) such as smart phones, tablets, PDA etc. Due to immense flexibility and scalability of content sharing, many researchers and developers are targeting to build an intelligent and smart content sharing applications using mobile phones. Most of these existing mechanisms enable sharing of data among smart phone users using Bluetooth (BT)/Device-to-Device (D2D)/Wireless Fidelity (WiFi) technologies, to reduce Internet tariff, battery consumption, and time to retrieve the shared contents [5,11,12,16]. These service enhancements are limited to their vicinity in absence of network signal. A prominent solution to overcome this situation is opportunistic data exchange. The importance of opportunistic data

© Springer Nature Singapore Pte Ltd. 2019
S. Nandi et al. (Eds.): ISEA-ISAP 2018, CCIS 939, pp. 3–16, 2019.
https://doi.org/10.1007/978-981-13-7561-3_1

exchange within challenged networks, delay tolerant network, ad-hoc network, etc., has been discussed in several works [7,10]. It is considered in [10] that opportunistic data exchange mechanism provides data transfer from source to destination via intermediate hops, opportunistically. These hops would be roaming user's smart devices, WiFi access points, Bluetooth communication, etc.

Security in opportunistic data exchange is a major issue, and there are multiple scenarios where improper security features have been shown to be compromising the integrity, confidentiality, and availability of the users' data. Moreover, distribution of unauthentic information via a network would cause heavy consumption of network resources, install viruses like unwanted software, denial of service attack, etc. To address this issue, research proposals including [3,6,8,14,15] have been presented to secure data exchange among D2D communication under Long-Term Evolution (LTE) network through suitable authentication key management. These mechanisms are flexible with inter-operator and roaming (or non-roaming) scenarios but operates in primary network signal cellular regions.

In this work, we propose a security framework to provide secure content update facility to the smart devices of interrupted cellular network signal through opportunistic data exchange. The idea is inspired from the kerberos system [9]. It uses a DHT based architecture [12] to communicate among overlay smart devices and eNodeBs under LTE-network. The overlay provides an efficient way to retrieve the shared file among member peers. The proposed secure opportunistic data exchange work under non-DHT environment. Analysis of the results shows that the proposed security framework requires less communication overhead and security is verified through AVISPA simulator.

Rest of the paper is organized as follows. Section 2 describes the related work on secure D2D communication in cellular networks. System model and security assumption for our proposed protocol are mentioned in Sect. 3. The proposed security protocol framework is presented in Sect. 4. Security analysis along with formal verification is presented in Sect. 5, and performance of the proposed mechanism is evaluated and compared with the existing scheme in Sect. 6. Finally, Sect. 7 concludes our work.

2   Related Work

Recently, several works on secure D2D communication while roaming have been presented. Alam et al. [3] discussed secure D2D communication among D2D smart devices in three scenarios: (1) a necessity of data offloading to reduce network traffic, (2) social networking, and (3) communication during fault network infrastructure due to disaster. To secure these communications, the authors used the existing LTE-A security mechanisms. Network and application controlled authentication are required before setting up secret keys in scenarios 1 and 2, while in scenario 3, a pre-distributed hard-coded shared key is considered.

As per the patent [6], a secure framework is set up between two D2D users using Diffie-Hellman Key Exchange algorithm (DHKE) to perform authentication and secure communications. In this, each user requests a certificate from their previously associated home networks and uses that certificate to perform mutual authentication. But, the requirement of certificate increases the deployment cost.

Liu et al. [8] proposed a key agreement protocol for D2D communications in LTE-A. It obtains a shared secret key between a UE and the associated core network that is used to generate the session key for D2D communications. The protocol is compatible with the existing LTE-A system. However, the session key of D2D communications is transmitted from the core network to one UE, instead of deriving the session key in the UE locally.

Wang et al. [14] proposed an authentication protocol for D2D communications under LTE network that deals with UE registration, key distribution, and mutual authentication between UEs. Their protocol depends on *eNodeB* which sends a shared master key to each UE. Master key is used to drive the session keys. However, due to its dependence on a single master key, their protocol suffers from the key escrow problem.

Wang et al. [15] proposed a universal authentication and key agreement protocol for D2D communications (UAKA-D2D) to establish a secure communication session. This mechanism has considered user roaming and inter-operator operations as well. The protocol uses DHKE to generate secure session key, and employs message authentication codes to achieve secured data sharing agreement between D2D users.

Unfortunately, most of the aforementioned security protocols operate under the availability of network signals while authenticating D2D devices, and not suitable for no signal networks during adverse situations such as flood or earthquake etc. Developing a secure framework in no network signal zone is the crux of this paper.

3   System Model and Security Assumption

This section illustrates system model and security assumptions of our proposed authentication and key agreement scheme. Used notations and their definition in this work are summarized in Table 1.

3.1   System Model

Figure 1 depicts a scenario of an interrupted cellular network which consists of three kinds of components: (1) D2D (or BT) enabled UE without data service facility, (2) UE with enabled data service (or WiFi) and (3) *eNodeB*. UEs with good battery status, enabled data service and roaming interest over cellular infrastructure would be assigned with the role of pilot. Each pilot maintains a vicinity which consists of D2D (or BT) enabled UEs within its range. Members in the range of pilot prefers to communicate via BT/D2D/WiFi communication mediums to access data update to save network bandwidth. A DHT overlay ring consisting of UE (including pilot) and eNodeB is setup as shown in Fig. 1. Each *eNodeB* provides meta data for authentication and key agreement to the

Table 1. System notation

Notation	Definition
UE_i/UID_i	Smart device i and its identity
P_i/PID_i	Pilot i and its identity
V_i/VID_i	Vicinity i and its identity
$eNodeB_i/BID_i$	eNodeB i and its identity
$Auth_i^j$	Authentication is generated by i for j
$Token_i^j$	Token is generated by i for j
MK_{ij}	Secret key between $eNodeB_i$ and $eNodeB_i$
MK_{Pi}	Secret key between $eNodeB_i$ and P_i
MK_{Pj}	Secret key between $eNodeB_j$ and P_j
K_{iPi}	Secret temporary key for P_i
K_{jPj}	Secret temporary key for P_j
K_{ij}	Secret session key between P_i and P_j
T_i	Issued time by $eNodeB_i$ for Auth and Token
T_j	Issued time by $eNodeB_j$ for Auth and Token
L_p	Length of security parameter
H	Hash function

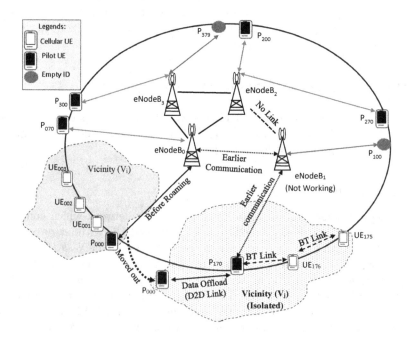

Fig. 1. A sample scenario for our system model.

associated pilots during overlay setup phase to enable it to communicate the pilot of other region. These meta data would be updated periodically in presence of good network signal.

In Fig. 1, two vicinity regions V_i (with $eNodeB_i$, i = 0) and V_j (with $eNodeB_j$, j = 1) are considered. Let $eNodeB_i$ is operational while $eNodeB_j$ is not functioning because of disaster or some unfavorable situations. At this instance, V_j is disconnected from rest of the world, whereas, member UEs of V_j can exchange their data with the help of pilot P_j (j = 170) within its vicinity through BT/D2D link. In this situation, the alternative approach to provide data sharing (or updating) using inter vicinity (or region) pilot UEs is through opportunistic data exchange would be executed.

Assume that P_i (i = 000) wishes to roam towards isolated region V_j from V_i. In this regard, it sends a roaming request to its associated $eNodeB_i$ before moving from its vicinity. It is also assumed that $eNodeB_j$ provides roaming agreement to facilitate P_i to authenticate and communicate with P_j while they have good network signal. The assigned token helps P_i to communicate with a pilot (P_j) belong to V_j.

3.2 Security Assumption

It is assumed that the communication between $eNodeB_i$ and $eNodeB_j$, as well as between P_i and $eNodeB_i$ are secured using same security schemes like network domain security protocols [1,2]. Thus, there exists a shared key MK_{ij} between $eNodeB_i$ and $eNodeB_j$ is established securely. Also, a shared key MK_{Pi} (MK_{Pj}) exists between $eNodeB_i$ ($eNodeB_j$) and P_i (P_j) securely. All these key establishment operations are performed during setup phase and the signal is assumed to be better at this time. Further, It is considered that there exist D2D spectrum to communicate inter-operator pilots after authenticating each other.

Our primary goal is to develop a security framework to secure data exchange for isolated smart devices using an appropriate authentication and key agreement under 3GPP defined LTE network.

4   The Proposed Security Framework

The proposed framework provides a secure data exchange within no signal network region. The proposed protocol for data exchange operates in two phases: (1) setup phase, and (2) opportunistic data exchange phase.

Phase 1: Setup phase. This phase assumes that the eNodeBs are operating. In this, each eNodeB generates an authenticator and a token for neighbor eNodeBs to communicate with its pilots. We consider two neighbor eNodeBs, ($eNodeB_i$ and $eNodeB_j$) having member pilots (P_i and P_j) respectively. For this, $eNodeB_i$ selects a time stamp (T_i) and a secret key K_{iPi} and generates $Auth_i^j$ and $Token_i^j$ for $eNodeB_j$ as follows:

$$Auth_i^j = Enc_{(MK_{ij})}\{BID_i||T_i||K_{iPi}\} \tag{1}$$

$$Token_i^j = Enc_{(MK_{Pi})}\{BID_i||T_i||K_{iPi}\} \tag{2}$$

Similarly, $eNodeB_j$ selects a time stamp (T_j) and a secret key K_{jPj} and generates $Auth_j^i$ and $Token_j^i$ for $eNodeB_i$ as follows:

$$Auth_j^i = Enc_{(MK_{ij})}\{BID_j||T_j||K_{jPj}\} \tag{3}$$

$$Token_j^i = Enc_{(MK_{Pj})}\{BID_j||T_j||K_{jPj}\} \tag{4}$$

Phase 2: Opportunistic Data Exchange Phase. This phase is extended when an eNodeB $(eNodeB_j)$ became non-functional due to some disasters, and the pilot of other eNodeB $(eNodeB_i)$ wishes to securely exchange data with this isolated region. This phase has following four steps.

(1) **Session Request** - Pilot (P_i) sends a roaming request, containing own ID (PID_i), to its associated $eNodeB_i$.

(2) **Session Response** - After receiving a session request from its pilot, $eNodeB_i$ finds the isolated (temporarily non-functioned) neighbor $(eNodeB_j)$. $eNodeB_i$ decrypts the received $Auth_j^i$ (obtained from $eNodeB_j$) with the shared secret MK_{ij} and computes an authenticator for pilot P_i as follows.

$$Auth_i^{P_i} = Enc_{(MK_{Pi})}\{BID_j||T_j||K_{jPj}\} \tag{5}$$

where, $Auth_i^{P_i}$ denotes that the authenticator (provided by $eNodeB_i$) to pilot P_i. Next, $eNodeB_i$ sends $Auth_i^{P_i}$ and $Token_j^i$, to P_i.

(3) **Authentication and key agreement** - While disconnecting outside world, P_j broadcasts data exchanging request message to provide an opportunity for updating or sharing contents. The request message includes its $eNodeB$ ID. To authenticate itself at P_j, the visitor pilot P_i decrypts $Auth_i^{P_i}$ to obtain time stamp T_j and key K_{jPj}. After getting the values, P_i generates a random number $r \xleftarrow{U} \mathbb{Z}_p^*$ and computes A_1 for authentication as

$$A_1 = Enc_{(K_{jPj})}\{r||T_j\} \tag{6}$$

P_i sends $< A_1||Token_j^i >$ to P_j. After receiving the response from P_i, P_j decrypts $Token_j^i$ with its private key MK_{Pj} to obtain key k_{jPj}, T_j, and earlier associated $eNodeB_j$ ID. Further, P_j decrypts A_1 and verifies whether T_j (obtained from $Token_j^i$) $\overset{?}{=} T_j$ (obtained from A_1). Successful verification authenticates P_i at P_j. P_j generates a random number $s \xleftarrow{U} \mathbb{Z}_p^*$ and computes A_2 as follow, and sends to P_i.

$$A_2 = Enc_{(K_{jPj})}\{(r+1)||s\} \tag{7}$$

(4) **Secure data exchange** - Both P_i and P_j drive a session key K_{ij} as

$$K_{ij} = H(r||s||K_{jPj}) \tag{8}$$

where H is a hash function. Hereafter, P_i and P_j exchange data securely using the session key K_{ij} (Figs. 2 and 3).

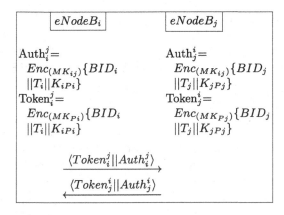

Fig. 2. Setup phase.

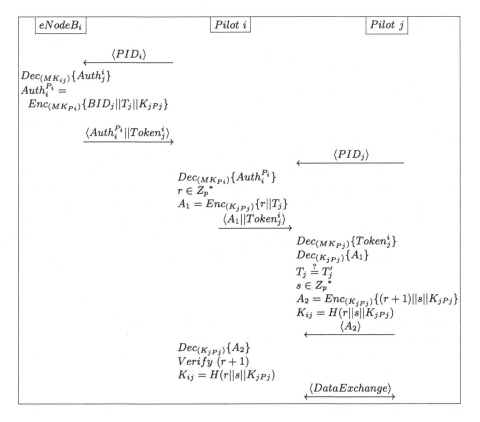

Fig. 3. Data exchanging phase.

5   Security Evaluation

This section analyses the security objectives of our proposed authentication and key agreement protocol such as mutual authentication, secure session key generation and attack resistance.

5.1   Mutual Authentication

Mutual authentication is important to avoid MITM attacks this could force to access false data or leak confidential data. The proposed scheme achieves mutual authentication between two pilots (P_i and P_j) through their corresponding $eNodeB$ which is assumed to be trusted. $Auth_j^i$ generated by $eNodeB_j$ (operational) which can be decrypted by P_j only, and no one can decrypt A_1 without knowing K_{jPj}. So P_j is assured to be authentic if A_2 is generated properly (using correct r value). Similarly, $Token_j^i$ generated by $eNodeB_j$ is decrypted and regenerated by $eNodeB_i$ only. This can be decrypted by P_i only and no other party than P_i can decrypt or know K_{jPj}. Thus, P_i is assured to be authentic if A_1 is generated properly (correct BID_j and T_j value).

5.2   Secure Session Key Generation

The proposed mechanism distributes the shared keys in a secure manner, i.e., the key K_{jPj} is not known to any party other than P_i, P_j, $eNodeB_i$, and $eNodeB_j$. As the MK_{ij} is a prior and shared between $eNodeB_i$ and $eNodeB_j$; $eNodeB_i$ only can decrypt and re-encrypt the $Auth_j^i$. Similarly, MK_{Pi} is shared between $eNodeB_i$ and P_i, so, no other party except P_i can determine K_{jPj} from $Auth_i^{Pi}$. Moreover, MK_{Pj} is shared between $eNodeB_j$ and P_j, so, only P_j can extract K_{jPj} from $Token_j^i$. As $eNodeBs$ are trusted, both P_i and P_j can extract the same K_{jPj}, respectively from $Auth_i^{Pi}$ and $Token_j^i$. Also, no other party can extract K_{jPj} due to lack of MK_{Pi}/MK_{Pj} and MK_{jPj}.

5.3   Data Confidentiality

The communication messages from P_i to P_j are encrypted with a shared secret key between them whenever they would meet opportunistically. Since, intruders do not have the key, they can not decrypt the message. Therefore, the proposed scheme preserves the data confidentiality for Pilots.

5.4   Attack Resistance

As the channel between $eNodeBs$ and that with Pilot UE and $eNodeB$ are secured using the existing network security mechanisms at presence of good network signal [1,2]. We only need to analyze the security resistance between visiting Pilot (P_i) and host Pilot (P_j). Random number r generated by P_i and the time stamp T introduced by $enodeB_j$ prevent replay attack. Meanwhile, verification and validation of the shared temporary key (K_{jPj}) with a generated random number at P_j (s) make the scheme to generate a shared secured session key K_{ij} withstand against MITM attacks.

```
% Role of roaming pilot (Pi)
role pilotPi(Pi, Pj, Ei : agent, MKpi : symmetric_key,
H, Succ: hash_func, PIDi, PIDj, NodeBi, NodeBj : text,
SND, RCV: channel(dy)) played_by Pi
def=
local State:nat,

KjPj, KiPi, KIj: symmetric_key,
T, R, S : text,
AuthiPi, Tokenij, Tokenji, BroadCast, DataExchangeReq, Temp1:
message

const pj_pi_t, kjPj: protocol_id

init State:=0
transition
    step1. State = 0 ∧ RCV(start) =|>
        State' := 1  % Roaming Request to eNodeBi
                     ∧ SND(PIDi.NodeBi)
                     ∧ BroadCast' := new()
                     % For data exchange request
                     ∧ SND(BroadCast')

    step2. State = 1 ∧ RCV(DataExchangeReq')
                     ∧ RCV(AuthiPi'.Tokenji') =|>
        State' := 2   ∧ Temp1':= ({AuthiPi'}_MKpi)
                      ∧ R' := new() ∧ T' := new()
                      ∧ SND({R'.T'}_KjPj.Tokenji')
                      ∧ witness(Pj,Pi,pj_pi_t,T')
                      ∧ secret(KjPj, kjPj, {Pi,Pj})

    step3. State = 2 ∧ RCV({Succ(R'). S'}_KjPj)
                     ∧ in(Succ(R'), {Succ(R'). S'}_KjPj) =|>
        State' := 3   % Secure Data exchange between Pi and Pj
                      ∧ KIj' := H(R'.S'.KjPj)
```

```
role pilotPj(Pj, Pi: agent, MKpj : symmetric_key,
H, Succ: hash_func, PIDi, PIDj, NodeBi, NodeBj: text,
SND, RCV: channel(dy))
played_by Pj
def=
local State:nat,
KjPj, KiPi, Kij: symmetric_key,

T, R, S: text,
Temp2, Tokenji, BroadCast, DataExchangeReq:
message
const pj_pi_t, kjPj: protocol_id

init State:=0
transition
    step1. State = 0 ∧ RCV(BroadCast') =|>
        State' := 1  ∧ DataExchangeReq' := new()
                     % Data exchange req
                     ∧ SND(DataExchangeReq')

    step2. State = 1 ∧ RCV({R'.T'}_KjPj.Tokenji')
=|>
        State' := 2  ∧ Temp2':= ({Tokenji'}_MKpj) ∧
S' := new()
                     ∧ SND({Succ(R'). S'}_KjPj)
                     ∧ Kij' := H(R'.S'.KjPj)
                     ∧ request(Pi,Pj,pj_pi_t,T')

end role
```

(a)   (b)

Fig. 4. Role specification: (a) for pilot P_i and (b) for pilot P_j.

5.5   Formal Security Verification

Our proposed secure data exchange mechanism is verified/validated using "Automated Validation of Internet Security Protocol and Applications" (AVISPA [4]) simulator. It provides automatic security verification for Internet security mechanisms and analyze according to the specified goals, which measures whether the mechanism is SAFE or UNSAFE. It supports High Level Protocol Specification Language (HLPSL [13]), which can be tested through back-end servers. AVISPA integrates four different back-end servers for automatic security verification and analysis, they are: (1) On-the-Fly Model-Checker (OFMC), (2) Constant-Logic-based Attack Searcher (CL-AtSe), (3) SAT-based Model-Checker, and (4) Tree Automata based on Automatic Approximation for the Analysis of Security Protocol (TA4SP).

```
% Role of eNodeBi                              % Role of eNodeBj
role eNodeBi(Pi, Ei, Ej : agent, MKpi, MKij :   role eNodeBj(Ej, Ei : agent, MKpj, MKij : symmetric_key,
symmetric_key, PIDi, PIDj, NodeBi, NodeBj: text,  PIDi, PIDj, NodeBi, NodeBj: text, SND, RCV: channel(dy))
SND, RCV: channel(dy))                          played_by Ej
played_by Ei def=                               def=
local State:nat, KiPi: symmetric_key,           local State:nat, KjPj: symmetric_key,
T: text,
A1, Authij, Authji, AuthiPi, Tokenij, Tokenji: message   T: text,
init State:=0                                    Authij, Tokenij, Authji, Tokenji: message
transition
        step1. State = 0 ∧ RCV(PIDi.NodeBi) =|>  init State:=0
        State' := 1 %Forwards the request to eNodeBj   transition
        ∧ SND(PIDi.NodeBi.NodeBj)                        step1. State = 0 ∧ RCV(PIDi.NodeBi.NodeBj) ∧
        step2. State = 1 ∧ RCV(NodeBi.Authji'.Tokenji') =|>   RCV(NodeBi.Authij'.Tokenij')=|>
        State' := 2  ∧ A1':= ({Authji'}_MKij)                   State' := 1 % generate Auth and Token for Pi
                     ∧ AuthiPi':= ({A1'}_MKpi)                       ∧ KjPj' := new() ∧ T' := new()
                     ∧ SND(AuthiPi'.Tokenji') % send to Pi          ∧ Authji':= ({PIDi.PIDj.T'.KjPj'}_MKij)
                     % generate Auth and Token for Pi              ∧ Tokenji':= ({PIDi.PIDj.T'.KjPj'}_MKpj)
                     ∧ KiPi' := new() ∧ T' := new()                ∧ SND(NodeBi.Authji'.Tokenji')
                     ∧ Authij':= ({PIDi.PIDj.T'.KiPi'}_MKij)               % To eNodeBi
                     ∧ Tokenij':= ({PIDi.PIDj.T'.KiPi'}_MKpi)   end role
                     ∧ SND(NodeBj.Authij'.Tokenij') % To eNodej

end role

        (a)                                              (b)
```

Fig. 5. Role specification: (a) for $eNodeB_i$ and (b) for $eNodeB_j$.

We firstly specified different roles of the players (i.e., pilots P_i, P_j, and eNodeBs $eNodeB_i$, $eNodeB_j$) in the proposed mechanism using HLPSL language in Figs. 4a, b, and 5a, b respectively. All specifications used type declaration channel (dy) which stands for the Dolev-Yao intruder model. In this verification model, intruder provided knowledge of the all roles and overlay Ids for the participating players and common system parameters. Finally, we defined the security goals "$secrecy\_of\ K_jP_j$" and "$authentication\_on\ p_j\_p_i\_t$" for our proposed scheme. It is verified that the proposed scheme provides secrecy for generated session key (K_{jPj}) and the mutual authentication, using a random number (r), between two DHT-D2D users (i.e., P_i and P_j). The $secrecy\_of\ k_{jPj}$ represents that the session key (K_{jPj}) are maintained secret to $\{P_i$ and $P_j\}$. The $authentication\_on\ p_j\_p_i\_t$ and $(in(Succ(R'), \{(Succ(R'))\}\_ K_{jPj})$ verified that P_i and P_j can authenticate mutually.

The results show in Fig. 6a and b are executed the security test based on OFMC and CL-AtSe back-end respectively. The results confirm that our scheme achieves the session key secrecy and mutual authentication goals. So, the proposed framework defend MITM and usage of random nonce and time-stamp avoid the replay attacks.

```
% OFMC                                    SUMMARY
% Version of 2006/02/13                     SAFE
SUMMARY                                   DETAILS
  SAFE                                      BOUNDED_NUMBER_OF_SESSIONS
DETAILS                                     TYPED_MODEL
  BOUNDED_NUMBER_OF_SESSIONS              PROTOCOL
PROTOCOL                                    /home/span/span/testsuite/results/
  /home/span/span/testsuite/results         DataExchange.if
/DataExchange.if                          GOAL
GOAL                                        As Specified
  as_specified                            BACKEND
BACKEND                                      CL-AtSe
  OFMC                                     STATISTICS
COMMENTS                                     Analysed  : 10 states
STATISTICS                                   Reachable  : 8 states
  parseTime: 0.00s                           Translation: 0.02 seconds
  searchTime: 0.16s                          Computation: 0.00 seconds
  visitedNodes: 132 nodes
  depth: 7 plies
            (a)                                        (b)
```

Fig. 6. Simulation results by (a) the OFMC back-end and (b) the SL-AtSe back-end.

6   Performance Evaluation

We analyze the communication and network traffic overhead after using the proposed scheme and compare with the existing mechanism [15].

6.1   Communication Overhead

We analyze the communication cost in our proposed scheme during session request, confirmation response, key agreement request and key agreement response to perform secure data exchange between UEs. We consider size of the different network entities and their parameters in bits as mentioned in Table 2. We consider the size of parameters to be same for the existing scheme UAKA-D2D [15]. In UAKA-D2D, HNID, SID, HINT, and RAND represent for home

Table 2. Parameters in the proposed and UAKA-D2D security schemes.

Parameters	Length (in bits)
Security parameter	L_p
UID/PID	128
VNID/VID	64
HNID/BID	64
r, s, R, K, RAND	L_p
MAC	256
T	64

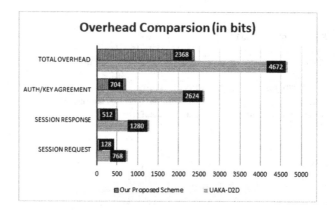

Fig. 7. Communication overheads during each phase of AKA process with 128 bits security parameter (L_p).

Table 3. Communication during AKA process.

	Communication	Message	Total (in bits)
		UAKA-D2D [15]	
Session request	$UE1 \rightarrow VN1$	$<UID_1, HNID_1>$	192
	$VN1 \rightarrow HN1$	$<UID_1, VNID_1>$	192
	$UE2 \rightarrow VN2$	$<UID_2, HNID_2>$	192
	$VN2 \rightarrow HN2$	$<UID_2, VNID_2>$	192
Session response	$HN1 \rightarrow VN1$	$<K_1, VNID_1, RAND_1>$	$64 + 2L_p$
	$VN1 \rightarrow UE1$	$<K_{r1}, VNID_1, RAND_1>$	$64 + 2L_p$
	$HN2 \rightarrow VN2$	$<K_2, VNID_2, RAND_2>$	$64 + 2L_p$
	$VN2 \rightarrow UE2$	$<K_{r2}, VNID_2, RAND_2>$	$64 + 2L_p$
Key agreement	$VN1 \rightarrow VN2$	$<UID_1, UID_2, r_1, SID_1>$	$320 + L_p$
	$VN2 \rightarrow VN1$	$<UID_1, UID_2, r_1>$	$256 + L_p$
	$VN1 \rightarrow UE1$	$<UID_2, R_k, SID_1>$	$320 + L_p$
	$VN2 \rightarrow UE2$	$<UID_1, R_k, SID_1>$	$320 + L_p$
Authentication	$UE1 \rightarrow UE2$	$<HINT_1, MAC_1, T_1>$	$320 + L_p$
	$UE2 \rightarrow UE1$	$<HINT_2, MAC_2, T_2>$	$320 + L_p$
		Our proposed scheme	
Setup process	$BID_i \rightarrow BID_j$	$<Auth_i^j, Token_i^j>$	$256 + 2L_p$
	$BID_j \rightarrow BID_i$	$<Auth_j^i, Token_j^i>$	$256 + 2L_p$
Session request	$PID_i \rightarrow BID_i$	$<PID_i>$	128
Session response	$BID_i \rightarrow PID_i$	$<Auth_i^j, Token_i^j>$	$256 + 2L_p$
Authentication/key agreement	$PID_i \rightarrow PID_j$	$<r, T, Token_i^j>$	$192 + 2L_p$
	$PID_j \rightarrow PID_i$	$<r, s>$	$2L_p$

network, visiting network, D2D session, session hint, and a random number respectively.

The communication overhead of UAKA-D2D and our proposed scheme are summarized in Table 3. Our mechanism consumes significantly less communication overhead during key agreement and authentication phase. Although, proposed scheme takes extra communication to perform setup phase. The overall bandwidth consumption is lesser than other schemes. The comparative study during all phases to perform AKA operations, considering 128 bits security parameter (L_p) size, are depicted in Fig. 7. The effects of communication overhead by increasing L_p size is showed in Fig. 8a and b. It shows that our protocol generates comparatively less overhead while incrementing the size of security parameter (L_p).

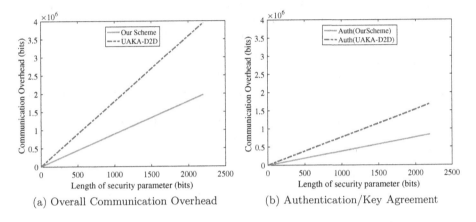

(a) Overall Communication Overhead   (b) Authentication/Key Agreement

Fig. 8. Comparison of communication overheads.

7   Conclusion

Content sharing in interrupted network signal of cellular networks is a challenging issue for the Internet users. Many mobile applications using BT/D2D/WiFi have been proposed as an alternative to Internet access. In this paper, we proposed a secure data offloading mechanism among smart phone users in the 5G/LTE-A networks. The proposed scheme uses secured authentication and token based user verification system that lets them to connect to the roaming pilot for data updating. It requires less communication and bandwidth overhead, and therefore more suitable for mobile phones. The scheme is analyzed through AVISPA simulator and showed to be safe (or secure). In future, we aim to design an android application to implement our protocol in real network.

References

1. 3rd Generation Partnership Project. Technical Specification Group Services and System Aspects; 3G security; Network Domain Security (NDS); IP network layer security (Rel 13), 3GPP TS 33.210 V13.0.0, December 2015
2. 3rd Generation Partnership Project. Technical Specification Group Services and System Aspects; Network Domain Security (NDS); Authentication Framework (AF) (Rel 13), 3GPP TS 33.310 V13.0.0, December 2015
3. Alam, M., Yang, D., Rodriguez, J., Abd-alhameed, R.: Secure device-to-device communication in LTE-A. IEEE Commun. Mag. **52**(4), 66–73 (2014)
4. Armando, A., et al.: The AVISPA tool for the automated validation of internet security protocols and applications. In: Etessami, K., Rajamani, S.K. (eds.) CAV 2005. LNCS, vol. 3576, pp. 281–285. Springer, Heidelberg (2005). https://doi.org/10.1007/11513988_27
5. Draishpits, G.: Peer-to-peer communication in wireless networks as an alternative to internet access. Ph.D. thesis, The Open University (2016)
6. Ekberg, J.E., Uusitalo, M.A., Li, Z.: Device-to-device communication security with authentication certificates. US Patent 9,960,922, 1 May 2018
7. Fall, K.: A delay-tolerant network architecture for challenged internets. In: Proceedings of the 2003 Conference on Applications, Technologies, Architectures, and Protocols for Computer Communications, pp. 27–34. ACM (2003)
8. Liu, Y., et al.: Methods and apparatus for generating keys in device-to-device communications. US Patent 9,660,804, 23 May 2017
9. Neuman, B.C., Ts'o, T.: Kerberos: an authentication service for computer networks. IEEE Commun. Mag. **32**(9), 33–38 (1994)
10. Pelusi, L., Passarella, A., Conti, M.: Opportunistic networking: data forwarding in disconnected mobile ad hoc networks. IEEE Commun. Ma. **44**(11), 134–141 (2006)
11. Tetarave, S.K., Tripathy, S., Ghosh, R.K.: GMP2P: mobile P2P over GSM for efficient file sharing. In: Negi, A., Bhatnagar, R., Parida, L. (eds.) ICDCIT 2018. LNCS, vol. 10722, pp. 217–231. Springer, Cham (2018). https://doi.org/10.1007/978-3-319-72344-0_18
12. Tetarave, S.K., Tripathy, S., Ghosh, R.: V-Chord: an efficient file sharing on LTE/GSM network. In: Proceedings of the 19th International Conference on Distributed Computing and Networking, p. 38. ACM (2018)
13. HLPSL Tutorial: A beginners guide to modelling and analysing internet security protocols (2005). Available at [AH-03] (2009)
14. Wang, J.T., Lin, T.M.: Authentication system for device-to-device communication and authentication method therefore. US Patent 9,232,391, 5 January 2016
15. Wang, M., Yan, Z., Niemi, V.: UAKA-D2D: universal authentication and key agreement protocol in D2D communications. Mob. Netw. Appl. **22**(3), 510–525 (2017)
16. Zulhasnine, M., Huang, C., Srinivasan, A.: Towards an effective integration of cellular users to the structured peer-to-peer network. Peer Peer Netw. Appl. **5**(2), 178–192 (2012)

Bloom Filter Based Privacy Preserving Deduplication System

Jay Dave[1(✉)], Vijay Laxmi[1], Parvez Faruki[2], Manoj Gaur[3], and Bhavya Shah[2]

[1] Malaviya National Institute of Technology Jaipur, Jaipur, India
jaydaveadms@gmail.com, vlgaur@gmail.com
[2] Government MCA College, Ahmedabad, India
parvezfaruki.kg@gmail.com, shahbhavya5800@gmail.com
[3] Indian Institute of Technology Jammu, Jammu, India
gaurms@gmail.com

Abstract. Deduplication is a data reduction technique which eliminates uploading and storing redundant data. Therefore, it is widely adopted in cloud storage services to reduce communication and storage overhead. However, deduplication can be used as a side channel to learn the existence of a particular data in cloud storage thereby raising significant privacy issues. The existing solutions delay deduplication process to hide information regarding the presence of data. These solutions increase communication overhead as the client needs to send data even if it is present on storage. In this paper, we present a novel privacy preserving deduplication approach using bloom filter. In our approach, bloom filter (containing blocks of data) is used as a deduplication identity. When a client sends an upload request, the server responds by sending a genuine bloom filter (if data exists) along with some dummy filters. Now, that client who genuinely owns the data, can learn the existence information by computing bloom filter of the data. Further, client does not need to send the data if it exists on storage. Security analysis proves that our approach provides privacy to data at deduplication system. We implement the approach and demonstrate that communication overhead is significantly less in our approach than the existing approaches.

1 Introduction

Cloud storage services have emerged as an essential part of organizations due to its scalable and low-cost online services. The Cisco Global Cloud Index reports that the size of digital data on cloud storage will reach upto 19.5 ZB in 2021 [21]. Such enormous growth of data demands an efficient data reduction approach. Deduplication is a data reduction approach which eliminates storing redundant data. In this approach, when a client requests to upload data, the server first checks existence of the data on storage. Server stores data only if it does not exist on storage.

Deduplication process can be classified into (i) Client-server side deduplication, (ii) File-chunk level deduplication, and (iii) Intra-inter user deduplication.

© Springer Nature Singapore Pte Ltd. 2019
S. Nandi et al. (Eds.): ISEA-ISAP 2018, CCIS 939, pp. 17–34, 2019.
https://doi.org/10.1007/978-981-13-7561-3_2

(i) In client side deduplication, the client computes and sends deduplication identity (generally, hash value of data) to check presence of the data at cloud storage. Client uploads data only if it is not present at storage. In server side deduplication, client is unaware about deduplication and always sends data to the server. Further, server takes care of deduplication. However, this approach suffers from communication overhead since a client requires to upload data even if it exists. (ii) In file level deduplication, storage is scanned file by file to detect redundancy. Chunk level deduplication splits the file into chunks and scans the storage chunk by chunk. (iii) Intra user deduplication allows to detect and remove redundancy from a client's individual data only. On the other hand, inter user deduplication considers data of all clients for removing redundancy. In this paper, we consider client side, file level, inter user deduplication.

From a security point of view, deduplication process reveals information regarding presence/absence of the file at storage [3]. For e.g. Tom, an adversary, suspects that Bob owns a sensitive file. Tom wants to collect the evidences. For that, Tom needs to learn just a deduplication identity (i.e. Hash of file). He can learn it by listening the communication link or compromising Bob's machine. Generally, deduplication identity is not secured by clients. Further, Tom sends deduplication identity to various cloud storages. Server responds yes/no for presence/absence of the file at storage. Now, Tom may appeal in court or just blackmail Bob regarding that suspicious file. Similarly, law enforcement officials can leverage deduplication process to check presence of the file and get a list of suspicious file uploaders from cloud storage providers.

The research community has proposed various solutions to the aforementioned security issue. In some proposals [3–5, 10, 18], the information regarding presence of file is obfuscated by delaying the deduplication process. In other words, server asks the client to send the file even if it exists in storage. On the other hand, gateway server based approaches were proposed in [6, 11, 15]. In these approaches, client is unaware about deduplication and sends file to the gateway server. Further, the gateway server will take care of the deduplication process. In aforementioned methodologies, client needs to transfer the file even if it is present at storage. Hence, it increases the communication overhead.

In this paper, we propose a privacy preserving deduplication approach. In our approach, bloom filter (BF) that is generated using file blocks, is used as a deduplication identity of the file. When a client requests for file upload, server responds with the genuine BF along with dummy filters and metadata. Here, we note that server does not reveal existence information of the file directly by responding Yes/No to upload request. Further, client generates BF by file blocks and searches it in received set of filters. If the client does not find file's BF, she encrypts the file using secure random encryption mechanism [23] and uploads encrypted file along with metadata. On the other hand, if the client finds file's BF in received BFs, she retrieves the encryption key from metadata and get access to existing file at storage. Hence, BF data structure is useful to restrict the access of file to only genuine owners. In other words, that client who owns the file, is able to generate the correct BF using file blocks and learn presence/absence of the file. Moreover, the client does not need to upload the file if it exists on storage.

Hence, communication overhead is less in our approach as compared to existing approaches. Moreover, for protection against eavesdropping, we include a random nonce in communication between client and server. As a result, an adversary who is listening the channel, cannot reuse the captured deduplication identity. We explain the proposed approach in detail in Sect. 4.

Contribution of this paper is:

- A novel Privacy Preserving Deduplication approach using bloom filter.
- Security analysis of proposed approach which proves that our proposal provides privacy to Deduplication system.
- We implement Bloom Filter based Privacy Preserving Deduplication System which provides following services: (a) Upload, (b) Download, (c) Delete, and (d) Update file. We evaluate the performance of implemented system.

The rest of paper is organized as follows. Section 2 briefly explains cryptographic definitions which are used in our approach. In Sect. 3, we discuss system model, threat model, and security goals. Section 4 describes a novel Privacy Preserving Deduplication approach using bloom filter. In Sects. 5 and 6, we evaluate security and performance of our approach. Section 7 discusses existing state-of-the-art on privacy of deduplication. And, we conclude our paper in Sect. 8.

2   Preliminaries

In this section, we discuss a brief of cryptographic definitions i.e., "Secure Random Encryption for Deduplicated Storage" and "Bloom filter".

2.1   Secure Random Encryption for Deduplicated Storage

Conventional encryption mechanisms for deduplication (i.e., Convergent Encryption, Message Locked Encryption) are vulnerable to dictionary attack [3]. In [23], authors propose "Secure Random Encryption for Deduplicated Storage". In this approach, client encrypts the file with a random key ($\mathcal{RK}$). Encryption with the random key provides semantic security to ciphertext. For deduplication, $\mathcal{RK}$ is encrypted with set of cryptographic hash values H_1, H_2,...,H_n generated from the file as shown in Fig. 1. Client uploads ciphertext of file along with ciphertext of random key(C_K) if file is not present on server. On the subsequent upload request, server responds with C_K. Further, client generates cryptographic hash values H_1, H_2,...,H_n from the file and decrypts the C_K. In this way, only a genuine file owner is able to learn the secret random key. In [23], authors prove that an adversary needs to execute a large number of attempts to perform successful dictionary attack on this mechanism as compared to existing mechanisms.

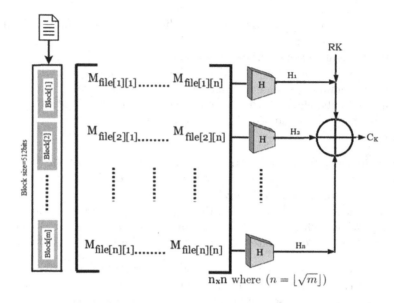

Fig. 1. Encryption of random key [23]

2.2 Bloom Filter

Bloom filter is a probabilistic data structure which is used to represent membership of elements [1]. The major advantage of BF is space efficiency. In other words, BF occupies less storage space as compared to other data structures. In our approach, we leverage BF as deduplication identity of the file. Size of BF can be determined as

$$B_{size} = \lceil \frac{-E \times ln(p)}{ln(2)^2} \rceil$$

where E = Number of file blocks = $\frac{Filesize}{512}$, p = False positive probability. The number of bloom hash functions are $B_{Hash} = \lceil \frac{B_{size}}{E} \times ln(2) \rceil$.

Initially, the file is split into blocks of 512 bits. Each block is inserted into BF by executing bloom hashes (B_{Hash}) on each block. It results a vector having size = B_{size}. BF is stored at server as the identity of file. In our approach, BF is useful to limit the access of file to only genuine owners. The client who possesses the file, can generate the BF using file blocks and requests for access to the file using BF. Further, we discuss usage of BF in detail in Sect. 4.

3 Problem Statement

In this section, we discuss system model, threat model and security goals of our proposal.

3.1   System Model

We consider three major entities of system model: Client, Server, and Storage as shown in Fig. 2.

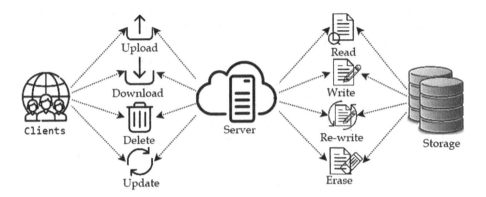

Fig. 2. System model

1. Client($\mathcal{C}$): Client owns the file and wishes to outsource the file due to limited storage and computation capacities at local site. $\mathcal{C}$ invites cross user, client side deduplication to reduce storage and communication cost. For security of file, $\mathcal{C}$ encrypts it by random encryption approach [23] before uploading.
2. Server($\mathcal{S}$): Server provides the following storage services: Upload, Download, Delete, and Update. $\mathcal{S}$ performs cross user deduplication to reduce storage overhead.
   (a) *Upload*: $\mathcal{C}$ sends tag of file as discussed in Sect. 4. $\mathcal{S}$ responds with set of BFs and encryption keys corresponding to the tag. If file is present on server storage, then file's BF exists in received set. Further, $\mathcal{C}$ computes the BF for her file and searches it in received set of BFs. If BF is not present, then $\mathcal{C}$ encrypts the file and uploads it with metadata. If BF is present, then $\mathcal{C}$ learns the corresponding encryption key for further access.
   (b) *Download*: $\mathcal{C}$ sends the hash value of encrypted file. $\mathcal{S}$ checks whether $\mathcal{C}$ is owner of the file or not. $\mathcal{S}$ sends ciphertext of file and $\mathcal{C}$ decrypts it with secret random key.
   (c) *Delete*: $\mathcal{C}$ sends hash value of encrypted file. $\mathcal{S}$ verifies the ownership of $\mathcal{C}$ on the file. If $\mathcal{C}$ is owner, then $\mathcal{S}$ removes her entry from owners' list. In case, owners' list gets empty, then $\mathcal{S}$ removes file and metadata from Storage.
   (d) *Update*: Update operation consists of (1) Delete operation on the old version of file, and (2) Upload operation on the new version of file.
3. Server storage: It is a physical storage environment which performs (i) Read, (ii) Write, (iii) Re-write, and (iv) Erase operations.

3.2   Threat Model

In this paper, we concentrate on following adversaries: (1) Semi-trusted Server, (2) Malicious Client.

- Semi-trusted Server: We assume that S is a semi-trusted entity. S honestly performs the storage operations requested by Cs, although S is interested in learning plaintext of outsourced files. S may perform dictionary attack.
- Malicious Client: Malicious client can misuse deduplication process to learn the presence of file at storage. Suppose, Tom suspects that Bob possesses a sensitive file X. Tom learns deduplication identity of file X by listening the communication links or compromising Bob's machine. Now, Tom can leverage deduplication process to check the presence of file X. Tom uploads deduplication identity to various cloud storages and learns about presence/absence of the file. Next, he file a case on Bob or just blackmail Bob regarding the suspicious file.

  Secondly, law enforcement officials can use deduplication process to detect illegal activities on the cloud storages. They learn deduplication identity of the sensitive file, send it to various cloud storages and observe the deduplication. In this way, they get a list of cloud storages having sensitive file. Further, they can get information about file uploaders from cloud storage providers.

  Thirdly, the malicious C is also interested in learning plaintext of other clients' files by performing dictionary attack.

3.3   Security Goals

Our approach achieves the following security goals:

1. Privacy: The primary goal of the proposed approach is to provide privacy of data at deduplication system. In other words, an adversary should not be able to learn any information regarding the file (i.e., plaintext, presence of file). The C encrypts the file with a random key before outsourcing for protection against dictionary attack.

   Moreover, when a C enquirers about the presence of file, S responds with a set of BFs instead of "Yes/No" as a response. Further, the C needs to generate BF using file blocks and learn about file existence by searching the computed BF in the received set. Hence, an adversary cannot learn the existence information without knowledge of the complete file.

   An adversary can eavesdrop the communication between C and S to learn the deduplication identity of a file. For protection against eavesdropping, we include a random nonce in communication between C and S.
2. Integrity: Data may be intercepted and modified at the time of communication or storage. In our approach, we link hash value with stored/sent content. Hence, the receiver is able to identify unexpected modification in data.

4 Proposed Approach

In this section, we present a novel approach "Bloom filter based privacy preserving Deduplication system". We discuss basic processes of storage services: (1) *Upload*, (2) *Download*, (3) *Delete*, and (4) *Update*.

1. **Upload**: Firstly, Client($\mathcal{C}$) computes hash value of the file. $\mathcal{C}$ extracts first t bits from that hash value. Let's define it as *tag*. $\mathcal{C}$ sends tag to server($\mathcal{S}$). $\mathcal{S}$ extracts bloom filters BF_1, BF_2,..., BF_k and ciphertext of keys CK_1, CK_2,..., CK_k which are corresponding with received tag. If tag does not exist, then $\mathcal{S}$ inserts an entry of tag, dummy BFs and dummy keys. Next, $\mathcal{S}$ generates a random nonce R and replies $\mathcal{C}$ with {tag, R, BF_1, BF_2,..., BF_k, CK_1, CK_2,..., CK_k}. Here, we can see that $\mathcal{S}$ does not reply Yes/No directly for Presence/Absence of file.

   Further, $\mathcal{C}$ generates an empty BF. $\mathcal{C}$ splits file into 512 bits blocks and inserts them into BF. Then $\mathcal{C}$ checks whether the computed BF exists in the set of received BFs. If the computed BF exists in the received set of BF, then file is present on storage. Hence, a $\mathcal{C}$ who genuinely owns the file, can compute the correct BF and learn about presence/absence of file. Here, upload operation is categorized into (1) First upload, and (2) Subsequent upload as shown in Fig. 3.

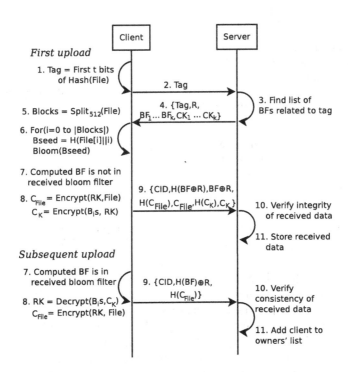

Fig. 3. Upload operation

Algorithm 1. Upload

1: **procedure** CLIENT: UPLOAD(File)
2:     Tag ← Extract(Hash(File), k)
3:     {tag, R, BF_i, CK_i} ← SearchBloom(Tag)
4:     {Blocks} ← Split(File)
5:     BF ← BloomGenerate()
6:     **for** i=1 to {Blocks}.Length **do**
7:         BloomInsert(BF, $Blocks[i]\|i$)
8:     n ← $\sqrt{|\{Blocks\}.Length|}$
9:     M_{File} ← $Matrix(\{Blocks\}_{n \times n})$
10:     **for** i=1 to n **do**
11:         H_i ← Hash($M_{File}[i][1] \| M_{File}[i][1] ... \| M_{File}[i][n]$)
12:     **if** BF∈{BF_i} **then**
13:         RK ← $CK_i \oplus H_1 \oplus H_2 ... \oplus H_n$
14:         C_{File} ← Encrypt(RK, File)
15:         SUpload(CID, Hash(BF)⊕R, Hash(C_{File}))
16:     **else**
17:         RK $\xleftarrow{\$}$ KeyGen(1^λ)
18:         C_{File} ← Encrypt(RK, File)
19:         C_K ← RK $\oplus H_1 \oplus H_2 ... \oplus H_n$
20:         FUpload(CID, Hash($BF \oplus R$), $BF \oplus R$, Hash(C_{File}), C_{File}, Hash(C_K), C_K)
21: **procedure** SERVER: SEARCHBLOOM(tag)
22:     **if** tag ∈ TagList **then**
23:         {BF_i,CK_i} ← ExtractBlooms(tag)
24:         R ← Random()
25:         Return {tag, R, BF_i,CK_i}
26:     **else**
27:         Return "False"
28: **procedure** SERVER: FUPLOAD(CID, Hash($BF \oplus R$), $BF \oplus R$, Hash(C_{File}), C_{File}, Hash(C_K), C_K)
29:     **if** (Hash(BF) ≠ ReceivedHashBF ‖ Hash(C_{File}) ≠ ReceivedHashCFile ‖ Hash(C_K) ≠ ReceivedHashRK) **then**
30:         Return "False"
31:     **else**
32:         Store(Hash(BF), BF, Hash(C_{File}), C_{File}, Hash(C_K), C_K)
33: **procedure** SERVER: SUPLOAD(CID, Hash(BF)⊕R, Hash(C_{File}))
34:     Hash(C_{File}) ← Retrieve(Hash(BF))
35:     **if** Hash(C_{File}) ≠ ReceivedHashCFile **then**
36:         Return "False"
37:     **else**
38:         Ownershiplist[Hash(BF)] ← Ownershiplist[Hash(BF)] ∪ CID

– First upload: $\mathcal{C}$ does not find BF in received set {BF_1, BF_2,..., BF_k}. Hence, $\mathcal{C}$ needs to upload the file along with BF. Before outsourcing the file, $\mathcal{C}$ encrypts the file using secure random encryption mechanism, as we discussed in Sect. 2. $\mathcal{C}$ uploads {CID, $Hash(BF \oplus R)$, $BF \oplus R$, $Hash(C_{File})$, C_{File}, $Hash(C_K)$, C_K}, where CID = client's id, C_{File} = ciphertext of file, and C_K = ciphertext of key. $\mathcal{S}$ verifies the integrity of received data and $\mathcal{S}$ stores the received data.

– Subsequent upload: C searches a match of computed BF in the received BFs. C learns CK_i corresponding to that BF_i. C decrypts the key with set of hash values which are generated from file. C encrypts the file using the key and computes hash value of ciphertext of file, Hash(C_{File}). C sends $\{Hash(BF)\oplus R$, Hash(C_{File})$\}$ to S. S retrieves the Hash(C_{File}) corresponding to Hash(BF) and compares with received value. If it is matched, then S adds C in owners' list of file. Otherwise, S rejects the upload request.

2. **Download:** C sends Hash(C_{File}) to S (Algorithm 2). S verifies whether C resides in the owners' list of file. If C is owner of the file, then S responds with $\{C_{File}$, Hash(C_{File})$\}$. Further, C checks the integrity of received file and decrypts it with the secret random key.

Algorithm 2. Download

1: **procedure** CLIENT: DOWNLOAD(File)
2:      $\{C_{File}$, Hash(C_{File})$\} \leftarrow$ SDownload(CID, Hash(C_{File}))
3:      **if** Hash(C_{File}) $\neq$ ReceivedHash **then**
4:           Return "False"
5:      **else**
6:           File $\leftarrow$ Decrypt(RK, C_{File})
7: **procedure** SERVER: SDOWNLOAD(CID, Hash(C_{File}))
8:      **if** CID $\in$ Ownershiplist(Hash(C_{File})) **then**
9:           Return (C_{File}, Hash(C_{File}))
10:     **else**
11:          Return "False"

---

3. **Delete File:** C sends Hash(C_{File}) to S. S checks whether C resides in the file's owners' list. If C is owner of the file, then S erases entry of C from owners' list. If owners' list gets empty, then S removes the file and its metadata from the storage.
4. **Update File:** When C request to update a file, our system performs Delete operation on the older version of file and Upload operation on the updated version of file.

5 Security Analysis

In this section, we discuss security aspects "Privacy" and "Integrity" of our approach.

5.1 Privacy

In our approach, we assume that client(C) and server(S) are untrusted entities. These entities are interested in learning plaintext of file outsourced by other Cs.

For that, $\mathcal{C}$ encrypts the data before upload. However, conventional encryption mechanisms for deduplication are vulnerable to dictionary attack. In this paper, we adopt "Secure Random Encryption mechanism" [23] which protects against the dictionary attack. In this mechanism, the file is encrypted with a random key. Therefore, the ciphertext of file is semantically secure. For deduplication, the random key is encrypted by set of hash values computed from the file. Thus, only those $\mathcal{C}$s who own the file, are able to decrypt the ciphertext and learn the key. In [23], authors prove that an adversary needs to perform a significantly large number of attempts to perform successful dictionary attack on the proposed encryption mechanism.

In the following, we discuss privacy of information regarding presence/absence of file. We explain the security game where adversary tries to learn about presence of file by guessing relevant BF as shown in Table 1.

Table 1. Security game

$EXP_A()$	$Bloom(File, Tag, a)$
$a \xleftarrow{\$} \{0, 1\}$	$\{Blocks\} \leftarrow Split(File)$
	$BF \leftarrow BloomGenerate()$
$Tag \leftarrow \mathcal{A}$	for i = 1 ... $\{Blocks\}$.Length
	$\quad BloomInsert(BF, Blocks[i]\|i)$
$a' \leftarrow \mathcal{A}^{Bloom}()$	$b \xleftarrow{\$} \{1, ..., k\}$
	for i=1...k
$return\ a' = a$	$\quad$ if i = b and a = 1 then
	$\qquad BF_i \leftarrow BF$
	$\quad$ else
	$\qquad BF_i \leftarrow \{0, 1\}^n$
	return BFs

Advantage of adversary to win this security game is:

$$Adv_A = |(Pr[Exp_A = 1]) - \frac{1}{2}| \tag{1}$$

Theorem 1. *Our approach provides privacy to information regarding the presence of file.*

Proof. We assume that Adversary($\mathcal{A}$) knows deduplication tag (i.e., Hash value) and wants to learn about presence/absence of a particular file. In the security game, challenger first chooses a random value a from 0 to 1. $\mathcal{A}$ calls an oracle "Bloom". On each query, Bloom oracle generates a BF and inserts blocks of the file in it. Oracle also generates dummy BFs having random strings of 0s and 1s. If 'a' is 0, then it shows that file is not present at storage. In this case, oracle replies with the set of k dummy BFs. If a is 1, then it shows that file is present at storage. Hence, oracle replies with the set of BFs including the real BF at random position and $k - 1$ dummy BFs.

Now, $\mathcal{A}$ tries to learn whether the file is present at cloud storage. For that, $\mathcal{A}$ tries to check whether file's BF is present in received BFs and guess the value of a'. Here, if $a' = a$, then $\mathcal{A}$ wins the security game. Otherwise, $\mathcal{A}$ loses the security game.

In our approach, cryptographic BF is computed by inserting file blocks. In other words, an adversary needs to have knowledge about the complete file for generating BF. When $\mathcal{A}$ sends upload request with tag, $\mathcal{S}$ responds with a set of k BFs. Here, $\mathcal{A}$ does not have knowledge about file except tag. Hence, it is hard to guess whether file's BF is present in set of k BFs. The probability of $\mathcal{A}$'s winning or $(Exp_A = 1)$ is $\frac{1}{2} + \epsilon(n)$, where $\epsilon(n)$ is negligible function. Therefore, advantage of $\mathcal{A}$ to win the security game is

$$Adv_A = |(Pr[Exp_A = 1]) - \frac{1}{2}| = |\frac{1}{2} + \epsilon(n) - \frac{1}{2}| = \epsilon(n).$$

Hence, we prove that $\mathcal{A}$ has the negligible advantage to learn about presence/absence of file in our approach. In other words, our approach provides privacy to information regarding presence/absence of the file.   □

False Positive Anomaly: BF data structure suffers from the false positive anomaly. The membership verification process may declare an element as a member of BF even if it is not. However, in our approach, we consider BF as deduplication identity of the file. $\mathcal{C}$ generates BF from file blocks and compares it with BFs which are received from the $\mathcal{S}$, to learn about the presence/absence of file. In this way, we leverage BF generation process and output vector of BF, but not BF's membership verification process in deduplication. Hence, the false positive anomaly of BF will not appear in our approach.

In BF, the sequence of inserting elements does not influence the output vector. For instance, two files (File 1 and File 2) are permutation of each other as shown in Fig. 4. Hence, BFs for both files are identical. Suppose, file 1 is present at cloud storage. When a $\mathcal{C}$(owner of file 2) requests to upload file 2, she may receive BF of file 1 in the set of received BFs from the $\mathcal{S}$. In such case, $\mathcal{C}$ finds a same copy of BF in received set and believes that file 2 is present at cloud storage. In this way, it causes the false positive anomaly.

As a solution, our approach file block with its position and executes BloomInsert($Block_i\|i$). Hence,

- BF_1 of file 1: BloomInsert($B1\|1$), BloomInsert($B2\|2$), BloomInsert($B3\|3$)
- BF_2 of file 2: BloomInsert($B2\|1$), BloomInsert($B1\|2$), BloomInsert($B3\|3$)

Since inserted elements are distinct in both cases, it results distinct filter vectors for these files.

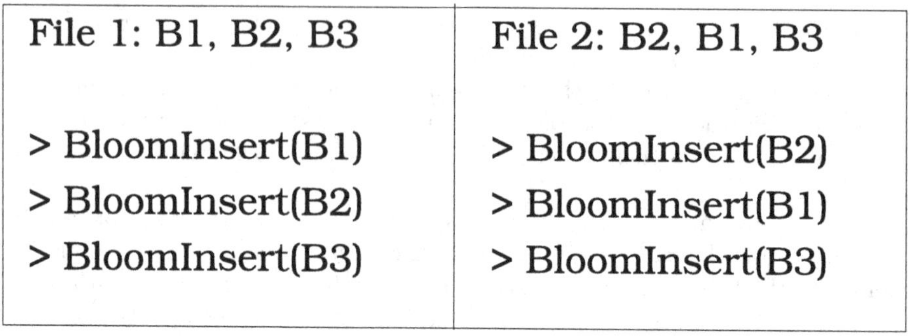

File 1: B1, B2, B3	File 2: B2, B1, B3
> BloomInsert(B1) > BloomInsert(B2) > BloomInsert(B3)	> BloomInsert(B2) > BloomInsert(B1) > BloomInsert(B3)

Fig. 4. Permuted files

Eavesdropping: An adversary can eavesdrop the communication between $\mathcal{C}$ and $\mathcal{S}$ and learn the deduplication identity of a file. Further, she can use it to learn the existence information of the file as discussed in Sect. 3.2. In our approach, for each upload request, the $\mathcal{S}$ responds with a set of BFs including dummies. Here, an adversary who is eavesdropping, cannot detect a file's BF in the received set without having knowledge about the complete file.

To protect the communication from $\mathcal{C}$ to $\mathcal{S}$, we leverage random nonce phenomena. Here, $\mathcal{C}$ sends $BF \oplus R$ and $Hash(BF) \oplus R$ in place of BF and Hash(BF) (where R = a random nonce generated by $\mathcal{S}$ for each upload request). Since R is uniformly random for each upload request, adversary cannot reuse the captured deduplication identity, whereas the $\mathcal{S}$ can retrieve BF by $(BF \oplus R)_{recv.} \oplus R$.

5.2 Integrity

Active attackers can attack communication links and modify the data. So, receiver will get modified data in place of original one. On the other hand, data may be accidentally changed while transmitting/storing.

For security against such unintended modification, we link hash values along with data while transmitting/storing. As a result, receiver is able to verify the integrity of received data using hash values.

6 Performance Analysis

We implement "Client" of our approach in C# Microsoft visual studio with ASP.NET on Intel i3 processor with 2.40 GHz and 4 GB RAM. "Server" code is implemented in C# Microsoft visual studio with Microsoft SQL Database services on Intel i5 processor with 3.19 GHz and 8 GB RAM. We execute our system over files having size 10 KB, 20 KB, 30 KB, 50 KB, and 100 KB. In the following, we evaluate (1) Time consumed by upload operation, and (2) Communication cost of proposed approach with BF's false positive probability = 0.001.

– Upload time: In upload operation, $\mathcal{C}$ generates and sends tag of the file. $\mathcal{S}$ responds with the set of bloom filters and metadata. $\mathcal{C}$ splits the file into blocks and generates BF using it. Further, $\mathcal{C}$ checks whether computed BF is matched with anyone of received BFs or not. If she does not find a match, then she uploads file and metadata. Otherwise, she extracts the encryption key from metadata, encrypts the file using it and uploads hash digest of the encrypted file and the bloom filter. In Fig. 5, we discuss time consumed by first upload and subsequent upload operations.

– Communication cost: In the existing approaches, $\mathcal{C}$ needs to send the file and metadata even if the file is present on storage. However, in our approach, $\mathcal{C}$ needs to send only hash values of bloom filter and encrypted file (i.e., only 512 bits) if the file is present. Figure 6 demonstrate that communication cost in our approach is significantly less than existing approaches for subsequent upload.

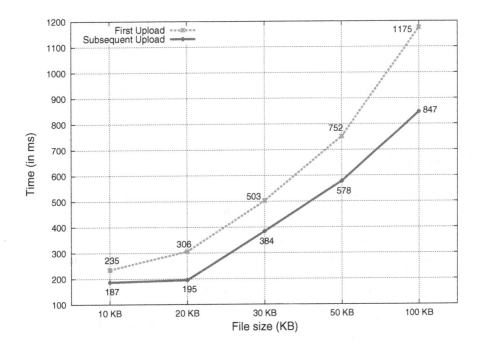

Fig. 5. Upload time

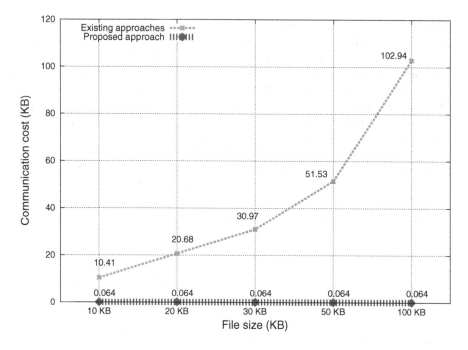

Fig. 6. Communication cost of subsequent upload

7 Related Work

In cloud storage services, data is to be encrypted before outsourcing for providing secrecy. Conventional encryption mechanisms conflict with deduplication. As a solution, Douceur et al. [2] introduced "Convergent Encryption" for deduplicated storage. In this approach, a file is encrypted with the hash value of it. Hence, all owners are able to compute the same key. However, convergent encryption is vulnerable to dictionary attack. For the security against dictionary attack, Bellare et al. [7] presented random convergent encryption (RCE). RCE encrypts the file with a random key for semantic security. However, the random key is weakly encrypted with the hash value of file. Hence, ciphertext of random key is still vulnerable to dictionary attack. Various state-of-the-art leverages additional server phenomena to improve security level.

In [16], Liu et al. proposed a scheme which provides security against dictionary attack without additional servers. In this scheme, clients need to be online for key exchange with new uploaders. In other words, key exchange overhead is on file owners. In [23], authors presented an approach "Secure Random Encryption for Deduplicated Storage". This approach encrypts the file with a random key for semantic security. For deduplication purpose, the random key is encrypted with the hash values derived from the file. Authors prove that an adversary needs to perform significantly huge number of attempts to compromise the secrecy of this approach. We adopt aforementioned encryption approach in this paper. In [24], authors present a secure proof of ownership (POW) mechanism. POW mechanism restricts deduplicated file's access to such users who own the complete file.

However, deduplication is vulnerable to side channel attacks even after applying encryption [3]. In [17], Hovhannisyan et al. proposed a scheme to send a complete message using the side channel attack. Adversary can leverage deduplication process for learning about the presence of file at storage. Adversary captures the deduplication identity (i.e., Hash of file) which is not generally secured by entities. She sends deduplication identity to server and server directly responds Yes/No for the Presence/Absence of file at storage. In this way, adversary can successfully learn about the existence of file. Server-side deduplication can provide protection against such information leakage. In this approach, a client is unaware about deduplication and always sends the file to server. Further, server takes care of deduplication on received file. However, a client needs to send the file even if it is present at storage. In this way, server side deduplication increases significant communication overhead.

In [3,5], authors proposed a threshold based solution. In this approach, clients need to send the file up to 't' uploads, where 't' is randomly chosen by the server. Hence, an adversary is not able to detect the presence of file up to t uploads. In [4], Pulls et al. formalized the attacks on cross-user deduplication. Further, they suggested dummy traffic between Client and Server to hide the information between client and server to hide information regarding the existence of file.

For providing semantic security to unpopular data, Stanek et al. proposed secure data deduplication scheme [10,20]. In this scheme, a file is encrypted with multiple security layers. Outer layer is semantically secure. And inner layer is convergent layer. Server invites upload until file reaches popularity. After reaching popularity, the server removes outer layer from ciphertext and file is now encrypted by convergent encryption. In this approach, two fully trusted entities ("Identity server" and "Indexing server") are employed for managing the file owners list and defining the popularity of file.

In [18], Puzio et al. proposed a scheme "PerfectDedup". In this scheme, client first learns the popularity of file by querying server. If file is not popular, then client uploads semantically encrypted ciphertext. And if file is popular, then client uploads convergently encrypted file. Further, server replaces semantically encrypted ciphertext with convergently encrypted ciphertext.

In various state-of-the-art [6,11,15], authors appointed gateway server between client and server. Client sends the file to gateway server and gateway server takes care of deduplication. In these proposals, clients needs to send the file to server even if it is present. Hence, it increases the communication cost. In Table 2, we discuss comparison between existing approaches and the proposed solution.

Table 2. Comparison with existing approaches

Existing approaches	Methodology	Limitation
Server side deduplication	Client always sends the file. And server takes care of deduplication on the received file	Communication overhead: Clients need to send the file even if it is present at storage
Threshold based solution [3,5]	Server decides a threshold t and keeps a counter c for each file. Server hides the existence information by asking client to upload the file until $c < t$	
Popularity based solution [10, 18, 20]	Initially, server permits clients to upload the file encrypted by own secret key. Further, server replaces all versions with convergently encrypted version when file uploads reach popularity threshold	
Gateway server based approach [6, 11, 15]	An additional gateway server is equipped for deduplication. Client always sends the file and gateway server performs deduplication on the file	
Proposed approach	Server hides the existence information by responding with set of BFs including dummies to each upload request	–

In [8, 9, 12, 14, 19], authors proposed solutions to detect on-device and remote host malware via statistical signatures. In [13, 22], authors presented secure sql mechanism for database as a service model. In future, we will work on applying deduplication in malware detection and sql as a service mechanism.

8   Conclusion

In this paper, we discuss a significant privacy issue in the deduplication system. The adversary can leverage deduplication process to learn about presence/absence of a particular file. We propose a privacy preserving deduplication approach which obfuscates the information regarding presence of the file. In this approach, Bloom filter (having blocks of a file as members) is considered as a deduplication identity of the file. When a client requests to upload a file, the server responds with the genuine bloom filter (if file exists) along with dummy filters. Now, if a client has knowledge about the complete file, then only she can compute file's bloom filter and learn the file existence information using it. We prove that our approach provides privacy to information regarding the existence of file. In other words, an adversary can learn presence/absence of the file with negligible advantage. Moreover, we demonstrate that our approach has significantly less communication overhead than existing approaches.

References

1. Bloom, B.H.: Space/time trade-offs in hash coding with allowable errors. Commun. ACM **13**(7), 422–426 (1970)
2. Douceur, J.R., Adya, A., Bolosky, W.J., Simon, P., Theimer, M.: Reclaiming space from duplicate files in a serverless distributed file system. In: Proceedings of 22nd International Conference on Distributed Computing Systems, pp. 617–624. IEEE (2002)
3. Harnik, D., Pinkas, B., Shulman-Peleg, A.: Side channels in cloud services: deduplication in cloud storage. IEEE Secur. Privacy **6**, 40–47 (2010)
4. Pulls, T.: (More) side channels in cloud storage. In: Camenisch, J., Crispo, B., Fischer-Hübner, S., Leenes, R., Russello, G. (eds.) Privacy and Identity 2011. IAICT, vol. 375, pp. 102–115. Springer, Heidelberg (2012). https://doi.org/10.1007/978-3-642-31668-5_8
5. Lee, S., Choi, D.: Privacy-preserving cross-user source-based data deduplication in cloud storage. In: 2012 International Conference on ICT Convergence (ICTC), pp. 329–330. IEEE, October 2012
6. Heen, O., Neumann, C., Montalvo, L., Defrance, S.: Improving the resistance to side-channel attacks on cloud storage services. In: 2012 5th International Conference on New Technologies, Mobility and Security (NTMS), pp. 1–5. IEEE, May 2012
7. Bellare, M., Keelveedhi, S., Ristenpart, T.: Message-locked encryption and secure deduplication. In: Johansson, T., Nguyen, P.Q. (eds.) EUROCRYPT 2013. LNCS, vol. 7881, pp. 296–312. Springer, Heidelberg (2013). https://doi.org/10.1007/978-3-642-38348-9_18
8. Faruki, P., Laxmi, V., Ganmoor, V., Gaur, M.S., Bharmal, A.: Droidolytics: robust feature signature for repackaged android apps on official and third party android markets. In: 2013 2nd International Conference on Advanced Computing, Networking and Security (ADCONS), pp. 247–252. IEEE, December 2013
9. Faruki, P., Ganmoor, V., Laxmi, V., Gaur, M.S., Bharmal, A.: AndroSimilar: robust statistical feature signature for Android malware detection. In: Proceedings of the 6th International Conference on Security of Information and Networks, pp. 152–159. ACM, November 2013
10. Stanek, J., Sorniotti, A., Androulaki, E., Kencl, L.: A secure data deduplication scheme for cloud storage. In: Christin, N., Safavi-Naini, R. (eds.) FC 2014. LNCS, vol. 8437, pp. 99–118. Springer, Heidelberg (2014). https://doi.org/10.1007/978-3-662-45472-5_8
11. Meye, P., Raipin, P., Tronel, F., Anceaume, E.: A secure two-phase data deduplication scheme. In: 2014 IEEE International Conference on High Performance Computing and Communications, 2014 IEEE 6th International Symposium on Cyberspace Safety and Security, 2014 IEEE 11th International Conference on Embedded Software and Syst (HPCC, CSS, ICESS), pp. 802–809. IEEE (2014)
12. Faruki, P., Kumar, V., Ammar, B., Gaur, M.S., Laxmi, V., Conti, M.: Platform neutral sandbox for analyzing malware and resource hogger apps. In: Tian, J., Jing, J., Srivatsa, M. (eds.) SecureComm 2014. LNICST, vol. 152, pp. 556–560. Springer, Cham (2015). https://doi.org/10.1007/978-3-319-23829-6_43
13. Dave, J.: Secure SQL with access control for database as a service model. Doctoral dissertation, Dhirubhai Ambani Institute of Information and Communication Technology (2014)

14. Faruki, P., Bharmal, A., Laxmi, V., Gaur, M.S., Conti, M., Rajarajan, M.: Evaluation of android anti-malware techniques against dalvik bytecode obfuscation. In: 2014 IEEE 13th International Conference on Trust, Security and Privacy in Computing and Communications (TrustCom), pp. 414–421. IEEE, September 2014

15. Shin, Y., Kim, K.: Differentially private clientside data deduplication protocol for cloud storage services. Secur. Commun. Netw. 8(12), 2114–2123 (2015)

16. Liu, J., Asokan, N., Pinkas, B.: Secure deduplication of encrypted data without additional independent servers. In: Proceedings of the 22nd ACM SIGSAC Conference on Computer and Communications Security, pp. 874–885. ACM, October 2015

17. Hovhannisyan, H., Lu, K., Yang, R., Qi, W., Wang, J., Wen, M.: A novel deduplication-based covert channel in cloud storage service. In: 2015 IEEE Global Communications Conference (GLOBECOM), pp. 1–6. IEEE, December 2015

18. Puzio, P., Molva, R., Önen, M., Loureiro, S.: PerfectDedup: secure data deduplication. In: Garcia-Alfaro, J., Navarro-Arribas, G., Aldini, A., Martinelli, F., Suri, N. (eds.) DPM/QASA -2015. LNCS, vol. 9481, pp. 150–166. Springer, Cham (2016). https://doi.org/10.1007/978-3-319-29883-2_10

19. Faruki, P., et al.: Android security: a survey of issues, malware penetration, and defenses. IEEE Commun. Surv. Tutorials 17(2), 998–1022 (2015)

20. Stanek, J., Kencl, L.: Enhanced secure thresholded data deduplication scheme for cloud storage. IEEE Trans. Dependable Secure Comput. 15, 694–707 (2016)

21. Networking, C.V.: Cisco Global Cloud Index: Forecast and Methodology, 2016–2021. White paper. Cisco Public, San Jose (2016)

22. Dave, J., Das, M.L.: Securing SQL with access control for database as a service model. In: Proceedings of the Second International Conference on Information and Communication Technology for Competitive Strategies, p. 104. ACM, March 2016

23. Dave, J., Saharan, S., Faruki, P., Laxmi, V., Gaur, M.S.: Secure random encryption for deduplicated storage. In: Shyamasundar, R.K., Singh, V., Vaidya, J. (eds.) ICISS 2017. LNCS, vol. 10717, pp. 164–176. Springer, Cham (2017). https://doi.org/10.1007/978-3-319-72598-7_10

24. Dave, J., Faruki, P., Laxmi, V., Bezawada, B., Gaur, M.: Secure and efficient proof of ownership for deduplicated cloud storage. In: Proceedings of the 10th International Conference on Security of Information and Networks, pp. 19–26. ACM, October 2017

A Semantic Notion of Secure
Information-Flow

N. V. Narendra Kumar[1]([⊠]) and R. K. Shyamasundar[2]

[1] Centre for Payment Systems, IDRBT, Hyderabad, India
naren.nelabhotla@gmail.com
[2] Department of Computer Science and Engineering,
Indian Institute of Technology Bombay, Mumbai, India
shyamasundar@gmail.com

Abstract. It is highly desirable to have a safety property characterizing a general notion of secure information flow that succinctly captures the underpinnings of language-based security for general purpose programming languages. Such a notion must necessarily consider both implicit and explicit flows, and the need to provide labeled outputs. The notion must also embed access control and information-flow control considering that the program output is usually a set of multilevel labeled outputs. Finally, it must be based on a notion of security violations, as the latter plays a vital role in compositionality of security properties. The widely used notion of non-interference does not meet many of these criteria, and its use has crippled the progress of secure programming systems and operating systems. A notion of security that takes the desired criteria into account is proposed, and its advantages in comparison with non-interference and other related notions is established. We further relate our notion to the early works of Fenton and Denning to highlight its succinctness in defining language-based security, and also with that of Boudol's notion of secure information flow as a safety property. An added advantage of our approach compared to Boudol's approach is that it generalizes to non-deterministic systems and systems with rich constructs such as exceptions etc.

Keywords: Secure information-flow · Semantics · Non-interference

1 Introduction

The notion of non-interference [8,9] championed the characterization of Multi-Level Secure (MLS) systems. Essentially, it tries to capture the leakage of information when multiple users with multi-level authorizations are enrolled on an MLS system. To establish an end-to-end security, two key properties are involved (ignoring side channels for the moment), access control and information flow in the system.

McLean [14] was one of the first persons to examine the classical noninterference and its variants like generalized noninterference, restrictiveness etc. He

© Springer Nature Singapore Pte Ltd. 2019
S. Nandi et al. (Eds.): ISEA-ISAP 2018, CCIS 939, pp. 35–52, 2019.
https://doi.org/10.1007/978-981-13-7561-3_3

argues that protecting only high-level input is insufficient for ensuring security since in many systems high-level output is generated solely from low-level input. Ryan et al. [20], argue that non-interference is such an abstract formulation that it seems remote from real concerns of security managers, policy makers and the developers of systems and it has not made any effective impact in practice.

On another plane, requirements of fine-grained security specification at a program level have led to certification semantics of programming languages [5,6]. Volpano et al. [23], used a purely value-based interpretation of non-interference as a semantic characterization of information-flow. Volpano et al.'s notion of non-interference and its extensions have become the de-facto standard for the semantics of information-flow in the literature on language-based security. Generalizations of Volpano et al.'s non-interference to concurrent systems [12], and non-deterministic systems [2] have also been explored. However, researchers [13,14] have questioned whether the notion of non-interference is relevant for defining security of programs, particularly in programming languages as they are usually not deterministic.

Boudol [3] argues that non-interference is inappropriate as a semantics for secure programming languages because: (i) it does not support dynamic policies, and (ii) it is not easy to explain the security errors. Further, inspired by Fenton's work [7], he argues that the notion of information-flow security can be cast as a safety property which makes it a lot easier to comprehend and reason about. Based on this notion, he proposed a security semantics for a *while* programming language as a safety property and showed that for his chosen language it is strictly stronger than non-interference of Volpano et al. [23]. The emphasis of Boudol's work [3] has been to demonstrate the notion of a *security error*[1], that can be captured by a standard security type system. Thus, he did not address the nuances of dynamic labelling of objects /processes in the context of language constructs where one needs to consider non-termination, failures etc., and also the access control requirements of labelled data.

The main objective[2] of this paper is to refine Boudol's work [3] by defining a notion of information-flow security referred to as IF-Secure, as a safety property for general computing systems and explore a class of systems for which our new notion will be strictly stronger than non-interference of Volpano et al. [23]. Further, we arrive at a method for automatically deriving the monitoring semantics of any computational system w.r.t IF-Secure, and demonstrate its application for both static and dynamic (run-time) analysis. Note that while Boudol demonstrated the possibility for a specific deterministic programming system, IF-Secure is applicable for non-deterministic systems, and also for deterministic systems with rich constructs such as exceptions etc.

---

[1] Typically illustrated by the guidance that one should not place in a public location a value arrived at using confidential information.

[2] In this paper, we shall confine to the notion of non-interference that is widely used for security analysis of programs and do not discuss the vast amount of work related to the decentralized label model [16], its variations (cf. an early survey [21]) and its applications.

The main contributions of this paper are:

- Defining a strong notion of flow security called IF-Secure as a safety property,
- For finite deterministic computing systems, establish that IF-Secure is strictly stronger than non-interference (a generalization of Boudol's result),
- Present systematic approaches for deriving run-time monitors and program certification semantics using the proposed notion.

The rest of the paper is organized as follows: Sect. 2 introduces our notion of information-flow security as a safety property, and establishes that it is strictly stronger than non-interference for finite deterministic systems. Approaches to derive run-time monitors and program certification semantics based on the proposed notion are presented in Sect. 3. Section 4 discusses related work, and the paper concludes in Sect. 5 with a discussion on whether the proposed notion of security is better suited for supporting the various aspects needed for language-based security.

2   A Notion of Information-Flow Security

In this section, we arrive at a notion of information-flow security based on the sequence of accesses caused due to the execution of commands of a machine.

Definition 1 (Computing Machine). *A computing machine, $\mathcal{M}$, is defined as a transition system, $(\mathcal{Q}, \mathcal{C}, \mathcal{S})$, where $\mathcal{Q}$ denotes the set of states in the system, $\mathcal{C}$ denotes the set of commands/instructions of the machine, and $\mathcal{S} : \mathcal{Q} \times \mathcal{C} \to \mathcal{Q}$, denotes the semantics of the commands.*

For the purposes of this paper, we can consider the state to be defined by either values of variables, or contents of memory locations, i.e., $\forall q \in \mathcal{Q}, q : V \to \mathcal{V}$, where V denotes the set of variables (or addresses), and $\mathcal{V}$ denotes a semantic domain of values.

Definition 2 (Execution). *Given a state q, and a command c of a machine, the detailed process by which the state is changed to $\mathcal{S}(q, c)$ is referred as execution of c in q.*

Execution of a given command in a given state involves a sequence of accesses (reads or updates) to variables, and is implied by the semantics - a description not-only of what the state change is, but also how the state changes. Let r denote read and u denote update, and $A = \{r, u\}$ denote the set of possible accesses. X^* denotes the Kleene-closure of a set X, i.e., the set of all finite sequences of elements of X. For a sequence s, $|s|$ denotes its length, and for $1 \leq i \leq |s|$, s_i denotes the ith element in s.

Definition 3 (Access Sequence of an Execution). *Access sequence of an execution of a computing machine is defined as a function $ASeq : \mathcal{Q} \times \mathcal{C} \to (V \times A)^*$.*

Let p denote the process executing in a computing machine. Variables accessed by p during its execution cause information-flow in the following ways: (i) when p reads a variable v, information is said to flow from v to p, and (ii) when p updates a variable v, information is said to flow from p to v. We obtain the information-flow sequence of an execution by replacing each element of the form (v, r) appearing in its access sequence by (v, p) to depict the flow of information from v to p, and (v, u) by (p, v) to depict the flow of information from p to v. Let $V' = V \cup \{p\}$. The definition of information-flow sequence of an execution is:

Definition 4
(Information-Flow Sequence of an Execution). *Information-flow sequence of an execution of a computing machine is a function IFSeq $: \mathcal{Q} \times \mathcal{C} \to (V' \times V')^*$, defined by*
$|IFSeq(q, c)| = |ASeq(q, c)|$, *and* $\forall 1 \leq i \leq |ASeq(q, c)|$,
$IFSeq(q, c)_i = (v, p)$ *if* $ASeq(q, c)_i = (v, r)$, *and*
$IFSeq(q, c)_i = (p, v)$ *if* $ASeq(q, c)_i = (v, u)$.

To begin with, let us restrict our attention to information-flow between variables. In this case, we say that information flows from a variable v_1 to a variable v_2 during the execution of c in q, if v_2 is updated after reading v_1. A formal definition is given below.

Definition 5 (Information-Flows caused by an Execution). *Information-flows caused by an execution of a computing machine is a function*
$IF : \mathcal{Q} \times \mathcal{C} \to 2^{(V \times V)}$, *defined by*
$IF(q, c) = \{(v_1, v_2) \mid \exists\ 1 \leq i \leq j \leq |IFSeq(q, c)|\ IFSeq(q, c)_i = (v_1, p) \wedge IFSeq(q, c)_j = (p, v_2)\}$.

Denning's seminal work [4] gives us the definition of an information-flow policy or permissible information flows.

Definition 6 (Information-Flow Policy). *Information-flow policy, $\mathcal{P}$, defines the permissible information flows in a system, and is denoted by a four tuple $(\mathcal{L}, \leqslant, \oplus, \lambda)$, where $\mathcal{L}$ is a set of security classes/labels, $\leqslant \subseteq \mathcal{L} \times \mathcal{L}$ is a partial-order over $\mathcal{L}$ denoting the permissible flows, $\oplus : \mathcal{L} \times \mathcal{L} \to \mathcal{L}$ is the least upper bound operator, and $\lambda : V \to \mathcal{L}$ is an assignment of security labels to variables.*

Given a computing machine and an information-flow policy, we now define a notion of information-flow security referred to as *IF-Secure*.

Definition 7 (Information-Flow Security (IF-Secure)). *A command $c \in \mathcal{C}$ of a computing machine $\mathcal{M} = (\mathcal{Q}, \mathcal{C}, \mathcal{S})$ is said to be IF-Secure with respect to an information-flow policy $\mathcal{P} = (\mathcal{L}, \leqslant, \oplus, \lambda)$ if and only if*
$\forall q \in \mathcal{Q}, v_1, v_2 \in V \big[[(v_1, v_2) \in IF(q, c)] \Rightarrow [\lambda(v_1) \leqslant \lambda(v_2)]\big]$,
where $\Rightarrow$ denotes logical implication.

A computing machine is said to be secure with respect to an information-flow policy if and only if all its commands are IF-Secure with respect to the policy.

Note that our notion of IF-Secure, is a safety property. This is because of the simple fact that for any two commands c_1 and c_2, $\text{IF}(q, c_1) \subseteq \text{IF}(q, c_1; c_2)$, where ';' denotes sequential composition.

In the rest of this section, we shall illustrate and provide more intuitions for the notion of IF-Secure through examples, compare it with Boudol's notion of security, and also show that IF-Secure is stronger than non-interference.

2.1   Illustrative Examples

Example 1: Let us consider the Copy1 example of Denning [5] given below:

```
procedure copy1(x: integer; var y: integer);
"copy x to y"
var z: integer;
begin
y := 0;
z := 0;
if x=0 then z:=1;
if z=0 then y:=1;
end
end copy1
```

Let c_1 denote the procedure copy1. Let q_0 denote the state where $x = 0$, and q_1 denote the state where $x = 1$ (the values of y and z are immaterial as they are anyway initialized to 0 at the start of the procedure).

An elaborate description of the execution of c_1 in q_0 is: read the constant 0, update y with 0, read the constant 0, update z with 0, read x, read 0, compare x and 0, since they are equal, read 1, update z with 1, read z, read 0, compare z with 0, since they are unequal do nothing. The description of the execution of c_1 in q_1 is similar. It is important to note that irrespective of whether the tests succeed or fail, the process executing c_1 always reads x and z. From the discussion above first we shall present the access sequences of executing c_1 in states q_0 and q_1.

$\text{ASeq}(q_0, c_1) = (0, r).(y, u).(0, r).(z, u).(x, r).(0, r).(1, r).(z, u).(z, r).(0, r)$
$\text{ASeq}(q_1, c_1) = (0, r).(y, u).(0, r).(z, u).(x, r).(0, r).(z, r).(0, r).(1, r).(y, u)$

Let p denote the process executing c_1. Then the information-flow sequences of executing c_1 in states q_0 and q_1 are given below. Recall that this is obtained by simply replacing tuples of the form (v, r) from ASeq with (v, p) to indicate the information-flow from variable/memory location v to program point p, and replacing tuples of the form (v, u) with (p, v) to indicate the information-flow from program point p to variable/memory location v.

$\text{IFSeq}(q_0, c_1) = (0, p).(p, y).(0, p).(p, z).(x, p).(0, p).(1, p).(p, z).(z, p).(0, p)$
$\text{IFSeq}(q_1, c_1) = (0, p).(p, y).(0, p).(p, z).(x, p).(0, p).(z, p).(0, p).(1, p).(p, y)$

Next, the information-flows caused by the execution of c_1 in q_0 and q_1 are computed as follows:

$\text{IF}(q_0, c_1) = \{(0, y), (0, z), (x, z), (1, z)\}$
$\text{IF}(q_1, c_1) = \{(0, y), (0, z), (x, y), (z, y), (1, y)\}$

Ignoring the trivially permissible flows from constants to variables, we will have:
$\text{IF}(q_0, c_1) = \{(x, z)\}$
$\text{IF}(q_1, c_1) = \{(x, y), (z, y)\}$

The command/program c_1 will be declared IF-Secure for only those flow-policies λ that satisfy $\lambda(x) \leqslant \lambda(z)$, and $\lambda(x) \leqslant \lambda(y)$, and $\lambda(z) \leqslant \lambda(y)$. In particular, this means that IF-Secure correctly identifies the flow of information from x to y in the procedure copy1.

2.2   Comparison with the Approach of Boudol [3]

There are two main differences between our approach and Boudol's. One is that in our approach, PC (the label of the program counter) is never reset, while in Boudol's approach, PC is reset immediately after a block. While this does not bear upon deterministic finite programs, this plays a vital role in extending the notion of security to generalized settings. For example, information leakage due to termination channels cannot be captured by Boudol's approach. Consider the program:

```
procedure copy2(x: integer; var y: integer);
"copy x to y"
begin
y := 0;
while x=0;
y := 1;
end
end copy2
```

Boudol's approach (Definition 2.4 in [3]) will declare this program to be secure w.r.t the class of memories where $x = 1$ and does not recognize the flow from x to y. In contrast, our approach captures this flow. This is because, while in our approach the label of the process captures the fact that it has read x and remembers it ever after, Boudol's approach resets the PC label once the control exits the while loop.

Second, IF-Secure defines the security of a command w.r.t a flow policy, whereas Boudol's notion of security (Definition 2.4 in [3]) allows talking about the security of a command w.r.t a class of memories. For example, Boudol's approach would declare the program c_1 to be secure w.r.t the policy λ where $\lambda(x) \leqslant \lambda(z)$ for the class of memories q_0 where $x = 0$, and similarly, it declares the program c_1 to be secure w.r.t the policy λ' where $\lambda'(z) \leqslant \lambda'(y)$ for the class of memories q_1 where $x = 1$.

2.3   IF-Secure is Stronger than Non-interference

In this section, we compare our notion of IF-Secure with that of non-interference due to Volpano et al. and establish that our notion is stronger than the other.
   First, let us formalize the notion of non-interference.

Definition 8 (L-equivalence of States). *Given two states $q_1 \in \mathcal{Q}$ and $q_2 \in \mathcal{Q}$ of a computing machine $(\mathcal{Q}, \mathcal{C}, \mathcal{S})$, and a label $L \in \mathcal{L}$ from the policy $(\mathcal{L}, \leqslant, \oplus, \lambda)$, q_1 and q_2 are said to be L-equivalent, written $q_1 \cong_L q_2$, if $\forall v \in V \left[(\lambda(v) \leqslant L) \Rightarrow (q_1(v) = q_2(v)) \right]$.*

   In the following, we capture the non-interference definition of [23] through our notation.

Definition 9 (Non-interference). *A command $c \in \mathcal{C}$ of a computing machine $\mathcal{M} = (\mathcal{Q}, \mathcal{C}, \mathcal{S})$ is said to be non-interfering with respect to an information-flow policy $\mathcal{P} = (\mathcal{L}, \leqslant, \oplus, \lambda)$ if and only if $\forall q_1, q_2 \in \mathcal{Q}, L \in \mathcal{L} \left[(q_1 \cong_L q_2) \Rightarrow (\mathcal{S}(q_1, c) \cong_L \mathcal{S}(q_2, c)) \right]$*

   In the following, we shall illustrate the relation between IF-Secure and non-interference through example traces.

Example 2: IF-Security/non-interference of some simple traces is illustrated below.

- The program $l := 0$ is both IF-Secure and non-interfering.
- The program $h := 0; l := h$ is non-interfering but not IF-Secure.
- The program $l := h$ is neither non-interfering nor IF-Secure.

Important Remarks

1. Note that the authority/capability of subjects plays a crucial role in the original notion of non-interference [8,9] due to Goguen and Meseguer. It is a subject's authority that determines his ability to execute commands and also his observation power of a state. These aspects have been totally ignored in the pure value based notion of non-interference due to Volpano et al. [23]. However, it is the latter that is predominantly used as the notion of information-flow security. Our notion of IF-Secure incorporates the necessary features to include subject's authority in the reasoning about security.
2. Consider the naive program $h := 0; l := h;$. It is a non-interfering program that is not IF-Secure. One could argue that the value of l will be 0 after all possible executions of the program, and therefore consider the program to be secure. While the above argument holds in a sequential context, it does not hold in a concurrent context where information-flow is much more subtle as illustrated in [15]. Particularly, if there are concurrent threads that share the variable h, then the above program can leak h. This example illustrates the importance of control information carried in the program counter, and also the holistic nature of our notion IF-Secure. Thus, IF-secure is a better semantic notion compared to non-interference and provides plausible information leaks

that could be used to build security models. The notion of IF-Secure also enables one to build assertions on individual components for their composition to be secure.

Now, we will present the main result that for deterministic systems that always terminate, IF-Secure is stronger than non-interference as interpreted by Volpano et al. [23]. Let $\Rightarrow$ denote logical implication.

Theorem 1 (IF-Secure is Stronger than Non-interference). *Given a finite command $c \in \mathcal{C}$ of a deterministic computing machine $\mathcal{M} = (\mathcal{Q}, \mathcal{C}, \mathcal{S})$, and an information-flow policy $\mathcal{P} = (\mathcal{L}, \leqslant, \oplus, \lambda)$,*
c is IF-Secure $\Rightarrow$ c is non-interfering.

Proof is by a case-by-case analysis and is provided at Appendix.

2.4 Advantages of IF-Secure over Non-interference

If we consider various examples from copy1 to copy5 from Denning [5], we find that "PC-reset" (PC stands for the label of the program counter which is typically used to track subtle information-flows encoded in the control flow path) after each block is not sufficient for certifying the security of programs. While the extreme information requirement for certifying the security of a program is PC-monotonic[3], for quite a large class of programs the extent of tracking the PC lies between PC-reset to PC-monotonic; in fact, we can transform iterative programs into semantically equivalent programs to derive both forward and backward security flow obligations. This is embedded in IF-Secure; in fact, the definition of security of a command captures these aspects. It may be noted that Boudol's mechanism uses the PC-reset option thereby already restricting the class of flow secure programs.

While it has not been easy to generalize the notion of non-interference to non-deterministic systems, the examples given earlier in the section clearly illustrate that our notion of information-flow security is a trace property that applies and extends naturally to general systems (nondeterministic or concurrent). Further, it is also unclear if and in what way the value-based notion of non-interference of Volpano et al. is connected to information-flow security in general systems. In summary, we contend that our notion of IF-Secure is more appropriate for information-flow security than non-interference of Volpano et al.

3   Mechanisms for Preserving/Enforcing IF-Secure

In this section, we first discuss a general approach for deriving mechanisms that preserve/enforce our notion of information-flow security, IF-Secure, and then show how it can be applied for specific systems.

First, we define the information-flow security preserving semantics of a computing machine.

---

[3] That is, PC is never reset.

Definition 10 (Security Preserving Semantics). *Given a computing machine* $\mathcal{M} = (\mathcal{Q}, \mathcal{C}, \mathcal{S})$, *its security preserving semantics with respect to an information-flow policy* $\mathcal{P} = (\mathcal{L}, \leqslant, \oplus, \lambda)$, *is a function*
$\mathcal{S}' : (\mathcal{Q} \cup \{MISUSE\}) \times \mathcal{C} \to (\mathcal{Q} \cup \{MISUSE\})$, *and is defined as*
$\forall\, c \in \mathcal{C}\; [\mathcal{S}'(MISUSE, c) = MISUSE]$, *and*
$\forall\, q \in \mathcal{Q}, c \in \mathcal{C}$
$\mathcal{S}'(q, c) = \mathcal{S}(q, c) \quad if\; \forall (v_1, v_2) \in IF(q, c)\; (\lambda(v_1) \leqslant \lambda(v_2))$
$\qquad\quad = MISUSE\; otherwise.$

Typically, a computing machine is described by providing a set of basic commands, and a set of operators for composing the basic commands to realize complex functionality. Direct application of the above definition for security preservation of compound commands is inefficient. Modular reasoning becomes possible by introducing a notion of a security context.

For supporting modular reasoning that simplifies the checks to be performed by the mechanisms, we keep track of the security context using a variable called the PCLabel whose possible values range over $\mathcal{L} \cup \{\varepsilon\}$, where $\mathcal{L}$ is the set of labels in the information-flow policy, and ε denotes an information misuse. At the start of each execution, PCLabel is set to $\perp$ representing the lowest label. Let $\mathcal{L}' = \mathcal{L} \cup \{\varepsilon\}$.

Definition 11 (IF-Secure Version of a Computing Machine). *The IF-Secure version of a computing machine* $\mathcal{M} = (\mathcal{Q}, \mathcal{C}, \mathcal{S})$ *is defined as the machine* $\mathcal{M}_{IF\text{-}Sec} = (\mathcal{Q}', \mathcal{C}, \mathcal{S}')$, *where* $\mathcal{Q}' = \mathcal{Q} \times \mathcal{L}'$, *and*
$\forall q \in \mathcal{Q}, c \in \mathcal{C}\; [\mathcal{S}'((q, \varepsilon), c) = (q, \varepsilon)]$
$\forall q \in \mathcal{Q}, c \in \mathcal{C}, L \in \mathcal{L}$
$\mathcal{S}'((q, L), c) = (\mathcal{S}(q, c), L \bigoplus_{(v_1, v_2) \in IF(q, c)} \lambda(v_1))$
$\qquad\qquad if\; \forall (v_1, v_2) \in IF(q, c)\; [(L \oplus \lambda(v_1)) \leqslant \lambda(v_2)],$
$\qquad\quad = (q, \varepsilon)\; otherwise,$
where λ *comes from an information-flow policy* $\mathcal{P} = (\mathcal{L}, \leqslant, \oplus, \lambda)$.

The above definition provides a constructive approach for deriving mechanisms for verifying and enforcing the security of systems. In the following sections, we illustrate the generality and utility of the above definition by applying it to derive IF-Secure versions of two distinct computing machines.

3.1 Run-Time Monitoring

In this section, we derive the IF-Secure version of Fenton's Data Mark Machine (DMM) [7] using our approach, and compare it with Fenton's semantics.

There are only three basic operations in the Minsky machine, increment, decrement, and check_zero. The access sequence of increment, $x := x + 1$, is $(x, r).(x, u)$ i.e., value of x is read and updated. Therefore the security check to be performed in the security context PCLabel is PCLabel $\oplus \lambda(x) \leqslant \lambda(x)$, and the security context is updated to PCLabel $\oplus \lambda(x)$. The same holds for decrement, $x := x - 1$. For checking whether a register x is zero, we need to read

x, i.e., the access sequence for check_zero is (x, r). Therefore for this operation, the security context is updated to PCLabel $\oplus \lambda(x)$. Similarly, for outputting the contents of the output register o, it needs to be read, therefore the security context is updated to PCLabel $\oplus \lambda(o)$. Further, the output will be labelled PCLabel (updated context), because it is executed in this security context.

From the discussion above, the IF-Secure version of the DMM using our approach is given in Table 1.

Table 1. IF-Secure version of DMM

Instruction	IF-Secure Semantics

x'	if PCLabel $\neq \varepsilon$ then
	  if PCLabel $\leqslant \lambda(x)$ then
	    PCLabel = PCLabel $\oplus \lambda(x)$,
	    x:=x+1
	  else PCLabel $= \varepsilon$

$x^-(n)$	if PCLabel $\neq \varepsilon$ then
	  if $(x == 0)$ then
	    PCLabel = PCLabel $\oplus \lambda(x)$,
	    goto n
	  else if PCLabel $\leqslant \lambda(x)$ then
	      PCLabel = PCLabel $\oplus \lambda(x)$,
	    x:=x-1
	    else PCLabel $= \varepsilon$

Halt	if PCLabel $\neq \varepsilon$ then PCLabel = PCLabel $\oplus \lambda(o)$ Output the contents of o with label PCLabel

Comparison with the Approach of Fenton [7]. The main difference between our semantics of DMM and that of Fenton's, is his introduction of two new commands x^*, and Return. Note that in the original Minsky machine, the "true" branch of the instruction $x^-(n)$ need not return to the instruction immediately following it. The two new commands added by Fenton combine to simulate the standard if-then-else command, wherein it is guaranteed that irrespective of which branch was taken, the code following the command will be executed, and therefore cannot be used to leak information about the condition variable. In our understanding, this is the analysis Fenton used to restore the process data mark to its previous value upon returning from the "true" branch. In our opinion, this restoring is inappropriate for sound reasoning of information-flow security as discussed in detail in the next section. Further, from his semantics of the "Halt" instruction, it looks as if the output was intended to be always public, thus not truly supporting the notion of computing on MLS data.

3.2   Static Program Certification

Program certification is a mechanism to determine whether a given program specifies invalid flows. Note that in the ideal case, this approach is sound but not precise as the program may never execute instructions causing the invalid flows. The certification process can be easily incorporated into the analysis phase of a compiler, when variables have immutable labels declared in the program. The mechanism is presented in the form of *certification semantics* - actions for the compiler to perform, along with usual semantic actions such as type checking and code generation, when a string of a given syntactic type is recognized.

In this section, we derive the certification semantics of a simple language using our approach, and compare it with the semantics given by Denning [5].

For certifying a program to be secure, it is to be verified that the information-flow policy is preserved in all possible executions. With this in mind, let us derive the certification semantics for the standard *while* language. For a statement S, let S^u and S^r denote the greatest lower bound of the labels of variables that could be modified in some execution of S, and the least upper bound of the labels of variables that could be accessed in some execution of S, respectively. Let eLabel and PCLabel denote the label of an expression (the least upper bound of the labels of all the variables appearing in the expression), and the security context of the program point respectively.

First, we shall derive the semantics for base statements, then reason about their composition. From the semantics of the assignment statement $v := e$, it is immediate that it always causes the following access sequence $(v_1, r). \cdots .(v_n, r).(v, u)$, where $v_1, \ldots, v_n$ are all the variables occurring in e. Therefore it causes information flow from v_i to v for all $1 \le i \le n$, and the condition eLabel $\le \lambda(v)$ needs to be checked for its security. For the branching statement, "if e then S_1", the possible access sequences are $(v_1, r). \cdots .(v_n, r)$ followed by some access sequence of S_1. For this statement to be secure, in addition to the security of the flows in S_1, it needs to be verified that the flow from e to S_1 is secure, and therefore the condition eLabel $\le S_1^u$ needs to be checked. Similarly, for the security of "if e then S_1 else S_2", in addition to the security of S_1 and S_2, it needs to be verified that eLabel $\le S_i^u$ for $i \in \{1, 2\}$, because its possible access sequences could be e followed by an access sequence of S_1 or S_2.

Access sequences generated by the statement "while e do S_1", are of the form $(v_1, r). \cdots .(v_n, r)$ followed by some access sequence of S_1 followed by some access sequence of S_1 and so on. For the security of this statement, in addition to the security of flows in S_1, it needs to be verified that (i) the flow from e to S_1 is secure, which is checked by eLabel $\le S_1^u$, and (ii) the sequential composition of S_1 with itself is secure, which is discussed below.

From the semantics of sequential composition, $S_1; S_2$, it is clear that S_2 starts executing only in the context in which S_1 finishes. In general, the program point itself contains some information encoded in it, which needs to be taken into account for verifying the security of the program executing in it. We use the variable PCLabel to denote this information. From the perspective of access sequences generated by $S_1; S_2$, it will be a concatenation of some access sequence of S_1 with some access sequence of S_2. So, for the security of $S_1; S_2$ in the context PCLabel, in addition to S_1 and S_2 being secure, the following needs to be verified: (i) information in the program point can flow into S_1, denoted by PCLabel $\leqslant S_1^u$, (ii) after S_1 finishes, the context is updated to PCLabel $\oplus S_1^r$, and in this context S_2 needs to be secure, verified by PCLabel $\leqslant S_2^u$. After the execution of S_2, the context is updated to PCLabel $\oplus S_2^r$. The certification semantics for the language is summarized in Table 2 - note that $\otimes$ denotes the greatest lower bound operator.

Table 2. Certification of the While language

Expression e	Semantic Actions
$f(a_1, \ldots, a_n)$	eLabel $= \lambda(a_1) \oplus \cdots \oplus \lambda(a_n)$

Statement S	Semantic Actions
$b := e$	$S^u = \lambda(b), S^r = $ eLabel verify: eLabel $\leqslant S^u$
$S_1; S_2$	$S^u = S_1^u \otimes S_2^u,$ $S^r = S_1^r \oplus S_2^r,$ verify: PCLabel $\leqslant (S_1^u \otimes S_2^u)$ verify: $S_1^r \leqslant S_2^u$ PCLabel $=$ PCLabel $\oplus S^r$
if e then S_1 [else S_2]	$S^u = S_1^u[\otimes S_2^u],$ $S^r = S_1^r \oplus $ eLabel$[\oplus S_2^r],$ verify: eLabel $\leqslant S^u$
while e do S_1	$S^u = S_1^u, S^r = S_1^r \oplus $ eLabel verify: $(S_1^r \oplus $ eLabel$) \leqslant S_1^u$

Comparison with the Approach of Denning [5]. In comparison to the certification semantics given by Denning, the only difference is in consideration of the PCLabel for deriving the semantics of sequential composition (which also impacts the semantics of iteration). Despite providing a rich set of examples/arguments illustrating the impact of the program context in security analysis, why both Fenton, and Denning ignored it remains a mystery. Perhaps, it was a step to avoid the accumulation of a lot of information in the program context (considered insignificant in terms of its observable impact), a phenomenon called "label creep" [21]. Note that label creep severely restricts permissible further actions of the program. However, from an analysis using IF-Secure, it is clear that label creep is a necessity for a sound information-flow analysis (manifests clearly in the context of concurrent/non-deterministic systems), and not a limitation as it is made out to be.

3.3   Trusted-Execution Platform

An important feature of our approach is that the output is labelled, and need not be only public information. It is the responsibility of the underlying system to enforce proper access controls on labelled data according to the multi-level security (MLS) policy. Thus, our approach cleanly captures the notion of computing on MLS data for any general lattice, and naturally leads to a clear definition of language-based security. In turn, this leads to a trusted execution platform - Figs. 1 and 2 - that realizes the capability based execution envisaged in [8,9].

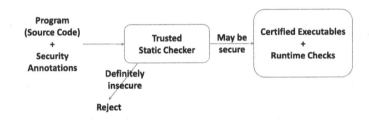

Fig. 1. Trusted static checker

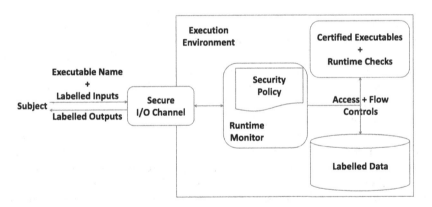

Fig. 2. Trusted execution platform

The trusted execution platform works as follows:

- A program (source code) with security annotations is presented to the trusted static checker.
- If the static checker deems the program to be insecure, the program is rejected - executable is not produced.
- Else, the static checker produces a certified executable, possibly with additional assertions to be verified at run time for program security.

- A certified executable, when executed in the system, consumes labelled inputs and data, and produces labelled outputs in such a way that the security policies are enforced throughout i.e., end-to-end.
- Further, it articulates the subjects that can indeed execute the certified executable.

4 Related Work

Askarov and Myers [1], present a semantic framework in a language-based setting for downgrading policies (declassification/endorsement) characterized in terms of the power downgrading lends to the attacker. Because of their static labeling approach, endorsement and declassification become necessary for specifying the permitted information flows.

In our opinion, having declassify and endorse as explicit unstructured language constructs opens up a lot of covert channels which are impossible to overcome. This is possibly the reason for having multiple semantics for these constructs in the literature. Apart from this, the approach of Askarov and Myers has the following issues: (i) static labels for all the variables - huge burden on the programmer to annotate all the variables. Besides, it is extremely challenging and error-prone to manually assign labels taking all desirable flows into account, (ii) trusted subjects capable of declassifying and endorsing, and (iii) cross-product of confidentiality and integrity lattice for supporting both simultaneously.

Porter et al. [18] introduced Laminar a system with special program constructs like security regions, explicit declassification and endorsement. There is a huge effort needed from the programmer to write secure programs in Laminar (applies to all security-typed languages including Jif [17]). In addition, the programmers are also burdened with the task of explicitly annotating all the program variables. Further, it is trivial for a motivated attacker to write a Laminar program that breaks the security of the whole system by abusing the power of declassification and endorsement.

Consider that we wish to write a program in Laminar for some joint computation between two mutually distrusting parties with the help of a third party. Note that an example of this was presented in the conference version of their paper [19]. What would happen in this case is that, the result computed by the third party would be inaccessible to both the parties, and further cannot be declassified by either of them. The only way the result would be of any use to the parties would be if they provide capabilities to declassify the result to the third party. Note that because of such power vested in the third party, he may leak the information about the two parties by declassifying them, if he so chooses. This is because there are no restrictions on using the privileges/capabilities that a principal possesses, and may be used purely discretionarily at any point during the computation. We suspect this may be the reason they presented a different version in [18] - to hide the inability of their labeling to cleanly address the problem highlighted above. Note that the new version does not contain these problems - except that in this case one party is forced to share his information with the other party.

Many label models in the literature including those described in [11] and [22] treat the two components of secrecy and integrity as independent of one another, while in reality they are interconnected. This adds to the complexity of annotating program variables with static labels that capture all the necessary flows to correctly represent the policy of interest.

Authors of Jifclipse [10] argue that it is extremely challenging to develop programs using security-typed languages, Jif in particular. Most important reason for this difficulty seems to be the fact that the programmer has to provide annotations to most of the variables in the program. They illustrate through the ExamRoom application as an example, that it is challenging to even understand the error messages that these languages provide.

Authors of [10] identify the following principles that should be supported by any ideal development environment for security-typed languages: principal, label inference, information-Flow resolution, constraint resolution, declassification, implicit flow, and rapid prototyping. We firmly believe that a trusted execution platform that adheres to the above principles can be constructed from our approach to information-flow security.

5 Conclusions and Future Directions

In this paper, we have defined a flow security notion called IF-Secure, and shown that it provides a firm compositional basis for language-based security keeping in mind that a secure program takes labelled inputs and produces labelled outputs; it must be noted that labelling of inputs and outputs explicitly brings out the underlying access control requirements for secure input and output. We have compared our notion of IF-Secure and shown that it is stronger than the value-based notions of non-interference in the literature. It may be noted that the definition caters to the generation of high-level outputs solely from low-level inputs as well – thanks to dynamic labelling. Furthermore, it provides a compositional basis for language-based security. It naturally satisfies the argument of Boudol [3] that intensional notion of security should better be based on the notion of a security violation. As already argued, IF-Secure is a refinement of Boudol's notion and captures a larger class of secure programs. Further, we have described a method for automatically deriving the monitoring semantics of any computational system w.r.t IF-Secure, and demonstrated its application to both static and dynamic (run-time) security analysis. Note that the same technique can be applied to non-deterministic systems, and also for deterministic systems with rich constructs such as exceptions etc. Of course, for an effective usage, a proper labeling cum analysis for classical "print" statement becomes essential in a practical setting. Based on our efforts in building secure certification platforms like Java and Python, we are of the opinion that:

- IF-Secure provides a basis for establishing soundness with the advantage of being compositional.
- Dynamic labelling will be essential for establishing security violations of a program without which the class of programs that can be certified for security

will reject widely used program patterns in practice. Further, it may be noted that the classical two-valued lattice (LOW < HIGH) does not clearly bring out the picture of labelled outputs and taking a cross product of lattices for confidentiality and integrity leads to explosion of lattice points, some of which may be unrealizable in practice. Thus, dynamic labelling using a general lattice structure becomes a necessity that can cater to confidentiality and integrity in a unified manner.

- IF-Secure enables us to define a notion of "program being securely executed in an environment", like an "app" executing in a virtual machine (VM).

Appendix

Proof. We prove this by proving its contrapositive, i.e., by proving that if c is not non-interfering, then it is not IF-Secure.

c is not non-interfering if

$$\exists q_1, q_2 \in \mathcal{Q}, L \in \mathcal{L}\big[(q_1 \cong_L q_2) \wedge (\mathcal{S}(q_1, c) \ncong_L \mathcal{S}(q_2, c))\big] \tag{1}$$

Without loss of generality, let q_1, q_2, and L be such that they satisfy (1). We now consider a case-by-case analysis.

Case(i): $\text{ASeq}(q_1, c) = \text{ASeq}(q_2, c)$.

Let $\sigma = \text{ASeq}(q_1, c)$, and $|\sigma| = n$. For $0 \leq i \leq n$, and $j \in \{1, 2\}$, let q_j^i denote the values of variables after the ith intermediate step in the execution of $\mathcal{S}(q_j, c)$, where $q_j^0 = q_j$, and $q_j^n = \mathcal{S}(q_j, c)$. From the hypothesis, we have $q_1^0 \cong_L q_2^0$ and $q_1^n \ncong_L q_2^n$. Let $1 \leq i \leq n$ be the integer such that $[\forall 0 \leq k < i \ (q_1^k \cong_L q_2^k)] \wedge (q_1^i \ncong_L q_2^i)$. This means that $\sigma_i = (v', u)$ for some variable v' with $\lambda(v') \leqslant L$, and that v' has been updated with different values at the ith step in the two executions. Since the machine and its commands are deterministic, and since $[\forall 0 \leq k < i \ (q_1^k \cong_L q_2^k)]$, this is possible only if $\exists v'' \in V, 1 \leq l < i \ \big[(\lambda(v'') \nleqslant L) \wedge (\sigma_l = (v'', r)) \wedge (q_1^l(v'') \neq q_2^l(v'')) \wedge [\forall l < m < i \ (\sigma_m \neq (v'', r))]\big]$.

$$(\sigma_l = (v'', r)) \wedge (\sigma_i = (v', u)) \wedge l < i \Rightarrow (v'', v') \in \text{IF}(q_1, c) \tag{2}$$

$$[(\lambda(v') \leqslant L) \wedge (\lambda(v'') \nleqslant L)] \Rightarrow (\lambda(v'') \nleqslant \lambda(v')) \tag{3}$$

From (2), and (3) we can immediately conclude that c is not IF-Secure.

Case(ii): $\text{ASeq}(q_1, c) \neq \text{ASeq}(q_2, c)$.

Note that because of the deterministic nature of the computing machine $\mathcal{C}$, it cannot diverge without accessing any inputs i.e., $\text{ASeq}(q_1, c)_1 = \text{ASeq}(q_2, c)_1$. Let $|\text{ASeq}(q_1, c)| = n_1$, $|\text{ASeq}(q_2, c)| = n_2$, and without loss of generality $n_1 \leq n_2$. Let $1 \leq i \leq n_1$ be such that $[\forall 1 \leq j \leq i \ (\text{ASeq}(q_1, c)_j = \text{ASeq}(q_2, c)_j) \wedge (\text{ASeq}(q_1, c)_{i+1} \neq \text{ASeq}(q_2, c)_{i+1})]$. Further note that due to the deterministic nature of c, the point of divergence can only occur because of a new information learnt i.e., $\text{ASeq}(q_1, c)_i = \text{ASeq}(q_2, c)_i = (v', r)$ for some $v' \in V$. Let σ denote the longest common prefix of the sequences $\text{ASeq}(q_1, c)$ and $\text{ASeq}(q_2, c)$ i.e., σ is the subsequence of $\text{ASeq}(q_1, c)$ consisting of its first i elements. For $j \in \{1, 2\}$, and $0 \leq i \leq n_j$, let q_j^i denote the values of variables after the ith intermediate step in the execution of $\mathcal{S}(q_j, c)$, where $q_j^0 = q_j$, and $q_j^{n_j} = \mathcal{S}(q_j, c)$.

Here, we further subdivide the proof into two cases.

Case(ii-A): $q_1^{i-1} \cong_L q_2^{i-1}$
In this case, only a variable $v' \in V$ such that $\lambda(v') \not\leq L$ can satisfy $q_1^{i-1}(v') \neq q_2^{i-1}(v')$, which is a necessity for the paths to diverge.

$$(q_1^{i-1} \cong_L q_2^{i-1}) \wedge (q_1^{n_1} = \mathcal{S}(q_1, c) \not\cong_L \mathcal{S}(q_2, c) = q_2^{n_2}) \Rightarrow \exists v'' \in V, i < k \leq n_2 \big[(\lambda(v'') \leq$$
$$L) \wedge (\text{ASeq}(q_2, c)_k = (v'', u))\big] \tag{4}$$
$$\text{ASeq}(q_2, c)_i = (v', r) \wedge \text{ASeq}(q_2, c)_k = (v'', u) \wedge i < k \Rightarrow (v', v'') \in \text{IF}(q_2, c) \tag{5}$$
$$[(\lambda(v') \not\leq L) \wedge (\lambda(v'') \leq L)] \Rightarrow (\lambda(v') \not\leq \lambda(v'')) \tag{6}$$

From (4), (5) and (6) we can immediately conclude that c is not IF-Secure.

Case(ii-B): $q_1^{i-1} \not\cong_L q_2^{i-1}$
This case is similar to Case(i). $\square$

References

1. Askarov, A., Myers, A.C.: Attacker control and impact for confidentiality and integrity. Log. Methods Comput. Sci. **7**(3) (2011). https://doi.org/10.2168/LMCS-7(3:17)2011
2. Barthe, G., D'Argenio, P.R., Rezk, T.: Secure information flow by self-composition. In: 17th IEEE CSFW, pp. 100–114 (2004)
3. Boudol, G.: Secure information flow as a safety property. In: Degano, P., Guttman, J., Martinelli, F. (eds.) FAST 2008. LNCS, vol. 5491, pp. 20–34. Springer, Heidelberg (2009). https://doi.org/10.1007/978-3-642-01465-9_2
4. Denning, D.E.: A lattice model of secure information flow. Commun. ACM **19**(5), 236–243 (1976)
5. Denning, D.E.: Cryptography and Data Security. Addison-Wesley, Boston (1982)
6. Denning, D.E., Denning, P.J.: Certification of programs for secure information flow. Commun. ACM **20**(7), 504–513 (1977)
7. Fenton, J.S.: Memoryless subsystems. Comput. J. **17**(2), 143–147 (1974)
8. Goguen, J.A., Meseguer, J.: Security policies and security models. In: IEEE S&P, pp. 11–20 (1982)
9. Goguen, J.A., Meseguer, J.: Unwinding and inference control. In: IEEE S&P, pp. 75–87 (1984)
10. Hicks, B., King, D., McDaniel, P.: Jifclipse: development tools for security-typed languages. In: Proceedings of PLAS, pp. 1–10 (2007)
11. Krohn, M.N., et al.: Information flow control for standard OS abstractions. In: Proceedings of the 21st ACM SOSP, pp. 321–334 (2007)
12. Mantel, H., Sands, D., Sudbrock, H.: Assumptions and guarantees for compositional noninterference. In: 24th IEEE CSF, pp. 218–232 (2011)
13. McCullough, D.: Noninterference and the composability of security properties. In: IEEE S&P, pp. 177–186 (1988)
14. McLean, J.: Security models and information flow. In: IEEE S&P, pp. 180–189 (1990)

15. Muller, S., Chong, S.: Towards a practical secure concurrent language. In: 27th ACM OOPSLA, pp. 57–74 (2012)
16. Myers, A.C., Liskov, B.: Protecting privacy using the decentralized label model. ACM Trans. Softw. Eng. Methodol. **9**(4), 410–442 (2000)
17. Myers, A.C., Zheng, L., Zdancewic, S., Chong, S., Nystrom, N.: Jif 3.0: Java information flow, July 2006. http://www.cs.cornell.edu/jif
18. Porter, D.E., Bond, M.D., Roy, I., McKinley, K.S., Witchel, E.: Practical fine-grained information flow control using laminar. ACM Trans. Program. Lang. Syst. **37**(1), 4:1–4:51 (2014). https://doi.org/10.1145/2638548
19. Roy, I., Porter, D.E., Bond, M.D., McKinley, K.S., Witchel, E.: Laminar: practical fine-grained decentralized information flow control. In: Proceedings of ACM PLDI, pp. 63–74 (2009)
20. Ryan, P., McLean, J.D., Millen, J.K., Gligor, V.D.: Non-interference: who needs it? In: 14th IEEE CSFW 2014, pp. 237–238 (2001)
21. Sabelfeld, A., Myers, A.C.: Language-based information-flow security. IEEE J. Sel. Areas Commun. **21**(1), 5–19 (2003)
22. Stefan, D., Russo, A., Mitchell, J.C., Mazières, D.: Flexible dynamic information flow control in the presence of exceptions. CoRR abs/1207.1457 (2012)
23. Volpano, D.M., Irvine, C.E., Smith, G.: A sound type system for secure flow analysis. J. Comput. Secur. **4**(2/3), 167–188 (1996)

Bad Signature Identification in a Batch Using Error Detection Codes

Apurva S. Kittur[✉], Swapnil Kauthale, and Alwyn R. Pais

Information Security Research Lab,
Department of Computer Science and Engineering,
National Institute of Technology Karnataka, Surathkal 575025, India
apurva.kittur@gmail.com, swapnilkauthale@gmail.com, alwyn.pais@gmail.com

Abstract. In today's digital communication world, authentication of data and the sender is very important before processing. Digital Signatures are the best way for verifying the authenticity of the message or document. When multiple signatures need to be verified together, we use batch signature verification. There are multiple batch verification algorithms for various digital signature schemes such as ECDSA, RSA, DSS and others. Most of the batch verification techniques fail to locate the position of the invalid signature/s in a batch. Hence there are multiple bad signature identification algorithms available to locate the bad signatures. The existing algorithms are inefficient in identifying position of bad signature, if the number of bad signatures increases in the batch or if the number of bad signatures are not known before verification. Hence such schemes are practically not suitable for real time environment. Our proposed CRC based verifier scheme overcomes these disadvantages, as well as outperforms the existing schemes in efficiently identifying the bad signature/s. The comparative analysis of the proposed scheme and the existing schemes, is also discussed in the paper.

Keywords: Digital signature · Batch verification ·
Cyclic Redundancy Check (CRC) codes · Error detection codes

1 Introduction

Multiple Digital Signatures can be verified at the same time in batch using various batch verification schemes. There are multiple batch verification schemes available for various digital signature algorithms [2,3,12]. Some of the most popular digital signature algorithms are RSA (Rivest, Shamir, Adleman) [5], DSS (Digital Signature Scheme) [4], ECDSA (Elliptic Curve Digital Signature Algorithm) [9], etc. The batch verification schemes accept a batch of signatures and verifies whether the batch has any faulty signature/s. If all the signatures are valid, then the output is *True* and if one or more bad signatures exist in the batch then it returns *False*.

Most of the batch verification techniques do not provide the location of the bad signature/s, if there exists two or more bad signature/s. Hence there are

© Springer Nature Singapore Pte Ltd. 2019
S. Nandi et al. (Eds.): ISEA-ISAP 2018, CCIS 939, pp. 53–66, 2019.
https://doi.org/10.1007/978-981-13-7561-3_4

multiple techniques introduced to identify the bad signature/s within a batch. The default way to find the faulty signature is, individual verification, where every signature is individually verified to find the faulty one. There are many other techniques such as Divide-and-Conquer [13,17], Hamming code verifier [17], etc.

In our proposed method, we are using the Error-Detecting code, Cyclic Redundancy Check (CRC). It is commonly used in digital communication for detecting the changes made to the data received. In CRC based verification, a CRC check code is attached along with the signature, which is the remainder of the polynomial division. The similar calculation is repeated at the receiver too to identify the faulty bit. Hence in a similar way, we can identify the faulty signature too. Therefore once the batch verification fails, our scheme performs CRC verification to identify the faulty one.

The major contributions of the paper are:

- Analyse the existing schemes along with their drawbacks.
- Proposed a CRC code based verifier to identify the invalid signature in a batch.
- Detailed analysis of our scheme and the existing schemes with respect to number of operations needed to identify the bad signature/s.

The flow of the paper is as follows: after the introduction and literature review of existing schemes in Sects. 1 and 2 describes the proposed scheme. Section 3 discusses the runtime analysis of proposed scheme and existing schemes. This is followed by conclusion in Sect. 4.

1.1 Preliminaries

In this subsection we are providing some of the important definitions which are referred later in the paper. We start with the definition of batch verification and other techniques.

Definition 1: Batch Verification Algorithm(x, t): *Given a batch instance* $x = ((m_1, s_1), (m_2, s_2), \ldots, (m_{t-1}, s_{t-1}), (m_t, s_t))$ *and the security parameter* l. The $GT(x, t)$ takes x and

1. returns $'True'$ when all signatures in a given batch are valid. The test is assumed to never make mistakes.
2. returns $'False'$ whenever there is presence of at least one bad signature. The probability of verifying a bad signature as valid is 2^{-l}, where l is the security parameter.

In [1], there are three efficient Generic Tests (GT) proposed, which are for modular exponentiation based digital signature algorithms. Hence with little modifications they can also be applied on other digital signatures algorithms too. These are the techniques which improve the security of batch verification algorithm.

Definition 2: Random Subset Test: *For a given batch of t digital signatures,* $((m_1, s_1), (m_2, s_2), \ldots, (m_t, s_t))$, *the receiver performs,*

1. *For every signature* $i = \{1, 2, \ldots, t\}$, *select* $b_i = \{0, 1\}$ *in random*
2. *Select signatures* s_i, *where* $b_i s$ *are equal to one*
3. *For all the selected* s_i, *perform standard batch verification.*
4. *If the batch verification succeeds, accept the signatures, otherwise reject and repeat the test for all sub-set of signatures*

Definition 3: Small Exponents Test: *In this test, we generate small random number* u_i *during verification*

1. *Generate random number* $u_i \in \{0, 1\}$ *for every signature* s_i.
2. *Apply the random number on both sides of standard batch verification equation.*
3. *If the verification succeeds, then accept all the signatures, otherwise reject.*

Definition 4: Bucket Test: *This test needs an extra parameter* $v \geq 2$ *and computes* $V = 2^v$, *which indicates that there are V buckets*

1. *For every signature* s_i, $i \in \{1, 2, \ldots, t\}$, *pick* V_j *from* $j \in \{1, \ldots, V\}$ *randomly. This means place all signatures randomly in the V buckets.*
2. *For every bucket* V_j *from* $j \in \{1, \ldots, V\}$, *apply standard batch signature verification algorithm on all signatures in the bucket.*
3. *Repeat the same batch verification test over all the signatures in every bucket* $V_j \in \{1, \ldots, V\}$

Next is to understand the algorithms to used to find the faulty signatures when the GT batch verification fails. Hence there are multiple schemes to identify the faulty signature/s in the failed batch. In Naive approach, the signatures in the batch are individually verified to identify the index of the bad signature/s. The batch verification fails, if one or more signatures are faulty. Then to identify the location of bad signatures, all the signatures are verified in sequence to identify the faulty signature/s location.

Definition 5: Naive Verifier: *For a received set of t message-signature pairs* $(m, s) = ((m_1, s_1), (m_2, s_2), \ldots, (m_t, s_t))$,

1. *First verify the batch of signatures using one of the GT techniques described. If* $GT(s, t) = 1$, *then accept all the signatures and exit, otherwise go to next step*
2. *For every signature* s_i *where* $i \in \{1, 2, \ldots, t\}$ *do,*
   (a) *Apply GT verification,* $GT(s_i, 1)$
   (b) *If* $GT(s_i, 1) = 1$, *then the signature is valid and go to next signature*
   (c) *If* $GT(s_i, 1) = 0$, *then the signature is invalid and add to the list L.*
3. *List all the signatures from the list L as invalid and exit*

The next approach in finding the index of the bad signature is, the Divide-and-Conquer (DC) verifier [17]. The entire batch of given signatures are verified through one of the GTs. If the test fails, then the batch is divided into sub-batches which are again independently verified through the same GT previously used. Then the sub-batches which fail the GT are again sub-divided recursively to locate the bad signature.

Definition 6: DC Verifier: *For a given batch of t signatures, $(m, s) = ((m_1, s_1), (m_2, s_2), \ldots, (m_t, s_t))$,*

1. *If the received batch contains only one signature, ie., $t = 1$, then verify the signature using the GT. If $GT(m, s, 1) = 1$, signature is valid, otherwise invalid and exit.*
2. *If the batch consists of more than one signatures, then perform GT. If GT $(m, s, t) = 1$, then all signatures are valid and exit, otherwise go to next step.*
3. *If the given batch has a few invalid signatures, then break the batch into α sub-batches, $\alpha_1, \alpha_2, \ldots, \alpha_\alpha$, where every sub-batch has a set of $\frac{s}{\alpha}$ signatures. Now invoke the DC Verifier for every sub-batch α_j, where $j \in \{1, 2, \ldots, \alpha\}$.*

There are batch verification techniques such as Hamming Code verifier [13], which identify the invalid signature provided there is only one bad signature in the given batch of signatures. Such batch verification techniques are very efficient since they batch verify all the signatures as well as point us to the faulty signature too.

Definition 7: Hamming Verifier: *For a given batch of t signatures, $(m, s) = ((m_1, s_1), (m_2, s_2), \ldots, (m_t, s_t))$, where $t = 2^k - 1$, for positive k*

1. *Apply GT on the received batch of signatures. If $GT(m, s, t) = 1$, accept the signatures and exit, otherwise go to next step.*
2. *Next is to create k sub-batches,*

$$(m_i, s_i) = \{(m_j, s_j) | h_{i,j} = 1\}$$

where $i = 1, \ldots, k$ and (m_i, s_i) are signatures from the given batch for which $h_{i,j}$ is equal to 1, otherwise ignored.
3. *Now perform the $GT(m_i, s_i, 2^{k-1}) = \sigma_i$, for $i = 1, \ldots, k$, depending on the result of verification, the value of σ_i is decided. The syndrome $(\sigma_1, \ldots, \sigma_k)$ indicates the bad signature positions.*
4. *Perform GT on the instances which are free from bad signatures. If the batch instance is accepted then return the index, else exit*

One more approach to finding the illegal signature/s, is based on ID codes [18]. It has the disadvantage of restriction on the maximum number of illegal signatures that the batch can have to efficiently locate them.

Definition 8: ID Codes: *For a given a batch instance $B^u = \{(m_i, s_i) | i = 1, \ldots, u\}$ of signed messages (m_i is the i-th message and s_i is the signature of*

m_i). The identification code $IC(u, n)$ identifies a maximum of n bad signatures in a collection of sub-instances $(B_1, B_2, \ldots, B_v)$ where $B_i \in B^u$, such that for any possible pattern of up to n bad signatures, the outcomes (the syndrome) $S = (T(B_1), \ldots, T(B_v))$ uniquely identify all bad signatures

Most of the schemes discussed previously are generic schemes and can be applied to any digital signature algorithms. But the algorithms proposed in [14, 19] are for RSA signatures.

Definition 9: Matrix Verifier: *For a given set of message-signature pairs,* $((M_1, s_1), (M_2, s_2), \ldots, (M_t, s_t)),$

1. *The verifier generates a $m \times n$ matrix such that $m \times n \geq t$, and t random numbers r_i where $i = 1, 2, \ldots, t$ and $r_i \in \{1, 2, \ldots, t\}$.*
2. *Now the verifier fills the matrix positions with the signatures according to the following equation,*

$$s(m, n) = \begin{cases} s(\lceil \frac{r_i}{n} \rceil, n), & \text{if } r_i \bmod n = 0 \\ s(\lceil \frac{r_i}{n} \rceil, r_i \bmod n), & \text{otherwise} \end{cases}$$

3. *Now the verifier uses GT verification to verify every row and every column individually.*
   At the row side,

$$(\prod_{i=1}^{n} s_{(m,i)})^e = \prod_{i=1}^{n} h(M_{(m,i)}) \bmod n \qquad (1)$$

   At the column side:

$$(\prod_{i=1}^{m} s_{(i,n)})^e = \prod_{i=1}^{m} h(M_{(i,n)}) \bmod n \qquad (2)$$

4. *Find the rows and columns which fail the GT, and their overlapping location points us to the location of bad signature.*

1.2   Literature Review

Many batch verification techniques have been proposed for RSA [7, 8, 11], DSS [6, 15, 16] and ECDSA [10]. The main disadvantage with most of the schemes is that, they fail to identify the index of the faulty signature. These schemes may be efficient in verifying the existence of bad signature/s in the given signature batch, but they do not discuss the efficiency in identifying the bad signature/s. The detailed study of various batch verification techniques have been studied in [12].

The Table 1 compares various bad signature identification schemes. We also have discussed the key features or characteristics of the those existing schemes as well as their disadvantages. We can observe that few are efficient in identifying bad signatures provided they have prior knowledge of the number of bad signatures in the given batch of signatures.

Table 1. Comparative analysis of bad signature identification techniques

Technique	Prior Information	Number of GT	Restriction on the number of bad signatures	Characteristics	Drawback
Naive	No	Fixed	No	Every Signature is carefully verified. Hence no chance of mistakes in verification	It is the most inefficient way of verification
DC Verifier [17]	No	Variable	No	Very efficient and secure for average case where a few of the signatures are bad in the batch	Performance decreases if all the bad signatures are distributed randomly in the batch
Hamming Verifier [13]	Yes	Fixed	Yes	Performs batch verification as well as identifies bad the index of the bad signature	Can be used only if the batch contains only one bad signature
IC Verifier [18]	Yes	Fixed	No	Uses Hamming weight for better identification of bad signatures	The bad signature identification time is directly proportional to the number of bad signatures
Li et al. [14]	No	Variable	Yes	Identifies the location of bad signature very accurately	Increases the number of computations and does not work for more than 2–3 bad signatures
Ren et al. [19]	No	Variable	No	Very efficiently identifies any number of bad signatures	With the increase in the bad signatures, computation also increases

We have compared the various existing schemes based on the three parameters.

– *Prior Information*: This parameter indicates whether the scheme requires the prior knowledge of the number of faulty signatures beforehand. Hence the techniques which require prior knowledge are mostly practically not possible to deploy.

- *Number of GT*: If the number of Generic Tests (GT) is fixed, then the scheme has number of GT fixed and it does not vary with the batch size.
- *Restriction on the number of bad signatures*: This parameter specifies whether the scheme is efficient for smaller as well as larger batch sizes.

2 Proposed Verification Scheme

The proposed verification scheme is based on Cyclic Redundancy Check (CRC), which is an error-detecting code used in digital network communication. Before introducing our verification scheme, first we will brief the CRC encoding and decoding in digital communication.

2.1 Cyclic Redundancy Check (CRC)

CRC codes are used in digital communication, and are based on binary division, where we append extra bits to the data before transmission. These redundant bits are Cyclic Redundancy Check bits which are appended at the end of the data, such that the entire data unit is exactly divisible by pre-agreed binary number between sender and verifier. We express the data to be sent, as a polynomial in x. The data $a = a_{n-1}a_{n-2}\ldots a_1a_0$ of length n is represented by the degree $n-1$ polynomial and is as shown below,

$$a(x) = \sum_{i=0}^{n-1} a_i x^i = a_{n-1}x^{n-1} + a_{n-2}x^{n-2} + \cdots + a_1 x + a_0$$

Suppose the agreed upon binary number also called Generator polynomial, with length l, can be expressed in polynomial as,

$$c(x) = c_{l-1}x^{l-1} + c_{l-2}x^{l-2} + \cdots + c_1 x + c_0$$

In order to calculate the CRC codes, first append the data with zeros of length $l-1$. Then divide the data by the binary number. The remainder is added as the appending CRC code to the original data. The zeroes which were earlier appended are replaced with the remainder of division. And this data unit is sent to the verifier. Suppose the remainder is $r(x)$, and the quotient is $z(x)$, then the data unit $d(x)$ to be sent can be written as,

$$d(x) = c(x)z(x) + r(x)$$

The receiver receives the data unit $d(x)$ which it has to verify using agreed upon binary number $c(x)$ of length l which is also known as Generator Polynomial. The verifier divides the received data unit by the generator polynomial (Fig. 1).

$$r(x) = d(x)/c(x)$$

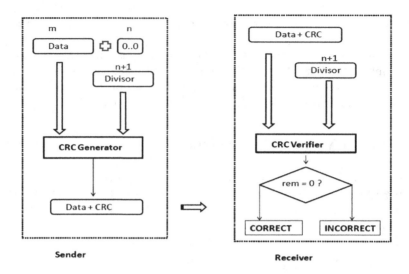

Fig. 1. CRC encoding and decoding at sender and receiver

If the remainder $r(x) = 0$, then the bits in the data unit are not modified and the signature is valid. If the remainder is greater than zero, $r(x) > 0$, then the data has been modified intentionally or unintentionally during transmission. Hence we are using the concept of error detection codes in batch verification to identify faulty signatures. Hence once the batch verification fails, it indicates that one or more signatures are faulty. Then we verify all the signatures individually through proposed CRC verification scheme, to identify the bad signature.

2.2   CRC Verification Algorithm

The signer generates the CRC redundancy bits for every signature generated for every message. The CRC bits are appended to the signature and sent across to the verifier.

Definition 10: CRC Signer: *The signer generates t signatures $s_1, s_2, \ldots, s_t$ for t messages $m_1, m_2, \ldots, m_t$ using his private key pk and also generates CRC polynomial bits for the signature $b(x)$*

1. Generate the message-signature pairs (m_1, s_i), for all the t messages using the signer's private key for every message m_i.
2. For every signature s_i, calculate the CRC polynomial bits $b_i(x)$ using the pre-agreed binary number of polynomial bit length $L - 1$ bits.
3. Finally append the CRC code bits b to every signature s_i respectively to create data unit $d_i(x)$. And then send the message and the data unit across the verifier.

The verifier receives the message-data unit pairs $(m_i, d_i(x))$ and performs batch verification. If the batch verification test fails, then the signatures are verified through their CRC codes, to identify the faulty signature.

Definition 11: CRC Verifier: *The verifier receives* $(m_i, d_i(x))$ *where* m_i *is the message and* $d_i(x)$ *is the data unit, which is combination of signature* s_i *and CRC polynomial code* $b_i(x)$.

1. *Stopping case: If the number of signatures in the instance is one, ie.,* $t = 1$, *then perform* $GT(x, 1)$. *If the* $GT(x, 1) = 1$, *then the signature is valid else is invalid.*
2. *If for the instance* x, *there are* $t > 0$ *signatures, verify them through* $GT(x, t)$ *on the received signatures. If* $GT(x, t) = 1$, *return 'True' which indicates that the signatures in instance* x *are valid. Otherwise go to next step.*
3. *Code Verify: For every message-data unit pair* $(m_i, d_i(x))$, *divide the data unit* $d_i(x)$ *of every signature by the polynomial bits* $b(x)$. *If the division leaves no remainder then the signature is valid, otherwise add it to bad signature list.*

The algorithms in Definitions 10 and 11 for signature verification describe the steps to identify the faulty signature among a batch of signatures. Once the batch verification fails, we perform binary division of data unit $d_i(x)$ by the Generation polynomial $b(x)$. If even a single bit is altered or modified, then the remainder will be non-zero which proves that the signature is faulty.

2.3   Trade-Off Between Signature Generation and Verification

The signature generated at the sender is (m, d) where m is the message to be signed and d is the data unit where the signature is appended with the CRC code. Therefore a standard CRC code which is either 16 or 32 bits extra, is added to the signature. Here in our scheme, an extra 32 bits are appended to the signature s. Hence there is extra time needed to generate these CRC code bits to be appended.

Table 2. Time taken for generation operation (msec)

Time (msec)	Batch size of signatures				
	2^2	2^4	2^6	2^8	2^{12}
Signature generation	10.2	11	12.06	27.8	148
CRC generation	1.15	1.27	2.81	8.59	137.4

The Table 2 gives the values of time needed for signature generation without CRC and time for CRC code generation. The CRC code generation adds minimum delay in signature generation. But this extra time for CRC generation saves more 50% of extra computation time to identify the faulty signature. Hence the generation of CRC code incurs minimum extra time and computation when compared to the amount of time and computation it saves at the verification.

2.4 Security Analysis

In case of Man-in-the-Middle attack, if the attacker modifies the signature intentionally or unintentionally, the CRC verification fails. When an attacker modifies one or more bits of signature, the polynomial division ends up with a remainder, which results in a conclusion that the signature is faulty.

If an attacker modifies the signature, then the received data unit is $d'(x)$. Then the batch verification using one of the GTs fails. Then we perform CRC verification.

$$r(x) = d'(x)/b(x)$$

$$r(x) \neq 0$$

Since $d'(x)$ is modified, the division does not end with zero remainder, and the faulty signature can be found.

The next attack can be the modification of CRC bits itself. But the verifier does not know the Generator Polynomial, which is shared between the signer and verifier beforehand. Hence without the knowledge of it, it cannot generate the CRC bits. Hence the attacker does not even have the knowledge of the length of CRC bits and signature. Hence the attacker does not exactly know which part of the data unit is signature and which part is CRC bit part.

3   Comparative Analysis

The proposed CRC verifier outperforms all other existing faulty signature identification schemes. We have not considered the schemes which require the count of faulty signatures at the beginning of verification, since in real time scenario, it is difficult to know the number of faulty signatures beforehand.

The proposed scheme outperforms the existing schemes in terms of computation time to identify the bad signature/s. The number of operations in the proposed scheme to locate the invalid signature is independent of the number of invalid signatures. Before the CRC verification, the verifier performs batch verification to check if the batch of signatures contains any bad ones. The verification fails if either one or more or even all the signatures are faulty. Then we use one of the verification techniques to locate this/these bad signatures, such as Naive verifier, DC verifier, CRC verifier.

Best Case

The best case scenario happens when all the signatures are valid and there are no invalid ones. In such a scenario, all the three techniques initially perform verification in a batch using one of the GTs. Since all the signatures are valid,

the batch verification does not fail. Hence we do not go for bad signature identification techniques. Hence the number of operations for all the techniques is,
No. of GT - 1

Average Case

The average case occurs when one more signatures are faulty. Suppose there is a batch of signatures of batch size t, and n signatures among them are faulty, then

1. In Naive verifier, after batch verification fails, every signature is individually verified to list out the faulty signatures. Hence the total number of operations needed to locate all the faulty signatures are,
   No. of GT - 1
   No. of Individual verifications - t

2. In case DC verifier, once the batch verification fails, we divide the given batch of signatures into α sub-batches. Then these sub-batches are again verified through batch verification using GT. We again further divide these sub-batches if they fail the GT. This division is continued until we find the faulty signatures.
   No. of GT - $\alpha^{r+1}(k - r + 1) - 1$,
   where $t = \alpha^k$ and $n = \alpha^r$

3. In CRC verifier, after the batch verification failure, each signature is verified through the CRC code appended to it. Each signature is verified through the CRC verifier as described earlier. Even though there are one or multiple number of faulty signatures n, the CRC verifier verifies every signature to locate the faulty ones.
   No. of GT - 1
   No. of CRC individual verifications - t

Worst Case

This is a scenario where all the signatures in a given batch are faulty. Hence the verification of batch using GT fails since there are faulty signatures in it. For a batch of t signatures, all t signatures are faulty, ie., $n = t$

1. In case of Naive verifier, since GT failed, all the signatures are verified to locate the bad signatures. Hence the total number individual verifications is the size of the batch. Hence the total number of operations is,
   No. of GT - 1
   No. of individual verifications - t

2. In case of DC verifier, after the verification by GT, the batch is divided and verified according to the Definition 6. Hence if all the signatures are faulty, then every sub-batch is recursively verified through GT to locate the faulty

ones. Hence the total number of operations is,

No. of GT - $\frac{n\alpha-1}{\alpha-1}$

3. For our proposed scheme, after the failure of GT, every signature is verified using CRC verification. Hence the total number of operations remains same in average case and worst case.

   No. of GT - 1

   No. of CRC verifications - t

The number of operations needed to locate the bad signatures in various techniques is already discussed. Next we study the verification time taken by these techniques in doing the same.

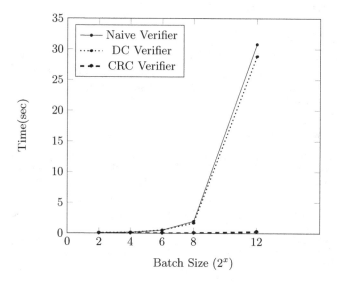

Fig. 2. Execution time when 50% signatures are faulty

The two Figs. 2 and 3 indicate the execution time taken by Naive verifier, DC verifier and CRC verifier. We can observe clearly from the graphs that, our proposed CRC verifier performs better than the other two schemes in both the average as well as worst cases. Hence the proposed technique proves to be the efficient technique among the available ones.

CRC verification takes very less verification times when compared to the techniques which depend on PKI (Public Key Infrastructure). Hence the Naive verifier and DC verifier require more time and our proposed scheme gains significant speed because of the CRC verification. Hence we can prove the same through the graphs.

For our experimentation purpose, we consider ECDSA digital signatures. Therefore we use the standard batch verification algorithm of ECDSA [10]. The

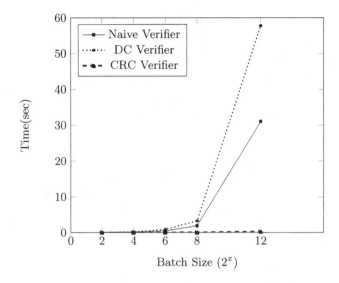

Fig. 3. Execution time when all signatures are faulty

experimentation is carried out on a Rock Cluster 6.0 with Intel® Xeon® E5-2650, 2.3 GHz processor. During simulation, we have only considered the time to verify the signature/s, once the they are received. Hence the verifier first performs the batch verification, then execute various schemes to identify the bad signature/s.

4   Conclusion and Future Plan

In this paper, we presented a new algorithm for locating the position of the bad signature in a given batch of digital signatures. We have also showed that our scheme performs evidentially better than the existing schemes. It reduces the computation time and load at the verifier significantly. Hence it is suitable for applications which have lightweight devices with low computation power.

Our future study involves experimenting with other error detection and control codes which can yield more efficient and secure results than the proposed CRC verifier.

References

1. Bellare, M., Garay, J.A., Rabin, T.: Fast batch verification for modular exponentiation and digital signatures. In: Nyberg, K. (ed.) EUROCRYPT 1998. LNCS, vol. 1403, pp. 236–250. Springer, Heidelberg (1998). https://doi.org/10.1007/BFb0054130
2. Cheon, J.H., Yi, J.H.: Fast batch verification of multiple signatures. In: Okamoto, T., Wang, X. (eds.) PKC 2007. LNCS, vol. 4450, pp. 442–457. Springer, Heidelberg (2007). https://doi.org/10.1007/978-3-540-71677-8_29

3. Fiat, A.: Batch RSA. In: Brassard, G. (ed.) CRYPTO 1989. LNCS, vol. 435, pp. 175–185. Springer, New York (1990). https://doi.org/10.1007/0-387-34805-0_17
4. Fips, P.: 186–2. Digital Signature Standard (DSS). National Institute of Standards and Technology (NIST) **20**, 13 (2000)
5. Goldwasser, S., Micali, S., Rivest, R.L.: A digital signature scheme secure against adaptive chosen-message attacks. SIAM J. Comput. **17**(2), 281–308 (1988)
6. Harn, L.: Batch verifying multiple DSA-type digital signatures. Electron. Lett. **34**(9), 870–871 (1998)
7. Harn, L.: Batch verifying multiple RSA digital signatures. Electron. Lett. **34**(12), 1219–1220 (1998)
8. Hwang, M.S., Lin, I.C., Hwang, K.F.: Cryptanalysis of the batch verifying multiple rsa digital signatures. Informatica **11**(1), 15–18 (2000)
9. Johnson, D., Menezes, A., Vanstone, S.: The elliptic curve digital signature algorithm (ECDSA). Int. J. Inf. Secur. **1**(1), 36–63 (2001)
10. Karati, S., Das, A., Roychowdhury, D., Bellur, B., Bhattacharya, D., Iyer, A.: Batch verification of ECDSA signatures. In: Mitrokotsa, A., Vaudenay, S. (eds.) AFRICACRYPT 2012. LNCS, vol. 7374, pp. 1–18. Springer, Heidelberg (2012). https://doi.org/10.1007/978-3-642-31410-0_1
11. Kittur, A.S., Jain, A., Pais, A.R.: Fast verification of digital signatures in IoT. In: Thampi, S.M., et al. (eds.) SSCC 2017. CCIS, vol. 746, pp. 16–27. Springer, Singapore (2017). https://doi.org/10.1007/978-981-10-6898-0_2
12. Kittur, A.S., Pais, A.R.: Batch verification of digital signatures: approaches and challenges. J. Inf. Secur. Appl. **37**, 15–27 (2017)
13. Lee, S., Cho, S., Choi, J., Cho, Y.: Efficient identification of bad signatures in RSA-type batch signature. IEICE Trans. Fundam. Electron. Commun. Comput. Sci. **89**(1), 74–80 (2006)
14. Li, C.T., Hwang, M.S., Chen, S.: A batch verifying and detecting the illegal signatures. Int. J. Innovative Comput. Inf. Control **6**(12), 5311–5320 (2010)
15. Lim, C.H., Lee, P.J.: Security of interactive DSA batch verification. Electron. Lett. **30**(19), 1592 (1994)
16. Naccache, D., M'Raïhi, D., Vaudenay, S., Raphaeli, D.: Can D.S.A. be improved? — Complexity trade-offs with the digital signature standard —. In: De Santis, A. (ed.) EUROCRYPT 1994. LNCS, vol. 950, pp. 77–85. Springer, Heidelberg (1995). https://doi.org/10.1007/BFb0053426
17. Pastuszak, J., Michałek, D., Pieprzyk, J., Seberry, J.: Identification of bad signatures in batches. In: Imai, H., Zheng, Y. (eds.) PKC 2000. LNCS, vol. 1751, pp. 28–45. Springer, Heidelberg (2000). https://doi.org/10.1007/978-3-540-46588-1_3
18. Pastuszak, J., Pieprzyk, J., Seberry, J.: Codes identifying bad signatures in batches. In: Roy, B., Okamoto, E. (eds.) INDOCRYPT 2000. LNCS, vol. 1977, pp. 143–154. Springer, Heidelberg (2000). https://doi.org/10.1007/3-540-44495-5_13
19. Ren, Y., Wang, S., Zhang, X., Hwang, M.S.: An efficient batch verifying scheme for detecting illegal signatures. IJ Netw. Secur. **17**(4), 463–470 (2015)

A Solution to "Confused Deputy" Problem Using RWFM Labels

Sandip Ghosal$^{(\boxtimes)}$ and R. K. Shyamasundar

Department of Computer Science and Engineering,
Indian Institute of Technology, Bombay, Mumbai 400076, India
sandipsmit@gmail.com, shyamasundar@gmail.com

Abstract. A client-server architecture mapped to a multi-level security (MLS) system maintain independent access restrictions for various system resources. Traditional access control mechanisms e.g., *discretionary access matrix* often lead to indirect access, therefore are incapable to enforce confidentiality and integrity at process-level. The *confused deputy* problem is well known in this regard where an unauthorized process may influence an authorized process to manipulate a protected object. In this paper, we propose a solution to *confused deputy* problem using a recently proposed novel mandatory access control (MAC) based security model RWFM. We demonstrate our approach through a *reference monitor* that adapts the proposed solution while performing process-level security check, and prevents indirect access to isolated sensitive objects. Further, we compare our solution with the existing literature towards the end of this paper.

Keywords: Confused deputy · Access control ·
Information flow control · Readers-writers flow model

1 Introduction

The operating system specification provides nice *abstraction* to camouflage underlying complexities. The chief abstraction is a process that arises when executing a program. One of the facets of abstraction is *encapsulation* that provides *separation* between two processes such that, a process cannot access address space that other process owns. The security provided by operating system introduces *access control* that defines access permissions for different subjects (e.g., processes) to objects (e.g., files). A classic example is a program when executed by a user creates a process that inherits the access rights e.g., *read, write, execute*, given to that user for certain files. Although this access control mechanism provides a rigid access policy while inter-process communication, however an unauthorized process might be able to influence a process that is authorized to access an object. The "Confused Deputy" problem envisage such an indirect access where an unauthorized entity compromises an authorized body.

© Springer Nature Singapore Pte Ltd. 2019
S. Nandi et al. (Eds.): ISEA-ISAP 2018, CCIS 939, pp. 67–76, 2019.
https://doi.org/10.1007/978-981-13-7561-3_5

The notion of *protection domain* is well known in access control where a set of privileges is associated with a process, that ease the implementation of *principle of least privileges*, i.e., granting a process the least privileges to perform specific operations. Operating systems, those empower protection domains enable domain transition for certain system calls e.g., changing from user mode to superuser mode. The set of privileges before and after a domain transition is either *attenuated* or *amplified* [10]. Changes in protection domain also often lead to "Confused Deputy" problem where the client's request might abuse the server's privileges that client does not hold. The problem was first reported by Norm Hardy [3] in 1988. The original problem description is summarized below.

A Unix like server operating system has a directory called SYSX that contains a compiler /SYSX/FORT, and a file /SYSX/STAT to obtain statistics about language usage. Another file named /SYSX/BILL is integrated into the compiler to generate billing information. The compiler is given permission to write into both the two files. A user can issue a command RUN /SYSX/FORT to the server along with an optional input file to receive the statistics. Additionally, server returns billing information based on the tasks it has performed. The scenario can be easily understood from the Fig. 1.

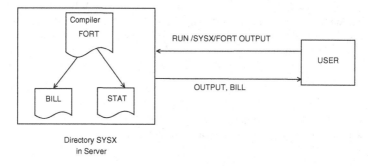

Fig. 1. User is issuing RUN command to server and receiving output and billing information after completion of the execution.

Now, a user input file, named same as BILL causes to confuse the compiler and writes the debugging output over billing information. Schneider [10] has exemplified the scenario through a lucid program shown in Table 1. The client sends a request to the server by passing a file output.text. Server processes the request and writes the results into the same file, and also creates a separate file writing the billing information that the client needs to pay. However, if the client somehow learns about the filename holding the billing information (s)he could pass the same (i.e. bill.text) while requesting to the server. Therefore, the statement S_5 would overwrite the bill.text and billing information will be lost by the server. Note that, although the client does not have any privilege to access the billing information (s)he can abuse the privileges given to the server.

Table 1. An abstract of the program that suffers from *confused deputy* problem (Cf. Schneider [10]).

```
Server:operation (output.text:file)
  S₁:buffer:=FileSys.Read(output.text)
  S₂:results:=F(buffer)
  S₃:charges:=calcBill(results)
  S₄:FileSys.Write(bill.text, charges)
  S₅:FileSys.Write(output.text, result)
end Server
```

In this paper, we propose a `RWFM` label based solution that a reference monitor can adapt while performing process-level security check to prevent indirect access to isolated server objects in client-server architecture. Further, we demonstrate that our solution is capable of handling the *confused deputy* problem and compare with the existing MAC based approach towards the end of this paper.

Structure of the Paper: Section 2 provides a brief introduction of `RWFM` security model. Section 3 presents our solution to *confused deputy* problem using `RWFM` labels. Section 4 describes the existing solutions to the problem and compares with the proposed solution. Finally, Sect. 5 summarizes the contributions along with the future work.

2   Readers-Writers Flow Model [5–7]: An Overview

The label of subjects and objects in the `RWFM` is a triple: (Owner/Authority, {Set of Readers}, {Set of Writers/Influencer}). The first component specifies the owner of information, the second component denotes the subjects who can read the information, and the third component represents the subjects who have contributed/influenced the information so far.

Definition 1 (Readers-Writers Flow Model (RWFM) [6]):

"RWFM is defined as the eight tuple $(S, O, SC, \leqslant, \oplus, \otimes, \top, \bot)$*, where* S *and* O *are the set of subjects and objects in the information system,* $SC = S \times 2^S \times 2^S$ *is the set of labels,* $\leqslant = (-, \supseteq, \subseteq)$ *is the permissible flows ordering,* $\oplus = (-, \cap, \cup)$ *and* $\otimes = (-, \cup, \cap)$ *are the join and meet operators respectively, and* $\top = (-, \emptyset, S)$ *and* $\bot = (-, S, \emptyset)$ *are respectively the maximum and minimum elements in the lattice."*

Consider the labelling function λ that maps a subject/object to its respective security label from the lattice, and defined as, $\lambda : S \cup O \rightarrow S \times 2^S \times 2^S$. Let $R_\lambda(e)$ and $W_\lambda(e)$ be the projection of the label ($\lambda(e)$) to the second and third component respectively.

Definition 2 (Flow Order). *For two given RWFM labels* $\lambda(e_1)$ *&* $\lambda(e_2)$*, we say the label* $\lambda(e_2)$ *is in flow order with the label* $\lambda(e_1)$ *written as,* $\lambda(e_1) \preceq \lambda(e_2)$ *iff* $R_\lambda(e_1) \supseteq R_\lambda(e_2) \wedge W_\lambda(e_1) \subseteq W_\lambda(e_2)$.

The state transition rules of RWFM as defined in [6] are given below:
READ Rule

"*Subject s with label (s_1, R_1, W_1) requests read access to an object o with label (s_2, R_2, W_2).*
If $(s \in R_2)$ then
change the label of s to $(s_1, R_1 \cap R_2, W_1 \cup W_2)$
ALLOW
Else
DENY"

WRITE Rule

"*Subject s with label (s_1, R_1, W_1) requests write access to an object o with label (s_2, R_2, W_2).*
If $(s \in W_2 \wedge R_1 \supseteq R_2 \wedge W_1 \subseteq W_2)$ then
ALLOW
Else
DENY"

CREATE Rule

"*Subject s labelled (s_1, R_1, W_1) requests to create an object o.*
Create a new object o, label it as (s_1, R_1, W_1) and add it to the set of objects O."

For a given security lattice, the above state transition rules precisely determine the labels of information at different stages of control flow.

3   Our Solutions to "Confused Deputy" Problem

We propose a solution a *reference monitor* at the server site could follow to address the *confused deputy* problem:

- **Process-level** monitoring: The security labels of arguments provided by the *user* is checked against the label derived from the discretionary access matrix the *server* possesses.

The effective solution we illustrate in this section distinguishes an object by its' name and security label e.g., $\langle x, \lambda(x) \rangle$. Let us consider a user (U) and server (S) process that represent the subjects *user* and *server* respectively are communicating after inheriting respective privileges. Further, assume that x is the argument supplied by the user while issuing the command i.e., RUN /SYSX/FORT x. The reference monitor recognizes the supplied argument as a tuple $\langle x, \lambda(U_x) \rangle$. The label $\lambda(U_x)$ is evaluated implicitly by the monitor. The monitor also evaluates the label of x, denoted by $\lambda(S_x)$ from the discretionary access matrix the server owns. Now, the reference monitor performs the check $\lambda(U_x) \preceq \lambda(S_x)$

i.e., whether the server owned label *is in flow order with* user provided label, and based on the predicate allows or denies the execution of command. In the remaining part of this section, we discuss the functionalities of reference monitor and technicalities of each of its' components.

3.1   Reference Monitor [1]

A reference monitor at the server side validates all requests made by the user processes to server objects. The reference monitor takes the user request as input, performs a validation against the security policy and outputs a binary decision allow/deny based on which the request is processed/rejected subsequently. The primary objectives of the individual component of reference monitor (shown in Fig. 2) are briefed below: (i) The monitor interface hooks are placed just before accessing a server object to ensure the access requests to sensitive objects are routed through the validation phase; (ii) Authorization module plays a crucial role to validate the user request. It accepts an input from the interface hooks and maps the object reference to a label. Further, it obtains the label of the same object the server possesses from the policy store, and sends an authorization query to the policy store for the purpose of validation. The module allows to execute the corresponding program for the request on receiving a positive response, otherwise rejects the request; (iii) The policy store is responsible to compute labels of the objects from the discretionary access matrix the server owns, and store the evaluated labels. Moreover, an authorization query from authorization module is answered by the policy store with the help of a given security policy.

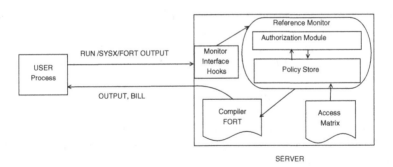

Fig. 2. A schematic diagram of the reference monitor [4] used for process-level monitoring.

3.2   Evaluate RWFM Labels for User Provided Arguments

The authorization module takes the onus to map each object reference to its label. The labels of the user supplied arguments can be derived implicitly based on the presumption that the user is the owner and must have permission to read and write on objects. Now, server must be able to read and write on the user supplied arguments to perform the requested task. Therefore, the supplied arguments have the RWFM labels of the form (U, {U, S}, {U, S}).

3.3   Access Permissions for Subjects to Objects

The discretionary accesses for subjects to objects the server holds are shown by the *access control matrix* (ACM) M (Table 2). It can be observed that the subject *User* has {read, write} permissions on both the FORT and OUTPUT files, but only read permission for BILL. On the contrary, *server* has {read, write} permissions for all the three objects.

Table 2. Access control matrix M.

| Objects→ | FORT | OUTPUT | BILL |
Subjects↓			
User	{read, write}	{read, write}	{read}
Server	{read, write}	{read, write}	{read, write}

In the next subsection we illustrate an algorithm that takes the matrix M as input and generates RWFM labels for each object the server owns.

3.4   Generate Server Objects' Label Enriched with RWFM

The policy store executes the steps shown in Algorithm 1 to compute the RWFM label of each server object from a given discretionary access matrix. The algorithm yields the objects' labels as: *FORT* (S, {S, U}, {S, U}), *OUTPUT* (S, {S, U}, {S, U}) and *BILL* (S, {S, U}, {S}). Note that, the usual meaning of RWFM writers set differs here as it represents the subjects who are allowed to influence the respective objects.

Now consider the problem reported by Norm Hardy given in Sect. 1, the user has provided BILL as the input argument instead of OUTPUT i.e., issued the command RUN /SYSX/FORT BILL. The reference monitor at server side would perform the following tasks:

1 Implicitly evaluates the label of user supplied arguments e.g., the objects FORT and BILL are labelled as (U, {U, S}, {U, S}).
2 Evaluates the label of the objects own by the server as discussed above, e.g., $\lambda(S_{FORT}) = (S, \{U, S\}, \{U, S\})$ and $\lambda(S_{BILL}) = (S, \{S, U\}, \{S\})$.
3 Performs the check if the labels of requested server objects i.e., $\lambda(S_{FORT})$ and $\lambda(S_{BILL})$ are *in flow order with* the label of user supplied objects i.e., $\lambda(U_{FORT})$ and $\lambda(U_{BILL})$ respectively.

Algorithm 1. Procedure to generate RWFM labels from a given access matrix. The algorithm takes input the access control matrix $M_{n \times m}$ and an empty map data structure L, and outputs L that maps each object to its' corresponding label.

Data: Matrix: $M_{n \times m}$, Map: $L \langle object : label \rangle$
Result: Map: L
for $j \leftarrow 1$ **to** m **do**
 Initialize each of *owner, readers, writers* with empty set;
 for $i \leftarrow 1$ **to** n **do**
  owner $\leftarrow$ *server*;
  if *read* $\in M_{ij}$ **then**
   readers $\leftarrow$ *insertIntoReaders*(*i*);
  end
  if *write* $\in M_{ij}$ **then**
   writers $\leftarrow$ *insertIntoWriters*(*i*);
  end
 end
 label $\leftarrow$ (*owner, readers, writers*);
 $L[j] \leftarrow label$;
end
return L;

It can be observed that, the user's request shall be rejected by the reference monitor as $\lambda(U_{BILL}) \not\preceq \lambda(S_{BILL})$.

The solution we just describe prevents to occur *confused deputy* problem at process-level. Moreover, the approach preserves confidentiality and integrity during inter-process communication in a decentralized labelling model. We discuss the differences with existing DAC/MAC based solutions in the next section.

4 Related Work

Norm Hardy in his article [3] discussed about the importance of capability based solutions to aid *confused deputy* problem. A filename designated by its capability helps to identify the file as well as authorizes compiler to write there. Now, while writing the debugging output on the user supplied file the compiler refers to the capability of the user. Therefore, the compiler will be prevented to write on BILL as the user would not have any capability to write on the file. While the solution is appropriate for a centralized system, but not adequate for a decentralized MLS system where the objects' labels are not maintained by any central authority.

Schneider [10] has extended this line of work and proposed to entitle only required sets of privileges to different statements in a program. E.g., in the program shown in Table 1, granting a *write* privilege on bill.text only to the statement S_4 and not to S_5 would prevent the execution of the statement S_5: FileSys.Write(bill.text, result). Schneider has presented a DAC model that dynamically hops among protection domains impromptu having amplified/attenuated privileges. However, conserving confidentiality and integrity in a decentralized MLS system still remains unclear.

A MAC security model called *Dual-Access Label* (DAL) has been proposed by Lu *et al.* [8] to combat the *confused deputy* problem in modern languages e.g., Java, CLR, etc. that performs *stack inspection* to capture intransitive access control. Further, the model also prevents information-flow based attacks. A variable or field maintains a DAL label that extends the access control model by specifying *accessibility* and *capability* of program code, i.e., $\phi = A.C$, and further restraint propagation of information among the variables/fields having different DALs in the multilevel security system. Accessibility specifies the privileges require to access the code, whereas capability indicates the privileges granted to the code. A programmer may write a fragment of the code specifying the accessibility, and a user may provide the capability while executing the code. Let us consider, $A_1.C_1$ as the DAL of the source of information, and $A_2.C_2$ is the DAL of the receiver. The information flow is secure if: (i) the receiver has the sufficient capability to satisfy the sender's accessibility (confidentiality) i.e., $A_1 \leqslant C_2$, and (ii) the sender has the sufficient capability to satisfy the receiver's accessibility i.e., $A_2 \leqslant C_1$.

Note that, the DAL model offers information flow relations induced by the security policy that does not have to be transitive. However, the transitivity in the *confused deputy* problem depends on the associated permissions that vary with different subjects. E.g., as the user and server process both have read permission on BILL, the transitive property holds good. On the contrary, the user may influence the server and server may write on the BILL, but the user cannot write on BILL directly, shows in-transitivity. Although the later case of intransitiveness is handled by the DAL security model, but could be modeled as a subset of problems arising due to indirect information flow. In this paper, we have highlighted the solution that precludes process-level indirect information flow, rather than language-level, because the later rectification has to be applied throughout the system instead of performing security check at some specific place. A generic solution that performs process-level security check using RWFM labelling as well as the polarity with DAL is demonstrated by the example discussed in the article [9].

Table 3. Discretionary access matrix for the example given in the article [9].

Objects→ Subjects↓	security_t	user_home_t
mozilla_t		{write}
sysadm_sudo_t	{write}	{read}

An access matrix for subjects (i.e., processes) mozilla_t (M) and sysadm_sudo_t (A) to objects (i.e., files) security_t (s) and user_home_t (u)

is shown in Table 3. The DAL labels derived from the access matrix is shown in Table 4. It can be observed that, an indirect write `mozilla_t.user_home_t` $\rightarrow$ `sysadm_sudo_t.` `user_home_t` $\rightarrow$ `sysadm_sudo_t.security_t` is allowed in DAL. Therefore, the subject `mozilla_t` is able to write into the object `security_t` although the subject does not have explicit *write* permission.

Table 4. DAL labels derived from the access matrix shown in Table 3.

Fields	Accessibility (A)	Capability (C)
mozilla_t.user_home_t	$\{\emptyset\}$	$\{\text{write}\}$
sysadm_sudo_t.user_home_t	$\{\emptyset\}$	$\{\text{read}\}$
sysadm_sudo_t.security_t	$\{\emptyset\}$	$\{\text{write}\}$

Let us model the above example in MAC based information-flow control model RWFM. Consider the initial labels for each subject M and A are (M, {A, M}, {M}) and (A, {A, M}, {A}) respectively, means both the participating subjects are legitimate readers and only the owner of the label has influenced the data so far. Algorithm 1 takes the access matrix shown in Table 3 as input, and computes the labels of s and u as (S, {}, {A}) and (S, {A}, {M}) respectively. An indirect write is performed by the series of operations shown in Table 5. Note that, the final write operation is prevented by the RWFM transition rules as the subject M does not have write permission to object s.

Table 5. An indirect write is prevented by the RWFM transition rules. Labels of the respective subjects/objects are shown in superscript.

Operations	Source label	Destination label	Changed label	Allow/Deny
$M \xrightarrow{\text{writes}} u$	$M^{(M,\{A,M\},\{M\})}$	$u^{(S,\{A\},\{M\})}$		Allow
$A \xleftarrow{\text{reads}} u$	$u^{(S,\{A\},\{M\})}$	$A^{(A,\{A,M\},\{A\})}$	$A^{(A,\{A\},\{A,M\})}$	Allow
$A \xrightarrow{\text{writes}} s$	$A^{(A,\{A\},\{A,M\})}$	$s^{(S,\{\},\{A\})}$		Deny

Therefore, in contrast to DAL based approach the proposed solution can track the indirect information flow at process-level thus enforce a stronger notion of confidentiality and integrity in MLS systems.

5   Conclusion

In this paper, we have proposed a RWFM label based solution that a reference monitor can incorporate to tackle the *confused deputy* problem at process-level. We have also demonstrated that our solution ensures end-to-end process-level confidentiality and integrity in a decentralized labelling system. Further, we have exemplified the shortcomings of existing solution that is based on an intransitive MAC security model, and highlighted the advantages of our approach in terms of tracking indirect information flow that comes naturally with the RWFM security model. One of the takeaways from this paper shows the application of RWFM labels at process-level in a decentralized label model. However, the work can be extended towards language-level to gain finer-grained access control. A foundation we have built for Python language using *dynamic labelling* algorithm [2] and RWFM state transition rules is the pioneer in this regard.

References

1. Anderson, J.P.: Computer security technology planning study, vol. 2. Technical report, Anderson (James P) and Co Fort Washington PA (1972)
2. Ghosal, S., Shyamasundar, R.K., Kumar, N.V.N.: Static security certification of programs via dynamic labelling. In: Proceedings of the 15th International Conference on Security and Cryptography (SECRYPT), pp. 234–245. INSTICC, SciTePress (2018)
3. Hardy, N.: The confused deputy: (or why capabilities might have been invented). ACM SIGOPS Oper. Syst. Rev. **22**(4), 36–38 (1988)
4. Jaeger, T.: Operating system security. Synth. Lect. Inf. Secur. Priv. Trust **1**(1), 1–218 (2008)
5. Kumar, N.V.N., Shyamasundar, R.K.: Realizing purpose-based privacy policies succinctly via information-flow labels. In: 2014 IEEE Fourth International Conference on Big Data and Cloud Computing (BdCloud), pp. 753–760. IEEE (2014)
6. Kumar, N.V.N., Shyamasundar, R.K.: Analyzing protocol security through information-flow control. In: Krishnan, P., Radha Krishna, P., Parida, L. (eds.) ICDCIT 2017. LNCS, vol. 10109, pp. 159–171. Springer, Cham (2017). https://doi.org/10.1007/978-3-319-50472-8_13
7. Kumar, N.V.N., Shyamasundar, R.K.: A complete generative label model for lattice-based access control models. In: Cimatti, A., Sirjani, M. (eds.) SEFM 2017. LNCS, vol. 10469, pp. 35–53. Springer, Cham (2017). https://doi.org/10.1007/978-3-319-66197-1_3
8. Lu, Y., Raghavendra, K.R., Zhang, C., Krishnan, P.: Secure information flow by access control: a security type system of dual-access labels. In: Proceedings of the 42nd International Conference on Very Important Topics, pp. 23:1–23:34, No. 23. LIPICS (2016)
9. Radhika, B.S., Kumar, N.V.N., Shyamasundar, R.K.: FlowConSEAL: automatic flow consistency analysis of SEAndroid and SELinux policies. In: Kerschbaum, F., Paraboschi, S. (eds.) DBSec 2018. LNCS, vol. 10980, pp. 219–231. Springer, Cham (2018). https://doi.org/10.1007/978-3-319-95729-6_14
10. Schneider, F.B.: Access control (2012). https://www.cs.cornell.edu/fbs/publications/chptr.DAC.pdf

BlockSLaaS: Blockchain Assisted Secure Logging-as-a-Service for Cloud Forensics

Sagar Rane$^{(\boxtimes)}$ and Arati Dixit$^{(\boxtimes)}$

Department of Technology, Savitribai Phule Pune University,
Pune, Maharashtra, India
scholarsaggy@gmail.com, adixit98@gmail.com

Abstract. Cloud computing has become a prominent and widespread technology nowadays. However, it agonized due to incremental serious security issues. To solve these issues forensic techniques needs to be applied in cloud. Log is a paramount element in forensic investigations to reveal 3W i.e. who, what, when of happened suspicious activity. That's the reason, secure preservation and investigation of different logs is an essential job for cloud forensics. Due to very little control over the clouds, it's very difficult to collect authentic logs from cloud environment while preserving integrity and confidentiality. Till today, forensic investigator has to trust Cloud Service Provider (CSP), who collect the logs from individual sources of cloud environment. However, untrusted stakeholders of cloud and malicious entities from outside the cloud can collude with each other to alter the logs after the fact and remain untraceable. Thus, validity of the provided logs for forensics can be questionable. In this paper, we proposed forensic aware blockchain assisted secure logging-as-a-service for cloud environment to securely store and process logs by tackling multi-stakeholder collusion problem and ensuring integrity & confidentiality. The integrity of logs is ensured using immutable property of blockchain technology. Cloud Forensic Investigator (CFI) can only be able to access the logs for forensic investigation by BlockSLaaS, which preserves confidentiality of logs.

Keywords: Secure logging · Forensics · Blockchain ·
Cloud computing

1 Introduction

CLOUD computing has unfolded scope of computing using its characteristics resiliency, ubiquitous access and measured service to various business fields. 83% of small and medium business fields workload will be in the cloud and it's projected to reach $411 billion market value by 2020 [1]. While using fascinating broad network access and economical computing model of cloud, security of these systems is ever growing and prime issue [9–11, 20]. Affordable pay per use model of cloud motivates malicious cloud service consumers and attackers to launch

© Springer Nature Singapore Pte Ltd. 2019
S. Nandi et al. (Eds.): ISEA-ISAP 2018, CCIS 939, pp. 77–88, 2019.
https://doi.org/10.1007/978-981-13-7561-3_6

attacks within and on cloud respectively. Massachusetts Institute of Technology (MIT) predicted in 2018 ransomware target will be on cloud and this will become biggest cyber threat [2]. Recently, a high profile DDOS attack is made on cloud using compromised amazon EC2 virtual machines [12].

Log is a documentation of recorded events happened in the system with timestamp, therefore it is very useful evidence to take legal action against suspect [13,17]. However, it is extremely difficult to collect and preserve logs in cloud due to reduced level of access control of cloud service consumers (CSC) on cloud. Till now there is no any technique through which we can preserve and verify integrity of logs. Cloud service consumers (CSC) and cloud forensic investigators (CFI) have to trust on cloud service provider (CSP) to get appropriate activities log. While the logs are essential element required for forensic investigation, the reliability of logs is doubtful as enemy can modify/add/delete/reorder these logs to remain untraceable. On other hand cloud forensic investigator (CFI) also can be malicious and can modify/add/delete/reorder the logs before presenting in the court [18].

In this paper we aim to solve cloud multi-stakeholders collusion problem while preserving integrity and confidentiality of logs. To solve above mentioned challenges we propose blockchain assisted secure logging-as-a-service (BlockSLaaS) for cloud. As VM resided data is volatile, BlockSLaaS extracts logs from suspected VMs and keep them in secondary storage while eliminating volatility problem. While doing this task encryption process takes place along with log anchoring on blockchain ledger with timestamp to maintain chronology of generated logs. After this no one can add/modify/reorder/remove the logs. BlockSLaaS provides appropriate logs to Law Enforcement Agency (LEA) with the help of fine gained access control mechanism.

Integration of BlockSLaaS in clouds will enable CFI to do reliable forensics. Elements of security i.e. CIA model (Confidentiality, Integrity and Availability) ensured by proposed BlockSLaaS and can be add-on feature for cloud to attract huge business enterprises. Secure transmission and preservation of logs over the secured network can make cloud more auditable, which is necessary requirement of SOX and HIPPA acts [3,4,22]. BlockSLaaS enabled cloud can reduce different malicious attacks. To understand cloud multi stakeholder collusion problem we present following hypothetical scenario.

Hypothesis: *Alice is an unsatisfied IT employee at a big multinational banking firm. Bank has its own cloud environment on which all bank employees' executing their day to day financial activities. Alice influenced by competitor bank did some alleged activities for her personal benefits and turned off her VMs. Due to this; there have been risk events while auditing which are non-compliant with regulations. Chief Security Officer (CSO) has tried to find out alleged one behind the scene but didn't have success. CSO asked a forensic investigator to investigate the case. Cloud Forensic Investigator (CFI) got to know that these events are happened from same cloud environment machines. Finally, CFI decreed Cloud*

Service Provider (CSP) for providing the logs of associated time period events. Even CSO has the logs, couldn't point anyone for being responsible because:

- Case 1: Alice influenced by Competitor Bank colluded with the Cloud Service Provider to create reputational risk on the bank. Afterwards, cloud forensic investigator had no way for correct log verification and thus Alice concealed herself from investigation.
- Case 2: Alice could claim that, Cloud Service Provider and Cloud Forensic Investigator colluded with each other to frame her by manipulating the logs.
- Case 3: Alice wiped out the traces of the alleged events by terminating her VMs to defame the bank. As a consequence Cloud Service Provider would unable to provide helpful logs to investigator (Fig. 1).

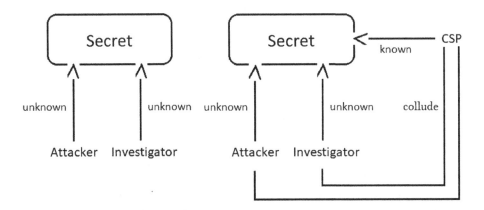

Fig. 1. A cloud multi stakeholder collusion problem

Contributions: Following are the contributions of this paper:

- We propose secured and reliable cryptographic technique for log items of potential evidences in cloud environment.
- We develop fine grained access control mechanism for forensic investigator in cloud system while preserving cloud users' logs integrity and confidentiality.
- We design blockchain based technique to solve cloud multi stakeholder collusion problem.
- We explain and use concept of proof of data possession along with blockchain under the theme of digital forensics.

Organization: The rest of the paper is organized as follows. Section 2 presents cloud log background, it's forensics challenges and blockchain. In Sect. 3, we present the associated literature work. Section 4 describes threat model, Sect. 5 represents implementation details of BlockSLaaS and its integrity & confidentiality preservation mechanism on open source cloud computing platform. Section 6 depicts Security Analysis of our technique And finally concluded in Sect. 7.

2   Background and Challenges

This section presents background of digital and cloud forensics. We listed few of the challenges of doing log based forensics in cloud.

2.1   Digital Forensics

It is a branch of forensic science that comprehends the recovery and examination of material found in digital devices. The process used to acquire, preserve, analyze and report on evidence using scientific methods that are demonstrably reliable, accurate, and repeatable such that it may be used in judicial proceedings [5, 14] (Fig. 2).

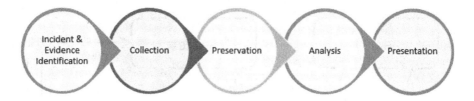

Fig. 2. Digital forensics steps

2.2   Cloud Forensics

According to NIST: Cloud Computing Forensic Science is the application of scientific principles, technological practices, derived and proven methods to process past cloud computing events through identification, collection, preservation, examination and reporting of digital data for the purpose of facilitating the reconstruction of these events [13].

2.3   Cloud Forensics Challenges

CSP Dependency for the Logs: While doing computer forensics, investigators have full control on suspected devices, e.g. computer hard drive and all computer logs. However, we have to depend on CSP to complete few steps of cloud forensics (collection of logs) in cloud. Cloud consumers have different and very less control level over three service models i.e. SaaS, PaaS and IaaS. Due to this evidence acquirement in cloud based system is most difficult task while doing investigation.

Volatile Nature of Logs: Generally every VM data (Network Logs, Setup Logs, and OS Logs) is volatile in nature unless CSP isn't shifting it on persistent storage. Sustainability of volatile logs is totally depending on power. If power goes on or someone terminated the VM, will lose the logs and there is no method to retrieve it again from shut down VM. An Attacker or Malicious employee would not be interested in preserving VM snapshots to remain clean [21].

Ease of Access to the Logs: In cloud, there are multiple service models i.e. SaaS, PaaS and IaaS. And in each service model there are multiple layers [24]. Logs generated in each service model and their sub layers should be accessible to various valid stakeholders of cloud system in a secure and easy way e.g. System Administrators, Developers and Forensic Investigators for their associated works. Log collection from these different layers itself big challenge in present scenario. However, preventing malicious employee or attacker from getting access to the potential evident logs is also an issue.

Decentralized Logs: Due to decentralized nature of cloud log information is not situated in centralized station. However, collecting logs from various destinations in a secure way is challenging task. Time Synchronization is also biggest problem [13] of decentralized cloud system, due to which receiver side logs doesn't match with provider side. Defending such evidences in court is also challenging.

Lack of Standard Log Formats: To apply various analytical algorithms well on cloud logs, it is necessary to have logs in standard format. Regrettably, standardization of log formats is lacking thing in cloud based system [22]. In cloud, logs are available in diverse formats in which not all providing vital information required for investigation. e.g. Who, What, When.

2.4 Blockchain

Blockchain is a chain of blocks where each block contains some data. Along with data it also contains hash of previous block and its own hash to maintain chronological records [6]. In our context, blockchain maintaining the chronological order of events happened in cloud computing environment. The intention behind using this technology is to design of scalable, cryptography enabled, tamper resistant, distributed logging service.

3   Related Work

Many researchers have explored cloud forensics on technical, legal and architectural aspects. Marty has proposed logging framework which involves enabling logging on potential sources, setup of log transport mechanism and tuned logging configurations. In the same work guidelines for when to log, what to log and how to log are also provided. As per these guidelines logging challenges can be solved. There is need of transport layer which having productive bandwidth, trustworthy, unreadable in nature [7]. A great level of trust is require in the cloud layers to acquire authentic data. Few tools and techniques are explored & evaluated for cloud forensics. FROST, a forensic tool is developed by Dykstra [15,23] to collect firewall and API logs. To provide various logs to cloud service consumers, read only APIs are developed [8] on the same line. Zafarullah proposed use of syslog generated by eucalyptus cloud computing software to detect DDOS attack on cloud. They were able to monitor internal and external behaviour of eucalyptus by doing analysis of bandwidth usage and processor usage logs [28]. Patrascu proposed management console which can be useful to acquire logs by communicating with VFS, network block and system call interfaces [16]. But another layer of management console can be one more place for vulnerability. Trusted Platform Module (TPM) is explored to perform digital forensics in cloud considering CSP as a trusted stakeholder [14].

Attention of these works is on enabling easy availability of logs without considering multi stakeholder collusion problem and analysis on logs for various attack detection. Integrity and Confidentiality of the logs is also questionable in above mentioned works. Happened-before relationship [29] to check consistency of virtual machine events will not work for all the time while doing cloud forensic investigations. Zawoad developed SecLaaS, a tamper evident scheme to provide integrity preserved logs for forensic investigation. In this work probabilistic data structures are used to create and verify proofs of past data which suffer from false positives [18,19]. Secure transmission of logs using cryptographic protocol on anonymous network (TOR) while preserving integrity and confidentiality delegates log management for cloud is cost effective [30,31]. But now organizations can bear cost of secure logging services. However, none of the above mentioned work proposed technique for securely storing logs in cloud and enabling availability of proofs of data possession publically. Cloud has complex virtual network configuration system and that is vulnerable to many incidents [25–27]. We design following threat model for the same.

4   Threat Model

In this section, we explain threat model of our system comprises of definition of different terms, General Attacks, Threat Categories and Risks factors.

4.1   Definition of Terms

1. CSC: A CSC is a consumer who is consuming cloud services to perform day to day activities; CSC can be malicious some times.
2. Log: A record of events generated in cloud computing environment, e.g. Network Log – recorded events of network.
3. CSP: A CSP is managerial entity of cloud system whose task is to prepare proofs of log possession, make it available in public, easy access control to collect logs.
4. CFI: A CFI is skilled forensic specialist and responsible for collection and investigation of evidences if malicious activity happened in cloud.
5. JSA: Generally, JSA is a judicial authority who will verify the truth of incidence using proofs of data possession created by blockchain.
6. BLC: Blockchain based log chain maintains the tamper resistant sequence of events.
7. PLP: To ensure integrity of logs, PLP holds proofs of log possession.
8. Regulator: A Regulator whose aim is to maintain integrity of the systems e.g. financial using some guidelines and restrictions.

4.2   General Types of Attacks

1. **Confidentiality Violation:** It will happen if unauthorized stakeholders or external attackers got access to the logs.
2. **Integrity Violation:** It will happen if a deceitful stakeholder of cloud self or colludes with each other to tamper the logs to frame someone i.e. either to protect attacker or to frame honest user.
3. **Availability Violation:** It will happen when CFI stopped from getting the logs for investigation i.e. availability of logs will get disrupted.
4. **Repudiation by CSP:** A malicious CSP can deny published PLP.
5. **Repudiation by CSC:** A CSC can claim that these logs are of other users and not mine considering comingled data of cloud.

4.3   Threat Categories

1. **Internal:** These types of threats can be done from persons having legitimate access to the system. These threats are difficult to recognize as malicious insiders might know the way to being non-recognized. To suite the requirements they can falsify the data.
2. **External:** These types of threats can be done from attackers, competitors. There are various ways through which it can be done.

4.4   Risks

Illicit Disclosure of Logs: This comprises illicit disclosure of private information of cloud users' logs which indicates the reputational damage of domain company e.g. Financial Bank.

Denial of Logging Services: Due to various threats on logging service itself, will create unavailability of logs problem which is required for further investigation.

Modification of Logs: Dishonest CSP and untrusted stakeholders of cloud can tamper to the logs to make their personal benefits.

5   The BlockSLaaS Technique

5.1   Overview

Using this technique we discuss working of BlockSLaaS i.e. Blockchain assisted Secure Logging-as-a-Service to store and process logs securely, gives fine grained access control to cloud forensic investigators and integrity verfication of the logs. According to our hypothesis, malicious employee or external attacker can make attack on cloud based systems. Activities happening on cloud infrastructure will generate logs for each VM activity e.g. Setup logs of VM, Network interactions of VM. These logs cannot sustain without power meaning if VM gets turn off data resided in VM will lose. BlockSLaaS extracts these logs from virtual environment and stores it into secondary storage to remove volatile nature of logs while preserving integrity and confidentiality of data (Fig. 3).

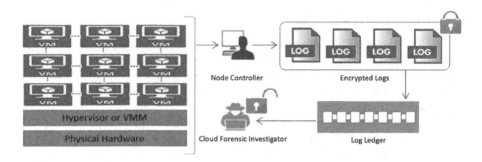

Fig. 3. Overview of BlockSLaaS

5.2 Implementation

We setup openstack, open source private cloud computing platform to run our blockchain based secure logging technique. We use following system setup for our implementation. Machine setup: Intel I7, 16 GB RAM, 1 TB Hard disk and Ubuntu 16.04 LTS 64-bit OS. Virtual Environment: Virtual Box 5.2.18. We used RSA algorithm for encryption and SHA-256 for hash generation. Following steps explain step by step working of BlockSLaaS.

Step 1: Node Controller collect the logs from all sources of virtual environment through libpcap log capturing library. After this process, Node Controller creates the log entry for each log which consist of (considering network log):

$$L = (fIP, tIP, T, port, userID) \tag{1}$$

where,
fIP is a IP of user who did the activity
tIP is a IP of user on which activity happened
T is a Timestamp of network activity
Port is a port used to perform activity
userID is a User ID of the cloud user/external attacker

Step 2: As per Service Level Agreement CSP and other stakeholders of cloud setup key generation and distribution environment. To ensure privacy of CSC's Node Controller encrypts each log entry using public key of cloud Forensic Investigator CFI_{PK}:

$$EL = encrypt(L, CFI_{PK}) \tag{2}$$

Step 3: Finally, Node Controller adds each EL on Blockchain. After every single day BlockSLaaS published these logs online to get more transparency. After this no one can tamper the logs and thus integrity will get preserved.

$$BLC = (EL, H<EL>, H<EL_p>) \tag{3}$$

where, BLC is Blockchain based LogChain which contains EL, Hash of current EL and Hash of Previous EL. It maintains chronology of logs.

Step 4: Using Eq. 3 system creates BLC Blockchain assisted LogChain. Block-SLaaS creates proofs of log possession which can be useful for forensic investigations in future.

$$PLP = (BLC_D, T_{PLP}) \tag{4}$$

Step 5: If any incident got happened, Clod Forensic Investigator can only get access to the blockchain as per decided in Service Level Agreements to perform investigation. CFI can use their secret key CFI_{SK} to decrypt the logs and this way confidentiality of CSCs' logs get preserved.

$$DL = decrypt(EL, CFI_{SK}) \tag{5}$$

5.3 PoC Using Hyperledger

We implement proposed BlockSLaaS technique using the Hyperledger. To create peer-to-peer network we used open source Hyperledger Fabric. This is platform for distributed ledger solutions [32]. As per our hypothesis, multiple branches of bank anchor entire logs on blockchain. BlockSLaaS anchor these encrypted logs on this private permissioned blockchain, so that no one can learn individual cloud consumer logs information. Composer tool of hyperledger is used to write the logic of proposed technique. By using this, stakeholders of cloud system can create, submit and query the transactions. In this way, we created PoC using Hyperledger.

6 Security Analysis

In this section, we made analysis of security elements e.g. Integrity, Confidentiality, Availability and Non-Repudiation. We considered general types of attacks, various threat categories, and risks mentioned in our threat model while doing this analysis (Fig. 4).

6.1 Integrity Perseverance

As shown in following diagram, each block of blockchain contains encrypted log entry EL, hash of EL and hash of previous block [6]. For the very first block of blockchain we have taken EL1, hash of EL1, previous hash is zero as it is genesis block. Next Block contains EL2, hash of EL2 and hash of EL1 and so on for all the logs as shown in Fig. 4. If any one tries to modify any log as previous hash will not match with the next block. No one can modify all the hashes as it is almost impossible. So, any stakeholder of cloud i.e. CSC/CSP/CFI cannot add/update/delete/modify/reorder the log entries.

Fig. 4. Integrity preservation in BlockSLaaS

6.2 Confidentiality Perseverance

In the BlockSLaaS technique only Law Enforcement Agency have secret keys. Thus, no one can add/modify/delete/reorder the logs. Our technique use one way hash function and thus, any malicious entity can not recover the original logs. So, from the above Eq. 5 we can say that only authorized peoples can access logs for investigation and thus, confidentiality get preserved.

6.3 Availability of PLP

The BlockSLaaS technique make proofs of log possession i.e. PLP publicly available. Law Enforcement Agency (LEA) can any time access past proofs of log possession and Judicial System Authority (JSA) can verify the correctness of the proofs.

6.4 Non-repudiation by CSP/CSC

While using BlockSLaaS technique a malacious CSP cannot deny published PLP as it is real time and tamper resistant. Also any CSC cannot claim that these logs are not belongs to me. Thus Non-Repudiation got achieved using our technique.

7 Conclusion

Log is impeccable source of evidence while doing forensic Investigations. Due to black box nature of cloud it is very difficult to collect logs in cloud based systems as compare to traditional systems. Forensic Investigator has to trust CSP while collecting the logs and till now there is no method to verify whether the CSP is providing accurate logs. Regrettably, there has been unavailability of technique to securely transfer logs to forensic investigator. In above mentioned work, we proposed BlockSLaaS which can key to securely store and process the logs which can be useful for forensics purpose later. Our technique preserving confidentiality of cloud consumers at the same time. Judicial system can verify integrity of the logs using blockchain based proof of data possession. This is feasible solution in current scenario as we ran it on open stack which is open source cloud computing platform. Our technique will make cloud more auditable and forensic friendly. Thus, cloud audit activities can always abide with regulatory acts like SOX, GLBA and HIPPA [22].

References

1. Columbus, L.: Cloud computing market projected to reach 411B dollar by 2020 (2017). https://goo.gl/hmKeK1. Accessed 09 July 2018
2. Ashford, W.: Ransomware to hit cloud computing in 2018, predicts MIT (2018). https://goo.gl/9JoHhj. Accessed 26 Apr 2018
3. Congress of the United States. Sarbanes-Oxley Act (2002). http://goo.gl/YHwujG. Accessed 20 Mar 2015
4. www.hhs.gov. Health Information Privacy. http://goo.gl/NxgkMi. Accessed 20 Mar 2015
5. Kent, K., Chevalier, S., Grance, T., Dang, H.: Guide to integrating forensic techniques into incident response. NIST Special Publication 800-86 (2006)
6. Nakamoto, S.: Bitcoin: a peer-to-peer electronic cash system. Consulted 1, 2012 (2008)
7. Marty, R.: Cloud application logging for forensics. In: Proceedings of the 2011 ACM Symposium on Applied Computing (SAC11), Taichung, Taiwan, pp. 178–184. ACM, March 2011
8. Birk, D., Wegener, C.: Technical issues of forensic investigations in cloud computing environments. In: SADFE, pp. 1–10. IEEE (2011)
9. Balduzzi, M., Zaddach, J., Balzarotti, D., Kirda, E., Loureiro, S.: A security analysis of Amazon's elastic compute cloud service. In: Symposium on Applied Computing, pp. 1427–1434. ACM (2012)
10. Subashini, S., Kavitha, V.: A survey on security issues in service delivery models of cloud computing. J. Netw. Comput. Appl. 34(1), 1–11 (2011)
11. Zissis, D., Lekkas, D.: Addressing cloud computing security issues. Future Gener. Comput. Syst. 28(3), 583–592 (2012)
12. Infosecurity-magazine. Ddos-ers launch attacks from Amazon ec2, July 2014. http://goo.gl/vrXrHE. Accessed 1 Jan 2018
13. Melland, P., Grance, T.: Nist cloud computing forensic science challenges. NIST Cloud Computing Forensic Science Working Group, Information Technology Laboratory, Draft NISTIR 8006, June 2014
14. Zawoad, S., Hasan, R.: Digital forensics in the cloud. J. Defense Softw. Eng. 26(5), 17–20 (2013)
15. Dykstra, J., Sherman, A.: Acquiring forensic evidence from infrastructure-as-aservice cloud computing: exploring and evaluating tools, trust, and techniques. J. Digit. Invest. 9, S90–S98 (2012). https://doi.org/10.1016/j.diin.2012.05.001
16. Patrascu, A., Patriciu, V.-V.: Logging system for cloud computing forensic environments. J. Control Eng. Appl. Inform. 16(1), 80–88 (2014)
17. Khan, S., Gani, A., Wahab, A., et al.: Cloud log forensics: foundations, state of the art, and future directions. ACM Comput. Surv. 49(1) https://doi.org/10.1145/2906149 (2016). Article 7

18. Zawoad, S., Dutta, A.K., Hasan, R.: SecLaaS: secure logging-as-aservice for cloud forensics. In: ASIACCS, pp. 219–230. ACM (2013)
19. Zawoad, S., Dutta, A., Hasan, R.: Towards building forensics enabled cloud through secure logging-as-a-service. IEEE Trans. Dependable Secure Comput. **13**(2), 148–162 (2016). https://doi.org/10.1109/TDSC.2015.2482484
20. Ruan, K., Carthy, J., Kechadi, T., Baggili, I.: Cloud forensics denitions and critical criteria for cloud forensic capability: an overview of survey results. Digital Invest. **10**(1), 34–43 (2013)
21. Zawoad, S., Hasan, R.: Cloud forensics: a meta-study of challenges, approaches, and open problems arXiv: 1302.6312v1 [cs.DC] 26 February 2013
22. Kent, K., Souppaya, M.: Guide to computer security log management. Technical report. NIST Special Publication 800-92 (2006)
23. Dykstra, J., Sherman, A.: Understanding issues in cloud forensics: two hypothetical case studies. Cyber Defense Lab, Department of CSEE, University of Maryland, Baltimore County (UMBC) (2011)
24. Cohen, F.: Challenges to digital forensic evidence in the cloud. In: Ruan, K. (ed.) Cybercrime and Cloud Forensics: Applications for Investigation Processes, pp. 59–78. IGI Global, December 2012
25. Khajeh-Hosseini, A., Greenwood, D., Sommerville, I.: Cloud migration: a case study of migrating an enterprise it system to IaaS. In: Proceedings of the 3rd International Conference on Cloud Computing (CLOUD), pp. 450–457. IEEE (2010)
26. Ruan, K., Carthy, J., Kechadi, T., Crosbie, M.: Cloud forensics. In: Peterson, G., Shenoi, S. (eds.) DigitalForensics 2011. IAICT, vol. 361, pp. 35–46. Springer, Heidelberg (2011). https://doi.org/10.1007/978-3-642-24212-0_3
27. Grispos, G., Glisson, W., Storer, T.: Calm before the Storm: the emerging challenges of cloud commuting in digital forensics. University of Glasgow (2012)
28. Zafarullah, Z., Anwar, F., Anwar, Z.: Digital forensics for eucalyptus. In: FIT, pp. 110–116. IEEE (2011)
29. Thorpe, S., Ray, I.: Detecting temporal inconsistency in virtual machine activity timelines. J. Inf. Assur. Secur. **7**(1), 24–31 (2012)
30. Thorpe, S., Ray, I., Grandison, T., Barbir, A., France, R.: Hypervisor event logs as a source of consistent virtual machine evidence for forensic cloud investigations. In: Wang, L., Shafiq, B. (eds.) DBSec 2013. LNCS, vol. 7964, pp. 97–112. Springer, Heidelberg (2013). https://doi.org/10.1007/978-3-642-39256-6_7
31. Ray, I., Belyaev, K., Strizhov, M., Mulamba, D., Rajaram, M.: Secure logging as a service delegating log management to the cloud. IEEE Syst. J. **7**(2), 323–334 (2013)
32. Hyperledger FabricDocs Documentation, Hyperledger. https://readthedocs.org/projects/hyperledger-fabric/downloads/pdf/latest/hyperledger-fabric.pdf

Keystroke Dynamics Authentication Using Small Datasets

Nataasha Raul, Royston D'mello, and Mandar Bhalerao[✉]

Sardar Patel Institute of Technology, Mumbai, India
mandar.bhalerao@spit.ac.in

Abstract. Keystroke dynamics is the analysis of timing information which describes exactly when each key was pressed or released by a user while typing. There have been various attempts to use this timing information to identify user's typing pattern and authenticate the user in a system, but mostly from a research perspective. We present a new methodology which focuses on solving the practical problems associated with deploying a keystroke dynamics authentication system. In our proposed methodology, a user's keystroke features are separated into two sets, namely high frequency and low frequency, based on the fraction of the total typing time the key takes. These two feature sets are then trained using OneClassSVM classifiers. Also, our proposed methodology requires minimal data and it is easily deployable on any computer.

Keywords: Keystroke dynamics · One class classification · Authentication

1 Introduction

Identification of a user as a credible user is a necessary condition, in order to allow access to any private or confidential information. Authentication works on three factors namely knowledge, possession and inherence where each factor gives partial information regarding validity of the user. Knowledge constitutes a token that a user knows prior to logging in (PIN, password, lock pattern). Possession includes something that a user has (mobile phone, card, license). Inherence includes what an individual has integrated in itself (Biometric). Biometrics is further classified into physiological characteristics and behavioural characteristics.

Success of biometric is determined by the factors such as universality, uniqueness, variance, measurability, performance, acceptability, circumvention [1].

Keystroke dynamics refers to the behavioural patterns found in a person's typing detected through their keystroke timestamps. Data needed to analyze keystroke dynamics is obtained by keystroke logging. These patterns are used to develop a unique biometric template of the user for future authentication [2]. These patterns are shown to possess cognitive qualities which are unique to each user and can be used as personal identifiers [3].

© Springer Nature Singapore Pte Ltd. 2019
S. Nandi et al. (Eds.): ISEA-ISAP 2018, CCIS 939, pp. 89–96, 2019.
https://doi.org/10.1007/978-981-13-7561-3_7

Keystroke dynamics can be used for both verification and identification. Verification refers to the process of proofing a validity of claimed identity. Identification is classifying a user to be to be among those in a database or not. Identification is generally more time consuming, slower in responsiveness, and require higher processing capacity [4]. In our experiment, we have dealt with verification of user identity.

In this paper we try to solve some of the problems associated with keystroke dynamics based authentication from a practical point of view. Most of the current literature focuses on classification on medium to large size datasets. However such datasets won't be available in a production system. The publicly available datasets are created over long durations of time at regular intervals. However, practically we can't wait to accumulate that much data for the system to work. Hence, we aim to solve the following objectives in this paper:

1. Authentication in an unsupervised way.
2. Training the model to work with a dataset as small as 10 data points.
3. Decrease the false rejection rate of the system.

In this paper, we thus present a system for authentication of users in an unsupervised way. The user logs in 10 times during the onboarding process using which we create the user's authentication model which is used thereafter to authenticate the user.

2   Related Work

Keystroke dynamics can either be applied to free (dynamic) text or a fixed (static) text. In our work, we focus on static text. User recognition using keystroke dynamics can be perceived as a pattern recognition problem and most of the methods can be categorized as machine learning approaches (37%), statistical (61%) and others (2%) [4].

In statistics, the most popular method is using a distance measure. In distance measure, the pattern of the user logging in is calculated. This pattern is compared to a precomputed reference pattern in the database to check for any similarity. Zhong et al. [5] give a new distance metric exploiting the advantages of Mahalanobis and Manhattan distance metrics, namely robustness to outliers (for Manhattan distance) and to feature correlation and scale variation (Mahalanobis distance). They treat user authentication as a one class classification problem and use a Nearest Neighbour classifier with their new distance metric to classify a sample as originating from a genuine or a false user. Using this algorithm on the CMU dataset, they have obtained an EER of 8.7% and ZMFAR of 42.3% across all 51 subjects. The error rate is reduced to 8.4% for EER and 40.5% for ZMFAR if outliers are removed from training data.

Similarly, [6] present their distance metric which addresses the problem of popularly used distance metrics such as Euclidean, Manhattan; which assume that each feature of data point is equally important and independent from others. With their new metric, they obtained an EER of 0.062 compared to EER of 0.110 obtained using Manhattan. Morales et al. [7] compares various score normalization techniques. Their work suggests that using score normalization techniques improves the overall performance of the system. The improvement, although, depends on the classifier and on dataset used.

Other than using distance measurement techniques, other statistical approaches include cluster analysis and probabilistic modelling.

Machine learning is widely used in the pattern recognition. The main idea is to identify a commonly occurring pattern and further classify data based on the pattern learned. This category includes various sub-domains like Neural Networks, Fuzzy Logic and Evolutionary Computing.

Among the listed sub-domains, neural network is claimed to give better results than statistical methods [8]. However, the classifiers require the genuine as well as the intruder's typing data to train. It is infeasible to specifically define and thus to obtain intruder's typing pattern, since any pattern other than the user's pattern is potentially an intruder's pattern. Furthermore, if the user's pattern changes, it would require the whole network to be retrained.

Another approach is by using anomaly detectors. Killourhy et al. [9] compared 14 anomaly detectors on a common dataset synthesized by them. Their experiments showed that Manhattan distance had the least EER of 0.096 and Nearest Neighbor (Mahalanobis) gave the least ZMFAR of 0.468.

Yu et al. [10] identified user authentication as a one-class classification problem, since getting the data of the imposter class is both infeasible and impractical. They used a GA-SVM based wrapper approach for feature selection and an SVM novelty detector, which fetched similar results as compared to neural networks. SVM maps the input vector into a high-dimensional feature space via the kernel function (e.g. linear, polynomial, sigmoid, or radial basis function). The algorithm will then search for a function that encapsulates the majority of patterns contained in the input vector and vector outside this region. As a result, the separating function is able to create more complex boundaries and to better determine which side of feature space a new pattern belongs.

3   Methodology

3.1   Data Collection

We have avoided the use of any public dataset which are usually created over predefined periods of time. We focus on creating our own dataset because our models need to work in an environment in which the user creates their dataset in one sitting during the registration process unlike the available public datasets. And the public datasets in which the users create the dataset in one sitting suffer from the short-time variance in a user's typing rhythm/speed. Using our preprocessing techniques described in the further sections, we solve this problem.

We used a Django web app for collecting keystroke data of each user. The keystroke values are recorded using Javascript. The password given is India@2018, which uses alphabets, numbers and special characters. Even though in this system the password choice is unconstrained, we have set a password for our experimental setup to maintain a uniformity across the dataset. This ensures that the choice of passwords doesn't influence the results. Each user is required to type this password 10 times. From a system point of view, we can't expect a user's onboarding process to last more than 10 password entries. So in this paper we focus on making the system work for 10 password entries during the model creation phase.

The timestamps are recorded in milliseconds, up to five decimal places. Using the press and release times, various other features (described below) are calculated and stored in a Pandas dataframe, through which it is exported to a CSV file. Along with the timestamp values, the files also contains a column for username.

3.2 Feature Extraction

We record the press and release time of each key for each sample. Using these two timestamps, we calculate the following features:

- Holdtime (Dwell time) = (KeyPress – KeyRelease)
- Flight UU = KeyUp - KeyUp(Previous key released)
- Flight DD = KeyDown - KeyDown(Previous key pressed)
- Flight UD = KeyDown - KeyUp(Previous key released)

These features (except hold time, press and release times) are calculated for a set of two consecutive keys (digraph), for each sample.

3.3 Preprocessing

Consistency Checking. We focus on creating our own dataset because often times a user doesn't enter their password consistently. One time the speed can be fast and the very next time it can slow down. This is the kind of short-time variance that can occur in a user's typing rhythm.

Since we have less amount of training data, we cannot afford any outliers in it. Yu et al. [10] find that preprocessing the data and removal of outliers improves the overall performance of the classifier. Thus we need to ensure that the 10 samples we collect are representative of the user's typing pattern. Hence, while recording each training sample, we consider it only if it matches the first 5 samples. The first 5 entries are assumed to be authentic (not consisting of outliers) which serves as a base for further detection of outliers.

The matching is done using Nearest Neighbor algorithm. First, the Kth nearest distance of each previously recorded training example is calculated. Euclidean distance is used as a distance measure. For two n dimensional points x and y, Euclidean distance (d) between them is defined as $d = \sqrt{(x - y)^2}$. For our purposes, we have chosen k = 3. Concretely, what Kth (3rd) nearest distance means is that we consider the nearest distances of a training example with other examples. Each example will differ from others by a certain value (i.e. the distance between them). Kth nearest distance is the distance between the example under consideration and the Kth most similar (Kth nearest) example to it. Thus, we will get n (n <= 10) such distances. The average value of 'n' distances recorded is chosen as a threshold value for incoming training example. Thus only if the Kth nearest distance of incoming training example is less than or equal to the threshold value, it is regarded as genuine training example. So the data is collected until there are 10 genuine training examples.

3.4   Separation of Keystrokes into High Frequency and Low Frequency

Instead of using all the features on one classifier, in this paper we have separated the feature set into two parts. Based on how close or further a keystroke is from its neighbours, in the time domain, we classify the keystrokes as high frequency and low frequency keystrokes respectively. And their features as high and low frequency features. For most users, the set of characters which they can type quickly will be very different. Hence we examine how separating the two kinds of features of a user can help in better identifying user patterns.

We consider the release timestamp only for all calculations of this module. We first normalise the dataset in the following way:

1. We first shift all the timings by the timing of the first key release. By doing this we make all the key release timings relative to the first one. This is to normalize the changes due to the user starting typing very late or early.
2. The relative timings are then converted into the fraction of the timing of the total duration of typing i.e. all the values are divided by the total time of typing which is found by the last release timestamp. This gives an indication of at what fraction of the typing time does that keystroke appear.

After this preprocessing the value of the first keystroke will always be 0 and that of the last keystroke will always be 1.

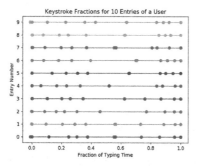

Fig. 1. Fractions at which a user's keystrokes occur for 10 entries

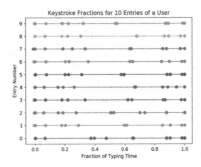

Fig. 2. The same plot for another user

From Figs. 1 and 2 it is evident that there are some regions that are distinct to the user. These regions may be low frequency regions or high frequency regions. There are clusters of low and high frequency regions in the plots.

The occurrence of these low and high frequency clusters may or may not be distinct to a user. In the graphs, most of the time bands look similar for both the users, except the time band between 'a' and 'shift', and '@' and '2'. For these two time bands it can be seen that the second user has wider time bands for these set of keys. Hence they can be used to distinguish the two users visually and show that it is also possible to identify them mathematically.

We then create a threshold to decide high and low frequency as $1/n$. This gives the average timing difference fraction. For every keystroke pair the timing difference is calculated and if that difference is lower than the average timing difference it is considered as high frequency region, otherwise it is considered as a low frequency region.

3.5   Training

Once we have collected 10 samples for a user, the next time the user logs in, the training is initiated. The data in the saved csv files is preprocessed as described in section preprocessing. The features are split into two groups and two classifiers are trained. It should be noted that the preprocessing is applied only for the calculation of high and low frequency features. This preprocessing is not used for the data that goes into training, since this kind of normalisation generally does not affect results of a learning algorithm. We then store the accuracies of the individual classifiers along with the list of high and low frequency features to disk with the two models as well.

The training is done in an unsupervised fashion. To do supervised learning we would need training samples from the intruder. We could create a negative training class with a handful of different users acting as intruders, but since the intruder's pattern could be anything we cannot accurately represent an intruder's typing pattern with such a dataset. Hence we have to train the data in an unsupervised way.

The data that we have for each user, although explicitly unlabeled, does have an implicit label of belonging to a genuine user or the positive class. Therefore this kind of learning is a kind of semi-supervised learning. The algorithm that we use for the same is a One Class SVM.

The Support Vector Method For Novelty Detection by Schölkopf et al. [11] separates all the data points from the origin and maximizes the distance from current hyperplane to the origin. This results in a binary function which captures regions in the input space where the probability density of the data is high. Thus the function returns +1 in a region where there are training data points and 1 elsewhere.

3.6   Authentication

When a new entry comes in for a particular user, we first load all their data use the low and high frequency lists to separate the incoming features accordingly. These features are then passed to the respective models and we get their individual predictions. We then take a weighted average of the individual predictions with the stored accuracies as weights. If the final result is positive we authenticate the user, else the user is rejected.

4   Results

To evaluate the results, we collect data from 7 users and keep one of them as an intruder profile. To evaluate the comparative performance of our proposed methodology we evaluate two kinds of results. For the first set of results we use a single feature set and train the model using a single OneClassSVM classifier. For the second set of results we evaluate the proposed methodology by splitting the features and training two classifiers.

For every profile we use the user's model and find prediction on the intruder's profile and find FAR. Using each of the user's profiles we find the FRR using all the incorrect predictions. We find the average FAR has decreased but the FRR has increased on splitting the feature set and creating weighted models. The results are shown in Table 1.

Table 1. Results

Type	FAR	FRR
Single classifier	0.3354	0.1200
High + low freq classifier	0.1032	0.2999

5   Conclusion

In this paper, we proposed a new authentication methodology using keystroke dynamics. Once deployed on a system, it would start authenticating users after 10 trials which are required for training purposes.

A new way of preprocessing keystroke timings was discussed, which separates the user's high frequency and low frequency sets. An FAR of 0.1032 and FRR of 0.2999 was obtained using this method.

In our approach, we ignore a change in user's typing pattern over a long time, which may invalidate the training data. Future efforts related to keystroke dynamics can be targeted to resolve this issue. Also, for the threshold used to define high and low frequency keystrokes we use the average time. This could be improved by trying multiple thresholds in combination with an optimisation algorithm to minimise FAR and FRR.

References

1. Jain, A.K., Bolle, R.M., Pankanti, S. (eds.): Biometrics: Personal Identification in Networked Society. Springer, New York (2006). https://doi.org/10.1007/978-0-387-32659-7
2. Deng, Y., Zhong, Y.: Keystroke dynamics user authentication based on gaussian mixture model and deep belief nets. https://www.hindawi.com/journals/isrn/2013/565183/
3. Obaidat, M.S.: A verification methodology for computer systems users. In: Proceedings of the 1995 ACM Symposium on Applied Computing, pp. 258–262. ACM, New York (1995)
4. Teh, P.S., Teoh, A.B.J., Yue, S.: A survey of keystroke dynamics biometrics. https://www.hindawi.com/journals/tswj/2013/408280/
5. Zhong, Y., Deng, Y., Jain, A.K.: Keystroke dynamics for user authentication. In: 2012 IEEE Computer Society Conference on Computer Vision and Pattern Recognition Workshops, pp. 117–123 (2012)
6. Ngoc, H.N., Nguyen, N.T.: An enhanced distance metric for keystroke dynamics classification. In: 2016 Eighth International Conference on Knowledge and Systems Engineering (KSE), pp. 285–290. IEEE, Hanoi (2016)
7. Morales, A., Luna-Garcia, E., Fierrez, J., Ortega-Garcia, J.: Score normalization for keystroke dynamics biometrics. In: 2015 International Carnahan Conference on Security Technology (ICCST), pp. 223–228 (2015)
8. Crawford, H.: Keystroke dynamics: characteristics and opportunities. In: 2010 Eighth International Conference on Privacy, Security and Trust, pp. 205–212 (2010)
9. Killourhy, K.S., Maxion, R.A.: Comparing anomaly-detection algorithms for keystroke dynamics. In: 2009 IEEE/IFIP International Conference on Dependable Systems Networks, pp. 125–134 (2009)
10. Yu, E., Cho, S.: Keystroke dynamics identity verification-its problems and practical solutions. Comput. Secur. **23**, 428–440 (2004)
11. Schölkopf, B., Platt, J.C., Shawe-Taylor, J.C., Smola, A.J., Williamson, R.C.: Estimating the support of a high-dimensional distribution. Neural Comput. **13**, 1443–1471 (2001)

ARBAC: Attribute-Enabled Role Based Access Control Model

Mahendra Pratap Singh$^{(\boxtimes)}$, S. Sudharsan, and M. Vani

Department of Computer Science and Engineering,
National Institute of Technology Karnataka, Surathkal,
Mangaluru, Karnataka, India
mahoo15@gmail.com

Abstract. Role Based Access Control (RBAC) is well-known for ease of policy administration, whereas Attribute Based Access Control (ABAC) is renowned for flexible policy specification and dynamic decision making capability. However, they both have some well-known limitations. In this paper, we present an approach that uniquely combines the benefits of RBAC and ABAC. Specifically, our approach associates attribute based rules with roles and permissions that enables the specification of multi-dimensional fine-grained attribute enabled role-based policies. These policies along with rules are also stored as in-memory data, which helps in minimizing the execution time of access requests. Experiments on a wide range of policy data sets demonstrate feasibility and scalability of the proposed approach.

Keywords: Access control · RBAC · Attributes ·
Context-based access control · Integration of RBAC and ABAC

1   Introduction

Over the last two decades, RBAC [15,17] has been a topic of research in the academia and industry, and is gained the attention of various organizations for its easier policy administration. In RBAC [17], a user can perform multiple tasks through roles which are composed of permissions. Permission represents an access right (e.g., read, write, etc.) on an object. Therefore, a role can directly influence the permissions available to a user. Though RBAC is easy to administrate, it has many limitations. One of it's the nature of role that is coarse-grained and does not suit fine-grained policy specification. More precisely, the need for small changes in the predefined set of permissions can lead to the creation of new roles. Additionally, a large number of roles might be needed for ensuring the fine-grained specification of policies. This issue is also known as role explosion that is one of the significant limitations of RBAC.

In large size organizations, objects for which access rights need to be defined can be considerable in number, resulting in a large number of permissions. In such scenario, fine-grained access control of objects might lead to role-permission

© Springer Nature Singapore Pte Ltd. 2019
S. Nandi et al. (Eds.): ISEA-ISAP 2018, CCIS 939, pp. 97–111, 2019.
https://doi.org/10.1007/978-981-13-7561-3_8

explosion issue that is another limitation of RBAC. Moreover, traditional RBAC does not support mobile-based environment where access is context-sensitive and is often associated with user's spatial and temporal contexts during which the access is requested.

Recently, ABAC model [7] is proposed that can overcome the limitations of RBAC. In it, policies are defined using attributes of various entities (e.g., user, object and environment), and such attributes can have one or more values. Therefore, access to an object can only be granted after the successful evaluation of the concerned policy. Though ABAC enables flexible policy specification and dynamic decision-making capability, its administration is difficult because to observe the effect of a change in policy, a large number of policies may need to be referred.

In essence, ABAC is flexible while RBAC is easy to administrative. Also, it is well known that RBAC is one of the widely adopted access control in the industry. Hence, the complete replacement of RBAC may involve a lot of migration issues that can be a hindrance for the deployment of the newer model. It would be ideal if the benefits of RBAC and ABAC can be combined. Recently, NIST announced an initiative [11] to integrate the concept of roles and attributes to build a flexible access control model. Following this, several approaches [5, 8–10] have been proposed to combine the benefits of RBAC and ABAC for nullifying their pitfalls. Most of these approaches either presented a modified RBAC or sophisticated and complex access control models.

In this paper, we present a unique approach which combines the benefits of RBAC and ABAC and enables the easier administration of policies. Specifically, we propose a new layer of functionality on top of the existing RBAC that not only enables the specification of flexible and context-sensitive policies but also minimizes migration efforts considerably. In the proposed approach, roles and permissions hold the same meaning as in RBAC, and the availability of them is further restricted by rules which can be composed of user attributes, object attributes and environment attributes.

Rest of the paper is organized as follows. Section 2 presents an approach for combining the benefits of RBAC and ABAC. Section 3 discusses few examples and illustrates the benefits of ARBAC. Section 4 presents experimental results and compares ARBAC performance with RBAC and ABAC. Section 5 reviews literature, and Sect. 6 concludes the paper.

2   Proposed Model

This section describes various components of ARBAC model shown in Fig. 1. Those components are also represented as relations in schemas shown in Figs. 2 and 3. These schemas together represent ARBAC model but for sake of clarity, they are shown separately. The discussion begins with representation and association of user attributes, object attributes, environment attributes and their values. Then several other components of ARBAC, such as Users, Objects, Roles, Permissions, Role Hierarchy, User-Role Assignment, Permission-Role Assignment and Sessions are defined along with the attribute-enabled access components Rule-Role Assignment (RuR) and Rule-Permission Assignment (RuP).

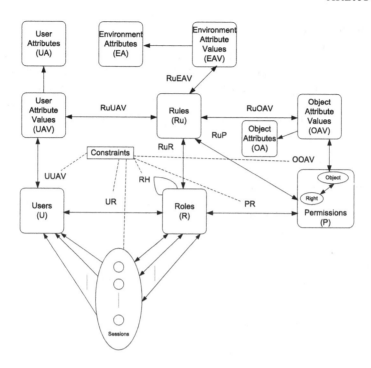

Fig. 1. Proposed ARBAC model

2.1   Users

A user is an entity that causes the flow of information and is captured in the relation *User*. Users can have one or more attributes, and each attribute can have one or more values that are captured in the relations *User_attribute* and *User_attribute_value*, respectively. Our model assigns one or more user attribute values to each user, which is captured in the following relation.

User_uav_assignment ⊆ Users × User_attribute_values

2.2   Objects

In an organization, objects contain or receive information and are captured in the relation *Object*. Objects can have one or more attributes, and such attributes can have one or more attribute values. The relations *Object_attribute* and *Object_attribute_value* capture object attributes and their values, respectively. Our model assigns one or more object attribute values to each objects. The object attribute values associated with objects are obtained through the following relation.

Object_oav_assignment ⊆ Objects × Objects_attribute_values

2.3 Environment

Environment, such as Time, location, etc., is an additional factor, independent of user and object, that can further restrict the availability of objects to users. Similar to user and object, environment can have one or more attributes and each attribute can have one or more values that are captured in the relations *Environment_attribute* and *Environment_attribute_value*, respectively.

2.4 Roles and Role Hierarchy

Roles define job functions that users suppose to perform in an organization. Unlike RBAC, a role in the ARBAC is further constrained by a set of rules which can be composed of user attributes and environment attributes. Thus, roles would only be available to those users who have the necessary attributes and satisfy at least one of the rules associated with those roles.

In RBAC, *Role hierarchy* define partial order relation on roles that enables the inheritance of roles. In ARBAC, the following relation captures the inheritance of roles.

Role_hierarchy $\subseteq$ Roles $\times$ Roles

2.5 Permissions

A permission defines the capability in the form of a right (e.g., read, write, etc.) on an object that empowers a user to perform a task through a role. In ARBAC, objects and rights associated with permissions are captured in the following relation.

Permission_object_assignment $\subseteq$ Permissions $\times$ Objects $\times$ Rights

2.6 User-Role Assignment (URA)

In ARBAC, a user can have one or more roles, and a role can be assigned to multiple users. The following relation capture the association of roles with users.

User_role_assignment $\subseteq$ Users $\times$ Roles

2.7 Permission-Role Assignment (PRA)

In ARBAC, a role can have one or more permissions, and permission can be assigned to multiple roles. The following relation capture the association of permissions with roles.

Permission_role_assignment $\subseteq$ Roles $\times$ Permissions

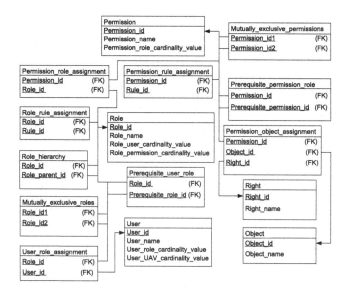

Fig. 2. Relation schema represents RBAC policies

2.8 Sessions

In RBAC, a session captures a subset of active roles from the set of roles assigned to a user. A user can activate one or more sessions, but each session would be assigned to a single user. In ARBAC, the activation of a subset of roles of users in sessions depends on the satisfiability of the rules associated with those roles.

2.9 Constraints

The proposed ARBAC can also specify different types of constraints that are captured in the following relations.

- **Mutually Exclusive Roles:** These are the critical roles in any organization and cannot be assigned to a single user. The relation given below expresses those roles which are mutually exclusive with other roles.

  Mutually_exclusive_roles ⊆ Roles × Roles

- **Mutually Exclusive Permissions:** These are the critical privileges in any organization and cannot be assigned to a single role. The following relation captures those permissions that are mutually exclusive with other permissions.

  Mutually_exclusive_permissions ⊆ Permissions × Permissions

- **Prerequisite user role:** In some of the organizations, a user can be a member of a role only if the user is assigned to the particular role. The following

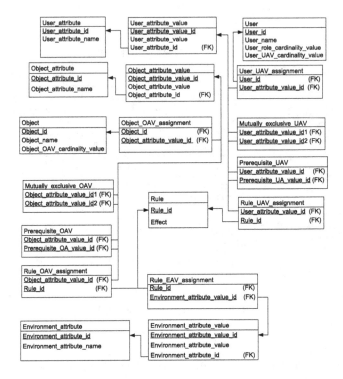

Fig. 3. Relation schema represents attribute-based rules

relation captures the prerequisite roles requirement for users.

prerequisite user role ⊆ Roles × Prerequisite Roles

- **Prerequisite permission role:** In some of the organizations, permission can be assigned to a role only if the role possesses the particular permission. The following relation captures the prerequisite permissions requirement for roles.

prerequisite role permission ⊆ Permissions × Prerequisite Permissions

- **Mutually Exclusive User attribute values:** These are the critical user attribute values that cannot be assigned to a single user. The following relation captures those user attribute values for each user.

Mutually_exclusive_UAV ⊆ User attribute values × User attribute Values

- **Mutually Exclusive Object attribute values:** These are the critical object attribute values that cannot be assigned to a single object. The following relation captures those object attribute values for each object.

Mutually_exclusive_OAV ⊆ Object attribute values × Object attribute Values

- **Cardinality Constraint:**
  In any organization, a user and a role can be assigned to a few roles and users, respectively. Similarly, a permission and a role can be associated with a few roles and permissions, respectively. Moreover, a user and an object can have a few user attribute values and object attribute values, respectively. The relations *User*, *Role*, *Permission* and *Object* capture the cardinality value for users, roles, permissions and objects, respectively.

2.10 Rules

Unlike RBAC, *Rule* is a new component in the ARBAC that can enable or disable roles and permissions. In ARBAC, rules which restrict the availability of roles to users can be composed of user attribute values and environment attribute values. The rules associated with roles are obtained through the following relations.

Rule_uav_assignment ⊆ Rules × User attributes values
Rule_eav_assignment ⊆ Rules × Environment attributes values

Similarly, rules which restrict the availability of permissions to roles can be composed of user attribute values, object attribute values and environment attribute values. The rules assigned to permissions are captured through the following relations.

Rule_uav_assignment ⊆ Rules × User attributes values
Rule_oav_assignment ⊆ Rules × Object attributes values
Rule_eav_assignment ⊆ Rules × Environment attributes values

2.11 Rule-Role Assignment (RuR)

RuR in ARBAC captures the association of rules with roles. A rule can be assigned to multiple roles, and a role can have multiple rules, which is obtained through the following relation.

Role_rule_assignment ⊆ Roles × Rules

Unlike the approach [4], we associate a set of attribute based rules with each roles that helps in reducing applicable rule space for a role and minimizes role availability evaluation time for a user. Thus, ARBAC can restrict roles, hence, differs from the [5].

2.12   Rule-Permission Assignment (RuP)

In ARBAC, RuP captures the associations of rules with permissions. A rule can be assigned to multiple permissions, and a permission can be associated with multiple rules, which is obtained through the following relation.

Permission_rule_assignment ⊆ Permissions × Rules

Unlike the approach [4], our approach directly associates a set of attribute based rules with permissions that helps in reducing applicable rule space for a permission and minimizes permission availability evaluation time for a role.

Instead of XACML, a unified database schema is designed to capture the ARBAC policies. For sake of clarity, the unified schema is divided into two different schemas shown in Figs. 2 and 3. The relations shown in Fig. 2 capture RBAC policies, whereas the relations shown in Fig. 3 capture attribute-enabled rules for roles and permissions. The execution time of user requests using the relations shown in Figs. 2 and 3 is discussed in the Sect. 4.

3   Discussion

This section demonstrates the specification of rules using attributes of various entities and also discuss how their association with roles and permissions can ensure the fine-grained availability of objects to users.

For example, consider a permission $p = (o) \land (read \lor write)$ assigned to a role *manager*, which states that a user associated with a role manager can read and write the object #o. Suppose permission #p is restricted by a rule $r_{cp} = (front\_desk\_service) \land (saving\_account) \land (working\_hour \land branch\_of\_posting)$ where *front_desk_service* is a user attribute value and *saving_account* is an object attribute value, whereas *working_hour* and *branch_of_posting* are environment attribute values. The rule (r_{cp}) states that, in order to be exercised the permission #p assigned to a user through the role manager, the user must be from front desk service, object must be a saving account, access time must be the office working hours and access location must be the branch of posting. Similarly, suppose that role *Manager* is restricted by a rule $r_{cr} = (working\_hour \land branch\_of\_posting)$ where *working_hour* and *branch_of_posting* are environment attribute values. The rule (r_{cr}) states that, in order to be exercised the role *Manager*, the access time must be office working hours and access location must be the branch of posting.

Let us consider another example of a classroom management system which is used to manage various courses. A course can be offered in multiple classes by one or more users, Who are Teacher, during a specified period and is identified by a unique id. If multiple teachers offer the same course in different classes, then they can manage only their course-class activities.

For instance, if the above-said scenario is specified through RBAC, then a *Teacher* role per class for that course would be needed that may result in the role-explosion issue. While our approach associates below-given attribute based

Table 1. Data sets details of RBAC

Parameters	Data set 1	Data set 2
Number of users	1000	5000
Number of objects	5000	25000
Number of rights	10	10
Number of roles	100	100
Number of permissions	7500	40000
Number of permission to role assignments	7500	40000
Number of user to role assignments	2000	10000

rule with the single role *Teacher* and ensures the fine-grained availability of that role to different users.

Rule 1:   (Class) $\land$ (Course) $\land$ (Course.Start-date $\leq$ Current.Date $\geq$ Course. End-date)

In *Rule 1*, class and course are user attributes, whereas duration represented by start-date and end-date is an environment attribute. *Rule 1* states that, in order to be exercised the role *Teacher*, the user must be handling the course in the class and access time must be the course duration.

A course may have a set of activities (e.g., assignments, course project, etc.), which students must complete within the specified duration. A particular type of access (e.g., modify, submit, view, etc.) on an activity defines permission. Once particular class students enrolled in a course, they can view the activities associated with that course and can provide their response within the course duration.

If RBAC is used to specify above-said requirements, then, clearly, the single role *Student* would not be able to provide fine-grained access of those requirements as permissions. Because the association of users with the *Student* role would enable them to exercise all the permissions of that role. Thus, to ensure the fine-grained access of permissions to users, a *Student* role per set of permissions needs to be created that may result in the role-permission explosion issue. In contrast to that, our approach associates the following attribute based rule with permissions and restricts the access of them to users through the single role *Student*.

Rule 2:   (Class $\land$ Course) $\land$ (Activity) $\land$ (Activity.Start-date $\leq$ Current.Date $\geq$ Activity.End-date)

In *Rule 2*, class and course are user attributes, and activity is an object attribute. The activity duration, which is represented by start-date and end-date, is an environment attribute. Assume that the *Rule 2* is associated with the permission #*p1*, in order to be exercised the #*p1* assigned to a user through the role *Student*, the user must be associated with the class, must be enrolled in the course, activity must be offered in the course and access time must be the activity duration.

As a result of Rule 1, users associated with the role *Teacher* can only access courses which are being currently handled by them. Similarly, Rule 2 ensures fine-grained access of course activities to students through the role *Student*. In either case, no additional roles are needed to ensure the fine-grained access of resources. Thus, the proposed model can minimize the role-explosion and role-permission explosion issues.

Table 2. Data sets details of ABAC

Parameters	Data set 1	Data set 2
Number of user attributes	50	250
Number of user attribute values	100	500
Number of user to user attribute value assignments	10000	50000
Number of object attributes	10	10
Number of object attribute values	100	500
Number of object to object attribute value assignments	10000	50000
Number of rules	250	1250

4   Experimental Results and Analysis

In this section, we present the implementation details and discuss the results of experiments on scalability and flexibility of the proposed approach. As a part of the experimental set-up, Oracle 12c in-memory database was used for storing the schemas shown in Figs. 2 and 3 of Sect. 2. The whole set-up was run on a 64-bit Windows 10 system empowered with an Intel i7 @3.40 GHz processor and 8 GB RAM.

4.1   Data Set Initialization

Scalability analysis of our model is done using two synthetic data sets of varying size. The specification of data sets related to RBAC and ABAC policies is presented in Tables 1 and 2, respectively.

To emulate the real-life situations, specific constraints were imposed on data sets that are as follows. For specifying RBAC policies, it was ensured that every user is assigned to at least one role, and each role is assigned to at least one user. Similarly, each permission is assigned to at least one role, and each role is given at least one permission. The number of rights is significantly lesser since there are not many scenarios where the number of different access rights in the system exceeds 10. The number of roles is maintained at 10% of the number of users across all data sets. The number of permissions is maintained around 15% of the number of objects taking into the possibility of multiple access rights for an object.

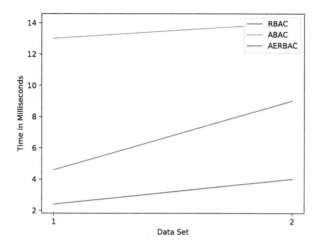

Fig. 4. Disk-based request evaluation time using RBAC, ABAC and ARBAC policies

For specifying ABAC policies, it was ensured that each entity (e.g., user, object and environment) has at least one attribute, and each attribute has at least one value. Assignments of user attribute values to users were done such that each user can access at least one object with a specific right. Object to object attribute values assignments were also done, similarly.

In ARBAC, rules for roles can be composed of user attributes and environment attributes, whereas rules for permissions can be composed of user attributes, object attributes and environment attributes. On the other hand, policies in ABAC are composed of user attributes, object attributes, environment attributes and rights. Thus, for analysis, we derived ARBAC rules as follows. For roles, rules were derived by extracting user and environment attribute values from ABAC policies. Similarly, for permissions, rules were obtained by extracting user, object and environment attribute values from ABAC policies.

In large organizations, users and objects would be in large number. Therefore, the fine-grained access of roles and permissions can only be ensured by associating multiple rules with them. In such a scenario, several rules may need to be evaluated for verifying a user request that would affect the system performance. In addition to that, there can be frequent modifications in policies to meet the evolving needs of organizations. Therefore, in-memory database was used to adequately address the above-said issues, which delivers higher performance and supports both reporting-style and transnational requests. In-memory database does not require the storage of entire data in main memory. Therefore, only the performance-critical data was stored in a compressed format that takes lesser space and can evaluate request as query directly, thus, enables higher performance.

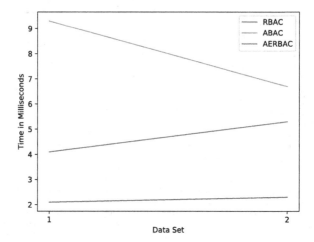

Fig. 5. In-memory based request evaluation time using RBAC, ABAC and ARBAC policies

4.2   Performance Analysis

Performance analysis of ARBAC along with RBAC and ABAC is done using two data sets shown in Tables 1 and 2. Time taken for executing a user access request is considered as a parameter for evaluating the performance of access control models. For eliminating the influence of any background process in the system and also to ensure the 95% confidence level and 5% margin of error, mean time of 73 evaluations of a request is considered as the final evaluation time.

For each access control model, a user request was executed 73 times for different inputs across two data sets. The disk-based and in-memory evaluation time of a request are shown in Figs. 4 and 5, respectively. In ABAC, a user access request was compared with the target of each policy until the applicable policy is found. In contrary, the number of rules to be referred for an access request was relatively less in our approach. In can be seen from Figs. 4 and 5, RBAC takes less time than ARBAC and ABAC but suffers from issues such as role explosion, role-permission explosion and lack of fine-grained policy specification, which cannot be represented in the figure under discussion. From Figs. 4 and 5, it can also be observed that disk-based and in-memory request execution using ARBAC policies take 8 ms and 5 ms, respectively. By taking all these into account, it can be concluded that ARBAC performs better than ABAC and would also perform better than fine-grained RBAC.

It may be observed that, 5 times increase in the number of users, objects and rules, the evaluation time of access requests do not grow significantly. Thus, it can also be concluded that, ARBAC is scalable and can specify flexible attribute-enabled role based access policies for ensuring the fine-grained access of resources at different levels of granularity.

5   Related Work

In past few years, several attempts have been made to integrate RBAC and ABAC for combining their benefits. A unified ABAC Model [9] proposed by Jin et al. demonstrates that ABAC is sufficient to encompass all the features of Discretionary Access Control (DAC) [19], Mandatory Access Control (MAC) [18] and RBAC [17]. Though the concept of roles is emulated by using attributes, the role explosion and role-permission explosion issues still exist an attribute level in the model.

Role-centric Attribute Based Access Control (RABAC) [10] is an extension of RBAC [17] that filters permissions based on user attributes and object attributes. For this purpose, a *Targetfilter* and a set of filter functions are defined. Each filter function is a boolean expression that is composed of user and object attributes. A *Targetfilter* determines a set of filter functions that apply to an object. Each function is then evaluated to determine whether a particular permission is to be filtered or not. These filtered set of permissions is the final set of permissions available to a user through a role. Both *Targetfilter* and filter functions are defined by using eXtensive Access Control Markup Language (XACML) [20]. Details of user and object attributes are ideally stored in a relational database. This way of defining some parts of the model in XACML and others in a relational database can become cumbersome. Another disadvantage of RABAC is that it is not suitable for context sensitive environment as the filtration of permissions has to be done each time whenever there is a change in the environment.

There are a few access control models which tried to accommodate the context sensitive policy specification, namely, Temporal RBAC [14], Spatio-Temporal RBAC [13] and Enhanced Spatio-Temporal RBAC [12]. These models also suffer from the issues of traditional RBAC, such as role explosion and role-permission explosion. Daniel et al. [2] and Fatima et al. [3] have listed the advantages and limitations of ABAC. Huang et al. [8] have proposed a mechanism which integrates ABAC with RBAC through two-layered approach that controls the availability of roles to users and permissions to roles based on environment based conditions along with user-role assignment and permission-role assignment. Though this model integrates the RBAC and ABAC, it does not eliminate the pitfalls of both the models. On the other hand, Giuri et al. [16] have presented an approach to parametrized privilege that associates object or context-related information based expression with each privilege to minimize the role-explosion issue.

Recently, an Attribute Enhanced Role-Based Access Control model (AER-BAC) [5] has been proposed, in which the definition of roles and association of permissions with roles are similar to RBAC. In AERBAC, objects are referred through object expressions which are directly associated with each object. An object expression is composed of object attribute values and refers to a set of objects which has the same attribute values as the object expression. In contrast to RBAC, a permission in AERBAC is defined as the association of object expression, access right and conditions. A condition can be composed of user attributes, object attributes and environment attributes. Thus, AERBAC grants permission only if at least one associated condition is satisfied. Hence, this model supports context-aware policy specification but complicates the administration of policies and requires modification in the core RBAC model. Qi et al. [4] have presented an approach for controlling the availability of roles and permissions based on attributes of entities, namely, user, object, role and environment. Hong et al. [1] have presented an approach that restricts the availability of sensitive data based on the time, user attributes and object attributes. Singh et al. [6] have presented an approach data warehousing based approach for enabling the specification, enforcement and maintenance of multi-dimensional multi-granular security policies. On the other hand, Our approach integrates ABAC with RBAC without any complications and nullifies their pitfalls.

6   Conclusion

In this paper, we have presented an extension of RBAC for ensuring the fine-grained availability of roles and permissions to users. Initially, rules are defined using attributes of various entities, namely, user, object and environment. To represent the ARBAC components, role rule assignment and permission rule assignment relations are defined along with RBAC relations. Next, the association of rules with roles and permissions are captured in the role rule assignment and permission rule assignment relations, respectively, and their impact is studied. It has been observed that 5 times increase in the number of users, objects, roles, permissions and rules, the execution time of access requests does not grow significantly.

We demonstrated the advantages of ARBAC in the discussion section through two different scenarios. In the future, we plan to propose an approach for automatic security analysis ARBAC policies. Further direction for future work includes the designing of a role-based administrative model for managing the various components of ARBAC.

References

1. Hong, J., et al.: TAFC: time and attribute factors combined access control for time-sensitive data in public cloud. IEEE Trans. Serv. Comput. 1–14 (2018)
2. Daniel, S., Osborn, L.S.: Current research and open problems in attribute-based access control. ACM Comput. Surv. 4(49), 65:1–65:45 (2017)
3. Fatima, A., Ghazi, Y., Shibli, M.A., Abassi, A.G.: Towards attribute-centric access control: an ABAC versus RBAC argument. Secur. Commun. Netw. 9, 3152–3166 (2016)
4. Qi, H., Luo, X., Di, X., Li, J., Yang, H., Jiang, Z.: Access control model based on role and attribute and its implementation. In: Proceedings of the International Conference on Cyber-Enabled Distributed Computing and Knowledge Discovery, pp. 66–71 (2016)
5. Rajpoot, Q.M., Jensen, C.D., Krishnan, R.: Attributes enhanced role-based access control model. In: Fischer-Hübner, S., Lambrinoudakis, C., Lopez, J. (eds.) Trust-Bus 2015. LNCS, vol. 9264, pp. 3–17. Springer, Cham (2015). https://doi.org/10.1007/978-3-319-22906-5_1

6. Singh, M.P., Sural, S., Atluri, V., Vaidya, J., Yakub, U.: Managing multi-dimensional multi-granular security policies using data warehousing. Network and System Security. LNCS, vol. 9408, pp. 221–235. Springer, Cham (2015). https://doi.org/10.1007/978-3-319-25645-0_15

7. Vincent, C.Hu., et al.: Guide to attribute based access control definition and considerations. National Institute of Standards and Technology (2014)

8. Huang, J., Nicol, D.M., Bobba, R., Huh, J.H.: A framework integrating attribute-based policies into RBAC. In: Proceedings of the Symposium on Access Control Models and Technologies, pp. 187–196 (2012)

9. Jin, X., Krishnan, R., Sandhu, R.: A unified attribute-based access control model covering DAC, MAC and RBAC. In: Cuppens-Boulahia, N., Cuppens, F., Garcia-Alfaro, J. (eds.) DBSec 2012. LNCS, vol. 7371, pp. 41–55. Springer, Heidelberg (2012). https://doi.org/10.1007/978-3-642-31540-4_4

10. Jin, X., Sandhu, R., Krishnan, R.: RABAC: role-centric attribute-based access control. In: Kotenko, I., Skormin, V. (eds.) MMM-ACNS 2012. LNCS, vol. 7531, pp. 84–96. Springer, Heidelberg (2012). https://doi.org/10.1007/978-3-642-33704-8_8

11. Kuhn, D.R., Coyne, E.J., Weil, T.R.: Adding attributes to role-based access control. IEEE Comput. **43**, 79–81 (2010)

12. Aich, S., Mondal, S., Sural, S., Majumdar, A.K.: Role based access control with spatiotemporal context for mobile applications. In: Gavrilova, M.L., Tan, C.J.K., Moreno, E.D. (eds.) Transactions on Computational Science IV. LNCS, vol. 5430, pp. 177–199. Springer, Heidelberg (2009). https://doi.org/10.1007/978-3-642-01004-0_10

13. Ray, I., Toahchoodee, M.: A spatio-temporal role-based access control model. In: Barker, S., Ahn, G.-J. (eds.) DBSec 2007. LNCS, vol. 4602, pp. 211–226. Springer, Heidelberg (2007). https://doi.org/10.1007/978-3-540-73538-0_16

14. Bertino, E., Bonatti, P.A., Ferrari, E.: TRBAC: a temporal role based access control model. ACM Trans. Inf. Syst. Secur. **4**(3), 191–233 (2001)

15. Ferraiolo, D.F., Sandhu, R., Gavrila, S., Kuhn, D.R., Chandramouli, R.: Proposed NIST standard for role-based access control. ACM Trans. Inf. Syst. Secur. **4**(3), 224–274 (2001)

16. Giuri, L., Iglio, P.: Role templates for content-based access control. In: Proceedings of the Workshop on Role-Based Access Control, pp. 153–159 (1997)

17. Sandhu, R., Coyne, E.J., Feinstein, H.L., Youman, C.E.: Role based access control models. IEEE Comput. **29**, 38–47 (1996)

18. Bell, E.D., LaPadula, J.L.: Secure computer systems: unified exposition and multics interpretation. Technical report MTR-2997, The Mitre Corporation, Bedford (1976)

19. Graham, G., Denning, P.: Protection principles and practice. In: Proceedings of the American Federation of Information Processing Societies Spring Joint Computer Conference, pp. 417–429 (1972)

20. OASIS eXtensible access control markup language (XACML). http://docs.oasis-open.org/xacml/3.0/xacml-profile-saml2.0-v2-spec-en.html

Malware Analysis

Malware Signature Generation Using Locality Sensitive Hashing

Hassan Naderi[1], P. Vinod[2], Mauro Conti[2], Saeed Parsa[1],
and Mohammad Hadi Alaeiyan[1]([✉])

[1] School of Computer Engineering, Iran University of Science and Technology,
Narmak, 16844 Tehran, Iran
{naderi,parsa}@iust.ac.ir, hadi_alaeiyan@comp.iust.ac.ir
[2] Department of Mathematics, University of Padua, 35122 Padua, Italy
{drvinodp,conti}@math.unipd.it

Abstract. Security threats due to malicious executable are getting more serious. A lot of researchers are interested in combating malware attacks. In contrast, malicious users aim to increase the usage of polymorphism and metamorphism malware in order to increase the analysis cost and prevent being identified by anti-malware tools. Due to the intuitive similarity between different polymorphisms of a malware family, clustering is an effective approach to deal with this problem. Clustering accordingly is able to reduce the number of signatures. Therefore, we have leveraged the Suffix tree structure and Locality Sensitive Hashing (LSH) to linearly cluster malicious programs and to reduce the number of signatures significantly.

Keywords: Malware clustering · Signature generation ·
Locality Sensitive Hashing (LSH) · Suffix tree

1 Introduction

Nowadays, malicious software has become a serious threat to computer systems. They have caused financial losses and casualties. In 2017, the number of new malware increased by 22.9% more than the samples discovered in 2016 [1]. Also, the number of new malware files, processed by Kaspersky lab to increased 11.5% over 2016 to 360,000 samples [2]. Malicious users increase the number of malware by using various techniques including obfuscation [6], encryption repackaging the software [7], to avoid the detection from antimalware tools. This growth has fundamentally challenged detection capabilities in terms of computing [14] and researchers had to use signature-based detection approaches to distinguish between malware and legitimate programs [9,18].

On the other side, the existence of a huge number of metamorphic and polymorphic malware collected by semi-automatic approaches are used to generate a large list of signatures. However, semi-automatically approaches are error-prone.

© Springer Nature Singapore Pte Ltd. 2019
S. Nandi et al. (Eds.): ISEA-ISAP 2018, CCIS 939, pp. 115–124, 2019.
https://doi.org/10.1007/978-981-13-7561-3_9

A perfect solution to overcome this problem is a reduction in the number of signatures. There are several static and dynamic methods that generate signature for a group of malware with identical behavior [4,12].

Clustering is a way to decrease the number of signatures and to determine malicious programs which are structurally similar [15]. The fundamental problem of clustering methods is the time of analysis. The minimum time required for clustering n elements is $O(n^2)$. Because distance between each pair of elements are calculated to group similar elements. Therefore, we have leveraged Locality-Sensitive Hashing (LSH) to identify similar elements with linear complexity [11]. The general idea of LSH is the selection of a number of elements as axes to be compared with other elements. A hash is defined by a similarity hash function. Those elements, having equal vectors are considered to belong to a cluster.

LSH requires a Locality-Sensitive Function (LSF). Despite the popular hash function which a small change in elements causes large variations in the amount of created hash value, LSF should be insensitive to variations of similar elements.

To put in a nutshell, in this paper, we statically extract opcode sequence of malicious codes to generate a set of signatures. Signatures identify the similar malware grouped by our proposed LSH method.

The remaining parts of this paper are organized as follows: In Sect. 2, related works in the field of malware detection with special emphasis on how to identify features is presented. Theory of LSH and LSF are presented in Sect. 3. The proposed algorithm for clustering malware based upon LSH is explained in Sect. 4. The signature generation algorithm is proposed in Sect. 6. Section 7 includes the evaluation of the proposed method. The concluding remarks are described in Sect. 8.

2   Related Works

A signature is a basic method for malware detection. However, the number of signatures increases with the increase in the number of malicious programs. But, clustering helps to reduce the number of malware signatures, as generate a signature from a group of malware with similar features.

Polygraph [13] is an automated signature generator for detecting polymorphic worms. It tokenizes the byte sequence and provides a set of tokens to be a conjunction byte signature. These conjunction byte signatures are scored by Bayesian probability and a threshold would classify worms.

Oprisa et al. [15] have defined a family of locality sensitive function and designed a blocked structure for malware clustering by LSH. This family of functions is defined by fixed-length strings as input. LSH compares malware by this function to determine the value of similarity, so, malicious programs which have a similar result, are the members of a cluster.

Wang et al. [17] have transferred the opcode sequence of malicious programs to images which they are compared with the image formed from the known malware sample code. Also, Kolosnjaji et al. [10] have leveraged the neural network consists of convolutional and feedforward layers. They extracted metadata of PE files, imported functions, and opcodes sequences to distinguish malicious from benign programs. Sharma et al. [16] have studied the frequency of opcode occurrence to detect unknown malware by using machine learning techniques. They leveraged the top 20 features obtained from Fisher score, information gain, gain ratio, Chi-square, and symmetric uncertainty feature selection methods. Consequently, Fisher score had the best classification result.

Drew et al. [8] have leveraged Strand gene sequence classifier and minhash to classify malicious programs. They classified the Kaggle dataset with a minimum accuracy of 95%. But, they have neglected to include benign programs in their evaluation.

All the previous works have neglected to reduce the number of signatures. In this paper, our main focus is not only the improvent of the classification performances but also, the decreastion of the number of signatures.

3   Locality Sensitive Hashing

Finding similar elements is one of the most important issues in different application domains. To group elements sharing similar properties diverse clustering algorithms are utilized. Unfortunately as the number of elements increase clustering samples turns out to be compute intensive. LSH selects a collection of malware as axes compared them with remaining samples. In-order to achieve this the similarity function must be a family of hash functions defined using Equation given below.

$$P(h(X) = h(Y)) = similarity(X, Y) \qquad (1)$$

where h is the specified hash function that is defined as Locality Sensitive Function (LSF). LSF is similarly sensitive. It means that, whatever two elements are more similar, they have the higher probability of having the same hash value.

Suppose S is a set of elements and d is a distance function. Therefore,

$$d : S \times S \rightarrow [0, \infty) \qquad (2)$$

The value of a distance function is a positive value. According to distance function d and the definition of LSF, we will have an LSH [11] which is defined as follow.

Definition 1. A hash function $h : S \rightarrow H$ is a (d_1, d_2, p_1, p_2)−sensitive if H is an infinite set and $d_1 < d_2$. We have the following conditions for $X, Y \in S$.

1. If $d(X, Y) \leq d_1$, then $P(h(X) = h(Y)) \geq p_1$
2. If $d(X, Y) \geq d_2$, then $P(h(X) = h(Y)) \leq p_2$

If the distance values of each pair of elements are less than d_1, then the probability is greater than p_1. In contrast, if the distance values of each pair of elements are greater than d_2, then the probability is less than p_2.

4   Hash Function for Sequential Data

Oprisa et al. [15], have presented a clustering algorithm by LSH. They have leveraged with distance function $\sigma(x) = a.x + b$ which a, b, and x are the vectors having fixed length. Two malware x and y are similar, if $\sigma(x)$ and $\sigma(y)$ are equivalent. The distance function is presented in Eq. 3. X and Y are two sequences and LCS is the longest common subsequence of X and Y.

$$d(X,Y) = |X| + |Y| - 2|LCS(X,Y)|. \tag{3}$$

The characteristics of this distance function are:

(a) Always $d(X,Y) \geq 0$.
(b) Always we have symmetry, $d(X,Y) = d(Y,X)$.
(c) There is triangle inequality, $d(X,Y) + d(Y,Z) \geq d(X,Z)$, in this function.

Moreover, Eq. 4 presents similarity function.

$$similarity(X,Y) = \frac{2 * |LCS(X,Y)|}{|X| + |Y|} \tag{4}$$

5   Malware Clustering Algorithm

Equation 4 is used as LSF to have an LSH cluster. We have leveraged the disassembled code of binary files to cluster malware. Therefore, the dataset is a sequence of the disassembled instruction set for each malicious or legitimate program. According to our experimental results, the length of these sequences is about 700000. Since our distance function requires to compute the longest common subsequence of two large strings which is time-consuming, Suffix tree largest common sequence algorithm, having time complexity of order of $O(|X| + |Y|)$.

Algorithm 1 presents the pseudocode of the proposed cluster algorithm. A list of malware paths, the sequences of malware, the number of malware, the similarity threshold and the number of axes are five input parameters of this algorithm. Also, the output of the algorithm is a list which contains groups of similar malware. LSH uses a hashtable in which each row shows the malware hash values obtained by axes. In the end, two or more rows which have similar values, are in the same group.

Therefore, this algorithm computes the values of the hashtable being presented by LSF. Malicious programs are disassembled and their sequence of instructions are extracted. Next, these sequences are compared with the sequences of malware which were selected as axes. We have utilized the Suffix tree algorithm to compare two sequences. If the length of longest common subsequence divides by the sum of lengths of two string is greater than the similarity threshold, T, then two malware are similar others they are not similar. Later, to find and group the similar rows of the hash table Algorithm 2 is invoked. Algorithm 2 has four input parameters, hashtable, the list of malware paths, the number of malware and the number of axes.

Data: malware paths $M[]$, Opcode sequences $S[]$, the length of S is $Slen$,
similarity threshold T, the number of axes A.
Result: groups of similar malware B
begin

> hashtable[Slen][A];
> List selected_index = Select_random_index(A, Slen);
> **for** $k = 0$ *to* A **do**
>
> > **for** $i = 0$ *to* $Slen$ **do**
> >
> > > LCS = Suffix_tree_get_LCS(S[i], S[selected_index[k]]);
> > > **if** *LCS.length / (S[i].length + S[selected_index[k]].length) > T* **then**
> > > > hashtable[i][k] = 1;
> > >
> > > **else**
> > > > hashtable[i][k] = 0;
> > >
> > > **end**
> >
> > **end**
>
> **end**
> return Groups-Generation(hashtable, M, Slen, A);

end

Algorithm 1. Cluster the malware based on locality sensitive hashing and
Suffix tree

Data: hashtable T, malware paths $M[]$, the number of malware $Slen$, the
number of axes A.
Result: Group B
begin

> Group B;
> List selected_index = Select_random_index(A, Slen);
> **for** $i = 0$ *to* $Slen$ **do**
>
> > **for** $j = i + 1$ *to* $Slen$ **do**
> >
> > > similar = true;
> > > **for** $k = 0$ *to* A **do**
> > >
> > > > similar = hashtable[i][k] == hashtable[j][k];
> > > > **if** *!similar* **then**
> > > > > break;
> > > >
> > > > **end**
> > >
> > > **end**
> > > **if** *similar* **then**
> > > > B[j].add(M[i]);
> > >
> > > **end**
> >
> > **end**
>
> **end**
> return B;

end

Algorithm 2. Groups-Generation

6   Generation of Cluster Signature

This section offers a signature generation algorithm for a group of malware which is gathered by Algorithm 1. Algorithm 3 is a recursive algorithm that generates a list of signatures for each group of malware that is grouped by Algorithm 1. This algorithm collects all common subsequences of this family of malware. We used the Suffix tree algorithm to collect all common subsequences. These common subsequences are arranged from greatest to least length of common subsequences. Then, the common subsequence, which is not the member of selected signatures and does not detect a benign file as a malware, is selected as a new signature. The new signature is inserted into the signature list. If there is not any signature which confirms these properties, then split the group into the two groups and re-invoke the algorithm. It can be repeated until there is only one malware into the group. Therefore, the sequence of this malware is selected as a malicious signature by the algorithm if it confirms both properties, does not detect a benign file as a malware and does not repeat in a signature list.

7   Evaluation

The proposed algorithm is written in C++ and is applied to a sequence of instructions of malware which is aggregated from sites Virusshare [3]. We have downloaded the VirusShare_00146.zip and VirusShare_00148.zip torrent files to evaluate this research. These files contains 501684 malware samples categorized into Trojan horses (121526 samples), Rootkits (79738 samples), Backdoors (110231 samples), Spywares (100017 samples), and Keyloggers (90172 samples). these classification is obtains by Kaspersky internet security. We perform this test with a system which has a 20 core, 2.4 GH CPU, and 48 GB memory.

In this section, the accuracy of our proposed method and the represented method in [15] is compared. Table 1 shows the performance of both methods based on the labeling to Kaspersky Internet security.

The maximum number of class for A axes is 2^A. While $A \to \infty$, there is not any limit on the number of classes. According to the experiment shown in Table 1, there are 4387 malicious clusters. This number is much less than 2^A. Moreover, the number of signatures, generated by Algorithm 3, is equal to 34239. On the other side, the accuracy of both methods are increased by the growth of the value of A.

As shown in Table 1, the number of signatures and the accuracy of our proposed method are better than those provided by [15], but our proposed methods had spent more processing time. However, our proposed method has fewer signatures.

T is an input parameter of Algorithm 1 and is a similarity measure of two samples. According to [5], it is rare to have a substring of two strings of length n and k characters. Also, malware authors use obfuscation or packing techniques to prevent from being detected by anti-malware tools. All of the above-mentioned points declares that T must be equal to a small probability.

Data: a Group of malware G.
Result: a list of signatures S
begin
   | List S;
   | List CS;
   | **if** $G.count >0$ **then**
   | | **if** $G.count==1$ **then**
   | | | **if** *!checkIsRepeatedSignature(G[0])* **then**
   | | | | S.add(G[0]);
   | | | **end**
   | | **else**
   | | | CS = G[o]; **for** $i=1$ to $G.count$ **do**
   | | | | CS = GetAllLongestSubSequences(CS, G[i]);
   | | | **end**
   | | | MakedSignature = false;
   | | | **if** $CS.count > 0$ **then**
   | | | | CS = DesSortbyLen(CS);
   | | | | **for** $i=0$ to $CS.count$ **do**
   | | | | | **if** *!checkIsRepeatedSignature(CS[i])* &&
   | | | | | *isnotinBenineFiles(CS[i])* **then**
   | | | | | | S.add(CS[i]); MakedSignature = true; break;
   | | | | | **end**
   | | | | **end**
   | | | **end**
   | | | **if** *!MakeedSignature* **then**
   | | | | S.addRange(Make_Signature(G[0, G.count/2]));
   | | | | S.addRange(Make_Signature(G[G.count/2+1, G.count]));
   | | | **end**
   | | **end**
   | **end**
   | return S;
end

Algorithm 3. Signature-Generation

As shown in Table 2, $T = 20$ provide optimal clustering and the number of signatures. While $T = 10$, the malicious programs which has less similarity are grouped together, it generate more signatures or to generate a signature for every single malware. While $T = 30$ or $T = 40$, the number of clusters is increased because of the strict selection of the same samples. However, it increases the number of signatures. Therefore, the number of clusters has a direct effect on the number of signatures.

Table 1. The comparison to proposed method and represented method in [15]. A is the number of axes and T is similarity percentage. $T = 20$.

Evaluation metrics	$A = 10^4$		$A = 2 * 10^4$		$A = 3 * 10^4$	
	Our method	Prior approach [15]	Our method	Prior approach [15]	Our method	Prior approach [15]
Accuracy	0.9094	0.8991	0.9172	0.9176	0.9559	0.9359
F-measure	0.9351	0.9304	0.9366	0.9423	0.9656	0.9580
Precision	0.9559	0.9576	0.9563	0.9776	0.9735	0.979
Recall	0.9152	0.9047	0.9176	0.9095	0.9578	0.9374
#clusters	3564	3754	3863	4023	4387	4543
#signatures	40549	49938	36493	47394	34239	46903

Table 2. Effect of T on the number of signature and clusters. $A = 3 * 10^4$.

	T = 10	T = 20	T = 30	T = 40
The number of clusters	4075	4387	4836	4914
The number of signatures	37253	34239	36365	36821

We have implemented the quadratic-clustering algorithm as in [14], to compare the required time. Comparing to the clustering time of quadratic-clustering, our proposed algorithm has better performance on malware clustering. Figure 1 shows the average time of both algorithms.

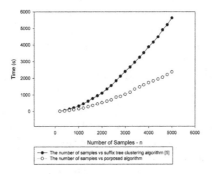

Fig. 1. Clustering time of Suffix tree clustering algorithm [14] vs proposed clustering algorithm.

8   Conclusion

The usage of signatures generation methods is inevitable to detect a huge number of malicious files. However, the number of signatures is the main problem of malware detection techniques. Therefore, in this paper, we present a hash function with higher accuracy than previous methods to cluster malware. Unlike the previous works that their features have a fixed-length, our hash function is based on dynamic-length features. But, computing fixed-length data are quicker than data with dynamic-length. Therefore, to improve performance a solution based on Suffix tree was implemented. It helps to extract the largest common subsequence of two strings and generate the signatures. We leveraged about 0.5 million samples to evaluate this research. Therefore, the achieved signature detected the dataset with an accuracy of 95.59% by saving 30% in the number of signatures. Future works include prototyping the proposed approach for deploying in a real-world online malware detection by reducing the number of signatures.

References

1. G-data. https://www.gdatasoftware.com/blog/2018/03/30610-malware-number-2017. Accessed 25 July 2018
2. Kaspersky lab. https://usa.kaspersky.com/about/press-releases/2017_kaspersky-lab-number-of-the-year. Accessed 25 July 2018
3. virusshare. www.virusshare.com. Accessed 6 Sept 2017
4. Abou-Assaleh, T., Cercone, N., Keselj, V., Sweidan, R.: N-gram-based detection of new malicious code. In: Proceedings of the 28th Annual International Computer Software and Applications Conference, COMPSAC 2004, vol. 2, pp. 41–42. IEEE (2004)
5. Chvatal, V., Sankoff, D.: Longest common subsequences of two random sequences. J. Appl. Probab. **12**(2), 306–315 (1975)
6. Collberg, C.S., Thomborson, C.: Watermarking, tamper-proofing, and obfuscation-tools for software protection. IEEE Trans. Softw. Eng. **28**(8), 735–746 (2002)
7. Dalla Preda, M.: Code obfuscation and malware detection by abstract interpretation. Ph.D. diss. (2007). http://profs.sci.univr.it/dallapre/MilaDallaPreda_PhD.pdf
8. Drew, J., Hahsler, M., Moore, T.: Polymorphic malware detection using sequence classification methods and ensembles. EURASIP J. Inf. Secur. **2017**(1), 2 (2017)
9. Gandotra, E., Singla, S., Bansal, D., Sofat, S.: Clustering morphed malware using opcode sequence pattern matching. Recent Patents Eng. **12**(1), 30–36 (2018)
10. Kolosnjaji, B., Eraisha, G., Webster, G., Zarras, A., Eckert, C.: Empowering convolutional networks for malware classification and analysis. In: 2017 International Joint Conference on Neural Networks (IJCNN), pp. 3838–3845. IEEE (2017)
11. Leskovec, J., Rajaraman, A., Ullman, J.D.: Mining of Massive Datasets. Cambridge University Press, Cambridge (2014)
12. Miao, Q., Liu, J., Cao, Y., Song, J.: Malware detection using bilayer behavior abstraction and improved one-class support vector machines. Int. J. Inf. Secur. **15**(4), 361–379 (2016)
13. Newsome, J., Karp, B., Song, D.: Polygraph: automatically generating signatures for polymorphic worms. In: 2005 IEEE symposium on Security and privacy, pp. 226–241. IEEE (2005)
14. Opriṣa, C., Cabău, G., Pal, G.S.: Malware clustering using suffix trees. J. Comput. Virol. Hack. Tech. **12**(1), 1–10 (2016)

15. Oprisa, C., Checiches, M., Nandrean, A.: Locality-sensitive hashing optimizations for fast malware clustering. In: 2014 IEEE International Conference on Intelligent Computer Communication and Processing (ICCP), pp. 97–104. IEEE (2014)
16. Sharma, S., Rama Krishna, C., Sahay, S.K.: Detection of advanced malware by machine learning techniques. In: Ray, K., Sharma, T.K., Rawat, S., Saini, R.K., Bandyopadhyay, A. (eds.) Soft Computing: Theories and Applications. AISC, vol. 742, pp. 333–342. Springer, Singapore (2019). https://doi.org/10.1007/978-981-13-0589-4_31
17. Wang, T., Xu, N.: Malware variants detection based on opcode image recognition in small training set. In: 2017 IEEE 2nd International Conference on Cloud Computing and Big Data Analysis (ICCCBDA), pp. 328–332. IEEE (2017)
18. Zhang, J., Qin, Z., Zhang, K., Yin, H., Zou, J.: Dalvik opcode graph based android malware variants detection using global topology features. IEEE Access 6, 51964–51974 (2018)

DroidDivesDeep: Android Malware Classification via Low Level Monitorable Features with Deep Neural Networks

Parvez Faruki[1(✉)], Bharat Buddhadev[2], Bhavya Shah[1],
Akka Zemmari[3], Vijay Laxmi[2], and Manoj Singh Gaur[4]

[1] Government MCA College, Ahmedabad, India
parvezfaruki.kg@gmail.com, shahbhavya5800@gmail.com
[2] MNIT Jaipur, Jaipur, India
bvbld@yahoo.com, vlaxmi@mnit.ac.in
[3] Indian Institute of Technology Jammu, Jammu, India
zemmari@labri.fr
[4] University of Bordeaux, Bordeaux, France
director@iitjammu.ac.in

Abstract. Android, the dominant smart device Operating System (OS) has evolved into a robust smart device platform since its release in 2008. Naturally, cyber criminals leverage fragmentation among varied major release by employing novel attacks. Machine learning is extensively used in System Security. Shallow Learning classifiers tend to over-learn during the training time; hence, the model under performs due to dependence on training data during real evaluation. Deep learning has the potential to automate detection of newly discovered malware families that learn the generalization about malware and benign files to be able to detect unseen or zero-day malware attacks.

Deep Neural Networks (DNN) have proven performance with image analysis and text classification. In this paper, our proposal DroidDivesDeep D^3, a malware classification and app categorization framework models' low level monitorable features (e.g., CPU, Memory, Network, Sensors etc.). Our proposal employs low level device runtime attributes unlike the existing techniques considering static extraction approach. D^3 evaluates a reasonable dataset consisting 24,343 genuine playstore apps against 8,779 real-world Android malware. In fact, the initial results of our proposal are quite encouraging with 98.65% detection rate with 99.79% accuracy during real evaluation. Our proposal improves upon existing techniques by 23%.

Keywords: Android malware · Improbable features · Code obfuscation · Similarity digest · Statistical features

1 Introduction

Android is the most popular operating system for smart and mobile devices. According to Gartner [19] and IDC statistical report [18], Android dominates mobile platform with more than 0.345 million devices worldwide, 86% market shares in Q3 2017. The

© Springer Nature Singapore Pte Ltd. 2019
S. Nandi et al. (Eds.): ISEA-ISAP 2018, CCIS 939, pp. 125–139, 2019.
https://doi.org/10.1007/978-981-13-7561-3_10

growing popularity comes at a cost. Android platform has become an attractive target of cyber-attacks with malware as a weapon [35]. The possibility of high monetary gains due fragmented OS versions within just a decade of its release (more than 14 stable version release), pose serious threat to the robust Android ecosystem. Android malware pose serious threat to network security and privacy protection. A recent research reports nine of ten mobile malware originating on Android platform [10, 32, 36]. Malware can possibly piggyback inside normal apps as a camouflaged Trojan; hence, malware detection has become challenging. Device users cannot review or understand the implications of group permissions at install time [12, 15].

Once the device is infected, we can detect malware via on-device dynamic analysis [13, 14, 17, 22]. However, the existing on-device solutions propose root privileges or modification to the OS or kernel code. Such modifications require technical intervention from the users. Furthermore, rooting the OS exposes device to other issues that may not be conducive to the Android platform architecture [9, 33]. The rate of Android OS upgrades is extremely fast, which makes modification to the kernel code highly unlikely, or difficult to achieving large user base without support from OEM and Google. Moreover, methods that require changes to the kernel code are unlikely to reach the common user unless OEM's and Google support such techniques.

Given the fragmented versions of Android devices (API version 14-25), and skewed distribution among users [5], malware detection approaches based on lower level monitorable attributes [22] is interesting. Such an approach can extract the features without necessitating root permissions or modification to the Android OS. Our previous proposal mimeoDroid [14] extracted important executable features on multiple virtual devices; however, there is a significant app behavior variation on virtual device generating incorrect classification [12, 13]. Features like processor execution traces, memory utilization pattern, various sensor activation details [38] and network attributes have a significant change in classification results.

In [30, 33] the authors explore the possible deployment of low privileged monitorable features to detect malicious activities. The low privileged features for Virtual/Cloned devices have been employed in different research [2, 14, 28] for malware detection, user data leakage detection [11, 16, 26], and user based operational authentication for behavior detection [38]. However, availability of reasonable dataset obtained for real Android devices remains a challenge.

Since Malware is predominantly used for cyberattacks, accurate detection, classification and categorization is very important. The existing state-of-the-art achieves favorable skewed results during training; however, real test does not realize desired accuracy. Furthermore, identifying targeted features that accurately classify rogue apps is of prime importance. In this paper, we propose [D^3], an overfitting resistant deep neural classification framework that enhances the real time test accuracy; unlike existing shallow learning techniques that perform well during training, but fail to deliver during real evaluation.

Our proposal leverages Dropout technique, to address the over-learning during training phase. Our proposal D^3 leverages the fact that, removal of some features at the training phase enforces the remaining features to train better; converging towards better classification accuracy in real time. Following are the contributions of our proposal D^3:

1. We identify low-level monitorable features that differentiate genuine apps from malware.
2. We trained more than a million genuine low-level monitorable features, and twenty thousand synthetic malware attributes at high sampling rate availed from real device data obtained from [12, 22]. Furthermore, we trained the deep neural network leveraging dropout technique combined with rectified linear unit activation to reduce the classification time training bias.
3. We classify collected features by improving the Dropout based DNN to achieve high detection rate. In fact, the chosen low-level features in various categories achieve significant improvement compared to existing state-of-the-art.
4. We evaluate D^3 with *tanH* and *ReLU* activation functions. To the best of our knowledge, D^3 leverages DNN and achieves significant improvement (more than 23%) in mobile malware classification.

The remainder of this paper is organized as follows. Section 2 present recent related work in malware classification. In Sect. 3, we formulate malware classification problem and stress upon the requirements of Deep Networks in mobile malware classification and categorization. In Sect. 4, we present our proposal architecture, experimental setup and evaluation of proposed technique. In Sect. 5, we discuss empirical results of D^3 classification accuracy and importance of activation functions in improving the real time classification accuracy. Finally, conclusion and future scope is presented in Sect. 6.

2 Related Work

Deep learning techniques are heavily used in image and speech classification. However, our proposal D^3 targets privileged low level features for malware classification via fully connected DNN. Yuan et al. proposed DroidDetector [37], a deep learning classification framework employing multi-dimensional app features. The proposed approach achieves classification accuracy with deep belief networks. However, we propose a dense connected network. employing dropout facility to achieve high detection rate. Faruki et al. [13] proposed low-level monitorable classification techniques for effective classification with shallow machine learning techniques. Dahl et al. [6] evaluated a neural network based classification using random projections; however, the technique has high error rate.

Dash et al. [7] propose DroidScribe, a runtime behavior based automatic shallow machine learning classification technique, a fusion of SVM with conformal prediction. Authors propose to reconstruct inter-process-communication rather than pure Linux system calls to improve classification accuracy. Our proposal considers low-level monitorable features from [22] to train the deep learning classifier. Furthermore, we evaluate real malware apps that have similarity with the training corpus. Suarez-Tangil et al. [31] proposed DroidSieve, a machine learning based classifier to detect unseen familial obfuscated variant of known malware families. Authors achieve a reasonable accuracy in malware detection. However, D^3 targets privileged features that does not require additional information to detect general class of malicious apps. Saxe et al. [27]

proposed a two-dimensional DNN based malware classification technique. However, the reported classification accuracy is low.

Deo et al. propose PreScience [8], a shallow machine learning classification technique that periodically retrains machine learning models using Venn-Abers probabilistic technique. Papernot et al. [25] identify attacks machine learning classifiers to reduce detection accuracy. MimeoDroid [14] improved upon the virtual device-based analysis approaches from Amos et al. [3] and Alam et al. [1]. The above approaches extract privileged features on virtual device rather than from real mobile. Our proposal D^3 creates a robust deep learning classification that avoids overfitting or skewed training time results.

Existing shallow machine learning and classification approaches become less accurate as malware evolves. Inaccurate updation techniques results in low detection in real world situation. The recent proposals fail to identify robust retraining techniques due to feature overfitting at training time. Furthermore, Shallow learning methods remain effective only case of few parameters and timely retraining. Deep Neural Networks permit computational models that are formed of many hidden and visible layers represented for data abstractions [21]. Deep Learning techniques have a profound effect in speech recognition, object recognition, and genome study due to its capabilities to discover intricacies, not feasible with shallow machine learning classification techniques. Hence, deep learning will become the new normal in cyber defense.

3   Problem Overviews

In the following, we discuss malware classification, a binary problem. Suppose, an equation as $\Sigma = \{\alpha_1, \alpha_2, \ldots \alpha_n\}$, is a universal set of Android apps. Σ consists of the $(G_{app}, M_{app}) \in U_{app}$; where malware intends to harm the users (e.g., data leakage, spying, file modification etc.). Each app $\alpha_i \in \Sigma$ is a pair:

$$\alpha_i = (F_i, C_i) \tag{1}$$

where F_i is set of feature vectors, and C_i is classified as (G_{app}, M_{app}) further defined as:

$$F_i = (\alpha_1, \alpha_2, \ldots, \alpha_n) \tag{2}$$

And

$$C_i \in (C_m, C_g, \ldots, C_u) \tag{3}$$

where C_g is classified genuine, C_m is labeled malware and C_u remains unclassified. α_j in Eq. 2 represent malware C_m, genuine C_g or unclassified C_u.

A classification algorithm Shallow (S) or Deep (D) learns the features during the training phase, then performs real time classification based on training time learning i.e., classifier CA learns the feature set during training C_t; then predicts the given unknown sample C_p as (C_m or C_g) based on previous learning. For each unseen test instance α_i the procedure is repeated subject to algorithm constraints. Our proposal mimeoDroid [14] employed shallow learning classifiers to predict class labels from virtual device execution features. The experimental evaluation revealed the limitations of shallow learning techniques. Similar problems have been reported among the recent machine learning based recent malware detection, classification and categorization proposals [3, 8, 11, 26, 30, 31].

3.1 Why Deep Neural Network

Deep Neural Networks have been highly expressive models has proven performance in speech analysis and modeling human learning [34]. Shallow learning methods such as Trees based learning, Bagging, Boosting work better with small dataset and fewer parameters [21, 27]. Moreover, too much dependence on training set results in over-fitting; hence, positively skewed training time results that seldom replicate during real test. The feature learning does not result into desired malware detection accuracy. Shallow learning classifiers require fine tuned feature set and additional efforts for parameter tuning during model preparation. Deep Neural Networks have expressive attributes (i.e., width, height and hidden layer(s)) to effectively learn the features from large corpus of parameters. During cross-validation the hidden layer(s) are forced to independently learn by removing random features from hidden layers. Self-dependence at learning time adepts NN classifiers achieve improved accuracy during real deployment. DNN algorithm shave the capability to distil the raw data representation.

In a typical deep learning system, there may be quite a few adjustable parameters and a number of labeled features with to train the machine. Convolution Neural Networks (ConvNets) have been deployed in speech and image recognition. They have been designed to process features extracted from multi-dimensional arrays (i.e., color image composed of three 2D arrays with pixel intensity for three colour channels). In our case the features are extracted from one dimensional binary file. If we shape it $1 \times 1 \times N$, it results in 1×1 convolution. Since 1×1 ConvNet is a fully connected network, we keep the connected DNN for classification and parameter tuning to improve classification accuracy.

Dropout can be thought of as a method which prevents overfitting in the deep learning networks. During training procedure few nodes are randomly dropped with their connections in the network without disturbing input and output layers neurons i.e. some neurons from hidden layers are temporarily switched off during training session. Every time the hidden layers run in model, they dropout different sets of neurons. So, dropout averages large number of different neural networks; hence, reduces overfitting. But in case of evaluation dataset, all the network units are utilized.

3.2 Enhancing DNN with Dropout Capability

Neural Network data structure is a directed graph where a node in the network represents bias and edge represents some weight. The neural networks perform an extensive hyper-parameter training. In classification terminology, an overfitting model performs well at (i.e., features tend to over-learn) at the training time; however, the model has a deteriorated performance during real deployment; thus, reduced detection rate. Dropout enforces the DNN make own inference at learning time by eliminating random feature blocks to reduce over dependence on input vectors.

Hence, we employ dropout within connected network to let the model enhance detection and classification capability at runtime. To improve the efficiency of DNN, we use dropout feature and perform ensemble-based learning at training time. Since, Dropout regulates the network at training time, reduces over-fitting, in turn achieve improved classification. Dropout takes more time to learn while comparing with standard neural network. However, the robust training improves the classification accuracy. Further, we improve the Dropout performance with heuristics like: (i) reduce neurons in the network; (ii) modify learning rate; and (iii) vary dropout rate.

4 Our Proposal: D^3

The Malware detectors employ varied features to detect, characterize, and classify malware and distinguish them from genuine apps. The first step towards malware detection is feature identification, then extraction and finally classification using appropriate learning model. Many popular anti-malware techniques employ feature selection to identify contributing features; hence, remove non-contributing attributes. Figure 1 gives an overview of D^3 which targets app resource utilization pattern including CPU usage, received and transmitted network data, resident set size (RSS), process scheduling time difference between User & Kernel mode, Dalvik private and shared dirty pages, and relative importance granted by OS to the running app.

We observed a significant deviation in behavior while we executed genuine and malware apps. Initially, we developed synthetic samples to identify the deviation in the attributes. Further, we leveraged a combined set of real malware feature set obtained from [22], significant data generated for over a year. We observed that, low-level monitorable features have the capability to differentiate malicious behavior from a normal behavior.

In the Training phase, the D^3 framework learns to differentiate execution behavior of malware from genuine app with following real device attributes availed from [22]. Appendix A lists important features differentiating genuine and malicious behavior.

Various researcher experiments report that specific malware family has unique differential behavior against monitorable resources [12]. Suarez-Tangil et al. [24, 30] proposed a mapping of malware categories against different sensors for detection. Our proposal D^3 evaluates the differential impact of malware and genuine app execution on low-privileged attributes. In particular, we focus low-level device resources which do not necessitate OS modification. Furthermore, attributes generate app profile for genuine/malware via low level features that does not require root privileges. As the root privileges are not needed, there is no issues related to security vulnerabilities; hence, analysis can be performed with real devices instead of emulators. To monitor low level features, Kernel level changes are not required.

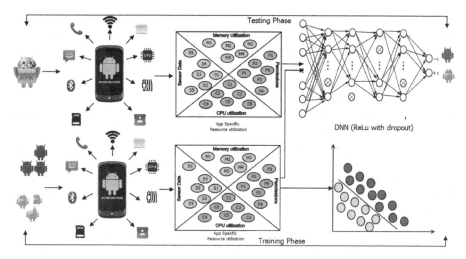

Fig. 1. Our proposal D^3: The diagram gives a conceptual overview of our proposal. We execute malware samples and log interaction with the monitorable features. We extract a wide range of data from low-privileged monitorable features and periodically upload the logs to server.

4.1   Experimental Setup

We believe that each malware family has a unique effect on device resources. Suarez-Tangil et al. [30] proposed a mapping of malware categories against a set of sensors to accurately classify Android malware. Our proposal evaluates differential impact of malware and genuine app execution on low-privileged attributes. The proposed framework is deployed on deployed HP ProLiant DL180G6 for experimental evaluation. The machine runs Intel^R, Xeon^R processor E5620 2.40 GHz with 128 GB Primary memory. Our proposal D^3 deployed H$_2$O package from R framework for data analysis, predictive modeling and visualization [4].

4.2   Performance Evaluation

An activation function produces output signal from input by introducing non-linearity. Since deep networks use gradient descent for backpropagation, they need differentiable activation functions. Rectified neurons biologically perform better than logistic *Sigmoids* which in turn are rational compared to tangent neurons [34]. Various research [20, 39] report rectifier function have improved performance if the number of hidden layers is three or more in DNNs. Rectifier non-linearity gives rise to real zeros during activation, which extracts scattered and robust features against minor changes. Hence, rectifier activation function can easily achieve sparse results, separating noise and signal in feature classification by learning the bias threshold.

Rectified Liear Unit (*ReLU*) is robust biological unit implemented as activation function to enhance the training capability of Deep Neural Networks. It works by thresholding values at zero, i.e. $f(x) = max\ (0,\ x)$. In simple words, we obtain zero as the output, when x is less than zero. Conversely, a linear function when $x = 0$. Rectified

Linear Unit (*ReLU*) solves the vanishing gradient problem since the rectifier activation allows a network to obtain sparse representation [23] actively learning even when the value of X turns negative. Unlike *Sigmoid* and *tanH*, *ReLU* deals with the gradient vanishing problem without any expensive mathematical operations since the activation is based on a simple threshold matrix.

Area under the Curve (AUC) is an area under the ROC curve for evaluation of performance metric. Our proposal DroidDivesDeep, a dropout assisted deep learning classification framework evaluation results are illustrated in Table 1. We compare SVM classifier, DNN with *tanH*, and *ReLU* activation functions. Table 1 illustrates that the SVM training results have (99.17%) training time classification accuracy. However, the actual classification drops to 60.48%, a drop of about 38% during real evaluation. The downgraded result is due to overfitting which results in positively biased training time output. Similarly, the DNN *tanH* activation reports low real time classification.

1. Sigmoid: It squashes a real-valued number into the range between 0 and 1. But these are used very rarely now a days because of their gradient vanishing and no-zero centric draw backs.
2. tanH: It squashes a real-valued number into the range between −1 and 1. The activation function also faces gradient vanishing problem; however, the output is zero centric.

Table 1. Comparison: shallow learners v/s D^3

Classifier	Training Accuracy	Test Accuracy
SVM (Shallow learner)	99.17%	60.98%
DNN with tanH	99.84%	56.72%
DNN with ReLU	**75.25%**	**99.65%**

We improved the DNN classification with *ReLU* activation by addressing the over-fitting issue. The training classification with *ReLU* is 75.25%, low compared to SVM during training. Since, dropout technique removes random features to improve classification at runtime, the classifier is forced to learn the features intelligently. Hence, real test classification accuracy is 99.56%, better by nearly 25% against training results. Furthermore, we can see that our proposal improves the existing classification by more than 40% during real test due to removal of over-fitting.

Figure 2 illustrates comparison of selected features and their contribution towards classification. We have used 0–100 epochs during the comparison. When the epochs reach 50, the root mean square (RMSE) reduces. This suggests, low RMSE values deviate when epochs increase, resulting in low predicted output. Once the epoch goes beyond 50, the ReLU root mean square error increases. Hence, we considered 50 epochs to evaluate the classification results. Figure 3 illustrates relative feature influence in classification. Relative variable importance shows relative influence of each variable, i.e. contribution towards real time predication. We see that *ppid, cutime* respond clearly towards predicting genuine features from malware.

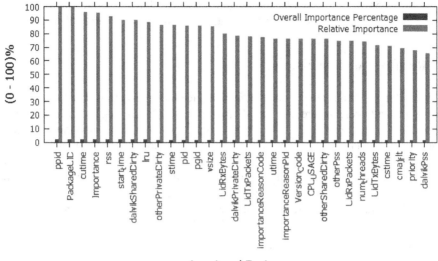

Fig. 2. Feature ranking

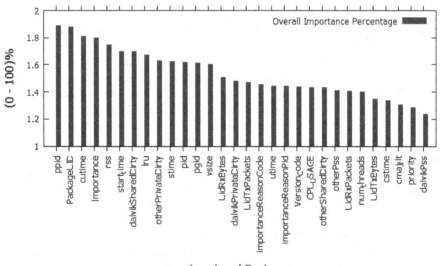

Fig. 3. Percentage importance

Percentage importance represents the overall percentage influence of specific predicator for response variable(s). Top 5 variables are Parent Process-Id, Package Identifier, CUTIME (Amount of time that this process's waited for children have been scheduled in user mode), Relative Importance granted to the process, Resident Set Size (number of pages the process has in real memory.). We observe four from five attributes (4/5) belong to CPU and Memory usage. Thus, experimental evaluation shows that CPU and memory utilization pattern is feature for anomaly detection.

5 Results and Discussion

Deep-learning methods are not dependent on the feature engineering. The feature layers and associated weights are not tuned manually. These are representation-learning methods with multiple levels. They begin from raw input and transform the representation at one layer to another. With multiple transformations, a complex function can be learned. The number of hidden layers amplify the prospect of better classification. DNN has proved to be very efficient in classifying the complex patterns in high-dimensional data. Hence, it is popular in speech and image recognition. DNN can easily take advantage of increase in the amount of available computation and data.

5.1 Discussions

A n hidden layered neural network has 2^n possible thinned neural networks. The possible networks share the weights; hence, parameters are $O(2^n)$ or less. For each presentation of training cases, a thinned network is sampled and trained. Training a neural network with dropout can be visualized as training a collection of 2^n thinned networks with extensive weight sharing, where each thinned network gets trained very rarely. Dropout can be thought of as a stochastic regularization technique, with deterministic counterpart obtained by marginalizing the noise [29].

Figure 4 compares ReLU based DNN with shallow learning SVM and DNN with *tanH* activation function. It is evident that DNN with *ReLU* out performs sigmoid and *tanH* activation functions during the real evaluation. Though, the training time evaluation is less on account of dropout, the real evaluation accuracy is above 98%. Further, we experimented on creating ensembled NNs with each one voting for best classifier. We trained 5 different neural networks using the with ReLU and tanH activation functions which achieved 99.6% accuracy and 98.6% detection rate. Even though, different NN have quite similar accuracy, they have varied errors on account of random initialization. Hence, an ensembled NNs improves overall accuracy. Our experimental evaluation show that voting among the five networks produces better results.

Further, we focused on the specific case of the popular rectified linear non-linearity for hidden units. Table 1 illustrates the same that drop out is accurate ensemble learning, when used in case of rectified linear networks. Further research is necessary to shed more light on the model averaging interpretation of dropout.

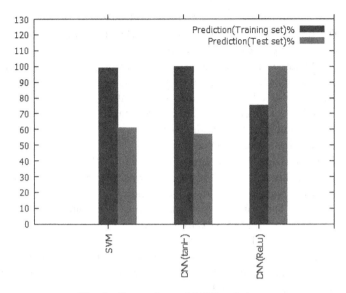

Fig. 4. Comparison of DNN techniques

6 Conclusion and Future Work

In this paper, we proposed a deep learning classification via low level monitorable features to classify malicious Android apps. To this end, we proposed a fully connected deep neural network equipped with dropout feature which is a robust learning technique to improve real-time detection. We record the impact of app execution on low level monitorable features by executing the genuine and malware apps. Furthermore, we train the fully connected deep network classifier based on the features recorded from low-privileged monitorable features.

The dropout technique employed in the proposal is an effective ensemble learning method paired accurately with rectified linear networks. We believe that, D^3 employs intelligent dropouts to achieve high classification accuracy. To the best of our knowledge, our proposal employing dense neural network for malware detection via device level low-privileged monitorable attributes as a significant improvement over existing proposals. In future, we plan to develop improved on-device anti-malware with deep learning capabilities without requirement of device rooting or kernel level modifications.

Appendix A

In the following, we briefly describe the important low-level monitorable features extracted for classification in our proposal DroidDivesDeep.

1. *cpu_usage* CPU utilization % to a constant CPU speed.
2. *cutime*: The time a process waited which are scheduled in user mode.
3. *importancereasoncode*: The reason for importance, if any.
4. *importance*: Status of a process i.e., background, foreground, service or sleeping.
5. *importancereasonpid*: For the specified values of importanceReasonCode, this is the process ID of the other process that is a client of this process.
6. *lru*: relative utility of processes within an importance category.
7. *num_threads*: Number of threads in this process.
8. *pgid*: Identifier of foreground process.
9. *priority*: Priority assigned to the process between 0–99.
10. *cmaj_flt*: Page faults a process and its children made the number of major faults that the process's waited-for children have made.
11. *otherprivatedirty*: The private dirty pages used by everything else.
12. *otherpss*: The proportional set size for everything else.
13. *othershareddirty*: Shared dirty pages.
14. *rss*: Resident Set Size: number of pages the process has in real memory.
15. *version_code:* An integer used as an internal version number for the Android app.
16. *packageuid*: An app package UID.
17. *uidrxbytes*: Bytes received by this application since the last time the T4 probe was activated.
18. *uidrxpackets*: Packets received by this application since the activated T4 probe.
19. *uidtxbytes*: Bytes transmitted by this application since the last time the T4 probe was activated.
20. *uidtxpackets*: Packets transmitted by this application since the last time the T4 probe was activated.
21. *dalvikprivatedirty*: The private dirty pages used by dalvik heap.
22. *dalvikpss*: The proportional set size for dalvik heap.
23. *dalvikshareddirty*: The shared dirty pages used by dalvik heap.
24. *start_time*: The time the process started after system boot.
25. *stime*: Clock tick time this process has been scheduled in kernel mode.
26. *utime*: Amount of time that this process has been scheduled in user mode, measured in clock ticks.

References

1. Alam, M., Vuong, S.T.: An intelligent multi-agent based detection framework for classification of android malware. In: Ślęzak, D., Schaefer, G., Vuong, S.T., Kim, Y.-S. (eds.) AMT 2014. LNCS, vol. 8610, pp. 226–237. Springer, Cham (2014). https://doi.org/10.1007/978-3-319-09912-5_19
2. Amos, B., Turner, H.A., White, J.: Applying machine learning classifiers to dynamic android malware detection at scale. In: 2013 9th International Wireless Communications and Mobile Computing Conference, IWCMC 2013, Sardinia, Italy, 1–5 July 2013, pp. 1666–1671 (2013)

3. Amos, B., Turner, H.A., White, J.: Applying machine learning classifiers to dynamic android malware detection at scale. In: Saracco, R., Letaief, K.B., Gerla, M., Palazzo, S., Atzori, L. (eds.) IWCMC, pp. 1666–1671. IEEE (2013)
4. R. Analytics. A comparison of deep learning packages for r (2017)
5. A. Brains. Android sdk version market share (2017)
6. Dahl, G.E., Stokes, J.W., Deng, L., Yu, D.: Large-scale malware classification using random projections and neural networks. In: ICASSP, pp. 3422–3426. IEEE (2013)
7. Dash, S.K., et al.: Droidscribe: classifying android malware based on runtime behavior. In: Mobile Security Technologies (MoST) (2016)
8. Deo, A., Dash, S.K., Suarez-Tangil, G., Vovk, V., Cavallaro, L.: Prescience: probabilistic guidance on the retraining conundrum for malware detection. In: Proceedings of the 2016 ACM Workshop on Artificial Intelligence and Security, AISec 2016, New York, NY, USA, pp. 71–82. ACM (2016)
9. Dini, G., Martinelli, F., Saracino, A., Sgandurra, D.: MADAM: a multi-level anomaly detector for android malware. In: Kotenko, I., Skormin, V. (eds.) MMM-ACNS 2012. LNCS, vol. 7531, pp. 240–253. Springer, Heidelberg (2012). https://doi.org/10.1007/978-3-642-33704-8_21
10. Dong, S., et al.: Understanding android obfuscation techniques: a large-scale investigation in the wild. CoRR, abs/1801.01633 (2018)
11. Faruki, P., Bhandari, S., Laxmi, V., Gaur, M., Conti, M.: DroidAnalyst: synergic app framework for static and dynamic app analysis. In: Abielmona, R., Falcon, R., Zincir-Heywood, N., Abbass, H.A. (eds.) Recent Advances in Computational Intelligence in Defense and Security. SCI, vol. 621, pp. 519–552. Springer, Cham (2016). https://doi.org/10.1007/978-3-319-26450-9_20
12. Faruki, P., et al.: Android security: a survey of issues, malware penetration, and defenses. Commun. Surv. Tutorials 17(2), 998–1022 (2015). Second quarter
13. Faruki, P., Ganmoor, V., Vijay, L., Gaur, M., Conti, M.: Android platform invariant sandbox for analyzing malware and resource hogger apps. In: Proceedings of the 10th IEEE International Conference on Security and Privacy in Communication Networks (Secur-eComm 2014), Beijing, China, 26–28 September 2014 (2014)
14. Faruki, P., Zemmari, A., Gaur, M., Vijay, L., Conti, M.: Mimeodroid: large scale dynamic app analysis on cloned devices via machine learning classifiers. In: 2016 46th Annual IEEE/IFIP International Conference on Dependable Systems and Networks Workshop (DSN-W), pp. 60–65 (2016)
15. Felt, A.P., Ha, E., Egelman, S., Haney, A., Chin, E., Wagner, D.: Android permissions: user attention, comprehension, and behavior. In: Proceedings of the Eighth Symposium on Usable Privacy and Security, SOUPS 2012, New York, NY, USA, pp. 3:1–3:14. ACM (2012)
16. Fratantonio, Y., Bianchi, A., Robertson, W., Kirda, E., Kruegel, C., Vigna, G.: TriggerScope: towards detecting logic bombs in android apps. In: Proceedings of the IEEE Symposium on Security and Privacy (S&P), San Jose, CA, May 2016
17. Hung, S.-H., Hsiao, S.-W., Teng, Y.-C., Chien, R.: Real-time and intelligent private data protection for the android platform. Pervasive Mob. Comput. 24(C), 231–242 (2015)
18. IDC. Idc: Smartphone market share 2016, 2015 (2017)
19. G. Inc. Gartner: Chinese vendor share q3 2016, 2015 (2017)
20. Keinert, B., Martschinke, J., Stamminger, M.: Learning real-time ambient occlusion from distance representations. In: Proceedings of the ACM SIGGRAPH Symposium on Interactive 3D Graphics and Games, I3D 2018, pp. 3:1–3:9. ACM, New York (2018)
21. Lecun, Y., Bengio, Y., Hinton, G.: Deep learning. Nature 521(7553), 436–444 (2015)

22. Mirsky, Y., Shabtai, A., Rokach, L., Shapira, B., Elovici, Y.: Sherlock vs moriarty: a smartphone dataset for cybersecurity research. In: Proceedings of the 2016 ACM Workshop on Artificial Intelligence and Security, AISec 2016, pp. 1–12. ACM, New York (2016)

23. Nair, V., Hinton, G.E.: Rectified linear units improve restricted boltzmann machines. In: Proceedings of the 27th International Conference on Machine Learning, ICML 2010, pp. 807–814. Omnipress (2010)

24. Neyshabur, B., Li, Z., Bhojanapalli, S., LeCun, Y., Srebro, N.: Towards understanding the role of over-parametrization in generalization of neural networks. CoRR, abs/1805.12076 (2018)

25. Papernot, N., McDaniel, P.D., Sinha, A., Wellman, M.P.: Towards the science of security and privacy in machine learning. CoRR, abs/1611.03814 (2016)

26. Rastogi, V., Qu, Z., McClurg, J., Cao, Y., Chen, Y.: Uranine: real-time privacy leakage monitoring without system modification for android. In: Thuraisingham, B., Wang, X., Yegneswaran, V. (eds.) SecureComm 2015. LNICST, vol. 164, pp. 256–276. Springer, Cham (2015). https://doi.org/10.1007/978-3-319-28865-9_14

27. Saxe, J., Berlin, K.: Deep neural network based malware detection using two dimensional binary program features. In: Proceedings of the 2015 10th International Conference on Malicious and Unwanted Software (MALWARE), MALWARE 2015, pp. 11–20. IEEE Computer Society, Washington, D.C. (2015)

28. Shabtai, A., Kanonov, U., Elovici, Y., Glezer, C., Weiss, Y.: "Andromaly": a behavioral malware detection framework for android devices. J. Intell. Inf. Syst. 38(1), 161–190 (2012)

29. Srivastava, N., Hinton, G., Krizhevsky, A., Sutskever, I., Salakhutdinov, R.: Dropout: a simple way to prevent neural networks from overfitting. J. Mach. Learn. Res. 15(1), 1929–1958 (2014)

30. Suarez-Tangil, G., Conti, M., Tapiador, J.E., Peris-Lopez, P.: Detecting targeted smartphone malware with behavior-triggering stochastic models. In: Kutyłowski, M., Vaidya, J. (eds.) ESORICS 2014. LNCS, vol. 8712, pp. 183–201. Springer, Cham (2014). https://doi.org/10.1007/978-3-319-11203-9_11

31. Suarez-Tangil, G., Dash, S.K., Ahmadi, M., Kinder, J., Giacinto, G., Cavallaro, L.: Droidsieve: fast and accurate classification of obfuscated android malware. In: 7th ACM Conference Data and Application Security and Privacy (CODASPY) (2017)

32. Suarez-Tangil, G., Stringhini, G.: Eight years of rider measurement in the android malware ecosystem: evolution and lessons learned. CoRR, abs/1801.08115 (2018)

33. Suarez-Tangil, G., Tapiador, J.E., Peris-Lopez, P., Ribagorda, A.: Evolution, detection and analysis of malware for smart devices. IEEE Commun. Surv. Tutorials 16(2), 961–987 (2014)

34. Szegedy, C., et al.: Intriguing properties of neural networks. CoRR, abs/1312.6199 (2013)

35. WeLiveSecurity. Trends (in) security everywhere (2017)

36. Wermke, D., Huaman, N., Acar, Y., Reaves, B., Traynor, P., Fahl, S.: A large scale investigation of obfuscation use in google play. CoRR, abs/1801.02742 (2018)

37. Yuan, Z., Lu, Y., Wang, Z., Xue, Y.: Droid-sec: deep learning in android malware detection. SIGCOMM Comput. Commun. Rev. 44(4), 371–372 (2014)

38. Zeng, M., Wang, X., Nguyen, L.T., Wu, P., Mengshoel, O.J., Zhang, J.: Adaptive activity recognition with dynamic heterogeneous sensor fusion. In: 6th International Conference on Mobile Computing, Applications and Services, MobiCASE 2014, Austin, TX, USA, 6–7 November 2014, pp. 189–196 (2014)

39. Zhang, L., Yi, Z., Yu, J., Heng, P.A.: Some multistability properties of bidirectional associative memory recurrent neural networks with unsaturating piecewise linear transfer functions. Neurocomput 72(16–18), 3809–3817 (2009)

40. Faruki, P., Laxmi, V., Ganmoor, V., Gaur, M.S., Bharmal, A.: DroidOLytics: robust feature signature for repackaged android apps on official and third party android markets. In: 2013 2nd International Conference on Advanced Computing, Networking and Security, pp. 247–252, December 2013. ISSN 2377-2506

41. Faruki, P., Zemmari, A., Gaur, M.S., Laxmi, V., Conti, M.: Android component vulnerabities: proof of concepts and mitigation. In: 2016 International Conference on Information Networking (ICOIN), pp. 17–22, January 2016

42. Faruki, P., Zemmari, A., Gaur, M.S., Laxmi, V., Conti, M.: MimeoDroid: large scale dynamic app analysis on cloned devices via machine learning classifiers. In: 2016 46th Annual IEEE/IFIP International Conference on Dependable Systems and Networks Workshop (DSN-W), pp. 60–65, June 2016

43. Faruki, P., Ganmoor, V., Laxmi, V., Gaur, M.S., Bharmal, A.: AndroSimilar: robust statistical feature signature for android malware detection. In: Proceedings of the 6th International Conference on Security of Information and Networks, SIN 2013, New York, NY, USA, pp. 152–159 (2013). ISBN 978-1-4503-2498-4

44. Faruki, P., Bharmal, A., Laxmi, V., Gaur, M.S., Conti, M., Rajarajan, M.: Evaluation of android anti-malware techniques against dalvik bytecode obfuscation. In: 2014 IEEE 13th International Conference on Trust, Security and Privacy in Computing and Communications, pp. 414–421, September 2014

45. Dave, J., Faruki, P., Laxmi, V., Bezawada, B., Gaur, M.: Secure and efficient proof of ownership for deduplicated cloud storage. In: Proceedings of the 10th International Conference on Security of Information and Networks, pp. 19–26 (2017)

46. Dave, J., Saharan, S., Faruki, P., Laxmi, V., Gaur, M.S.: Secure random encryption for deduplicated storage. In: Shyamasundar, R.K., Singh, V., Vaidya, J. (eds.) ICISS 2017. LNCS, vol. 10717, pp. 164–176. Springer, Cham (2017). https://doi.org/10.1007/978-3-319-72598-7_10

47. Dave, J., Das, M.L.: Securing SQL with access control for database as a service model. In: Proceedings of the Second International Conference on Information and Communication Technology for Competitive Strategies, p. 104 (2016)

48. Hou, S., Saas, A., Chen, L., Ye, Y., Bourlai, T.: Deep neural networks for automatic android malware detection, pp. 803–810 (2017). https://doi.org/10.1145/3110025.3116211

49. Wang, X., Zhang, D., Su, X., Li, W.: Mlifdect: android malware detection based on parallel machine learning and information fusion. Secur. Commun. Netw. **2017**, 14 (2017). Article ID 6451260

EvadePDF: Towards Evading Machine Learning Based PDF Malware Classifiers

Sukanta Dey[✉], Abhishek Kumar, Mehul Sawarkar, Pranav Kumar Singh, and Sukumar Nandi

Department of Computer Science and Engineering,
Indian Institute of Technology Guwahati, Guwahati 781039, Assam, India
{sukanta.dey,sukumar}@iitg.ac.in, snghpranav@gmail.com

Abstract. There have been significant developments in the application of Machine Learning based classifiers for identifying malware camouflaging as benign files (our study is based on PDF files) in recent times like PDFRate. However, unlike other fields where statistical techniques are used, malware detection lacks the fundamental assumption in ML-based techniques that the training data represents the perspective input. Instead, malware can be designed to specifically break the ML classifiers as an anomaly. We present a thorough study and the results of our improvement over the implementation of one such prominent project EvadeML, which is a Genetic Programming based technique to evade ML-based malware classifiers. EvadeML has shown 100% success rate for two target PDF malware classifiers PDFRate and Hidost. We have modified the EvadeML to have a better evasion efficiency for another PDF malware classifier AnalyzePDF and found significant improvement over the EvadeML. We have also tested our modified approach for the PDFRate malware classifier and found 100% success rate as in the original EvadeML.

Keywords: Adversarial machine learning · Benign ·
Malware classifiers · Genetic Programming · Malicious · Malware ·
PDF

1 Introduction

According to a recent survey [1], *Portable Document Format* (PDF) is one of the top 8 malicious attachments in 2017. It can be expected that there will be more opportunities for PDF malware attacks as 267 new vulnerabilities in Acrobat readers have been reported in CVE so far since 2017 (till 9th December 2018) [3].

Recently, one prominent attack is Jaff Ransomware [4] attack where the attacker hid malicious JavaScript snippets in a PDF document which was circulated by email and affected many people. To deal with such attacks Machine Learning (ML)-based malware classifiers have become very famous. Machine

© Springer Nature Singapore Pte Ltd. 2019
S. Nandi et al. (Eds.): ISEA-ISAP 2018, CCIS 939, pp. 140–150, 2019.
https://doi.org/10.1007/978-981-13-7561-3_11

Learning based malware classifiers work by applying algorithms like Decision Trees, Random Forest [13], SVM based classifiers [14] or Neural Networks on a feature set generated by tokenization of the PDF file like n-gram representation. The very basis of the ML-based classification is a feature set which can be increased or modified suitably while still preserving the malicious property of the PDF file, for example, a PDF file having a malicious JavaScript snippet can be appended with a large amount of benign text thus changing the feature set dramatically while still preserving the original malicious behavior. We discuss and suggest improvements to a Genetic Programming [6] based technique to figure out what mutations should be applied to the original file to make malware classifiers mistakenly classify it as benign owing to a deceiving feature set.

Motivation: Malicious code snippets like JavaScript snippets embedded in PDF files can be very dangerous for both security and integrity of any computer system. Owing to the broad reach of the ML-based classification algorithms, which can classify a very diverse set of malicious code snippets, unlike traditional malware classifiers which have hardcoded logic to identify only certain known viruses, breaking ML-based classifiers have become an increasingly important problem.

The major contribution of the paper,

- We have proposed a modification to the EvadeML approach of evading malware classification by incorporating changes in the Genetic Programming algorithm to achieve the evading for different PDF malware classifiers with an increase in evasion efficiency.
- We evaluate the proposed modification in the two PDF malware classifiers: PDFRate [13] and AnalyzePDF [2]. Our proposed modification is able to achieve 98% success rate in terms of evasion efficiency for the AnalyzePDF malware classifier compare to 93% success rate for the original EvadeML approach. A 100% success rate for the PDFRate classifier which shows the proposed modification does not reduce the impact of the actual EvadeML [16] method which also has a success rate of 100%.

The rest of the paper is organized as follows. The background of the paper is described in Sect. 2 which contains the a brief description of machine learning classifiers, the threat model used in this paper, and the related previous work. The working of the target PDF malware classifiers used in this paper is described in Sect. 3. The proposed improvement over the EvadeML approach is mentioned in Sect. 4. The experimental results are listed in Sect. 5. The work is concluded in Sect. 6.

2   Background

2.1   Machine Learning Classifiers

Machine Learning (ML) classifiers work on the data to classify. The Supervised Learning technique is the method where all the instances of the dataset are labeled. On the basis of the labeled dataset which is also known as the *training set*, the ML classier tried to formulate a hypothesis which would predict an unseen data sample as *benign* or *malicious* depending on different properties of the dataset. The properties of the dataset are characterized by an entity named called *feature*. All classification using the machine learning algorithms depend on the features.

2.2   Attack and Threat Model

The attack model used in this work is a black-box attack model, which means the attacker doesn't have any information about the working of the machine learning PDF malware classifier. However, for the threat model few assumptions need to be consider. The first assumption is that the attacker has the black-box access of the target classifier such that he can submit any PDF sample to the classifier and check the output. Secondly, the attacker can submit different malicious versions of the PDF file sample to the classier. Now, the aim of the attacker is to generate such a malicious PDF sample which would have the malicious behavior but it is miss-classified as benign by the target classifier. For each trial with the classifier, the attacker gets a maliciousness score between any real number between 0 and 1. A maliciousness score of 0.5 or more is considered as malicious PDF sample, else the sample is considered as benign.

2.3   Related Works

In recent years a number of ML-based Malware classifiers have been proposed e.g. Detection of Malicious PDF Files Based on Hierarchical Document Structure [14], Large-scale malware classification using random projections and neural networks [8], Malware Classification Using Euclidean Distance and Artificial Neural Networks [10].

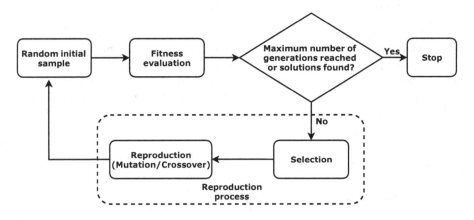

Fig. 1. Genetic Programming

With the importance and reach of the ML-based classifiers discussed above, there has been significant research lately in evading these classifiers like EvadeML [16]. On the other hand, based on the study of prior work in Secure Kernel Machines against Evasion Attacks by Russu et al. [12] and on the detection (statistical) of Adversarial examples by Grosse et al. [11]. It is clear from these works that performing statistical analysis of the crafted (generated to break a classifier) adversarial files might lead to more robust classifiers as all the crafted files are anomalous and share statistical peculiarities. Recently, Dang et al. [9] proposed an evading strategy where they have assumed the target classier is not available to them and attacker has to attack by morphing the samples. In this paper, we suggest one improvement to the EvadeML algorithm. Tong et al. [15] discussed about the feature space attack and problem space attack for the PDF malware classifiers. The work also showed that problem space attack imitates a more realistic way of attack on classifiers. However, the feature space attack is a basic attack for the problem space-based attacks, hence, it is important for the research community to study further about the feature space attack. Therefore, we have chosen an automated feature space based framework EvadeML by Xu et al. [16] which showed successful evasion with 100% evasion efficiency for two PDF malware classifiers Hidost [14] and PDFRate [13]. We studied the EvadeML algorithm critically and further proposed a replacement strategy over the EvadeML which can successfully evade the AnalyzePDF classifier with a better rate than the original EvadeML. A brief description of EvadeML is given as follows.

Algorithm 1. EvadeML [16]

1 Malicious file + Benign sample files → Random initial population;
2 Mutation and Crossover of the initial population to generate a file;
3 Ask an Oracle (MongoDB server in our implementation) if the generated file is benign or malicious;
4 **if** *benign* **then**
5 | Remove the file from population and add a new file from seed or random variant;
6 | go to step 2;
7 **else if** *malicious* **then**
8 | Compute its maliciousness score from the malware classifier being targeted;
9 | **if** *malicious score ≥ 0.5* **then** Evasive sample found ;
10 | **if** *Evasive sample found* **then**
11 | | success;
12 | **else**
13 | | **if** *maximum generation reached* **then**
14 | | | fail;
15 | | **else**
16 | | | Select variants from seed or random variants;
17 | | | go to step 2;

A Brief Review of EvadeML: EvadeML is a Genetic Programming based algorithm. Genetic Programming techniques work by starting with an initial population set and introducing changes in each iteration to the population set and selecting a subset of the population. This shows promising scores (a higher fitness value) until the desired sample is found (with fitness value above a threshold). Figure 1 shows the general paradigm of Genetic Programming algorithms.

EvadeML starts with a Malicious PDF file which is being correctly classified as malicious by a malware classifier and a set of benign files. Benign files are used for generating mutations to convert the malicious file to pseudo-benign file. It is in the sense that it still has its malicious behavior intact but it gets classified as benign by the malware classifier being targeted. The complete algorithm is listed in the Algorithm 1. For verifying the generated sample files as benign or malicious Oracle (MongoDB server in our implementation) has been used. From the features of the sample files a fitness score is generated and after many iterations of Genetic Programming evasive samples are found.

The motivation behind using Genetic Programming over Gradient Descent like approach is because in the evaluation of the cost function Genetic Programming doesn't stuck in the local optima and no parameter settings have to be done here. Depending on the parameter settings and learning-rates, the gradient descent may stuck in local optima and the convergence time may be longer. Hence Genetic Programming is preferred here.

3   PDF Malware and Classifiers

This section describes the fundamentals of PDF malware and the two target PDF malware classifiers used in this paper.

3.1   PDF Malware

The PDF file has been made open sourced and for public use in 2008. The structure of the PDF file is shown in Fig. 2. The *header* part contains the version number. The body is the most important part of a PDF file. All the visible content of the PDF file is inserted in the body section. It can contain eight different types of data which are Boolean, numbers, strings, names, dictionaries etc. The cross-reference table links all the elements and objects present in the PDF file. The trailer contains the link to the cross-reference table and also has the end of file (EOF) at the end. Any malicious code of JavaScript or other objects that can take advantage of the vulnerabilities of the PDF readers can be inserted in any of the four parts of a PDF file. When the user opens a malicious PDF file using a PDF reader, then malicious code inside it executes and can corrupt the system or brings in massive damage to the data.

3.2   Target Classifiers

The target classifiers PDFRate and AnalyzePDF have been discussed in the following section:

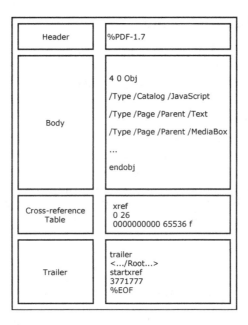

Fig. 2. PDF file structure

(a) PDFRate: PDFRate is a Random Forest based PDF malware classifier. In order to reduce the variations of the predictions, ensemble learning method is used which uses many decision trees to achieve effective predictions. Each decision tree is trained with a subset of training samples. PDFRate malicious classification score is ranging from 0 to 1. As mentioned PDFRate is trained with 5000 benign and 5000 malicious sample files from the Contagio data dump [7]. The number trees used is 1000 and the number of features in each tree is 43.

(b) AnalyzePDF: AnalyzePDF uses a rules-based PDF parser YARA [5]. It analyses the parsed tree generated from YARA rules which are certain heuristics about the nature of benign PDF files described in a particular format called YARA Rules. These rules help AnalyzePDF classify PDF files as benign or malicious by adding up a statistical score and a deterministic score based on YARA heuristics. Scores above 2.0 are considered malicious.

It is to be noted that we have modified some of the YARA rules as described in the original implementation of the AnalyzePDF. It was observed that some of the trivial modifications being done to the benign PDF files were getting classified as malicious by the AnalyzePDF due to the excessive restrictiveness of the YARA rules used by AnalyzePDF. Although, with sufficient trials, we have ensured that this change doesn't lead to malicious files being classified as benign. Most of the rules were trivial like 'carriage return' at the beginning of the PDF text.

4   Proposed Improvements

We have done modifications to the original algorithm to test the EvadeML's Genetic Programming algorithm described above on AnalyzePDF, a PDF malware classifier. The observations and improvements are discussed as follows:

4.1   Improvements Implemented

The evasion efficiency or the success rate can be defined as percentage of malicious PDF files which are classified as benign by the target classifier. As mentioned in the subsequent section, EvadeML is able to successfully evade (generate a corresponding seemingly benign file preserving the same maliciousness) about 93% of malicious files for AnalyzePDF while it can evade 100% of the files for PDFRate. Our aim is to improve the evasion efficiency for other target classifiers. We experimented with various parameters in the EvadeML algorithm, to key expects which came to our focus were:

– Mutation strategy of the successful evasive sample is stored and same mutation strategy is reused again which results in improved success rate or evasion efficiency.
– When a certain variant of sample is no longer malicious, then the benign sample can be replaced randomly by:
  • Initial seed
  • Best variant in previous generation
  • Best variant till now.

Mutation strategy storing method has improved the evasion efficiency or success rate to a greater extent. However, we have noticed a change in the evasion efficiency if the there is any change in the strategy of replacing benign samples. Therefore, to improve the evasion efficiency for other target malware classifiers we have used a strategy to replace benign PDF file samples when it is unable to find an evasive sample. Our replacing approach is summarized in Algorithm 2.

We defined three variables initial seed score (iS_{score}), best variant previous generation score (BVP_{score}), and best variant score till now (BV_{score}) corresponding to the three replacement strategy as discussed above. Initialize these variables iS_{score}, BVP_{score}, and BV_{score} by initial population size. Whenever an evasive sample is not found, follow the replacing strategy as mentioned in Algorithm 2. Instead of choosing uniformly randomly we used Algorithm 2 for replacing benign samples for the future generations of the genetic programming algorithm. Our proposed replacement strategy works on top of the original EvadeML algorithm as mentioned in Algorithm 1.

As it is clear from the above algorithm, we are making a selection in a weighted fashion, where each time a strategy gives good results its weight is increased. This is very much along the lines of what EvadeML had done for the mutation traces strategy. We have incorporated the above replacement strategy of Algorithm 2 in the main EvadeML algorithm which shows a significant improvement in the success rate for the AnalyzePDF malware classier over the original EvadeML approach.

Algorithm 2. EvadePDF: Replacing benign samples for future generations

---

1 We defined three variables initial seed score (iS_{score}), best variant previous generation score (BVP_{score}), and best variant score till now (BV_{score});
2 Initialize iS_{score}, BVP_{score}, and BV_{score} with the initial population size;
3 **while** *Evasive sample not found* **do**
4   Generate a random number between 0 and 1, say r;
5   **if** $r < \frac{iS_{score}}{iS_{score}+BVP_{score}+BV_{score}}$ **then**
6   replace by an initial seed value ;
7          $iS_{score} \leftarrow iS_{score} + 1$
8   **else if** $r < \frac{BVP_{score}}{iS_{score}+BVP_{score}+BV_{score}}$ **then**
9   replace by best variants of previous generation ;
10         $BVP_{score} \leftarrow BVP_{score} + 1$
11   **else**
12   replace by best variants till now ;
13         $BV_{score} \leftarrow BV_{score} + 1$
14   go to step 2 of Algorithm 1;

---

5 Experiments and Results

To showcase the improvements of our proposed EvadePDF approach, we have used two target classifiers PDFRate and AnalyzePDF for experiments.

5.1 Data Set and Experiment Setup

The simulation environment is setup as listed in Table 1. For the dataset, we have used 100 random malicious PDF files form the 10980 malicious file dumps of Contagio dataset [7]. These files are verified using MongoDB as the malicious file. All the initial parameters for Genetic Programming method is used, which is similar to the setup of EvadeML [16].

Table 1. System setup and details

Parameter	Values
Operating system	Ubuntu 14.04 (64 Bit) Linux
Memory (RAM)	8 GB
CPU	Intel (R) Core (TM) i7-6700 CPU 3.40 GHz
Language	Python
Performance metrics	Evasion efficiency
	Fitness score
PDF malware classifiers	PDFRate
	AnalyzePDF
Schemes implemented	Our proposed scheme: EvadePDF
	EvadeML proposal of Xu et al. [16]

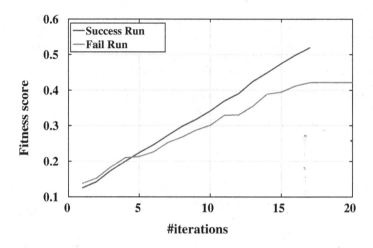

Fig. 3. The variation of fitness score with 20 iterations for a case of success run (classified as benign) and a fail run (classified as malicious) for AnalyzePDF classifier.

5.2   Results and Discussion

We conducted our experiments on the 100 random malicious PDF files of the Contagio dataset for the target classifiers PDFRate and AnalyzePDF. It is observed that the original EvadeML implementation was able to evade about 93% PDF files from 100 random files for the AnalyzePDF classifier. After implementing the changes in the replacement strategy of the benign samples as suggested in Algorithm 2, we are able to achieve about 98% success rate for the AnalyzePDF classifier.

The generation wise, maliciousness score (a score of more than 0.5 means file is benign) for a successful run and a failed run is shown in Fig. 3. It can be seen that the sample file initially has a malicious score of less than 0.5. In the successful run case, it manages to generate a benign version after 17 generations. In the fail run case, the maliciousness scores fails to achieve a score of 0.5 for the 20 generations and it failed to classify as benign. For the representation purpose we showed both success and fail run case in the Fig. 3. However, we have got just 2 files as failed run out of 100 files, for our approach when applying on the AnalyzePDF target classifier.

The evasion efficiency statistics is shown in Fig. 4. It is important to note that our modification doesn't impact EvadeML's performance on PDFRate where the evasion efficiency is already 100%.

We have concluded based on the results of our implementation that even in Genetic Programming based techniques different methods of selecting, mutating/ cross-over and eliminating variants might affect the results. Also, there is a further scope to check the robustness of this GP based algorithm on anti-evasion algorithms like Secure Kernel Machines against Evasion Attacks by Russu et al. [12].

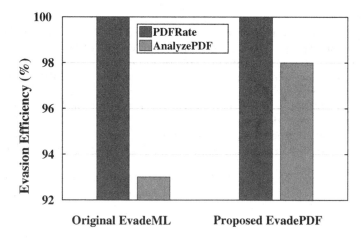

Fig. 4. Evasion efficiency comparison for the PDFRate and AnalyzePDF classifiers for the EvadeML and the proposed method.

6   Conclusion

In this paper, we have done the critical analysis of the EvadeML based approach for evading the machine learning based classifiers. We proposed an improvement to the EvadeML by incorporating the changes in the replacement policy of the Genetic Programming method of the EvadeML approach. Our proposed replacement method shows improvement in terms of evasion efficiency. We used two target classifiers PDFRate and AnalyzePDF to showcase the improvement of our proposed method. We have got an evasion efficiency of 98% for AnalyzePDF classifier using our approach in comparison to the evasion efficiency of 93% for the same classifier using the original EvadeML approach.

Acknowledgement. The research work has been conducted in the Information Security Education and Awareness (ISEA) Lab of Indian Institute of Technology, Guwahati, Assam, India. The authors would like to acknowledge IIT Guwahati, ISEA, and Ministry of Electronics and Information Technology (MeitY), Government of India for the support.

References

1. 2018 internet security threat report. https://www.symantec.com/security-center/threat-report
2. AnalyzePDF - bringing the dirt up to the surface. https://hiddenillusion.github.io/2013/12/03/analyzepdf-bringing-dirt-up-to-surface/
3. CVE details. Adobe acrobat reader—CVE security vulnerabilities, versions and detailed reports. https://www.cvedetails.com/product/497
4. Jaff ransomware hiding in a PDF document. https://www.vmray.com/cyber-security-blog/jaff-ransomware-hiding-in-a-pdf-document/

5. Yara rules. https://github.com/Yara-Rules/rules
6. Banzhaf, W., Nordin, P., Keller, R.E., Francone, F.D.: Genetic Programming: An Introduction, vol. 1. Morgan Kaufmann, San Francisco (1998)
7. Chenette, S.: Malicious documents archive for signature testing and research - contagio malware dump. http://contagiodump.blogspot.com/2010/08/malicious-documents-archive-for.html
8. Dahl, G.E., Stokes, J.W., Deng, L., Yu, D.: Large-scale malware classification using random projections and neural networks. In: IEEE International Conference on Acoustics, Speech and Signal Processing, ICASSP 2013, Vancouver, BC, Canada, 26–31 May 2013, pp. 3422–3426 (2013). https://doi.org/10.1109/ICASSP.2013.6638293
9. Dang, H., Huang, Y., Chang, E.C.: Evading classifiers by morphing in the dark. In: Proceedings of the 2017 ACM SIGSAC Conference on Computer and Communications Security, pp. 119–133. ACM (2017)
10. Gonzalez, L.E., Vázquez, R.A.: Malware classification using Euclidean distance and artificial neural networks. In: 12th Mexican International Conference on Artificial Intelligence, MICAI 2013, México, Mexico, 24–30 November 2013, pp. 103–108 (2013). Special Session Proceedings. https://doi.org/10.1109/MICAI.2013.18
11. Grosse, K., Manoharan, P., Papernot, N., Backes, M., McDaniel, P.D.: On the (statistical) detection of adversarial examples. CoRR abs/1702.06280 (2017). http://arxiv.org/abs/1702.06280
12. Russu, P., Demontis, A., Biggio, B., Fumera, G., Roli, F.: Secure kernel machines against evasion attacks. In: Proceedings of the 2016 ACM Workshop on Artificial Intelligence and Security, AISec@CCS 2016, Vienna, Austria, 28 October 2016, pp. 59–69 (2016). https://doi.org/10.1145/2996758.2996771
13. Smutz, C., Stavrou, A.: Malicious PDF detection using metadata and structural features. In: 28th Annual Computer Security Applications Conference, ACSAC 2012, Orlando, FL, USA, 3–7 December 2012, pp. 239–248 (2012). https://doi.org/10.1145/2420950.2420987
14. Srndic, N., Laskov, P.: Detection of malicious PDF files based on hierarchical document structure. In: 20th Annual Network and Distributed System Security Symposium, NDSS 2013, San Diego, California, USA, 24–27 February 2013 (2013). https://www.ndss-symposium.org/ndss2013/detection-malicious-pdf-files-based-hierarchical-document-structure
15. Tong, L., Li, B., Hajaj, C., Vorobeychik, Y.: Feature conservation in adversarial classifier evasion: a case study. CoRR abs/1708.08327 (2017). http://arxiv.org/abs/1708.08327
16. Xu, W., Qi, Y., Evans, D.: Automatically evading classifiers: a case study on PDF malware classifiers. In: 23rd Annual Network and Distributed System Security Symposium, NDSS 2016, San Diego, California, USA, 21–24 February 2016 (2016). http://wp.internetsociety.org/ndss/wp-content/uploads/sites/25/2017/09/automatically-evading-classifiers.pdf

Network Security

IP Traceback in Dynamic Networks

Sangita Roy[1], Hardik Chawla[1], and Ashok Singh Sairam[2(✉)]

[1] Thapar University, Patiala, Punjab, India
sangita.roy@thapar.edu, hardikisc@gmail.com
[2] Indian Institute of Technology Guwahati, Guwahati, Assam, India
ashok@iitg.ac.in

Abstract. IP traceback or identifying an attacker is an important step for post analysis of denial of service (DoS) attacks. In this work, we present techniques to traceback in networks with dynamic topology. We consider network scenarios where edges/nodes may get added or deleted in the attack path during the process of traceback. Due to the alteration in the attack path, the standard traceback procedures proposed in literature fail to construct the attack path. An exact algorithm, based on the branch and bound technique is proposed which guarantees to completely determine the attack path. An approximation of this algorithm is also presented which is shown to have a less computational complexity but introduces false positives.

Keywords: Denial of service attack · IP traceback · Dynamic network

1 Introduction

With the advent of new technologies and paradigms, distributed denial of service (DDoS) attacks have also evolved to target these new services. A number of tools and techniques have been devised to target Internet of Things devices, economic denial of service attacks targeting cloud services [1] and launching of DDoS attacks against software defined networks (SDNs) [2]. Counter measures to DDoS attack is a two-step process - attack reaction and source identification. In attack reaction, the aim is to mitigate the attack in real time by leveraging the upstream providers. Source identification involves tracing the origin of the attacker for post mortem analysis popularly known as IP traceback. The process of IP traceback is not limited only to DDoS attacks, but it can be used to identify the source of any packet on the Internet.

The challenge in IP traceback is primarily because attackers can easily spoof their IP address [3]. Thus to trace the origin of a packet, support is required from the underlying network. The support can be in the form of constructing an attack signature based on features of attack packets [4], logging of packets by en route routers [5], generating ICMP messages [6] and packet marking [3]. In this work, we use a packet marking technique based on distance-2 coloring [7] (also called star coloring).

© Springer Nature Singapore Pte Ltd. 2019
S. Nandi et al. (Eds.): ISEA-ISAP 2018, CCIS 939, pp. 153–165, 2019.
https://doi.org/10.1007/978-981-13-7561-3_12

Network topologies evolve rapidly in wireless networks due to fluctuating environment conditions. In the next generation wired networks such as SDN, the network topology changes dynamically in order to adapt to changing traffic conditions. The conventional traceback approaches will fail in such dynamic networks, since the original path followed by the packets would have changed during backtracking. In this paper, we propose an exact approach to trace the attacker in a dynamic network environment. The main contribution of the paper is in developing this function to find the next hop node of the traceback given that node and edge get deleted or added. We also propose an approximate approach which is computationally less expensive and has a success ratio of 75%.

The remainder of the paper is organized as follows. In Sect. 2, we review different packet marking techniques that have been proposed to traceback an attacker. The system model and the proposed dynamic traceback schemes are presented in Sects. 3 and 4 respectively. Numerical results are shown in Sect. 5. Finally the concluding remarks are presented in Sect. 6.

2   Literature Survey

In the literature a number of packet marking techniques [3,7] have been proposed to traceback an attacker. The basic idea is routers inject a *mark* or *color* probabilistically to en route packets. The mark may be a function of IP address of the router or independent of the router's address. The victim collect all packets containing marks of the attack path and use them to construct the attack path. These marks are overloaded in the IP header which is already constrained for space. Thus researchers have mainly concentrated in reducing the per packet space requirement and the total number of packets required for a successful traceback.

The first work on packet marking [3] proposed to embed the entire IP address. Rayanchu et al. [8] proposed to use a hash of the router's IP address to reduce the number of bits required for encoding the marks. Sairam et al. [7] proposed a scheme where the mark is a function of the network topology. In all of these traceback schemes, the network is assumed to be static. There are very few papers available in literature that consider the attack path can change during traceback.

Thing et al. [9] performed a qualitative analysis of the existing IP traceback schemes (including packet marking) in wireless ad hoc networks using proactive or reactive routing protocol. The authors show that the performance of traceback schemes depend on the underlying routing protocol. The authors simulated a dynamic network where the attacker as well as other nodes can move resulting in different attack paths. It was shown that all the traceback schemes had difficulty in constructing the attack path in such a dynamic scenario.

Dean et al. [10] re-framed the problem of attack path construction as a problem of polynomial reconstruction. In the full path encoding scheme, the first router in the path initiates the process of constructing the polynomial by using its IP address and a random variable. The polynomial so constructed as well as the random variable is encoded in the packet and passed on to the next router, who repeat the same steps. Finally, the victim receives the polynomial which includes encoding of IP address of all routers on the path. Using these polynomial, the victim can reconstruct the entire attack path. In order to dispense with the requirement of the first router initiating the marking process, the authors also proposed a random version, where any router can initiate the marking process based on the outcome of a random experiment.

Das et al. [11] capitalized on the robustness of the algebraic traceback approach [10], to propose an *incremental* traceback scheme for dynamic networks. The changes in the topology considered are addition or deletion of a single node in the attack path. The algebraic traceback approach allows to compute the IP address of a node at distance d from the attacker. The authors exploit this property to detect new value-pairs encoded by a new node in the path assuming that the victim has prior path information. The authors show that $O(d \log d)$ packets are required to detect a change in topology.

3   System Model

We consider the network as a graph $G(V, E)$, where the set of vertices V represent the routers and E represent the edges between the routers. The nodes are assumed to be distance-2 colored. In such a coloring scheme, each node is assigned a mark (also called color) such that no two nodes have the same color if the distance between them is equal to 2 hops or less. The mark of a node v is represented using $\varphi(v)$.

In packet marking technique, each node inserts its color to en route packets with a probability p. Let d be the distance between the attacker and the victim. The probability that the mark of a router at a distance d reaches the router is $p(1 - p)^{d-1}$. Let $X \subseteq V$ denote the set of routers on the attack path. In order to construct the attack path, the victim needs to receive at least one marked packet from each of these routers. We assume that the attack path is constructed using the IP traceaback scheme for distance-2 colored networks given in [7]. The constructed attack path will be the ordered set $(X, \prec)$.

In practice, the victim will not have the set X, but an ordered set of colors of the routers, represented as $\mathcal{C}$. This ordered set is a chain which we refer to as the *traceback chain*.

$$\mathcal{C} = (\{\varphi(x) | \forall x \in X\}, \prec) \tag{1}$$

Given this traceback chain, the task of the victim is to construct $(X, \prec)$. To trace the attacker, the victim needs to examine all the next hop routers and follow that router whose mark is equal to the next color in the chain. In Fig. 1, we show a star colored network, where the node labels denote the color of the nodes. The traceback chain $(\mathcal{C})$ available to the victim node (superscribed as s) is $\{1, 2, 3, 1, 2\}$. Given this chain, the victim can unambiguously traceback the attacker node (superscribed as r).

The procedure for traceback is shown in Algorithm 1. The function *next_hop()* (in line 6) fetches all the next hop nodes for the current node. For

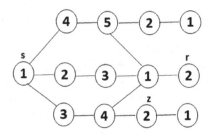

Fig. 1. Traceback process in a star colored network

each of these next hop routers, the algorithm checks if the color of the router matches the next color in the chain (lines 8–13). As we have assumed distance-2 colored, the color of all the next hop nodes will be distinct. Thus if the color of any of these router matches, then it must be the next router in the attack path. The algorithm will fail, if it cannot find a *matching* next hop router. Such a situation can arise if the network topology is dynamic. In such a scenario, it will call the *search()* function given in line 15, pseudo-code of which is presented in Algorithm 2.

```
 1: procedure TRACEBACK(a, v, C)                           ▷ a: attacker; v: victim
 2:     curr_node ← v
 3:     next_mark ← next(C, φ(curr_node))                  ▷ Get next color from chain
 4:     X ← v
 5: while φ(curr_node) ≠ φ(a) do
 6:     U ← next_hop(curr_node)                            ▷ Get all next hop nodes
 7:     is_next_hop ← FALSE
 8: foreach u ∈ U do
                                                           ▷ Examine each next hop node
 9:     if φ(u) == next_mark then
10:         X ← X ∪ u
11:         curr_node ← u
12:         next_mark ← next(C, φ(curr_node)
13:         is_next_hop ← TRUE
14:         break
        end
    end
    if is_next_hop == FALSE then
                                                           ▷ Next hop node not found
15:         search(curr_node,C)                            ▷ Search next hop node
    end
    end
16:     return X
17: end procedure
```

Algorithm 1: Procedure to traceback

4   IP Traceback in Dynamic Network Topology

In this section, we individually examine the case of edge deletion, node deletion, edge addition and node addition. For each such instance, we propose techniques to detect occurrence of the event as well as mechanisms to handle it. For successful traceback, we make the following assumptions:

- The routing table of each node in addition to storing IP address of the next hops, also stores *color* of the next hop.
- The network is a *connected* even after the event of edge deletion. In other words, if an edge between two nodes get deleted, there still exists an alternate path between the two nodes.

The first assumption facilitates in detecting the occurrence of an *abnormal* event. The second assumption ensures that the next hop node in the traceback chain can be reached through an alternate path.

4.1   Edge Deletion

In wired networks, an edge may get deleted not only due to disruption of the network link such as fibre cuts but also due to traffic conditions as in SDN. In wireless networks, due to dynamic channel conditions, edge failures are common. In this work, we only consider single edge deletions. During the traceback process as shown in Algorithm 1, the current node examines the color of all next hop forwarders and selects one whose color matches the next color in the traceback chain. In case no such forwarder exists, the node concludes the edge to the required next hop node is deleted. The subsequent step is to find an alternate path to the node. In this regard, we present the concept of *legal neighbourhood* of a node.

Definition 1. *Legal neighbours of a node are those nodes in the graph whose color is same as that of the next color in the traceback chain.*

Before edge deletion, each node will have only one legal neighbour among its first hop neighbours. A principal advantage of distance-2 coloring is that the marks can be reused which in turn reduces the number of bits required to encode the marks. The downside of color reuse is that a node can have multiple legal neighbours in its second hop neighbours and beyond. The challenge is to identify the actual router in the traceback path from among these multiple legal neighbours.

Definition 2. *Current node is the node at which the traceback process is presently active.*

The traceback process will start with the victim as the current node. At each iteration, the current node will attempt to find the next node in the traceback chain, which in turn will become the current node.

Exact Traceback During Edge Failures. We propose an exact algorithm to traceback an attacker during edge failures. The notations used as well as their meaning are given in Table 1. The notation $L(N(c, h), next(\mathcal{C}, \varphi(c)))$, can be thought of consisting of two parts. The first part $N(c, h)$ returns the set of nodes reachable from the node c in h hops. The second part $next(\mathcal{C}, \varphi(c))$ fetches the mark of next node of c from the traceback chain $\mathcal{C}$. Finally, the function $L()$, select those nodes from the first set whose color matches the result of the second part, which essentially is/are the legal nodes of c at hop h.

Table 1. Notations used and their meaning

Notations	Meaning
$N(c, h)$	Set of all nodes reachable from the node c in h hops
$next(\mathcal{C}, \varphi(c))$	Next mark with respect to current node c in the traceback chain
$L(N(c, h), next(\mathcal{C}, \varphi(c)))$	Set of all legal nodes of c at the hth hop

During edge failures, the current node will be unable to find the next hop node as indicated in the traceback chain among its first hop neighbours. The idea is to iteratively find the legal neighbours of the current node starting from the second hop nodes of the current node. Since each legal node can be potentially the next hop node, we assess them to check if they lie on the traceback path. The legal nodes are consecutively converted into a hypothetical current node and the traceback process is simulated starting from these conjectured current nodes. In case the simulation is successful, the legal node is designated as the current node.

In case the simulation fails and the set of legal nodes are exhausted, then we look for legal nodes at the subsequent hops of the original current node. In the worst case, the search for legal nodes may require searching the entire graph, which essentially mean *eccentricity* of the current node. In general, the upper bound to search the entire set of legal nodes will be the *diameter* of the graph. The steps of the search process are outlined in Algorithm 2.

Example to Illustrate Exact Traceback Under Edge Deletion. In Fig. 2, the traceback process is shown. The nodes are labelled with their assigned marks. The node superscribed with s is the victim node and the one superscribed with r is the attacker. The edges in the traceback path from s to r are marked. Let us assume that the first edge of the traceback path from the victim is deleted. The color of the node whose edge got deleted is 2. The victim node request color from all the second hop nodes and from amongst these nodes it finds that three nodes have the color code 2. These so called legal neighbours are shown as nodes superscribed with a, b and c. Each of these legal nodes are further examined.

procedure SEARCH$(c, \mathcal{C})$ ▷ c: current node
  for $(h \leftarrow 2; h \leq dia; h++)$ **do**
                                                                           ▷ dia: diameter of graph
    $legal\_nodes \leftarrow L(N(c, h), next(\mathcal{C}, \varphi(c)))$ ▷ Get legal nodes at hop h
    foreach $l \in legal\_nodes$ **do**
      $X' \leftarrow c' \leftarrow l$ ▷ Set legal node as the new current node c'
      do
        $\mathcal{U} \leftarrow next\_hop(c')$ ▷ Get next hop nodes
        $is\_next\_hop \leftarrow FALSE$
        if $\varphi(u \in \mathcal{U}) == next(\mathcal{C}, c')$ **then**
          $X' \leftarrow u$
          $c' = u$
          $is\_next\_hop \leftarrow TRUE$
        end
      while $is\_next\_hop == FALSE$ ▷ No more matches, abort loop
      if $\varphi(c) == \varphi(a)$ **then**
        return $X \cup X'$
      end
    end
  end
end procedure

Algorithm 2: An exact traceback process with edge deletion

Let us suppose, that we start with the legal node a. In the first hop of node a, a node with color 4 is present, which matches the next color in the traceback chain $\mathcal{C}$. The next to next node has the color 3, which does not match. Thus we do not explore this branch any further. Similarly, we will examine the legal node b and finally using legal node c, the whole attack path can be traversed. In case the search was unsuccessful, then we will examine the legal nodes at distance of hop 3 and so on the process will continue. The search process is similar to the branch and bound process [12], where the search is bounded by the help of the traceback chain.

Analysis of Exact Traceback Under Edge Deletion. In this section, we present a complexity analysis of Algorithm 2. The first step of the algorithm involves searching for legal nodes starting from the second hop and in the worst case may extend up to the diameter of the network. A upper bound on the diameter of the network [13] is given as

$$dia \leq n - \Delta + 1 \tag{2}$$

where n and Δ denote the order and degree of the graph respectively.

To compute a bound on the number of legal nodes, we assume the network to be color balanced star colored [7]. In color balanced star coloring, the objective is to reduce the number of colors used by balancing occurrences of the colors. A bound on the number of occurrence of the colors for such a coloring scheme is given in Eq. 3, where χ_s denote the star color chromatic number of the graph.

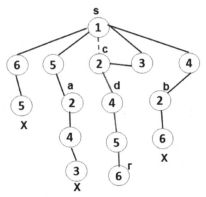

X: Not explored further
a, b, c : Legal nodes
s: victim, r: attacker
C: 1→2→4→5→6

Fig. 2. Example demonstrating exact traceback process

This equation, thus gives an upper bound on the number of legal nodes.

$$\left\lceil \frac{n}{\chi_s(G)} \right\rceil \tag{3}$$

The algorithm explores the first hop neighbour of the legal nodes by consulting their routing table. The maximum number of entries in the routing table can be Δ. In a graph of order n and maximum degree Δ, it has been shown that the vertex cover β is greater than or equal to $n/(\Delta + 1)$. Thus, in other words, a bound on Δ is given as

$$\Delta + 1 \geq \frac{n}{\beta} \tag{4}$$

Combining Eqs. 2, 3 and 4, we can deduce the running time complexity of the exact traceback algorithm is $\mathcal{O}(n^3)$.

Approximate Algorithm to Traceback During Edge Failures. In this section, we propose a low complexity solution approach to the problem of traceback under edge deletion. In the exact method, we search for legal nodes till the diameter of the network. However, in reality we are looking for a node, which before edge deletion was just one hop away. In real networks, we are likely to find the *target* legal node a lot closer to the current node. The other major overhead of the exact approach is that for each legal node, we simulate the traceback process till the attacker to check if the node under examination lies on the traceback path. The traceback process can be thought of as a process of traversing edges directed towards the attacker. In graph theory, assignment of direction to edges of a graph is nothing but an orientation of the graph. A well-known theorem by Gallai [14] - Roy [15] - Hasse [16] - Vitaver [17] provides a relation between the chromatic number of a graph and the longest path in the graph. Given Λ is orientation of a graph G with longest path $L(\Lambda)$, then

$$\chi_s \leq L(\Lambda) + 1 \tag{5}$$

Based on the above observations, we make the following two modifications to our search process

- Search for legal nodes up to the *mean path length* of the network. By definition such a path is the average of the shortest path length, averaged over all pair of nodes.
- During simulating path to the attacker, check for path lengths no greater than chromatic number of the graph.

4.2   Node Deletion

Analogous to edge failure, in the case of node failure we need to detect the event as well as come up with a counter measure. A simplified scenario of the edge deletion case is shown in Fig. 3a. In this example, the edge between s and x is assumed to be deleted and we attempt to find an alternate path to node x.

In the same example, assume that node x goes down. The scenario is shown in Fig. 3b. In this case, at least two edges will get deleted. Thus to detect a node failure, we first need to identify an edge failure. Next we attempt to find an alternate path to the next node. In case we fail to find an alternate path, we can presume the node to have become inoperative. However, such an approach will require searching the entire graph, which will be computationally expensive. Further, the traceback process too will be different than that of edge deletion. The traceback process has to commence from node y (instead of x), which is the next to next node of the current node.

The inference that we can draw from the above illustration is that if we can handle node failures, then edge failures will be automatically covered. The only exception will be the case where the next node in the traceback chain is the destination node. We can use the same search mechanism of edge deletion with two minor modifications. First, whenever we detect an edge deletion, we assume that it is a case of node deletion. Consequently, the traceback process attempts to recommence from the next to next node of the current node.

4.3   Node Addition

Addition of a node in the traceback path will generally have no effect in the traceback process except for the case where the edges are adjusted. In Fig. 3c, a new node u is added. In this example, we see that due to addition of the new node, there is no direct path from node s to node x. The same mechanism to handle node deletion can also be used to uncover node addition and thereby traceback. However, in the case of node addition, there will be only one legal node in the two hop neighbours of the current node. The legal node is in fact the actual traceback node, thus the traceback mechanism will converge faster.

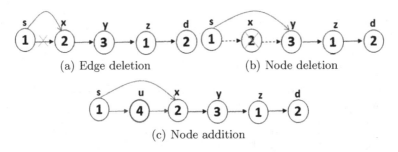

(a) Edge deletion   (b) Node deletion

(c) Node addition

Fig. 3. Dynamic network topology

5   Results

In this section, we empirically demonstrate the efficiency of our proposed approximate traceback scheme. We assume that routers on the attack path are not compromised. In the experiments conducted, we randomly picked an attacker and a victim node. From the attack path, an edge was randomly chosen and deleted. To ensure, the network is connected after edge deletion, we ensured that the two affected nodes have at least one incident edge. Two performance metrics were used - *success rate* and *false positive.*

For a given network topology, each experiment was repeated 50 times by selecting different attacker - victim pair during each iteration. Next we randomly select and delete an edge in the attack path. The graph is checked for connectivity and if so, then we start the traceback process. The success rate was measured by counting the number of successful tracebacks for each network topology.

In Fig. 4, we show the relation between the total number of nodes in the graph and success rate. The number of nodes were varied starting from 25 till 500. The success rate is close to cent percent for small number of nodes. As we increase the number of nodes, the success rate decreases. This is because in color balanced star coloring, the number of colors used to color the graph is not related to the number of nodes. For instance, in our experiments, we found that the number of colors used for 50 and 500 nodes graph is 23 and 27 respectively. Thus when the number of nodes increase, the *legal neighbours* will increase by a factor of 18, which in turn adversely affects the success rate. The average success rate is about 75%.

In star coloring, the number of colors required to color a graph is directly proportional to its degree. For a graph with degree Δ, the minimum number of nodes required is $\Delta + 1$. In the second experiment, we keep the number of nodes constant and vary the degree of the graph. Figure 5 show the relation between Δ and success rate. When the node degree is 10, the success rate is 42% and as we increase the node degree, the success rate increases exponentially. The success rate is above 90% when the degree of the graph is 100. The reason for this is that the number of alternate paths increase with increase in Δ.

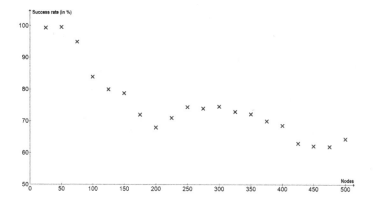

Fig. 4. Relation of success rate with number of nodes

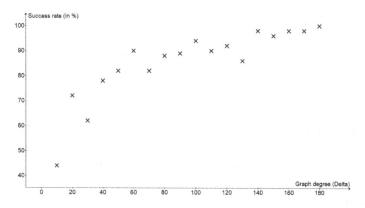

Fig. 5. Relation of success rate with Δ

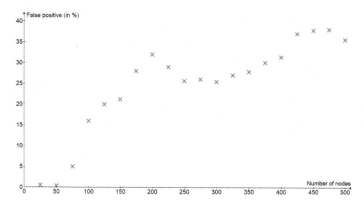

Fig. 6. Relation of false positive with number of nodes

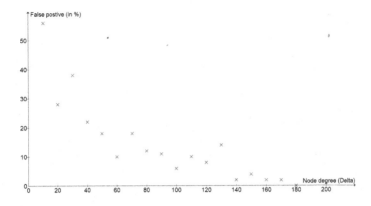

Fig. 7. Relation of false positive with Δ

In Fig. 6, we show the relation between number of nodes and false positives. A false positive is said to have occurred when a legitimate node is identified as an attacker. The number of false positives is close to 0 when the number of nodes is small and it increases almost linearly with the number of nodes. The average false positive rate is about 25%.

In Fig. 7, we show how the false positives change with node degree. The false positives almost linearly decrease as the degree of the graph increases. The false positive is highest when node degree is 10 and it is close to 0 for Δ values of 140 and beyond. The average false positive rate for this scenario is about 14.5%.

6   Conclusion

In this paper, we present techniques to perform traceback in networks with dynamic topology. We initially present an exact procedure to identify the attacker when an edge in the attack path gets deleted during traceback. The complexity of the exact algorithm is cubic, thus we present an approximate process which has quadratic complexity. Next, we examine the traceback process when a node gets deleted or added. We show that the traceback scheme to handle edge deletions can be extended to handle node deletions with minor modification. Experiments were performed for different network scenarios by varying the number of nodes as well as degree of the graph. The proposed approach has a success rate of 75%.

References

1. Shawahna, A., Abu-Amara, M., Mahmoud, A., Osais, Y.E.: EDoS-ADS: an enhanced mitigation technique against economic denial of sustainability (EDoS) attacks. IEEE Trans. Cloud Comput. 1 (2018). https://doi.org/10.1109/TCC.2018. 2805907

2. Yan, Q., Yu, F.R., Gong, Q., Li, J.: Software-defined networking (SDN) and distributed denial of service (DDoS) attacks in cloud computing environments: a survey, some research issues, and challenges. IEEE Commun. Surv. Tutor. **18**(1), 602–622 (2016)

3. Savage, S., Wetherall, D., Karlin, A., Anderson, T.: Network support for IP traceback. IEEE/ACM Trans. Netw. **9**(3), 226–237 (2001). https://doi.org/10.1109/90. 929847

4. Paxson, V.: An analysis of using reflectors for distributed denial-of-service attacks. SIGCOMM Comput. Commun. Rev. **31**(3), 38–47 (2001). https://doi.org/10. 1145/505659.505664

5. Snoeren, A.C., et al.: Single-packet IP traceback. IEEE/ACM Trans. Netw. **10**(6), 721–734 (2002)

6. Saurabh, S., Sairam, A.S.: ICMP based IP traceback with negligible overhead for highly distributed reflector attack using bloom filters. Comput. Commun. **42**, 60–69 (2014). https://doi.org/10.1016/j.comcom.2014.01.003

7. Sairam, A.S., Roy, S., Sahay, R.: Coloring networks for attacker identification and response. Secur. Commun. Netw. **8**(5), 751–768 (2015). https://doi.org/10.1002/ sec.1022

8. Rayanchu, S.K., Barua, G.: Tracing attackers with deterministic edge router marking (DERM). In: Ghosh, R.K., Mohanty, H. (eds.) ICDCIT 2004. LNCS, vol. 3347, pp. 400–409. Springer, Heidelberg (2004). https://doi.org/10.1007/978-3-540-30555-2_47

9. Thing, V.L.L., Lee, H.C.J.: IP traceback for wireless ad-hoc networks. In: IEEE 60th Vehicular Technology Conference, VTC2004-Fall, vol. 5, pp. 3286–3290 (2004)

10. Dean, D., Franklin, M.K., Stubblefield, A.: An algebraic approach to IP traceback. ACM Trans. Inf. Syst. Secur. **5**(2), 119–137 (2002). https://doi.org/10.1145/ 505586.505588

11. Das, A., Agrawal, S., Vishwanath, S.: On algebraic traceback in dynamic networks. In: IEEE International Symposium on Information Theory, pp. 1903–1907 (2010)

12. Mitten, L.G.: Branch-and-bound methods: general formulation and properties. Oper. Res. **18**(1), 24–34 (1970)

13. Buckley, F., Harary, F.: Distance in Graphs. Addison-Wesley Publishing, Redwood City (1990)

14. Gallai, T.: On directed graphs and circuits. In: Theory of Graphs (Proceedings of the Colloquium Tihany 1966), pp. 115–118 (1967)

15. Roy, B.: Nombre chromatique et plus longs chemins d'un graphe. R.I.R.O. **1**(5), 129–132 (1967). https://doi.org/10.1051/m2an/1967010501291

16. Hasse, M.: Zur algebraischen begrndung der graphentheorie. i. Mathematische Nachrichten **28**(56), 275–290. https://doi.org/10.1002/mana.19650280503

17. Vitaver, L.: Determination of minimal coloring of vertices of a graph by means of Boolean powers of the incidence matrix. Dokl. Akad. Nauk. SSSR **147**, 758–759 (1962)

Machine Learning Based Approach to Detect Position Falsification Attack in VANETs

Pranav Kumar Singh$^{(\boxtimes)}$, Shivam Gupta, Ritveeka Vashistha,
Sunit Kumar Nandi, and Sukumar Nandi

Department of Computer Science and Engineering, Indian Institute of Technology,
Guwahati 781039, India
snghpranav@gmail.com, sunitnandi834@gmail.com,
{shivam.gupta,ritveeka,sukumar}@iitg.ac.in

Abstract. VANETs is a major enabling technology for connected and autonomous vehicles. Vehicles communicate wirelessly with other vehicles, sensors, humans, and infrastructure, thereby improving decision making based on the information received from its surroundings. However, for these applications to work correctly, information needs to be authenticated, verified and trustworthy. The most important messages in these networks are safety messages which are periodically broadcasted for various safety and traffic efficiency related applications such as collision avoidance, intersection warning, and traffic jam detection. However, the primary concern is guaranteeing the trustworthiness of the data in the presence of dishonest and misbehaving peers. Misbehavior detection is still in their infancy and requires a lot of effort to be integrated into the system. An attacker who is imitating "ghost vehicles" on the road, by broadcasting false position information in the safety messages, must be detected and revoked permanently from the VANETs. The goal of our work is analyzing safety messages and detecting false position information transmitted by the misbehaving nodes. In this paper, we use machine learning (ML) techniques on VeReMi dataset to detect the misbehavior. We demonstrated that the ML-based approach enables high-quality detection of modeled attack patterns. We believe that the ML-based approach is a feasible and effective way of detecting such misbehavior in a real-world scenario of VANETs.

1 Introduction

Vehicular ad-hoc networks (VANETs) applications have great potentials to reduce the number of road accidents, diminish the carbon footprint, improve the traffic efficiency, and enhance the driving comfort and occupant's experience [1]. However, benefits usually come with challenges. Dealing with security threats such as fake data injections, messages alteration, replay attacks from insider attackers, and detecting such misbehaviors are the most significant challenges. Since the vehicular network is highly dynamic, the communicating vehicles are

© Springer Nature Singapore Pte Ltd. 2019
S. Nandi et al. (Eds.): ISEA-ISAP 2018, CCIS 939, pp. 166–178, 2019.
https://doi.org/10.1007/978-981-13-7561-3_13

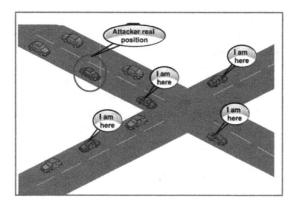

Fig. 1. Misbehavior in VANETs: position falsification

usually strangers and cannot fully trust each other. The problem becomes more dangerous when there are misbehaving/dishonest peers exist in the network. These peers may disseminate false/fake messages on purpose to gain something or to disturb normal functionalities.

Figure 1 demonstrates a scenario of position falsification attacks in VANETs [2]. Here, the misbehaving node uses the knowledge of the protocol semantics and create "ghost vehicles" in a particular road segment by broadcasting false position information in safety messages. In VANETs, the critical safety applications need to have reliable position information about its neighboring peers; thus, position falsification attack can create serious issues for road safety. Such attacks may also affect reliability for packet forwarding and lower the user acceptance of the system.

The public key infrastructure (PKI) is one of the highly recommended and used security framework. PKI facilitates the creation, management, distribution and revocation of keys and digital certificates for the proper and secure functioning of the system [3]. In the USA, Security Credential Management System (SCMS) is a leading candidate for the vehicular communication security which is based on PKI with unique features [4]. This security architecture was proposed by National Highway Traffic Safety Administration (NHTSA) for the vehicular network. The similar architecture was defined by European Telecommunications Standards Institute (ETSI) in Europe for intelligent transportation system (ITS). The specifications of these architecture are given in IEEE 1609.2 [5] and ETSI TS 102 940 [6] standards, respectively. However, the authenticity and verification process of these systems are not sufficient to guarantee the trustworthiness of the received message. Dealing with inside attackers or compromised entity and detection of any misbehaviors in the communication process are some of the biggest challenges of these security architectures.

Various data-centric and node-centric mechanisms for misbehavior detection can be found in the literature [7,8], however, most of them have their own set of challenges such as delay in detection, communication overhead, oversampling and cascading, etc. Machine Learning (ML) can be one of the potential solutions to it. ML-based paradigm allows us to build models that can help us to detect any unexpected behavior based on its learning. This data-driven mechanism can allow the onboard unit (OBU) of the vehicle to learn various data-centric relationship and detect any misbehavior in the vehicular plane of the VANETs. Thus, we employ the reliable predictive power of the supervised learning to predict a category whether each incoming message sample is correct or false based on the training. To demonstrate the effectiveness of the approach, we use the Vehicular Reference Misbehavior Dataset (VeReMi) [9] and focus on a specific attack instead of considering a wide range of attacks.

The rest of this paper is organized as follows. In Sect. 2, we discuss related works. Section 3 provides an overview of the system, communication, and adversary models. Section 4 describes details of machine learning mechanisms used in this work. In Sect. 5, we discuss the results obtained, and finally, we conclude our work in Sect. 6.

2   Related Work

In SCMS, the misbehavior detection (MD) is defined as the "process of identifying devices that are either malfunctioned or misbehaving" [4]. It requires two types of detection: (1) Local MD in vehicles to identify anomalies and to report this by devices to the SCMS, and (2) Global MD by the SCMS to analyze the reports of misbehavior and to decide which devices to revoke. However, the implementation of these MD processes for PKI frameworks in the USA and Europe is still in its research phase. In [9], the authors define misbehavior detection process as follows: "the lack of correctness in authentic messages is referred to as misbehavior detection."

PKI based cryptographic approach has already shown its efficiency in handling attack attempts from outside and unauthorized attackers. However, dealing with attacks or misbehavior from insider remains the biggest challenge to be addressed. The MD approach deal with inside attackers where PKI-based security fails. To this end, various mechanism have been proposed, which are listed in some of the surveys [7, 8, 10–13].

These solutions are based on various mechanism such as probabilistic approach [14], threshold-based [15], holistic approach [16], cooperative trust [17], game-theoretic [18], Kalman filter [19], extended Kalman filter [20], Bayesian Inference [21] etc. However, research using one of the strongest contenders for misbehavior detection, machine learning are much more deficient. We found few good studies [22–26] in which authors have proposed ML-based solutions to detect misbehavior in VANETs.

In [22], the authors proposed an ML-based approach to classify the behavior of the node, i.e. whether the node is honest or malicious. Authors implemented various types of misbehaviors by modifying information present in the propagated messages and used Naive Bayes, J-48, IBK, Random Forest and Ada Boost1 classifiers to classify the behavior. However, in their position forging attack, the attacker changes its ID randomly not the position. Kang et al. [23] proposed a deep neural network (DNN) based novel intrusion detection system (IDS) to detect attacks in a controller area network (CAN) network. In this work, the authors emphasize on the in-vehicle system rather than inter-vehicle communication. In the same line of thought, Loukas et al. [24] have proposed intrusion detection using deep learning to detect cyber-physical attacks inside the vehicle. However, their approach is cloud-based and consider attack vectors of the in-vehicle system only. Similarly, Taylor et al. [25] proposed Long Short-Term Memory (LSTM) neural network based anomaly detector to detect CAN bus attacks. This work also considers in-vehicle system vulnerabilities due to which CAN bus can be exploited. Ali et al. [26] proposed an intrusion detection system (IDS) to detect grey hole and rushing attacks in a vehicular network. The authors used both Support Vector Machines (SVM) and Feed Forward Neural Networks (FFNN) for attack detection.

To sum up this section, we see that there are only two good studies available that have used ML-based approach to detect inter-vehicle communication attacks. However, we believe that more such contributions are required because machine learning has great potential to address such issues in VANETs. To this end, our proposal is one such contribution.

3 Models: System, Communication and Adversary

3.1 System Model

As shown in Fig. 2, a VANET system architecture consists of three planes: Vehicular Plane, roadside unit (RSU) plane and Service plane.

Vehicular Plane. In the VANETs, the OBU of the vehicle has wireless connectivity options and a navigation option using Global Positioning System (GPS). Vehicles can communicate with all other devices equipped with wireless communication systems in their proximity such as pedestrians, other vehicles, RSUs, etc. Such type of communication is also referred to as Vehicle-to-Everything Communication (V2X).

RSU Plane. The fronthaul of the RSUs is wireless communication that provides connectivity with vehicles, which can be either Vehicle-to-Infrastructure (V2I) or I2V mode. The backhaul connectivity of RSUs are wired, which is connected to the gateway via switches and routers for packet forwarding to the service plane. Thus, RSUs facilitates communication between the vehicular plane and the services plane.

Service Plane. Various services in this plane can be of type Internet, payment, infotainment, traffic-related, etc. The requests generated by vehicles in the vehicular plane reach to the service plane via V2I connectivity and services are provided via the I2V mode of communication. The PKI-based certificate authority (CA) for VANETs is also deployed at the services plane.

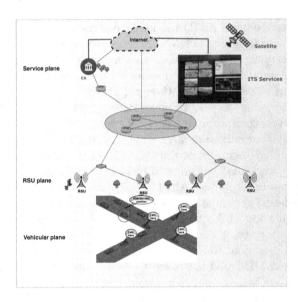

Fig. 2. VANET architecture

3.2 Communication Model

The Dedicated Short Range Communication (DSRC) is key radio access technology for V2V communication, specially designed for VANETs and standardized as IEEE 802.11p [27]. In the USA, 75 MHz frequency has been allocated to DSRC in 5.9 GHz frequency band. As shown in Fig. 3, the allocated spectrum is divided into seven channels of 10 MHz widths each. It supports data rates up to 27 Mbps (with 10 MHz) and can transmit up to 1000 m.

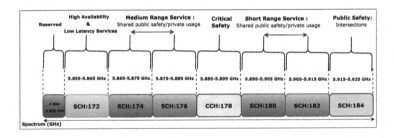

Fig. 3. DSRC frequency allocation in the USA for VANETs

Another very popular and emerging technology for VANETs is cellular-V2X (C-V2X), which is in its advancement phase. For V2I/I2V connectivity vehicles can use any available wireless access technology such as DSRC, Wi-Fi, mmWave, and LTE-A to which they are subscribed/authorized for access.

In the USA, Basic Safety Message (BSM) are defined in wireless access in vehicular environments (WAVE) protocol stack. BSM is periodically broadcasted (at 100 ms interval) over DSRC and contains information such as position, speed, direction, dimensions, and a pseudonym identifier to temporarily identifies the sender.

3.3 Adversary Model

In this work, we focus on an internal attacker that modify BSM to generate its false position and broadcast over DSRC. This malicious behavior is also known as position falsification attack.

As shown in the vehicular plane of the Fig. 3, the vehicle can overwhelm false information near intersections and create confusion for vehicles, which can severely affect critical safety applications of neighboring nodes. Since the message is from an insider, it gets accepted for processing by receiving vehicles. Thus, a wide variety of safety-related applications may get affected. Table 1 lists the types of attack modeled (parameters used) in the VeReMi dataset.

Table 1. Adversary parameters

Attack type	Description
Constant	Transmits a forged message with fixed position (pre-configured)
Constant offset	Transmits a forged message with fixed position by adding pre-configured offset
Random	Transmits a forged message with random position values from the simulation area
Random offset	Transmits a forged message with random position in a pre-configured rectangle around the node
Eventual stop	The vehicle behaves normally for a specified interval and then transmits the current position repeatedly

4 Proposed ML-Based Detection

In this section, we discuss our approach that includes ML-based models used, dataset, and feature description.

4.1 Machine Learning Models

Support Vector Machines (SVM). SVM is a supervised learning algorithm which is capable of solving both classification or regression challenges. However, it is more commonly used in classification problems. On a given training dataset

X, Y where X represents an input vector with n features and Y represents output data points are plotted on an n-dimensional plane with ith feature expressed as ith dimensional. Dataset is normalized to range 0 to 1 so that every feature are treated equally in the model and coefficients are not scaled differently according to the features magnitude. SVM tries to find a hyperplane to differentiate points into classes, and among different possible classification hyperplanes, it tries to find one which generalizes better to unseen test data by maximizing margin with the closest points.

Out of the whole dataset, only a few among them are close points, and hence only a subset of training points are required in actual classification process and needed to be kept in main memory which makes SVMs very efficient. SVM is mainly a 2-way Binary classifier, but it can be used for multiclass classification as well. In this paper, $|C|$ one-versus-rest binary classifiers are used to predict the class which gives maximum margin. Another strategy could be to use one-versus-one binary classifiers with all possible pairs of classes. At prediction time, class that is predicted by $(|C|(|C|+1))/2$. If the dataset is not linearly separable, then SVM transform these data points to a higher dimension using kernels such that data is separable by a hyperplane in the higher dimension. We used Radial basis function (RBF) kernel in our model, which is given by the following equation:

$$K(x,x') = exp(-||x - x'||^2/2\sigma^2) \tag{1}$$

Where $||x - x'||^2$ is the Euclidean distance between the two feature vector, original feature vector and feature vector with a higher dimension.

Logistic Regression. Logistic Regression is one of the basic algorithms to predict an classifying problem. The prediction is made using the logarithm of the "estimated odds of target variable". Given X as input vector, estimated probability is $p = 1/1 + e^{-(c+bX)}$. We have tried it by taking categorical features in one-hot representation.

4.2 VeReMi Dataset

The purpose of using the dataset is to have an initial baseline on which our detection mechanisms can be applied. We use open source dataset, which is made available for research studies. Use of existing dataset reduces the time required to perform simulation studies and makes things easier for us to apply the approach.

We used the VeReMi dataset [9] to train and test our models. This dataset is used as a reference for comparative studies between different ML-based misbehavior detection approach in VANETs. The dataset is based on Luxembourg traffic scenario (LuST) introduced by Codeca et al. [28] and used VEINS for the simulation of vehicles.

The VeReMi dataset consists of message logs for every vehicle in the simulation and a ground truth file that specifies the attacker's behavior. The local information from the vehicle is included through messages of a different type (representing periodic messages from a GPS module in the vehicle). The log file consists of local messages generated from traffic simulator SUMO and messages from other vehicles. Each log entry contains a reception time stamp, the claimed transmission time, the claimed sender, a simulation-wide unique message ID, a position vector, a speed vector, the RSSI, a position noise vector and a speed noise vector. Each time a message is sent it is also updated in the ground truth file which contains actual position/speed values and the attacker type. 0 is used for legitimate vehicles and 1, 2, 4, 8, 16 for 5 different types of attackers listed in Table 1 in respective order.

The dataset consists of 225 individual simulations with

- Five different attackers.
- Three different attacker densities.
- Three different traffic densities.
- Five repetitions for each parameter set (with different random seeds).

The dataset consists of a total of 225 simulation executions, split into three density categories.

- Low density has 35 to 39 vehicles.
- Medium density has between 97 and 108 vehicles.
- High density has between 491 and 519 vehicles.

Out of these vehicles, a subset of the vehicle is malicious. The decision is made by sampling a uniform distribution ([0; 1]) and comparing it to the attacker fraction parameter. All of the vehicles classified as attacker execute the same attack algorithm.

4.3   Feature Description

Feature selection plays a crucial role in machine learning classification accuracy can depend a lot on the features selected for training the model. Dimensionality relies on a number of features, it affects training time and is a powerful defense against overfitting.

We tried a different combination of features from the following set x, y, z position and speed coordinates, the difference between position and speed coordinates of sender and receiver. It is important to note that we only used those log entries which are received by a vehicle and not the ones generated by the vehicle itself. Various combination of features used in this work are listed in Table 2.

We used position as a feature because all the attacks are based on position falsification and hence attackers will have different trends of position values than legitimate vehicles. We added the difference of sender and receiver positions/speed to detect attackers of type 2 and 4. It should be considered because receiver cant receive signals from the certain physical threshold, hence if an attacker sends some random position which is beyond the theoretical range of communication, then the receiver would be able to detect that. We realized

Table 2. Combination of features used

Comb.	Features
1	a. x, y, z coordinates of a position
	b. x, y, z coordinates of speed
2	a. x, y, z coordinates of a position
	b. x, y, z coordinate difference of position between sender and receiver
3	a. x, y, z coordinates of a position
	b. x, y, z coordinates of speed
	c. x, y, z coordinate difference of position between sender and receiver
	d. x, y, z coordinate difference of speed between sender and receiver

that speed is not a useful feature because speed transmitted by both attackers and non-attackers is in a similar range. In the given dataset attacker tries doesn't make any falsification in its speed and hence it will not help the model distinguish between non-attackers and attackers. Our training time reduced significantly after removing speed from the features.

5   Results

In this section, we discuss the results that we achieved after the experiment. We used logistic regression (LR) without normalization and with normalization. We found that logistic regression achieves higher accuracy and works better with normalization. F1- the score is used as a metric for accuracy. The result graphs are shown in Figs. 4, and 5, respectively. Please note that we used logistic regression for binary classification (all attackers have attacker type 1 and 0 for non-attackers).

Our training time significantly reduced when we removed undesired features. As shown in Fig. 6, SVM binary classifier performed better than Logistic Regression. We achieved highest F1-score using SVM binary classifier, RBF() kernel and feature combination number 3.

F1 score is used for measuring accuracy when the distribution of positives and negatives in a dataset is highly skewed. F1 score is a combined metric as the harmonic average of both precision and recall. Precision is the ratio of correctly predicted positive (true positives) with total predicted positive data points (true positives + false positive). Recall is the ratio of correctly predicted positive values (true positives) with all data points that were actually in the positive class (true positive + false negative). In our experiments, we observed precision was slightly better than recall. Precision was close to 1 which means that out of vehicles predicted as attacker most of them were actual attacker which is a good sign that any non-attacker will not be discriminated in the network after getting misclassified. Recall in the observations were slightly lower compared to a precision which can be improved by adding more features and making the model more complex. The overall model is able to classify attackers with good recall and precision.

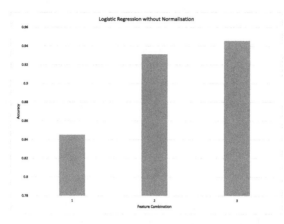

Fig. 4. LR without normalization

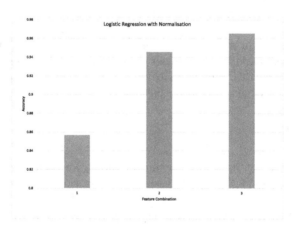

Fig. 5. LR with normalization

SVM performs better than logistic regression because it is less sensitive to outliers. A few outliers will significantly impact the loss function of logistic regression leading to distortion of the decision boundary with respect to general points. On the other hand, SVM tries to maximize the margin by taking a few points known as support vectors into consideration. Support Vector Machines generally trains faster than other regression models. And moreover, If a dataset

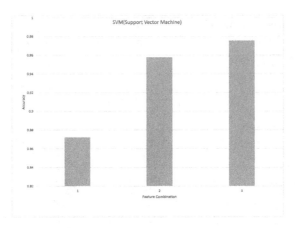

Fig. 6. SVM results

is not separable by a linear decision boundary then SVM outperforms linear regression. Different kernels can be used in SVM which transform data points to a higher dimensional space where transformed points can be linearly separable. We have used RBF (Radial Basis Function) kernel in our experiments which maps points to infinite dimensional space.

To further improve the performance of the model we can add features similar to simple speed check, which will train the model in such a way that vehicles which have inconsistencies between the rate of change of position and speed will be caught. We tested our model on the logs generated by the same simulation. We can test our model on a different dataset with different environmental conditions with the same log entries. Similar machine learning models can also be created for other types of misbehavior detection in VANETs.

6   Conclusion

In this paper, different machine learning methods are used to detect position falsification attack in VANETs. SVM with normalization performed better than logistic regression with or without normalization. Model accuracy depends a lot on feature selection. Further research work can be on multiple misbehavior modeling in VANETs and detection using the ML-based approach. Although traditional methods perform well, artificial neural networks can also be applied to evaluate the performance on the dataset.

Acknowledgments. The research work has been conducted in the Information Security Education and Awareness (ISEA) Lab of Indian Institute of Technology Guwahati. The authors would like to acknowledge IIT Guwahati and ISEA MeitY, India for the support.

References

1. Santa, J., Pereñíguez, F., Moragón, A., Skarmeta, A.F.: Experimental evaluation of CAM and DENM messaging services in vehicular communications. Transp. Res. Part C: Emerg. Technol. **46**, 98–120 (2014)
2. Kerrache, C.A., Calafate, C.T., Cano, J.C., Lagraa, N., Manzoni, P.: Trust management for vehicular networks: an adversary-oriented overview. IEEE Access **4**, 9293–9307 (2016)
3. Hasrouny, H., Samhat, A.E., Bassil, C., Laouiti, A.: VANet security challenges and solutions: a survey. Veh. Commun. **7**, 7–20 (2017)
4. Brecht, B., et al.: A security credential management system for V2X communications. IEEE Trans. Intell. Transp. Syst. (99), 1–22 (2018)
5. IEEE: IEEE Standard for Wireless Access in Vehicular Environments–Security Services for Applications and Management Messages. IEEE Std 1609.2-2016 (Revision of IEEE Std 1609.2-2013), pp. 1–240, March 2016
6. ETSI, T.: 102 940: Intelligent Transport Systems (ITS). Security; ITS communications security architecture and security management. Technical specification, European Telecommunications Standards Institute (2012)
7. Lu, Z., Qu, G., Liu, Z.: A survey on recent advances in vehicular network security, trust, and privacy. IEEE Trans. Intell. Transp. Syst. (2018)
8. Soleymani, S.A., et al.: Trust management in vehicular ad hoc network: a systematic review. EURASIP J. Wirel. Commun. Netw. **2015**(1), 146 (2015)
9. Van der Heijden, R.W., Lukaseder, T., Kargl, F.: VeReMi: a dataset for comparable evaluation of misbehavior detection in VANETs. arXiv preprint arXiv:1804.06701 (2018)
10. Van der Heijden, R.W., Dietzel, S., Leinmüller, T., Kargl, F.: Survey on misbehavior detection in cooperative intelligent transportation systems. arXiv preprint arXiv:1610.06810 (2016)
11. Khan, U., Agrawal, S., Silakari, S.: A detailed survey on misbehavior node detection techniques in vehicular ad hoc networks. In: Mandal, J.K., Satapathy, S.C., Sanyal, M.K., Sarkar, P.P., Mukhopadhyay, A. (eds.) Information Systems Design and Intelligent Applications. AISC, vol. 339, pp. 11–19. Springer, New Delhi (2015). https://doi.org/10.1007/978-81-322-2250-7_2
12. Zhang, J.: A survey on trust management for VANETs. In: International Conference on Advanced Information Networking and Applications (AINA), pp. 105–112. IEEE (2011)
13. Ma, S., Wolfson, O., Lin, J.: A survey on trust management for Intelligent Transportation System. In: Proceedings of the 4th ACM SIGSPATIAL International Workshop on Computational Transportation Science, pp. 18–23. ACM (2011)
14. Rawat, D.B., Bista, B.B., Yan, G., Weigle, M.C.: Securing vehicular ad-hoc networks against malicious drivers: a probabilistic approach. In: 2011 International Conference on Complex, Intelligent and Software Intensive Systems (CISIS), pp. 146–151. IEEE (2011)
15. Hsiao, H.C., Studer, A., Dubey, R., Shi, E., Perrig, A.: Efficient and secure threshold-based event validation for VANETs. In: Proceedings of the Fourth ACM Conference on Wireless Network Security, pp. 163–174. ACM (2011)
16. Zhuo, X., Hao, J., Liu, D., Dai, Y.: Removal of misbehaving insiders in anonymous VANETs. In: Proceedings of the 12th ACM International Conference on Modeling, Analysis and Simulation of Wireless and Mobile Systems, pp. 106–115. ACM (2009)

17. Leinmüller, T., Schmidt, R.K., Held, A.: Cooperative position verification-defending against roadside attackers 2.0. In: Proceedings of 17th ITS World Congress, pp. 1–8 (2010)
18. Bilogrevic, I., Manshaei, M.H., Raya, M., Hubaux, J.P.: Optimal revocations in ephemeral networks: a game-theoretic framework. In: 8th International Symposium on Modeling and Optimization in Mobile, Ad Hoc and Wireless Networks (WiOpt), pp. 21–30. IEEE (2010)
19. Stubing, H., Jaeger, A., Schmidt, C., Huss, S.A.: Verifying mobility data under privacy considerations in Car-to-X communication. In: 17th ITS World CongressITS JapanITS AmericaERTICO (2010)
20. Stübing, H., Firl, J., Huss, S.A.: A two-stage verification process for Car-to-X mobility data based on path prediction and probabilistic maneuver recognition. In: 2011 IEEE Vehicular Networking Conference (VNC), pp. 17–24. IEEE (2011)
21. Yang, Z., Yang, K., Lei, L., Zheng, K., Leung, V.C.: Blockchain-based decentralized trust management in vehicular networks. IEEE Internet of Things J. (2018)
22. Grover, J., Prajapati, N.K., Laxmi, V., Gaur, M.S.: Machine learning approach for multiple misbehavior detection in VANET. In: Abraham, A., Mauri, J.L., Buford, J.F., Suzuki, J., Thampi, S.M. (eds.) ACC 2011. CCIS, vol. 192, pp. 644–653. Springer, Heidelberg (2011). https://doi.org/10.1007/978-3-642-22720-2_68
23. Kang, M.J., Kang, J.W.: Intrusion detection system using deep neural network for in-vehicle network security. PloS One 11(6), e0155781 (2016)
24. Loukas, G., Vuong, T., Heartfield, R., Sakellari, G., Yoon, Y., Gan, D.: Cloud-based cyber-physical intrusion detection for vehicles using Deep Learning. IEEE Access 6, 3491–3508 (2018)
25. Taylor, A., Leblanc, S., Japkowicz, N.: Anomaly detection in automobile control network data with long short-term memory networks. In: 2016 IEEE International Conference on Data Science and Advanced Analytics (DSAA), pp. 130–139. IEEE (2016)
26. Ali Alheeti, K.M., Gruebler, A., McDonald-Maier, K.: Intelligent intrusion detection of grey hole and rushing attacks in self-driving vehicular networks. Computers 5(3), 16 (2016)
27. IEEE Std.: IEEE Standard for Information technology – Local and metropolitan area networks – Specific requirements – Part 11: Wireless LAN Medium Access Control (MAC) and Physical Layer (PHY) Specifications Amendment 6: Wireless Access in Vehicular Environments, pp. 1–51, July 2010
28. Codeca, L., Frank, R., Faye, S., Engel, T.: Luxembourg SUMO traffic (LuST) scenario: traffic demand evaluation. IEEE Intell. Transp. Syst. Mag. 9(2), 52–63 (2017)

Unsupervised Person Re-ID in Surveillance Feed Using Re-ranking

Mohit Kumar Singh[(✉)], Vijay Laxmi, and Neeta Nain

M.N.I.T Jaipur, Jaipur, India
{2017rcp9005,vlaxmi,nnain.cse}@mnit.ac.in

Abstract. With the increase of video feeds from the network of surveillance cameras and available sophisticated detection and bounding box techniques we have seen a jump in the use of deep learning models in the past years. These Deep Neural Network models are Supervised, in the sense that they require large labeled data samples. This hunger of more and more labeled data can be removed by moving on to Unsupervised learning. Despite of significant progress, very less attention is paid to unsupervised techniques. In our approach we tries to improve the accuracy of the Unsupervised Neural Network model by using re-ranking. K-mean algorithm is used to obtain the initial cluster as the samples are unlabeled initially and k-reciprocal nearest neighbor method is used to re-rank the output to remove false matches. Experiments are performed on DUKE and CUHK01 datasets.

Keywords: Supervised learning · Unsupervised learning ·
K nearest neighbour · CNN

1 Introduction

Person re-identification (re-ID) [1–6,36] has become very popular in the recent years due to its research significance and is primarily used in application areas such as video surveillance system, path detection, Activity-based human recognition and many other. Surveillance is the most crucial one as it includes object detection, object tracking, and classification of moving object or group of objects. The effectiveness of surveillance systems is judged by first how accurately (in shape and size) the system can detect an object or any suspicious behavior, and second by finding how reliable the system is with the change in environmental conditions such as lighting and background conditions.

Person re-id aims in identifying an object of interest in another viewing area or in the same when the object re-enters the frame after leaving it first. It is the need of today's world to identify terrorist attacks or other suspicious activities in the place of mass gatherings. Recently with the increase of video feeds available from the network of cameras installed in several smart cities for surveillance, we have significantly noticed the use of Deep Learning Systems for re-ID.

© Springer Nature Singapore Pte Ltd. 2019
S. Nandi et al. (Eds.): ISEA-ISAP 2018, CCIS 939, pp. 179–192, 2019.
https://doi.org/10.1007/978-981-13-7561-3_14

Person re-ID is primarily divided into Image-based and Video-based systems [1]. And the complete process of re-ID in a video-based system can be divided into Person Identification or Detection, Person Tracking and Person re-identification. Person identification and tracking in the video scene is a challenging task. We human masters this trick even if we losses the track of a person by checking for their appearance. This process becomes much more complicated in the case of a crowded scene. It will be cherry on the cake when we can master the capability of real-time re-identification in a crowded scene from surveillance video feeds with low-resolution availability.

However, real-time re-identification remains a challenging task as it is the process of matching correctly the two image of the same person having some commonness and uniqueness score [7] under substantial appearance, illumination, pose and viewing area changes. One of the reasons for using Deeply Trained Networks is that it is challenging to identify some of the low-level visible features for person identification such as skin color and other facial image feature due to very low-resolution availability.

Despite several impressive research on re-ID using Supervised methods, all these methods require a significant amount of training data, and less attention is given to unsupervised methods. In this paper, we provide an unsupervised approach to re-ID. This improved version of [38], make use of the trained model to extract deep features. Using clustering approach we obtained some original labels for our unlabelled data, we improve the clusters using the K-reciprocal method which is then used as input features to train the network. The advantage of this method is that it is a self-paced learning method as well as it provides the capability of refining the initial cluster which improves the training process significantly. The organization of the paper is as follow. Section 2 provides a brief insight into recent works, dataset and evaluation methods used. Section 3 provides details of the proposed algorithm and re-ranking approach. Section 4 includes implementation and results. Section 5 is the conclusion.

2   Recent Work

2.1   Image Based Re-ID Methods

Person re-ID is primarily divided into image, video and deep learning based systems.

Image based re-ID assumes that given a probe or query image q_j from query database having K images and the database of gallery $\mathcal{G}$ having N images, denoted by $(g_i)_{i=1}^N$ (Eq. 1). They belongs to M different identities.

$$\mathcal{G} = (g_i|i = 1, 2, \cdots N) \tag{1}$$

The identity of the query image q_j is obtained by checking the similarity between gallery images and the query image as in Eq. 2

$$q_j^{id} = arg\,min_{i \in 1,2,\cdots N} DIS(q_j, g_i), \quad id \in 1, 2, \cdots M \tag{2}$$

The distance function used (DIS), can be any of the distance metric [8]. Most commonly used metric is Mahalanobis distance (Eq. 3). Where M is a +ve semi definite matrix.

$$d(q_j, g_i) = (x_{q_j} - x_{g_i})^T M (x_{q_j} - x_{g_i}) \tag{3}$$

Image-based person re-ID is divided into Low-level feature based [9–17], and Attribute based approaches [18–23]. Colour and texture features are used as low-level features. Instead of using the low features it is better to use some mid-level descriptors that are more robust to image translation. Layne et al. [18] make use of 15 descriptors based on attire and soft biometric. Liu et al. [19] use improved Latent Dirichlet Allocation (LDA) method. Su et al. [21] use binary person semantic attributes of individuals with the same id from the different viewing area.

2.2 Deeply Learned Re-ID

The foundation stone for CNN based deep learning was laid down by LeCun in 1998 [24] by using LeNet-5, a 5-level CNN that can classify digits. Later on, Krizhevsky et al. [25] designed AlexNet and won the ImageNet Large Scale Visual Recognition Challenge (ILSVRC – 2012) by a large margin, and the race begins. Figure 1 depicts major milestone models for Deep Neural Network.

Broadly the CNN methods can be divided into two category Similarity Learning and Representation Learning [36]. Siamese model is used for similarity learning and is preferred when we have less number of training samples. The input to the Siamese model can be single image [26], the pair [27], triplet [28], or quadruplet [29] of images. Some of the initial works on CNN and Siamese model include [26–28, 30–33]. In [26] the input to the 2-CNN layers is horizontal overlapping parts of an image, and the outputs are combined to form a vector which is used to obtain the similarity between images using cosine similarity. Li et al. [30] make use of patch matching layer in different horizontal stripes. Wu et al. [31] use an even more extensive network called "PersonNet". Varior et al. [32] use LSTM (Long Short-Term Memory) module into a Siamese model which works as a memory. [27] use gating functions to enhance discriminative ability. Cheng et al. [28] proposed triplet loss function that takes three input images. A detailed justification of using triplet loss function can be found in [28].

Siamese model does not make use of the re-ID labels, and hence another model which seems promising is Classification model or identification model. Representation learning uses the classification model which is preferable when the training dataset is large enough. Softmax loss is mostly used in the classification model.

2.3 Dataset and Evaluation

Dataset. The bottleneck for deep learning model is the lack of training data. Several dataset for image based re-ID are available. Table 1 summarizes commonly used datasets. The smallest one is VIPeR, which consists of 632 ids with

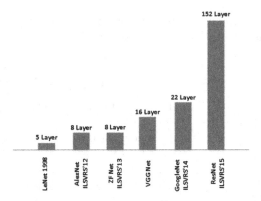

Fig. 1. Milestones models in the field of Deep Neural Network

2 images per ids. In order to reflect various scenarios GRID dataset was collected on a station, CUHK01, CUHK02, CUHK03 and Market-1501 were collected in a university campus. The datasets are improving by adding more and more ids and bounding box in order to provide ample amount of data to train deep CNN models.

As the size of the dataset increases, the bounding box are produced using detectors (DPM [28,35], ACF [34]) rather than hand-drawn. This can cause drop in re-ID accuracy, as the bounding box may deviate from the ideal position while using detectors. More detailed description of the dataset can be found in [6].

Table 1. Datasets used for image based re-ID

Dataset	Year	Individuals	No. of images
VIPeR	2007	632	1,264
iLIDS	2009	119	476
GRID	2009	250	1,275
CAVIAR	2011	72	610
PRID2011	2011	200	1,134
WARD	2012	70	4,786
CUHK01	2012	971	3,884
CUHK02	2013	1,816	7,264
CUHK03	2014	1,467	13,164
RAiD	2014	43	1,264
PRID 450S	2014	450	900
Market-1501	2015	1,501	32,668
DukeMTMC	2016	1,812	36,411

Evaluation. The evaluation of a re-ID system can be performed using Cumulative Match Curve (CMC) and Receiver Operating Characteristic Curve (ROC). CMC [39] is used as a measure to evaluate [1:m] identification system, where as ROC is used for [1:1] identification system. CMC give the performance of the query matching system that returns the ranked list of matching candidates from gallery $\mathcal{G}$. To obtain CMC, the query image is matched with every gallery image and a total K × M scores are obtained.

$$Score_j = [s(q_j, g_1), s(q_j, g_2), \cdots, s(q_j, g_M)], \quad j = 1, 2, \cdots, K \quad (4)$$

The scores are sorted as in Eq. 5 and a rank is provided to every query image based on the position of the matched image in the sorted list.

$$s(q_j, g_1) \geqslant s(q_j, g_2) \geqslant \cdots \geqslant s(q_j, g_M) \quad (5)$$

Now we have a rank associated with each query $Rank_{q_j}$ where $1 \leqslant Rank_{q_j} \leqslant M$. The CMC curve estimates the distribution of these ranks. Such that higher CMC(1) indicates better re-ID system.

$$CMC(1) = \frac{1}{n}(\text{Number of query image with rank} \leqslant 1) \quad (6)$$

The disadvantage of the CMC is that this method can not be used in the scenario when we have multiple ground truth for each query. Hence when multiple ground truth exist in the gallery [17] proposed a method Mean Average Precision (mAP) for the evaluation of the identification system.

3 Proposed Approach

3.1 Problem Definition

From the previous section, it is clear that intensive work has been done on deeply learned person re-ID using supervised learning method. The hunger of more and more data for training is the disadvantage of the supervised methods, and hence more effort has to be taken toward unsupervised learning methods.

In this section, we provide and improved unsupervised learning which is based on the progressive learning method [38]. This method use, an initial trained model (ResNet-50 trained on ImageNet). This initial model is fine tuned on some arbitrary unlabelled data other than the unlabelled dataset which is used for validation and testing. In step second, this fine tuned model is used for unsupervised learning, to extract some features from the unlabelled data. As the data are unlabelled, in step third we have to use some clustering algorithms to obtain initial clusters. Using some threshold on the distance matric use by the clustering algorithm, few samples are selected known as Reliable samples (Samples having significant similarity with cluster center). In step four, only Reliable samples are used to fine tune the original model to generate a new trained model. Step second, third and fourth are repeated until the model stabilizes. And at last the trained model obtained through subsequent refining is used to extract the feature from the samples used for testing.

The effectiveness of this process depends on the clustering approach used and the number of Reliable features generated which are used to train the model. This improved Unsupervised Learning approach increases the number of Reliable samples generated in each step and in turn improves the training. Less Reliable sample means more iterations of step second, third and fourth. Higher Reliable sample generation means fast and improved training.

3.2   Formulation

Let us consider that we are provided with N unlabelled dataset or images denoted by x_i. These images may belongs to K different individuals. Our task is to assign labels or ids to every unlabelled sample as in Eq. 7, using some model $M_{CNN+Classification}(.; pram)$, which takes as input the samples x_i and initial parameter $pram$.

$$x_i^{id} = M_{CNN+Classification}(x_i; pram), \text{Where } i = 1, 2, \cdots, N \qquad (7)$$

The label vector X_ID will contains all the assigned labels to the input samples (Eq. 8)

$$X\_ID = \left[(x_1^{id}, x_2^{id}, \cdots, x_N^{id}), |(1 \leqslant x_i^{id} \leqslant K) \right] \qquad (8)$$

The model $M_{CNN+Classification}$ used here consists of CNN module with initial learned parameter θ and a classification module with parameter w at the end. The CNN module takes x_i as input and generates corresponding features f_i using parameter θ.

$$f_i = M_{CNN}(x_i; \theta), \text{Where, } i = 1, 2, \cdots, N \qquad (9)$$

Few Reliable features out of the N features generated, are selected and before training these feature are refined using automatic Re-ranking to get final refined reliable features which are then used for training. All the features are assigned a selection indicator value $v_i \in \{0, 1\}$, such that if $v_i = 1$ means the feature is selected else rejected ($v_i = 0$). A selection indicator vector V is used which contains all the values as $V = [v_1, v_2, \cdots v_N]$. After repeated t training's, the final learned model $M_{CNN}(.; \theta_t)$ is used to extract features from the testing samples which are then fed to the classification module $M_{Classification}(.; w)$ to obtain the final class labels. θ_t is the improved parameter obtained by the subsequent training of the CNN model on the training set. The process is depicted in Fig. 2.

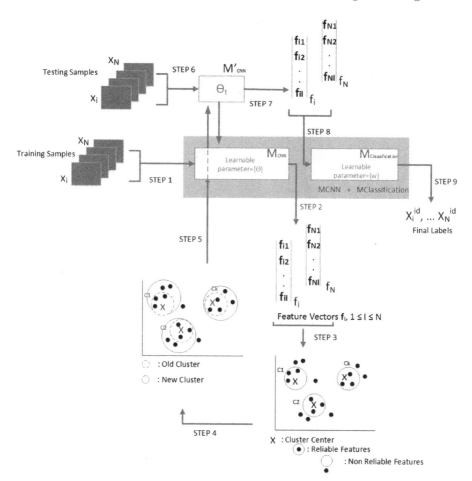

Fig. 2. Illustration of the complete process. The model $M_{CNN} + M_{Classification}$ is ResNet-50 pretrained on ImageNet. STEP 1: Unlabelled training sample are used as input. STEP 2: M_{CNN} submodule of the trained model is used to extract feature vector from each training samples. STEP 3: K-means clustering is used to obtain initial clusters and using distance metric the features are grouped into individual clusters. STEP 4: Features selected to form cluster are reliable features and those left are Non-reliable. Using K-reciprocal neighbourhood some of the non reliable features are selected to refine old clusters and their labels are defined using K-means approach. STEP 5: Clustered features and labels are used to generate a fine-tune submodule M_{CNN}. After $'t'$ iteration of the STEP 2, 3, 4 and 5 a new fine-tuned module with new parameter θ_t is obtained. STEP 6: This fine-tuned model of STEP 5 is used to extract features from testing samples in STEP 7. STEP 8: The extracted features are classified using classification submodule $M_{Classification}$ to generate labels for the testing samples.

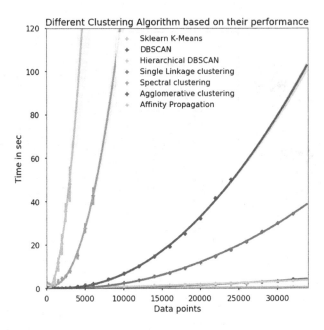

Fig. 3. Performance comparision of different clustering approaches

The idea of this approach is to minimize the equations below:

$$\arg\min_{x_i^{id}, C_k} \Sigma_{k=1}^{K} \Sigma_{x_i^{id}=k}(DIS(x_i^k, C_k)) \tag{10}$$

Where, $DIS(x_i^k, C_k) = ||(M_{CNN}(x_i; \theta) - C_k)||^2$

$$\arg\min_{V} \Sigma_{k=1}^{K} \Sigma_{x_i^{id}=k} v_i DIS(x_i^k, C_k) - \lambda ||V||_1 \tag{11}$$

Such that, $v_i \in \{0, 1\}$, and $\Sigma_{x_i^{id}=k} v_i \geqslant 1, \forall k$

The step in Eq. 10 infers to the label generation process using the clustering method. After feature generation in Eq. 9, these features are clustered using K-means clustering approaches. The clusters should be such that it minimizes the distance between the feature and the cluster center. There are several available approaches such as K-means, Affinity Propagation, Mean Shift, Agglomerative, DBSCAN, and HDBSCAN. The performance analysis for the clustering algorithms is illustrated in Fig. 3. HDBSCAN is a density-based clustering approach and is faster compared to K-means, but K-mean is best suited for data samples where no. of clusters are known in advanced.

After generating initial clusters and labels using K-means, Eq. 11 is used to select reliable features that are close enough to the cluster center. A sample is reliable, if the distance of its feature from the cluster center is smaller than λ.

λ is the threshold that defines which sample or feature to consider reliable, the value should be small as possible to remove the false matches from considering as reliable samples. Specially $\lambda = 0.85$ yields superior accuracy [38]. The condition $\Sigma_{x_i^{id}=k} v_i \geqslant 1, \forall k$ makes sure that the clusters are not blank, and at least one sample (Cluster center) must be there.

As we are dealing with unlabelled data, clustering and reliable features selection is very crucial for this algorithm. First of all, the feature selection must be pure and must not contain any False Matches. We are completely dependent on K-means and distance metric for reliable feature generation, but quality of cluster is dependent on the selection of initial cluster centroid which are generated using k-mean++ algorithm. Second, we are only checking for the distance between the cluster centers and feature. What if a feature which is not close enough to the cluster centers, but bears enough resemblance with the neighbouring reliable features. Now this is where we can increase the number of reliable features generated, having a check that no false matches should be included.

3.3   Re-ranking

After an initial ranking list is obtained it is a good practice to include the re ranking step to improve the ranks. No further requirement of training samples is the main advantage of this step and can be directly applied to the previous step. The underlying assumption is that if an image is returned as the true match of the query image, than it can subsequently be used to find other true matches in its neighbourhood. Inclusion of False Matches may be a problem in K nearest neighbour searching approach and to deal with it we applied a check using distance threshold (λ). In literature, the K- reciprocal nearest neighbour [37] is the effective solution to the problem of false match.

3.4   K-Reciprocal Nearest Neighbour

We can define $N(q, k)$ as the k-nearest neighbour of the query image as:

$$N(q, k) = (g_1, g_2, \cdots, g_k), |\# \text{ of samples in } N(q, k) = k \tag{12}$$

The K-reciprocal nearest neighbour can be defined as,

$$\mathcal{R}(q, k) = \{g_i | (g_i \in N(q, k)) \wedge (q \in N(g_i, k))\} \tag{13}$$

Equation 13 states that the if g_i is selected as the true match for query q, we can find other true matches in the neighbourhood of g_i with the condition that q must also be there. K-reciprocal nearest neighbour can be easily implemented in our approach to improve the generation of reliable features, by considering our cluster center as query q and selected reliable features as $g_i \in N(q, k)$. The new distance between q and g_i can be calculated using Jaccards metric of K-reciprocal approach as given in Eq. 14. Here $\mathcal{R}^*$ is the improved version of Eq. 13, so that no False match is included due to variation in illumination, pose and view.

$$d_J(q, g_i) = 1 - \frac{|\mathcal{R}^*(q, k) \cap \mathcal{R}^*(g_i, k)|}{|\mathcal{R}^*(q, k) \cup \mathcal{R}^*(g_i, k)|} \tag{14}$$

In order to consider the importance of Euclidean distance in re-ranking the final distance is changed to the one in Eq. 15 and is used to refine the reliable feature selection step.

$$d^*(q, g_i) = (1 - \lambda_J)d_J(q, g_i) + \lambda_J d(q, g_i) \tag{15}$$

Where, $\lambda_J \in [0, 1]$ is different than the KNN distance threshold (λ) one used in Eq. 11, and is used to penalize the features g_i that are far away from the query q. When $\lambda_J = 0$, K-reciprocal distance $d_J(q, g_i)$ is used and when $\lambda_J = 1$ Euclidean distance $d(q, g_i)$ is used. The K-reciprocal approach is depicted in Fig. 4. Figure 5 shows the improvement in the no. of reliable feature generation using the re-ranking method.

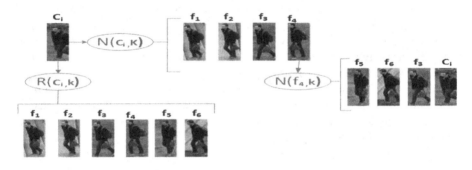

Fig. 4. Illustration of K-reciprocal neighbours approach. C_i is the cluster center and $N(C_i, K)$ is K-nearest neighbour to the cluster center. $\mathcal{R}(C_i, K)$ is the K-reciprocal neighbour to the cluster center. Feature f_4 lies in the K-nearest neighbour of the cluster center C_i. This illustration shows that we can add more reliable features in the cluster of C_i from $N(f_i, K)$ using $\mathcal{R}(C_i, K)$ based on Eq. 13

After repeated clustering and feature selection process of Eqs. 10, 11 and 15 which are used to fine tune the model, Eq. 16 is used to calculate the loss for the classification module.

$$\Sigma_{i=1}^{N} v_i \mathcal{L} M_{Classification}(x_i^{id}, M_{CNN}(x_i; \theta_t); w) \tag{16}$$

Here, $\mathcal{L}$ denotes the loss from the classification model. The inputs to the classification model are the labeled samples x_i^{id} (which is obtained using the fine tuned CNN model $M_{CNN}(x_i; \theta_t)$), classification parameter (w) and the selection indicator v_i.

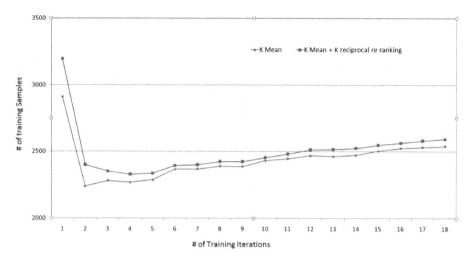

Fig. 5. Impact of using K-reciprocal re-ranking to improve the numbers of reliable feature generation. During iteration 1 only 2910 samples out of the total 3500 are selected using the threshold λ, in order to remove some false match cases. The drop in the reliable sample generation from iteration 1 to 2 is because initially the CNN model was trained on the dataset other than the training dataset and hence classifies more samples as reliable during iteration 1. After first training iteration on actual training set number of reliable features decreases. After subsequent training the model becomes more and more trained and hence from iteration 2 onwards the number of reliable features increases.

Table 2. Improved re-ID tested on Duke dataset

Method	CUHK01				
	rank-1	rank-5	rank-10	rank-20	mAP
Duke	0.375673	0.525135	0.600987	0.6669666	0.205698

4 Experiments

A ResNet-50 model pre-trained on ImageNet is used as our initial CNN model. A dropout of 0.5 is set just after the CNN layer. Every image is resized to 224×224. Parameter λ, which is used to select reliable features is set to 0.85. Parameter λ_J used in jaccards distance is set to 0.3. We have trained our model for 18 iterations with 10 epochs/iteration. The maximum saturation limit achieved was 2,593 reliable image out of 3,884 total images used for training.

The trained model was fine-tuned on CUHK01 dataset having only 3,884 images and is tested on Duke dataset with 17,661 gallery images and 2,228 query images. The result is summarized in Table 2 with Mean Average Precision (mAP) and rank outputs.

5 Conclusion

As discussed earlier that the hunger of more and more labeled samples is the disadvantage of Supervised learning algorithm. It is very tedious to gather labeled sample and have various problems when using automated tools.

In this paper we discussed an unsupervised approach of person re-id and tried to improve the reliable feature generation step using K-reciprocal nearest neighbour method. The reliable features are used to train the deep neural network model, and improving feature generation helps improving the training. The experimental results are provided using small datasets and can be further improved by providing training on larger datasets available such as Market and DukeMTMC.

References

1. Zheng, L., Yang, Y., Hauptmann, A.G.: Person re-identification: past, present and future. arXiv preprint arXiv:1610.02984, 10 October 2016
2. Martinel, N., Foresti, G.L., Micheloni, C.: Person reidentification in a distributed camera network framework. IEEE Trans. Cybern. **47**(11), 3530–3541 (2017)
3. Ma, A.J., Yuen, P.C., Li, J.: Domain transfer support vector ranking for person re-identification without target camera label information. In: Proceedings of the IEEE International Conference on Computer Vision, pp. 3567–3574 (2013)
4. Ma, A.J., Li, J., Yuen, P.C., Li, P.: Cross-domain person reidentification using domain adaptation ranking SVMs. IEEE Trans. Image Process. **24**(5), 1599–1613 (2015)
5. Liao, S., Hu, Y., Zhu, X., Li, S.Z.: Person re-identification by local maximal occurrence representation and metric learning. In: Proceedings of the IEEE Conference on Computer Vision and Pattern Recognition, pp. 2197–2206 (2015)
6. Bedagkar-Gala, A., Shah, S.K.: A survey of approaches and trends in person reidentification. Image Vis. Comput. **32**(4), 270–86 (2014)
7. Xu, Y., Ma, B., Huang, R., Lin, L.: Person search in a scene by jointly modeling people commonness and person uniqueness. In: Proceedings of the 22nd ACM International Conference on Multimedia, 3 November 2014, pp. 937–940. ACM (2014)
8. Yang, L., Jin, R.: Distance metric learning: a comprehensive survey, vol. 2, no. 2, p. 4. Michigan State Universiy, 19 May 2006
9. Farenzena, M., Bazzani, L., Perina, A., Murino, V., Cristani, M.: Person re-identification by symmetry-driven accumulation of local features. In: 2010 IEEE Conference on Computer Vision and Pattern Recognition (CVPR), 13 June 2010, pp. 2360–2367. IEEE (2010)
10. Gheissari, N., Sebastian, T.B., Hartley, R.: Person reidentification using spatiotemporal appearance. In: Null, 17 June 2006, pp. 1528–1535. IEEE (2006)
11. Gray, D., Tao, H.: Viewpoint invariant pedestrian recognition with an ensemble of localized features. In: Forsyth, D., Torr, P., Zisserman, A. (eds.) ECCV 2008. LNCS, vol. 5302, pp. 262–275. Springer, Heidelberg (2008). https://doi.org/10.1007/978-3-540-88682-2_21
12. Mignon, A., Jurie, F.: PCCA: a new approach for distance learning from sparse pairwise constraints. In: 2012 IEEE Conference on Computer Vision and Pattern Recognition (CVPR), 16 June 2012, pp. 2666–2672. IEEE (2012)

13. Shen, Y., Lin, W., Yan, J., Xu, M., Wu, J., Wang, J.: Person re-identification with correspondence structure learning. In: Proceedings of the IEEE International Conference on Computer Vision, pp. 3200–3208 (2015)
14. Das, A., Chakraborty, A., Roy-Chowdhury, A.K.: Consistent re-identification in a camera network. In: Fleet, D., Pajdla, T., Schiele, B., Tuytelaars, T. (eds.) ECCV 2014. LNCS, vol. 8690, pp. 330–345. Springer, Cham (2014). https://doi.org/10.1007/978-3-319-10605-2_22
15. Pedagadi, S., Orwell, J., Velastin, S., Boghossian, B.: Local fisher discriminant analysis for pedestrian re-identification. In: Proceedings of the IEEE Conference on Computer Vision and Pattern Recognition, pp. 3318–3325 (2013)
16. Liu, X., Song, M., Tao, D., Zhou, X., Chen, C., Bu, J.: Semi-supervised coupled dictionary learning for person re-identification. In: Proceedings of the IEEE Conference on Computer Vision and Pattern Recognition, pp. 3550–3557 (2014)
17. Zheng, L., Shen, L., Tian, L., Wang, S., Wang, J., Tian, Q.: Scalable person re-identification: a benchmark. In: Proceedings of the IEEE International Conference on Computer Vision, pp. 1116–1124 (2015)
18. Layne, R., Hospedales, T.M., Gong, S., Mary, Q.: Person re-identification by attributes. In: BMVC 2012, vol. 2, no. 3, p. 8, September 2012
19. Liu, X., Song, M., Zhao, Q., Tao, D., Chen, C., Bu, J.: Attribute-restricted latent topic model for person re-identification. Pattern Recogn. **45**(12), 4204–4213 (2012)
20. Liu, C., Gong, S., Loy, C.C., Lin, X.: Person re-identification: what features are important? In: Fusiello, A., Murino, V., Cucchiara, R. (eds.) ECCV 2012. LNCS, vol. 7583, pp. 391–401. Springer, Heidelberg (2012). https://doi.org/10.1007/978-3-642-33863-2_39
21. Su, C., Yang, F., Zhang, S., Tian, Q., Davis, L.S., Gao, W.: Multi-task learning with low rank attribute embedding for person re-identification. In: Proceedings of the IEEE International Conference on Computer Vision, pp. 3739–3747 (2015)
22. Shi, Z., Hospedales, T.M., Xiang, T.: Transferring a semantic representation for person re-identification and search. In: Proceedings of the IEEE Conference on Computer Vision and Pattern Recognition, pp. 4184–4193 (2015)
23. Li, D., Zhang, Z., Chen, X., Ling, H., Huang, K.: A richly annotated dataset for pedestrian attribute recognition. arXiv preprint arXiv:1603.07054, 23 March 2016
24. LeCun, Y., Bottou, L., Bengio, Y., Haffner, P.: Gradient-based learning applied to document recognition. Proc. IEEE **86**(11), 2278–2324 (1998)
25. Krizhevsky, A., Sutskever, I., Hinton, G.E.: Imagenet classification with deep convolutional neural networks. In: Advances in Neural Information Processing Systems, pp. 1097–1105 (2012)
26. Yi, D., Lei, Z., Liao, S., Li, S.Z.: Deep metric learning for person re-identification. In: 2014 22nd International Conference on Pattern Recognition (ICPR), 24 August 2014, pp. 34–39. IEEE (2014)
27. Varior, R.R., Haloi, M., Wang, G.: Gated siamese convolutional neural network architecture for human re-identification. In: Leibe, B., Matas, J., Sebe, N., Welling, M. (eds.) ECCV 2016. LNCS, vol. 9912, pp. 791–808. Springer, Cham (2016). https://doi.org/10.1007/978-3-319-46484-8_48
28. Cheng, D., Gong, Y., Zhou, S., Wang, J., Zheng, N.: Person re-identification by multi-channel parts-based CNN with improved triplet loss function. In: Proceedings of the IEEE Conference on Computer Vision and Pattern Recognition, pp. 1335–1344 (2016)
29. Chen, W., Chen, X., Zhang, J., Huang, K.: Beyond triplet loss: a deep quadruplet network for person re-identification. In: IEEE Conference on Computer Vision and Pattern Recognition (CVPR), 1 July 2017, vol. 2, no. 8 (2017)

30. Li, W., Zhao, R., Xiao, T., Wang, X.: DeepReID: deep filter pairing neural network for person re-identification. In: Proceedings of the IEEE Conference on Computer Vision and Pattern Recognition, pp. 152–159 (2014)

31. Wu, L., Shen, C., Hengel, A.V.: PersonNet: person re-identification with deep convolutional neural networks. arXiv preprint arXiv:1601.07255, 27 January 2016

32. Varior, R.R., Shuai, B., Lu, J., Xu, D., Wang, G.: A siamese long short-term memory architecture for human re-identification. In: Leibe, B., Matas, J., Sebe, N., Welling, M. (eds.) ECCV 2016. LNCS, vol. 9911, pp. 135–153. Springer, Cham (2016). https://doi.org/10.1007/978-3-319-46478-7_9

33. Liu, H., Feng, J., Qi, M., Jiang, J., Yan, S.: End-to-end comparative attention networks for person re-identification. arXiv preprint arXiv:1606.04404, 14 June 2016

34. Su, C., Zhang, S., Xing, J., Gao, W., Tian, Q.: Deep attributes driven multi-camera person re-identification. In: Leibe, B., Matas, J., Sebe, N., Welling, M. (eds.) ECCV 2016. LNCS, vol. 9906, pp. 475–491. Springer, Cham (2016). https://doi.org/10.1007/978-3-319-46475-6_30

35. Felzenszwalb, P.F., Girshick, R.B., McAllester, D., Ramanan, D.: Object detection with discriminatively trained part-based models. IEEE Trans. Pattern Anal. Mach. Intell. **32**(9), 1627–1645 (2010)

36. Dollár, P., Appel, R., Belongie, S., Perona, P.: Fast feature pyramids for object detection. IEEE Trans. Pattern Anal. Mach. Intell. **36**(8), 1532–1545 (2014)

37. Zhong, Z., Zheng, L., Cao, D., Li, S.: Re-ranking person re-identification with k-reciprocal encoding. In: 2017 IEEE Conference on Computer Vision and Pattern Recognition (CVPR), 21 July 2017, pp. 3652–3661. IEEE (2017)

38. Fan, H., Zheng, L., Yan, C., Yang, Y.: Unsupervised person re-identification: clustering and fine-tuning. ACM Trans. Multimed. Comput. Commun. Appl. (TOMM) **14**(4), 83 (2018)

39. Bolle, R.M., Connell, J.H., Pankanti, S., Ratha, N.K., Senior, A.W.: The relation between the ROC curve and the CMC. In: Null, 17 October 2005, pp. 15–20. IEEE (2005)

An Approach to Meta-Alert Generation for Anomalous TCP Traffic

Deeksha Kushwah[1(✉)], Rajni Ranjan Singh[1],
and Deepak Singh Tomar[2]

[1] Department of CSE and IT,
Madhav Institute of Technology and Science, Gwalior, India
deekshakushwah0@gmail.com, rrsingh@mitsgwalior.in
[2] Department of CSE, Maulana Azad National Institute of Technology,
Bhopal, India
deepaktomar@manit.ac.in

Abstract. This is the era of digitization. Almost every service is online these days. As per an estimate till 2020, there will be 730 million internet users, 175 million online shoppers, 70% E-commerce transaction will be via mobile, and 50% travel transactions will be online in India [1]. Along with the growth of online services, the percentage of online crime is also increasing. Online services utilize internet protocols for functioning. TCP is the most commonly used transport layer protocol over the web. Many attackers utilize anomalous TCP flags to scan a system. Therefore it is crucial to research and adopt ways to detect and prevent the TCP packets which contains anomalous TCP flags. Intrusion Detection System is a hardware/software system which is used to detect and prevent attacks. However, it may generate many/false alerts. It is a time-consuming process to manually examine these huge numbers of alerts. Hence, it would be beneficial to generate meta-alerts for similar alerts. In this research work, an approach has been proposed to detect, log and generate meta-alerts for the packets, which contain anomalous TCP flags. To analyze the performance and usefulness of the proposed method an experiment has been carried out using real network traffic, and four well-known datasets i.e. MIT/LL 1998, MIT/LL 1999, Honeynet, and MACCDC dataset. It is observed that overall 99.96% alerts have been reduced. A comparative analysis has been carried out between the proposed work and existing work and it is observed that the proposed method gives better result.

Keywords: Intrusion detection system · Meta-alert generation ·
Alerts reduction · DARPA dataset

1 Introduction

From the very beginning of the internet, nobody could have imagined that the development of technologies would have lead to radical change in everyday lives. Online services like online trading, online marketing, online banking etc., is increased exponentially in the past few years. As a result of the boost in online services there exists an uncalculated risk because of the variety of attack that is being performed over the

© Springer Nature Singapore Pte Ltd. 2019
S. Nandi et al. (Eds.): ISEA-ISAP 2018, CCIS 939, pp. 193–216, 2019.
https://doi.org/10.1007/978-981-13-7561-3_15

internet every day. The infinite numbers of attacks make network systems security under potential violation. Consequently, the protection of network systems, organizations, and government agencies are strongly required. So it is utmost important to secure the cyberspace. Online services make connections using protocols. The Protocol is a set of rules which are used for governing communication. TCP & UDP are the two most important protocols for communicating over the cyberspace. Between these two, TCP is a highly used protocol because of its reliability. Generally, 90% of connections over the internet are made by TCP. The brief description of TCP protocol is given below.

A. Transmission Control Protocol

TCP is one of the transport layer protocols in the TCP/IP suite [2]. It provides full duplex, process-to-process, and connection-oriented service. Connection establishment, data transfer, and connection termination are the three phases of a TCP connection. In TCP protocol, a packet is called a segment. A segment consists of two fields namely; header fields and a data field for the application program. The size of a header is 20 bytes without the option. A header of a segment consists of several fields. The proposed work is focused on the Anomalous TCP flags. There are 6 different control fields/flags are defined by the control fields, which are shown in Fig. 1.

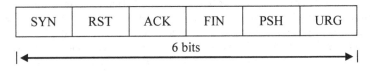

Fig. 1. Control field.

A brief description of the functionality of the TCP flags are shown here-

(1) **SYN flag.** It is used for synchronizing the sequence numbers. The two TCP must synchronize on one another's initial sequence number for a connection to be established. This is completed with an exchange of segments carrying initial sequence numbers and SYN (for Synchronize) control bit. An SYN segment consumes one sequence number but it cannot carry data.

(2) **ACK flag.** A successful receipt of the packet is indicated by ACK (used for Acknowledgement) flag. It depicts that acknowledgment is valid in a particular segment. If carrying no data an ACK segment does not consume sequence number.

(3) **FIN flag.** During an established connection, when the last packets are exchanged between two entities, then FIN flag appears. This flag is used to terminate the successfully created connection. It can be just a control segment or can include the last chunk of data. If it does not carry data then it consumes one sequence number.

(4) **RST flag.** A segment, which is not intended for the existing connection, whenever arrives an RST (for RESET) must be sent. This flag is used for reset the connection. A reset is sent in response to any incoming segment except another reset

if the connection does not exist. A TCP should permit data to be included in received RST segment.

(5) **URG flag.** This control flag implies that the urgent field is significant. The urgent pointer set segments do not have to wait until previously arrived segments are consumed by the receiver rather they sent directly and processed immediately. To yield the urgent pointer this field must be added to the segment sequence number. At least one data octet to be sent to send the urgent indication. To sum up, segments sent to the destination TCP will have the urgent pointer set, if the URG (for URGENT) flag is set. The urgent condition is signaled by the receiving TCP, to the receiving process, if the urgent pointer indicates that the data pre-existing the urgent pointer has not been consumed by the receiving processes.

(6) **PSH flag.** PSH (for PUSH) flag is used to assure the sender that all the data they have submitted to the TCP, has been transmitted. A push causes the TCP to forward and deliver data up to the receiver. Each time a push flag is associated with data it causes the buffer to promptly send the data to the application even if the buffer is not filled. This method is extensively used in real-time applications because of its significance in avoiding the TCP buffering mechanism.

Although TCP flags are used to indicate the function of the connection but a lot of intruders use them to invade a system. The intruders use anomalous flags to scan a system. Anomalous flags usually contain an invalid combination of flags and do not appear in normal traffic. An attempt to invade a system by violating various aspects such as the qualities of the services, confidentiality, availability, or integrity in the system is called intrusion. For example - Port scanning is the technique used to probe a host or server for open ports. The port scan method a machine sends packets to a target machine with TCP flags set and then on the basis of the target machine's response it decides the state of a port. It is one of the reconnaissance technique attacker used to intrude into a system. There are several ways in which an intrusion can be detected. Intrusion detection systems (IDS) are the one way to detect intrusions. Here, we discussed an intrusion detection system, their types based on analyzed activity and detection method.

B. Intrusion Detection System

Intrusion detection systems attempt to detect system abuse or intruders by gathering information from a computer network. It can be hardware, software, or a combination of both. It is employed to detect suspicious activity both at the host level or network level. It may have different capabilities. These capabilities are depending on how complex and sophisticated the components are. It can be classified based on the detection method or analyzed activity.

Snort is a cost-effective, high performance, libpcap-based [3] packet sniffer and logger. It works as a network intrusion detection system. It was originally intended to work as a packet sniffer. It is developed by Roesch in 1998 [4]. It fulfills the needs of many organizations because of its robust and cost-effective NIDS solutions.

It is open-source software and free of cost available on the internet. It is used for scanning the data in transmission on the network. Snort uses the libpcap library for filter parsing, packet capture, and opening the interface. It is divided logically into different components.

The main issue with existing intrusion detection systems is that they generate a high volume of low-level alerts which are hardly manageable. The analysis and management of this much amount of information is a time-consuming task. So we need to fuse those alerts in order to process more rapidly. In the presented paper, a method is presented by us to fuse the same type of alert and generate a high level of alert called meta-alerts. So instead of analyzing the whole lot of alerts in a great amount of time, we can analyze them in less time and in a hassle-free way.

The rest of this paper is managed as follows: Sect. 2 related works have been discussed. Section 3 presents the data sets that were analyzed. Section 4 introduces the method we proposed to generate meta-alerts based on the TCP flags. Section 5 confers a detailed description of the experimental setup and the results we have got. In Sect. 6 conclusion and future work are discussed.

2 Related Work

In this section, a review of the existing literature has been carried out.

Debar and Wespi [5] designed an aggregation and correlation algorithm which acquire and merge intrusion alerts together. Their algorithm is divided into three phases; processing of alerts, the correlation relationship, and the situation. In the first phase, the incoming alerts processed by extracting common information. In the second phase, it creates a correlation relationship by checking duplicate and consequences. Further, in the third phase, the aggregation relationships created through the situations. In their proposed technique, the alerts are aggregated into situations, which are based on any of the combinations of the three attributes i.e. alert class, target, and source. Author slices time to 2 s as a time window and the aggregation should only be performed within a time window.

Siraj and Vaughn [6] discuss the use of cognitive modeling of cause and effect relationship in a distributed environment to correlate alerts. The authors presented cognitive modeling as a generalization over repeated experiences where knowledge acquires through perception and experience. In the presented work, a casual knowledge-based inference technique with fuzzy cognitive modeling is used to correlate alerts by discovering the causal relationship in alert data. However, the presented approach is not able to deal with unknown alerts.

Siraj and Vaughn [7] presented a new alert correlation technique that utilizes fuzzy cognitive modeling with generalization to correlate alerts that are linked in multi-staged attacks. Their proposed technique has developed an abstract incident model for alert correlation with generalized security events to deal with scalability issues in sensor fusion. In the abstract incident model, an event can cause other event to occur or it can occur because of other events occurring in the system. The positive advantage of their alert correlation technique with abstract incident modeling has been to link together alerts that are involved in multi-staged coordinated attacks by considering both evidence of attacks presented in the sensor reports and the possible occurrence of such attacks.

Tedesco and Aickelin [8] demonstrate an algorithm which protects network intrusion detection systems from alert flooding attacks. The developed algorithm adjoins two algorithms, i.e. an existing alert correlation algorithm and the throttling algorithm. The throttling algorithm is a token bucket filter algorithm which controls the rate of data flow. The main objective of the author is to reduce the alert throughput if any alert flooding attack is performed whilst minimize the odds of missing crucial alerts.

Harang and Guarino [9] developed a forward greedy algorithm. The purpose of the algorithm is to detect the set of distinct factors, which increases the number of elements in an aggregated alert. Whilst reducing the hamming distance between any pair of alerts in the aggregate. The authors apply this method on 30 days of snort data and get average 83.2% reduction in analyst-visible snort alerts.

Cuppens [10] presented a cooperation module for intrusion detection within the project MIRADOR. The purpose of the presented work is an intrusion detection environment with several IDS that generate alerts when abnormal events occur. Their cooperation module consists of five functions but the author focus on only three functions in demonstrated work. The remaining two functions are presented in [11]. The three functions are Alert management function, alert clustering function, and alert merging function. Alert management function receives the alerts generated by different IDS and stores them. In Alert clustering function alert mapping to the same occurrence of an attack are recognized and gathered into the same cluster. In alert merging function a global alert is generated for each cluster identified by the clustering function. The author implemented these three functions using Gnu-Prolog.

Cuppens and Miege [11] developed a cooperative module CRIM for intrusion detection systems. The module consists of five main functions i.e. alert base management, alert clustering, alert merging, alert correlation and intention recognition. The first three functions are specified by the authors in previous work [10]. The next function of CRIM is alert correlation function. The aim of the correlation function is to correlate alerts in order to provide the security administrator with more synthetic information. Further, the aim of intention recognition function is to extrapolate these candidate plans in order to anticipate the intruder action. In the presented work [11] only alert correlation function is presented by authors.

Farhadi et al. [12] presented a system to correlate intrusion alerts and extract attack scenario as well as to predict the next attacker action. The presented alert correlation system contains two components; Attack Scenario Extraction Algorithm (ASEA) and Hidden Markov Model (HMM). The ASEA mines the stream of alerts for attack scenario. And HMM predicts the next attack class of the intruder also called plan-recognition. The ASEA is able to operate in the real-time environment. And it consumes low memory and low computational overhead. On the other hand, ASEA is not tested to detect new attack scenario.

Julisch and Dacier [13] presented a semi-supervised approach to reducing false positive. The false positive reduction is done via automatically generated episodic rules and clustering is done via a modification of attribute-oriented induction (AOI).

Treinen and Thurimella [14] examine a production data set from a security service provider. This dataset involves output from over thousand sensors. They focused on the automated generation of pattern matching rules from the incoming data stream. Along with this, they have shown that the framework can be used to flag suspicion network activity.

Chyssler *et al.* [15] present an architecture in which intrusion detection systems are combined as sensors. The alarms, provided by this architecture, are improved from the point of view of both quality and quantity. They achieved alarm reduction using adaptive and static filtering. They demonstrated aggregation and correlation utilizing real data from sensors like Syslog, Samhain, and Snort.

Valeur *et al.* in [16] demonstrate a comprehensive approach to alert correlation. The correlation process explained by the authors is containing various components i.e. normalization, preprocessing, fusion component, verification component, thread reconstruction component, attack session reconstruction component, focus recognition component, multistep correlation components, impact analysis component and prioritization component. The author claims that the described approach integrates the most complete set of components in the correlation process.

Hoffman and Sick [17] proposed an approach for online alert aggregation and generation of meta-alerts. Their alert aggregation approach is based on a probabilistic model of the current situation. In this paper first author discuss in brief about their intrusion framework then, they described the generation of alerts and the alert format. After that, they demonstrated a new clustering algorithm for offline alert aggregation. Then they extend their offline model to an algorithm for data stream clustering, which applied to online alert aggregation.

Morin *et al.* in [18] proposed a data model M2D2 for intrusion detection alert correlation. Authors supplies M2D2 with four information type i.e. information related to the characteristic of the monitored information system, information about the vulnerabilities, information about the security tools used for the monitoring and information about the events observed. The author further claims that no other formal model includes the vulnerability and alerts apart from M2D2.

Ning *et al.* [19] proposed a framework to correlate intrusion alerts using prerequisites of intrusions. The author proposes three Utilities i.e. adjustable graph reduction, focused analysis, and graph decomposition. These utilities facilitate the simplification of the analysis process of the large set of correlated alerts.

Ning *et al.* [20] demonstrated a method that constructs attack scenario through correlating alerts. This is done by using conditions and results of attacks. The idea behind the method is that by examining a range of attacks the author concluded that the attacks are not distinct but connected with each other at some stage.

Siraj *et al.* [21] demonstrate a decision engine which fuses information collected from distinct intrusion detection modules by using a casual knowledge-based inference technique to make an intelligent intrusion detection system. For acquisition of casual knowledge fuzzy rule bases and fuzzy cognitive maps were used by authors.

3   Data Sets

In this work following datasets have been utilized- DARPA, Honeynet, MACCDC dataset and the real network traffic captured from the internet. In Table 1 the summary of these datasets is presented.

(I) DARPA DATASET

To accurately test the functions of the intrusion detection systems a huge pattern of real computer attacks was needed. The different classes of attacks must be covered by this sample pattern. For this purpose, DARPA dataset is simulated. The DARPA IDS valuation program contains a huge sample of computer attacks with normal background traffic. DARPA dataset is a benchmark dataset for intrusion detection. ARPA dataset consists of traffic archive captured in the year 1998 and 1999. The dataset contains training and testing traffic archives. In the presented work, DARPA datasets MIT/LL 1998 [22] and MIT/LL 1999 [23] is used. The MIT/LL 1998 dataset contains seven week of training data and two weeks of testing data. And MIT/LL 1999 dataset contains three weeks of training data and two weeks of testing data.

Table 1. Dataset summary.

Dataset	Total Captured Packets	Total TCP Packets	Total Alert Generated
MIT/LL 1998	1144393	831115	1214
MIT/LL 1999	1456347	1377167	1030
HONEYNET	163832	163816	8851
MACCDC	8635943	8485246	879
Real Network Data	22183	9534	2563

(II) Honeynet Dataset

This dataset is collected from the honeynet organization's website which is a nonprofit security research organization [24]. The size of this dataset is 11 MB and the format is tcpdump traffic archive. On this dataset, five type of port scanning attacks were performed by the researchers. A honeynet on the internet is made and attacks were performed on that honeynet. The traffic of these attacks was captured by the tool snort in tcpdump format.

(III) MACCDC Dataset

This dataset was created during the Mid-Atlantic Collegiate Cyber Defense Competition (MACCDC) [25]. The utilized dataset is generated in 2012. The size of the dataset utilized in this paper is 1 GB and the format is tcpdump traffic archive. This dataset contains a port scanning attack embedded in real network traffic. These attacks are performed during a competition to teach simulate the real network scenarios for the students.

4 Proposed Work

Network administrator/forensic investigator utilize alert log data as an input to find out attack patterns in order to find out the source of the attack. However, IDS may generate millions of alerts. Therefore, it is a tiresome & time taking process to analyze these huge numbers of alerts.

In this work, a framework has been proposed to reduce the number of alerts. The proposed framework is shown in Fig. 2. The packets have anomalous TCP flags are captured and alerts have been generated in online mode. This benefit in reduce the analysis time. The proposed framework consists of four modules i.e. capturing, marking, logging and meta-alert generation. The description of these modules is given in the following section.

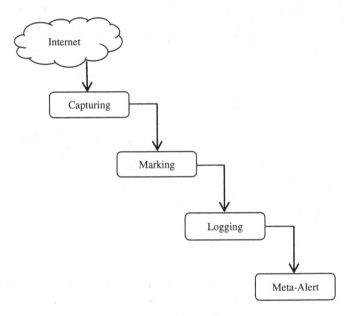

Fig. 2. Proposed framework.

A Capturing

It is the first module of the proposed framework. Capturing module intercepts the packets that are in transition on the network. As data streams flow across the network, the module captures every packet that is in transition on the network irrespective of the protocol and the data being carried. The packet capturing is done by a sniffer. Packet sniffing is a utility that sniffs without modifying the packet in any way. The capturing module has information about almost all packets that have been passed over that network. Afterward, the captured packets are sent to the next module for further processing.

B Marking

In the marking module, all captured packets are marked relevant or irrelevant. The packets are marked on the basis of anomalous TCP flags combinations. Anomalous flags or flag combinations do not occur in normal traffics. These combinations only occur during an attack. A list of anomalous TCP flags has been constructed and shown in Table 2. All the packets having the same flags or combination of flags as Table 2 are marked as relevant and send to the third module. Remaining packets are marked as irrelevant and dropped. The marking module works as follows-

(i)   Check the protocol of the received packet; if not TCP then mark it irrelevant and break; else go to step ii.
(ii) If a packet does match from any rules listed in Table 2 then go to step iii; else mark the packet irrelevant and break;
(iii) Mark it as relevant.
(iv) Repeat these steps for all captured packet.

Table 2. Anomalous TCP flag combinations.

No.	Anomalous Flags	No.	Anomalous Flags
1.	NULL	28.	SYN-PSH-FIN-URG
2.	URG	29.	SYN-ACK-PSH-FIN
3.	PSH	30.	SYN-ACK-FIN-PSH-URG
4.	PSH-URG	31.	SYN-RST-FIN
5.	SYN-URG	32.	SYN-RST-FIN-URG
6.	SYN-ACK-URG	33.	SYN-RST-ACK-FIN
7.	SYN-PSH	34.	SYN-RST-ACK-FIN-URG
8.	SYN-PSH-URG	35.	SYN-RST-PSH-FIN
9.	SYN-ACK-PSH	36.	SYN-RST-FIN-PSH-URG
10.	SYN-ACK-PSH-URG	37.	SYN-ACK -RST-PSH-FIN
11.	SYN-RST	38.	SYN-ACK-RST-PSH-FIN-URG
12.	SYN-RST-URG	39.	RST-URG
13.	SYN-RST-ACK	40.	RST-ACK-URG
14.	SYN-RST-ACK-URG	41.	RST-PSH
15.	SYN-RST-PSH	42.	RST-PSH-URG
16.	SYN-RST-PSH-URG	43.	RST-ACK-PSH
17.	SYN-RST-ACK-PSH	44.	RST-ACK-PSH-URG
18.	SYN-RST-ACK-PSH-URG	45.	ACK-FIN-URG
19.	FIN	46.	ACK-FIN-PSH-URG
20.	FIN-URG	47.	RST-FIN
21.	FIN-PSH	48.	RST-FIN-URG
22.	FIN-PSH-URG	49.	RST-ACK-FIN
23.	SYN-FIN	50.	RST-ACK-FIN-URG
24.	SYN-FIN-URG	51.	RST-FIN-PSH
25.	SYN-ACK-FIN	52.	RST-FIN-PSH-URG
26.	SYN-ACK-FIN-URG	53.	RST-ACK-FIN-PSH
27.	SYN- PSH-FIN	54.	RST-ACK-FIN-PSH-URG

C Logging

In this module alerts are generated for all the packets that are marked relevant in the previous module. Here, for each packet, a single alert is generated. Thus the number of generated alerts is massive. The generated alerts logged into a separate file. The generated log file is a binary file in nature. The log file contains information about each packet that is marked relevant in the previous phase. The log file contains information of packets in a list. The list contains the time, source IP address, Source port address, protocol, destination IP address, destination port address, sensor number, length of the packet and flags. The log file is sent to the next module for Meta-Alert generation.

D Meta-Alert Generation

In this module meta-alerts are generated. The Meta-Alert is the combination of two or more than two similar or related alerts. The process of combining alerts is referred to the merging of two or more than two similar alerts as a single meta-alert that compromises the information contained in all alerts. A meta-alert represents a cluster of the same type of alerts. The packets with the similar anomalous TCP flag combination belong to the same cluster, and for each cluster, a meta-alert is generated. The generated meta-alert, stand for a whole cluster of similar types of alerts.

In our research work, a data-structure MetaAlertList has been developed to visualize the result (i.e. meta-alerts). The data-structure MetaAlertList is shown in Table 3. By the help of this data structure, all meta-alerts are represented. This data structure consists of seven fields, namely; TotalRows, RuleId, RuleMessage, Sensor, Timestamp, SourceIP, and DestinationIP. These fields are briefly discussed below-

(1) **TotalRows.** This field defines the total number of alerts a meta-alert represented. The number of rows meta-alert contains is number of alerts that meta-alert represented.

(2) **RuleId.** RuleId is the id to recognize each meta-alert separately. It is a unique number that is assigned to the meta-alert at the time of rule generation. For a specific attack type, a specific number is assigned.

(3) **RuleMessage.** RuleMessage is a message of a higher level to show the information about meta-alert. RuleMessage is assigned at the time of rule generation. A RuleMessage is also unique like RuleId. It is a short message, about the type of alerts, are in the meta-alert. In our work, RuleMessage shows the flag combination of packets a meta-alert contains.

(4) **Sensor.** It is the id of the sensor indicating that the presented packets are captured through the respected sensor. In a distributed network environment usually, more than one sensor is deployed for intrusion detection. So, in that case, it becomes difficult to know the sensor of the particular packet when they are clustered in a group. At that time this field becomes significant. So for simplicity, the sensor contains a unique ID by which the sensor of the particular packet is identified.

(5) **Timestamp.** A timestamp contains the time of a packet captured by the capturing module. If this field contains more than one value than the total number of distinct value is shown by this field.

(6) **SourceIP.** SourceIP contains the IP address of the source of the packet. It shows the IP address of the source in the dotted-decimal notion. It shows the IP address or a number of distinct IP addresses of the source of a particular attack in a meta-alert. The significance of this field is that it tells that the origin of the attack is from one IP address or it is from more than one IP addresses. It helps a network administrator to know more about a particular attack, in a network originated from one place or more than one place.

(7) **DestinationIP.** This field stores the IP address of the destination of the packet. It shows the IP address of the destination in the dotted-decimal notion. It gives the IP address or sum of numbers of distinct IP addresses of the destination of a particular attack in a meta-alert. The importance of this field is that it tells that the destination of a single attack is same or same attack is performed on multiple hosts in the network or one system is attacked by how many systems at a time. It helps a network administrator to more about the target of single or multiple attacks.

Table 3. Data-structure MetaAlertList

--- rows:	
RuleID	----------
RuleMessage	----------
Sensor	----------
Timestamp	----------
SourceIP	----------
DestinationIP	----------

5 Experimental Setup and Results

The proposed architecture has been tested and implemented on a small LAN. A testbed is built compromised of a victim machine/server, two chat client and 3 systems that work as scanners as shown in Fig. 3. The configuration summary of all the machines involved in a testbed is shown in Table 4.

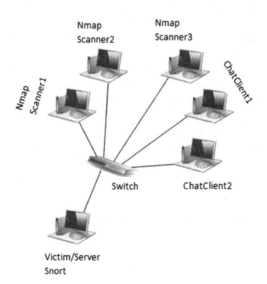

Fig. 3. Test-Bed Topology.

Table 4. Configuration summary of Test-bed machines.

Name	IP Address	OS	Hardware Configuration	Applications	Application Configuration/ Command
Victim Machine/ Server	172.16.50.110	Microsoft Windows 7 Professional	Intel® Core™ i7-3770 CPU@3.40 GHz	Snort 2.9.9.0 JAVA 1.8.0.162 JDK 8.0	NIDS Mode with fast alert Snort Rule : Table5 Protocol: TCP
ChatClient1	172.16.49.192			JAVA 1.8.0.162 JDK 8.0	javac chatclient.java
ChatClient2	172.16.49.176				java chatclient
Scanner1	172.16.51.234			Nmap 7.60 (an Windows verson of Nmap)	Nmap –sN –p 1-1024 172.16.50.110
Scanner2	172.16.50.167				Nmap –sF –p 1-1024 172.16.50.110
Scanner3	172.16.51.92				Nmap –sX –p 1-1024 172.16.50.110

Scanners 1, 2, 3 are equipped with Nmap [26]. Scanners preform FIN, NULL, and XMAS attack on the victim machine. In order to perform relevant packet capturing and scanning traffic, an intrusion detection system, Snort has been installed on the server/victim machine. Snort was configured to the proposed system. It can be configured in three main modes: network intrusion detection, packet logger, and sniffer. It will detect and analyze all network traffic against the user-defined rule set in intrusion detection mode. While, in packet logger mode, this program simply log all packet to the disk. And in sniffer mode, all network packets are intercepted and displayed on the console by the program. Further, specific actions are taken by the program based on what has been identified.

In proposed work packet marking and capturing performed by the Snort IDS. Snort was configured in NIDS mode (to activate NIDS mode option –c is utilized). And the rules were introduced in snort to detect the flag combination of a TCP packet. The rules used to detect the combination are shown in Table 5. It is developed and configures to capture TCP packets which contain anomalous combinations of TCP flags. The all captured packets are compared against the user-defined rule-set and if any packet is matched with the rule-set, then it will be stored in a log folder and an entry is made in the alert file. The structure of a snort alert, in fast mode, is as follows-

(a) <Timestamp>
(b) <Alert message (Configurable through rules)>
(c) <Source IP address>
(d) <Source port>
(e) <Destination IP address>
(f) <Destination port>

Ex- 03/09-19:14:19.099505 [**] [1:100000034:0] FIN [**] [Priority: 0] {TCP} 153.37.134.17:49724 -> 172.16.114.50:2.

Chat Server and Clients is for producing real network traffic. These programs, has been written in Java, and implemented on two systems namely chatclient1 and chatclient2.

In the experiment, scanner 1, 2, 3 perform port scanning simultaneously to the victim machine. And using both chat clients, normal traffic is produced. All packets are efficiently captured by snort. Snort process total 22183 packets and 9534 TCP packets. After the capturing process packets are marked as relevant or irrelevant on the basis of rules presented in Table 5. The packets that are marked as irrelevant are dropped while the packets marked as relevant forwarded for further execution. The relevant packets are logged into a separate file called log file. The meta-alerts are generated for these logged file. We created a data structure, MetaAlertList, to visualize these meta-alerts. Apart from normal traffic various datasets are used for validating the results. The results show a significant reduction.

In result, tcpdump file is created with a log file. In the proposed work, an offline analysis is carried out too. We have taken various recognized datasets along with real network traffic for validating our results. The tcpdump file is collected from the internet of various datasets. The tcpdump processed with the snort. Only the packets matched are sent forward. The meta-alerts are generated with these forwarded packets.

The overview of the process is showing in Fig. 4.

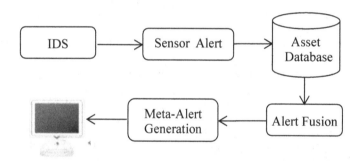

Security Administrator

Fig. 4. Meta-alert generation process overview.

In the alert fusion process, the network traffic is introduced with an IDS. The Sensor alerts are generated by the IDS. Sensor alerts are low-level alert which contains an entry for every anomalous packet. The sensor alerts are stored in a log file in the log database. In the next step, the data in the log file is taken to next level for alert fusion. In alert fusion process, similar type of alerts is fused in one-another. After alert fusion, the fuse alerts are taken into the next step and meta-alert are generated by convenient methods. In proposed work, meta-alerts are generated with the help of a data structure. These meta-alerts are then processed by the network administrator. Compare to all alerts these meta-alerts are less in size. Meta-alerts offer a high-level view of alerts. Furthermore, meta-alerts are less in numbers so processing these alerts do not take much time and can be done efficiently.

Table 5. Snort rules.

S. No.	Snort Rules
1	alert tcp any any -> any any (msg:"NULL"; flags: 0; sid:100000016;)
2	alert tcp any any -> any any (msg:"URG"; flags: U; sid:100000017;)
3	alert tcp any any -> any any (msg:"PSH"; flags: P; sid:100000018;)
4	alert tcp any any -> any any (msg:"PSH-URG"; flags: PU; sid:100000019;)
5	alert tcp any any -> any any (msg:"SYN-URG"; flags: SU; sid:100000020;)
6	alert tcp any any -> any any (msg:"SYN-ACK-URG"; flags: SAU; sid:100000021;)
7	alert tcp any any -> any any (msg:"SYN-PSH"; flags: SP; sid:100000022;)
8	alert tcp any any -> any any (msg:"SYN-PSH-URG"; flags: SPU; sid:100000023;)
9	alert tcp any any -> any any (msg:"SYN-ACK-PSH"; flags: SAP; sid:100000024;)
10	alert tcp any any -> any any (msg:"SYN-ACK-PSH-URG"; flags: SAPU; sid:100000025;)
11	alert tcp any any -> any any (msg:"SYN-RST"; flags: SR; sid:100000026;)
12	alert tcp any any -> any any (msg:"SYN-RST-URG"; flags: SRU; sid:100000027;)
13	alert tcp any any -> any any (msg:"SYN-RST-ACK"; flags: SRA; sid:100000028;)
14	alert tcp any any -> any any (msg:"SYN-RST-ACK-URG"; flags: SRAU; sid:100000029;)
15	alert tcp any any -> any any (msg:"SYN-RST-PSH"; flags: SRP; sid:100000030;)
16	alert tcp any any -> any any (msg:"SYN-RST-PSH-URG"; flags: SRPU; sid:100000031;)
17	alert tcp any any -> any any (msg:"SYN-RST-ACK-PSH"; flags: SRAP; sid:100000032;)
18	alert tcp any any -> any any (msg:"SYN-RST-ACK-PSH-URG"; flags: SRAPU; sid:100000033;)
19	alert tcp any any -> any any (msg:"FIN"; flags: F; sid:100000034;)
20	alert tcp any any -> any any (msg:"FIN-URG"; flags: FU; sid:100000035;)
21	alert tcp any any -> any any (msg:"FIN-PSH"; flags: FP; sid:100000036;)
22	alert tcp any any -> any any (msg:"FIN-PSH-URG"; flags: FPU; sid:100000037;)
23	alert tcp any any -> any any (msg:"SYN-FIN"; flags: SF; sid:100000038;)
24	alert tcp any any -> any any (msg:"SYN-FIN-URG"; flags: SFU; sid:100000039;)
25	alert tcp any any -> any any (msg:"SYN-ACK-FIN"; flags: SAF; sid:100000040;)
26	alert tcp any any -> any any (msg:"SYN-ACK-FIN-URG"; flags: SAFU; sid:100000041;)
27	alert tcp any any -> any any (msg:"SYN-FIN-PSH"; flags: SFP; sid:100000042;)
28	alert tcp any any -> any any (msg:"SYN-FIN-PSH-URG"; flags: SFPU; sid:100000043;)
29	alert tcp any any -> any any (msg:"SYN-ACK-FIN-PSH"; flags: SAFP; sid:100000044;)

(continued)

Table 5. (*continued*)

30	alert tcp any any -> any any (msg:"SYN-ACK-FIN-PSH-URG"; flags: SAFPU; sid:100000045;)
31	alert tcp any any -> any any (msg:"SYN-RST-FIN"; flags: SRF; sid:100000046;)
32	alert tcp any any -> any any (msg:"SYN-RST-FIN-URG"; flags: SRFU; sid:100000047;)
33	alert tcp any any -> any any (msg:"SYN-RST-ACK-FIN"; flags: SRAF; sid:100000048;)
34	alert tcp any any -> any any (msg:"SYN-RST-ACK-FIN-URG"; flags: SRAFU; sid:100000049;)
35	alert tcp any any -> any any (msg:"SYN-RST-FIN-PSH"; flags: SRFP; sid:100000050;)
36	alert tcp any any -> any any (msg:"SYN-RST-FIN-PSH-URG"; flags: SRFPU; sid:100000051;)
37	alert tcp any any -> any any (msg:"SYN-RST-ACK-FIN-PSH"; flags: SRAFP; sid:100000052;)
38	alert tcp any any -> any any (msg:"SYN-RST-ACK-FIN-PSH-URG"; flags: SRAFPU; sid:100000053;)
39	alert tcp any any -> any any (msg:"RST-URG"; flags: RU; sid:100000054;)
40	alert tcp any any -> any any (msg:"RST-ACK-URG"; flags: RAU; sid:100000055;)
41	alert tcp any any -> any any (msg:"RST-PSH"; flags: RP; sid:100000056;)
42	alert tcp any any -> any any (msg:"RST-PSH-URG"; flags: RPU; sid:100000057;)
43	alert tcp any any -> any any (msg:"RST-ACK-PSH"; flags: RAP; sid:100000058;)
44	alert tcp any any -> any any (msg:"RST-ACK-PSH-URG"; flags: RAPU; sid:100000059;)
45	alert tcp any any -> any any (msg:"ACK-FIN-URG"; flags: AFU; sid:100000060;)
46	alert tcp any any -> any any (msg:"ACK-FIN-PSH-URG"; flags: AFPU; sid:100000061;)
47	alert tcp any any -> any any (msg:"RST-FIN"; flags: RF; sid:100000062;)
48	alert tcp any any -> any any (msg:"RST-FIN-URG"; flags: RFU; sid:100000063;)
49	alert tcp any any -> any any (msg:"RST-ACK-FIN"; flags: RAF; sid:100000064;)
50	alert tcp any any -> any any (msg:"RST-ACK-FIN-URG"; flags: RAFU; sid:100000065;)
51	alert tcp any any -> any any (msg:"RST-FIN-PSH"; flags: RFP; sid:100000066;)
52	alert tcp any any -> any any (msg:"RST-FIN-PSH-URG"; flags: RFPU; sid:100000067;)
53	alert tcp any any -> any any (msg:"RST-ACK-FIN-PSH"; flags: RAFP; sid:100000068;)
54	alert tcp any any -> any any (msg:"RST-ACK-FIN-PSH-URG"; flags: RAFPU; sid:100000069;)

The data captured from the real network traffic and processed with Snort IDS. In this dataset, there are 22183 packets. The number of TCP packets is 9534 packets. The alerts generated from these are 2563 alerts. These generated alerts consists 1025 TCP packets which have no flag set, 513 TCP packets with FIN-PSH-URG flag set and 1023 TCP packets with only FIN flags set. So in a nutshell, three types of scanning are done here i.e. NULL scan, XMAS scan, and FIN scan. The graphical representation of these alerts is shown in Fig. 5. The meta-alert generated for this dataset are shown in Tables 6, 7 and 8.

Table 6. Real network traffic meta-alert 1.

1025 rows:	
RuleID	/100000016
RuleMessage	/NULL
Sensor	/Sensor-001
Timestamp	#1025 Distinct Value
SourceIP	172.16.51.234
DestinationIP	172.16.50.110

Table 7. Real network traffic meta-alert 2.

513 rows:	
RuleID	/100000037
RuleMessage	/FIN-PSH-URG
Sensor	/Sensor-001
Timestamp	#513 Distinct Value
SourceIP	172.16.51.92
DestinationIP	172.16.50.110

Table 8. Real network traffic meta-alert 3.

1025 rows:	
RuleID	/100000034
RuleMessage	/FIN
Sensor	/ Sensor-001
Timestamp	#1023 Distinct Value
SourceIP	172.16.50.67
DestinationIP	172.16.50.110

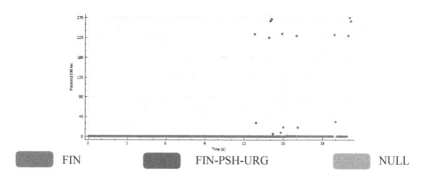

Fig. 5. Real network traffic alerts graph.

Here, four datasets are being utilized, apart from real network traffic dataset, namely, DARPA MIT/LL 1998 dataset, DARPA MIT/LL 1999 dataset, Honeynet dataset, and MACCDC dataset. The tcpdump files of these datasets are retrieved from the internet. Later we processed these tcpdump's from snort IDS and again repeat the whole process of generating meta-alerts for each dataset separately. The results show a significant reduction in alerts. Below we have discussed the results and generated meta-alerts. The generated Meta-alerts for DARPA 1998 dataset given in Tables 9, 10 and 11, DARPA 1999 dataset are given in Table 12, Honeynet dataset is given in Tables 13, 14 and 15, MACCDC dataset is given in Tables 16, 17 and 18. The impact of meta alert generation process is given in Table 19.

The DARPA MIT/LL 1998 dataset (data of two days) consist total 1144393 packets. Among these packets, 831115 packets are TCP packets. Alert generated from these packets are 1214. These generated alerts consists 1075 TCP packets which have only FIN flag set, 94 TCP packets with SYN-FIN flag set and 45 TCP flags with SYN-ACK-FIN flags set. Which further classify into FIN scan, SYN-FIN scan, SYN-ACK-FIN scan. So, to summarize the dataset consist total three types of scanning attacks. The graphical representation of these alerts is shown in Figs. 6 and 7. In Tables 9, 10 and 11 the meta-alerts generated from MIT/LL 1998 dataset are shown.

Table 9. DARPA 1998 data-set meta-alert 1.

1075 rows:	
RuleID	/100000034
RuleMessage	/FIN
Sensor	/Sensor-001
Timestamp	#1075 Distinct Value
SourceIP	202.72.1.77
DestinationIP	172.16.112.50

Table 10. DARPA 1998 data-set meta-alert 2.

94 rows:	
RuleID	/100000038
RuleMessage	/SYN-FIN
Sensor	/Sensor-001
Timestamp	#93 Distinct Value
SourceIP	202.49.244.10
DestinationIP	#45 Distinct Value

Table 11. DARPA 1998 data-set meta-alert 3.

45 rows:	
RuleID	/100000040
RuleMessage	/SYN-ACK-FIN
Sensor	/Sensor-001
Timestamp	#45 Distinct Value
SourceIP	#32 Distinct Value
DestinationIP	202.49.244.10

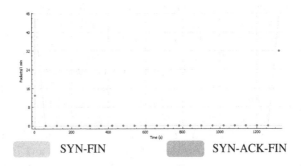

SYN-FIN   SYN-ACK-FIN

Fig. 6. DARPA 1998 data-set alert graph 1.

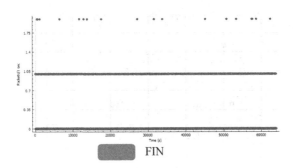

FIN

Fig. 7. DARPA 1998 data-set alert graph 2.

In the DARPA MIT/LL 1999 dataset (data of one day), there are total 1456347 packets. The number of packets of the TCP protocol is 1377167. The number or alerts generated is 1030 alerts. The alert packets contain 1030 TCP packets with only FIN flag set. So, to summarize the dataset consist only one scanning attack i.e. FIN scan. The graphical representation of these alerts is shown in Fig. 8. The generated meta-alert for DARPA MIT/LL 1999 dataset is shown in Table 12.

Table 12. DARPA 1999 data-set meta-alert.

1030 rows:	
RuleID	/100000034
RuleMessage	/FIN
Sensor	/Sensor-001
Timestamp	#1030 Distinct Value
SourceIP	153.37.134.17
DestinationIP	172.16.114.50

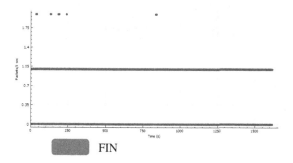

FIN

Fig. 8. DARPA 1999 data-set alert graph.

In the Honeynet dataset, there are total 163832 packets. The total number of TCP packets is 163816. The alerts generated from these packets are 8851. These generated alerts consists 1335 TCP packets which have No flag set, 7513 TCP packets with FIN-PSH-URG flag set and 3 TCP flags with SYN-FIN-PSH-URG flags set. To conclude, dataset consists three types of scan i.e. NULL scan, XMAS scan, and SYN-FIN-PSH-URG scan. The graphical representation of these alerts is shown in Fig. 9. The generated meta-alerts are shown in Tables 13, 14 and 15.

Table 13. Honeynet data-set meta-alert 1.

1335 rows:	
RuleID	/100000016
RuleMessage	/NULL
Sensor	/Sensor-001
Timestamp	#1335 Distinct Value
SourceIP	192.168.0.9
DestinationIP	192.168.0.99

Table 14. Honeynet data-set meta-alert 2.

7513 rows:	
RuleID	/100000037
RuleMessage	/FIN-PSH-URG
Sensor	/Sensor-001
Timestamp	#7513 Distinct Value
SourceIP	#4 Distinct Value
DestinationIP	192.168.0.99

Table 15. Honeynet data-set meta-alert 3.

3 rows:	
RuleID	/100000043
RuleMessage	/SYN-FIN-PSH-URG
Sensor	/Sensor-001
Timestamp	#3 Distinct Value
SourceIP	192.168.0.9
DestinationIP	192.168.0.99

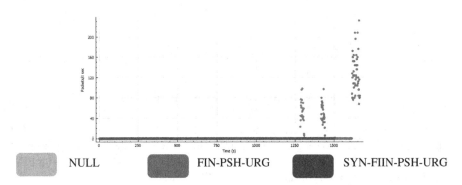

Fig. 9. Honeynet data-set alert graph.

The Mid-Atlantic Collegiate Cyber Defense Competition (MACCDC) data set contains total 8640136 packets. Among these packets, 8485246 packets are TCP packets. Total 879 alerts are generated from IDS for this data set. The generated alerts contains 293 TCP packets with no flag set, 295 TCP packets with FIN-PSH-URG flags set and 291 TCP packets with SYN-FIN-PSH-URG flags set. In conclusion, there are three types of scanning attacks performed over this dataset those are namely NULL scan, XMAS scan, and SYN-FIN-PSH-URG scan. The graphical representation of these alerts is shown in Fig. 10. The meta-alerts for this data set are shown in Tables 16, 17 and 18.

Table 16. MACCDC data-set meta-alert 1.

293 rows:	
RuleID	/100000016
RuleMessage	/NULL
Sensor	/Sensor-001
Timestamp	#128 Distinct Value
SourceIP	#5 Distinct Value
DestinationIP	#62 Distinct Value

Table 17. MACCDC data-set meta-alert 2.

295 rows:	
RuleID	/100000037
RuleMessage	/FIN-PSH-URG
Sensor	/Sensor-001
Timestamp	#134 Distinct Value
SourceIP	#5 Distinct Value
DestinationIP	#63 Distinct Value

Table 18. MACCDC data-set meta-alert 3.

291 rows:	
RuleID	/100000043
RuleMessage	/SYN-FIN-PSH-URG
Sensor	/Sensor-001
Timestamp	#129 Distinct Value
SourceIP	#5 Distinct Value
DestinationIP	#62 Distinct Value

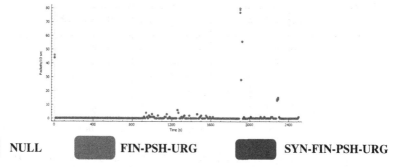

NULL   FIN-PSH-URG   SYN-FIN-PSH-URG

Fig. 10. MACCDC data-set alert graph.

The Overall Impact of Meta-Alert Generation is given in the Table 19.

Table 19. Impact of Meta-Alert Generation

	MIT/LL 1998	MIT/LL 1999	Honeynet	MACCDC	Real Network Traffic
Input Packets	1144393	1456347	163832	8640136	22183
Output Alerts	1214	1030	8851	879	2563
Meta Alerts	3	1	3	3	3
Reduction	99.75%	99.90%	99.97%	99.66%	99.88%

6 Conclusion and Future Work

In the proposed work, a framework has been developed to reduce the number of alerts. The developed framework consists of four modules i.e. Capturing, Marking, Logging and Meta-alert generation. Each module is dedicated to a specific task. The capturing module intercepts all the packets that are in transition on the network. Capturing is performed by a sniffer. The Marking is completed by a set of developed snort rules. And for Meta-Alert a data-structure i.e. MetaAlertList, has been developed, which helps in visualize the results (i.e. Meta-Alerts). The proposed work has shown that the huge amount of alerts that must be analyzed by a human administrator can be reduced significantly. An experiment is carried out using real-network traffic and some well-known data sets. The utilized datasets are MIT/LL 1998, MIT/LL 1999, Honeynet, and MACCDC dataset. In all datasets, it is observed that the number of resulted alerts reduced substantially. An average reduction of 99.96% is observed for the proposed method. At the same time, the number of missing alerts is negligible. Here, one thing should be kept in mind, that is, in this work; the research is conducted on the invalid flag combination, not on the invalid packet sequence. A comparative analysis has been carried out using MIT/LL 1999 dataset and it is observed that the proposed method do better result and less time consuming than the existing one.

The proposed work is based on the anomalous TCP flags combination. However, in the future, we will plan to extend the work for various other protocol and attacks.

References

1. Saraswat, V.K.: Cyber Security Presentation [PowerPoint slides] (2018). Accessed http://www.niti.gov.in/writereaddata/files/document_publication/NationalStrategy-for-AI-Discussion-Paper.pdf
2. Forouzan, B.A.: TCP/IP Protocol Suite, 4th edn. McGraw Hill Education, Delhi (2010)
3. Jacobson, V., Leres, C., McCanne, S.: LIBPCAP. Lawrence Berkeley Laboratory, Berkeley, CA (1994). Initial public release June

4. Roesch, M.: Snort: lightweight intrusion detection for networks. In: Lisa, vol. 99, no. 1, pp. 229–238, November 1999
5. Debar, H., Wespi, A.: Aggregation and correlation of intrusion-detection alerts. In: Lee, W., Mé, L., Wespi, A. (eds.) RAID 2001. LNCS, vol. 2212, pp. 85–103. Springer, Heidelberg (2001). https://doi.org/10.1007/3-540-45474-8_6
6. Siraj, A., Vaughn, R.B.: A cognitive model for alert correlation in a distributed environment. In: Kantor, P., et al. (eds.) ISI 2005. LNCS, vol. 3495, pp. 218–230. Springer, Heidelberg (2005). https://doi.org/10.1007/11427995_18
7. Siraj, A., Vaughn, R.B.: Alert correlation with abstract incident modeling in a multi-sensor environment. IJCSNS Int. J. Comput. Sci. Netw. Secur. 7(8), 8–19 (2007)
8. Tedesco, G., Aickelin, U.: Data reduction in intrusion alert correlation. arXiv preprint arXiv: 0804.1281 (2008)
9. Harang, R., Guarino, P.: Clustering of Snort alerts to identify patterns and reduce analyst workload. In: Military Communications Conference, MILCOM 2012, pp. 1–6. IEEE, October 2012
10. Cuppens, F.: Managing alerts in a multi-intrusion detection environment. In: ACSAC, p. 0022. IEEE, December 2001
11. Cuppens, F., Miege, A.: Alert correlation in a cooperative intrusion detection framework. In: Proceedings 2002 IEEE Symposium on Security and Privacy, p. 202. IEEE, May 2002
12. Farhadi, H., AmirHaeri, M., Khansari, M.: Alert correlation and prediction using data mining and HMM. ISC Int. J. Inf. Secur. 3(2), 77–101 (2011)
13. Julisch, K., Dacier, M.: Mining intrusion detection alarms for actionable knowledge. In: Proceedings of the Eighth ACM SIGKDD International Conference on Knowledge Discovery and Data Mining, pp. 366–375. ACM, July 2002
14. Treinen, J.J., Thurimella, R.: A framework for the application of association rule mining in large intrusion detection infrastructures. In: Zamboni, D., Kruegel, C. (eds.) RAID 2006. LNCS, vol. 4219, pp. 1–18. Springer, Heidelberg (2006). https://doi.org/10.1007/11856214_1
15. Chyssler, T., Burschka, S., Semling, M., Lingvall, T., Burbeck, K.: Alarm reduction and correlation in intrusion detection systems. In: Detection of Intrusion and Malware & Vulnerability Assessment, DIMVA, pp. 9–24, June 2004
16. Valeur, F., Vigna, G., Kruegel, C., Kemmerer, R.A.: Comprehensive approach to intrusion detection alert correlation. IEEE Trans. Dependable Secure Comput. 1(3), 146–169 (2004)
17. Hofmann, A., Sick, B.: Online intrusion alert aggregation with generative data stream modeling. IEEE Trans. Dependable Secure Comput. 8(2), 282–294 (2011)
18. Morin, B., Mé, L., Debar, H., Ducassé, M.: M2D2: a formal data model for IDS alert correlation. In: Wespi, A., Vigna, G., Deri, L. (eds.) RAID 2002. LNCS, vol. 2516, pp. 115–137. Springer, Heidelberg (2002). https://doi.org/10.1007/3-540-36084-0_7
19. Ning, P., Cui, Y., Reeves, D.S.: Analyzing intensive intrusion alerts via correlation. In: Wespi, A., Vigna, G., Deri, L. (eds.) RAID 2002. LNCS, vol. 2516, pp. 74–94. Springer, Heidelberg (2002). https://doi.org/10.1007/3-540-36084-0_5
20. Ning, P., Cui, Y., Reeves, D.S., Xu, D.: Techniques and tools for analyzing intrusion alerts. ACM Trans. Inf. Syst. Secur. (TISSEC) 7(2), 274–318 (2004)
21. Siraj, A., Bridges, S.M., Vaughn, R.B.: Fuzzy cognitive maps for decision support in an intelligent intrusion detection system. In: 2001 Joint 9th IFSA World Congress and 20th NAFIPS International Conference, vol. 4, pp. 2165–2170. IEEE, July 2001
22. M.I.T. Lincoln Laboratory: 1998 DARPA Intrusion Detection Evaluation Dataset. https://www.ll.mit.edu/r-d/datasets/1998-darpa-intrusion-detection-evaluation-data-set. Accessed 05 May 2018

23. M.I.T. Lincoln Laboratory: 1999 DARPA Intrusion Detection Evaluation Dataset. https://www.ll.mit.edu/r-d/datasets/1999-darpa-intrusion-detection-evaluation-data-set.   Accessed 05 May 2018
24. The Honeynet Project. http://www.honeynet.org/. Accessed 05 May 2018
25. Mid-Atlantic Collegiate Cyber Defense Competition (MACCDC). http://www.netresec.com/?page=MACCDC. Accessed 05 May 2018
26. Lyon, G.: Nmap–free security scanner for network exploration & security audits (2009)

Privacy Preservation

APPLADroid: Automaton Based Inter-app Privacy Leak Analysis for Android

Vineeta Jain[1(✉)], Vijay Laxmi[1], Manoj Singh Gaur[2], and Mohamed Mosbah[3]

[1] Malaviya National Institute of Technology, Jaipur, Jaipur, India
{2015rcp9051,vlaxmi}@mnit.ac.in
[2] Indian Institute of Technology Jammu, Jammu, India
director@iitjammu.ac.in
[3] LaBRI, CNRS, Bordeaux INP, University of Bordeaux, Talence, France
mohamed.mosbah@labri.fr

Abstract. An app named "Aqua Mail" is a Google play store app with millions of downloads. It allows the user to manage Google account mails. For caching purposes, it stores the mails in a content provider protected with a custom permission rather than Android defined permission to access mails (MANAGE_ACCOUNTS). Another app named "Enhanced SMS and call" can access mails directly by obtaining the permission of reading the custom content provider of Aqua Mail. Google is not aware of the fact that any other app is accessing the mails. In order to detect such flows, a precise inter-app analysis is needed to identify leakage from source in one app to sink in another app.

In this paper, we present an extension of a static analysis technique named SniffDroid to detect the inter-app privacy leaks in Android. Our technique models Android apps and Android permissions as the automaton and utilizes the intersection property of automaton to detect privacy leakage. To assess the performance of the proposed approach, we analyzed Droidbench samples, self-made apps and Google playstore apps. We created novel samples of leakage through a chain of apps and analyzed them using open-source existing state-of-art approaches. We found that none of them could detect the leakage paths. The proposed approach detects the inter-app privacy leakage with 100% accuracy.

1 Introduction

The Inter-component communication (ICC) mechanism of Android enables communication among components of the same app and different apps through various ICC mediums (such as intents, content providers, shared preferences)[1]. Unfortunately, ICC incorporates an erroneous information passing mechanism between components of apps, which can be exploited by malicious apps to exfiltrate information outside app boundaries, without the consent of user [1]. Hence,

---

[1] In the paper, ICC mediums refer to intents, content providers and shared preferences.

© Springer Nature Singapore Pte Ltd. 2019
S. Nandi et al. (Eds.): ISEA-ISAP 2018, CCIS 939, pp. 219–233, 2019.
https://doi.org/10.1007/978-981-13-7561-3_16

it poses an enormous threat to the user's security and privacy. According to OWASP Android Testing Cheat Sheet 2017 [2], `Improper Platform Usage` is one of the top 10 serious risks in Android apps.

This paper focuses on conducting ICC analysis to detect inter-app privacy leak via ICC mediums using the automaton approach. We define privacy leak as a transmission of sensitive information via ICC mediums from an app accessing source (holding permission to access source) to an app accessing sink (not holding the permission to access source but holding the permission to access sink) through a chain of apps of length > 1. We define source as an external resource protected by dangerous permissions from which information is read (Example: READ_PHONE_STATE) and sink as an external resource protected by dangerous permissions from which information is transmitted outside app boundaries (Example: INTERNET) [3]. The information obtained by accessing source is termed as sensitive information [3].

Prior approaches to detecting information leakage paths mainly focus on single app analysis [4–6]. Malware writers have outsmarted the single app analysis techniques by discovering alternative ways to conduct information leakage. One such way is using a chain of apps to accomplish the goal, i.e. source in one app and sink in another app. Recent efforts on detecting inter-app privacy leaks fail to detect all flows. The reason being three-fold - (1) Most of the techniques target only intents [1,7]. However, communication among apps can also occur through content providers and shared preferences. (2) The techniques can detect leakage only through two apps [3]. But the leakage can be performed using more than two apps (explained in Sect. 2). (3) The runtime overhead of already existing approaches such as the ones using formal methods, model checking, is very high [8]. Thus, the approaches are not practically scalable for a chain of apps.

In this paper, we present a static information flow analysis technique named APPLADroid (**A**utomaton based inter-a**P**p **P**rivacy **L**eak **A**nalysis for **Android**) for conducting ICC analysis to detect inter-app privacy leak using automaton approach.

The contribution of the work is as follows:

- We capture privacy leaks by describing ICC using Non-deterministic finite automaton (NFA) named as *Application Automaton*. We initially create a database of malicious flows by performing control, data flow and taint analysis and further model these flows using graphs. The app graphs are unioned and pruned to detect sensitive information flow and this flow is modeled as Application Automaton. The apps form the states of the automaton[2]. This reduces inter-component data sharing to inter-app data sharing and, thus, the approach becomes scalable. We describe the permission mapping from source to sink using *Policy Automaton*. Inter-app privacy leak is symbolized as a final state in the intersection automaton of Application automaton and Policy automaton.
- We created novel samples of privacy leakage through a chain of apps of length > 2.

---

[2] Automaton refers to NFA in the paper.

– We have tested APPLAdroid on the dataset created by us consisting of 31
apps, droidbench samples, and 2000 Google playstore apps. APPLAdroid
identifies all the ICC flows among the created dataset and droidbench samples
with 100% accuracy, and outperforms the existing state-of-art approaches. By
evaluating Google playstore apps on APPLAdroid, we have identified that
real-world apps leak information through ICC mediums.

The paper is organized as follows: Sect. 2 explains the threat scenario. Section 4
introduces APPLADRoid and Sect. 5 explains design and implementation of the
proposed approach in detail. Section 6 shows the experimental results and Sect. 7
compares the work with existing state-of-the art. Section 8 concludes the work.

2   Threat Model

Suppose there is an app named Medium1 which obtains permission -
READ_CONTACTS (source) from the user. The app creates a public content provider named *cte* with read permission and saves the contacts (sensitive information) of the user in it. Suppose there is another app named
Medium2 which also holds permission - READ_CONTACTS. It queries the public content provider of Medium1 using the content URI *content://com.pro/cte*
and inserts the obtained information as a payload in intent with action
string *com.demo.intent*. Further, Medium2 sends the intent to Medium3 which
also contains the permission READ_CONTACTS. Medium3 extracts the data
from the intent and stores it in shared preferences named *myPref* created
in MODE_WORLD_READABLE. Subsequently, Medium4 accesses the shared
preferences *myPref* and obtains the contacts of the user and writes in external storage (sink). Importantly, Medium4 does not holds the permission
READ_CONTACTS, but still it is able to access the contacts of the user. Thus,
the sensitive information flows from source to sink through a chain of apps. This
shows that information can be leaked using multiple apps and multiple ICC
mediums. Figure 1 describes the leakage scenario.

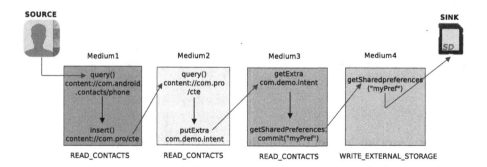

Fig. 1. Privacy leakage scenario

3   Preliminaries

In order to fathom the working of APPLADroid thoroughly, we provide a concise description of NFA and intersection model of NFA.

3.1   Non-deterministic Finite Automaton

NFA is a simple state machine used to represent a sequential logic. It is represented as M with the following specifications:

$M = (Q, \Sigma, \triangle, q_o, F)$ where
Q = finite set of states
Σ = finite set of input symbols known as the alphabet
$\triangle$ = transition function represented as $Q \times \Sigma \longrightarrow Q$
q_o = initial state
F = set of final states, $F \subseteq Q$

Let us assume no. of states in M is n. Hence, the size of M is equal to n. Let $w = b_1, b_2, b_3........b_n$ represent a word over Σ. M accepts w if a sequence of states $p_0, p_1.....p_k \in Q$ fulfill following 3 conditions - (1) $p_0 = q_0$ (first alphabet of $w = q_o$), (2) for $i = 0, 1...n-1$: $p_{i+1} \in \triangle(p_i, b_{i+1})$ (for every alphabet in string w, M transits from state to state according to $\triangle$) and (3) $p_n \in F$ (w is accepted if it halts on one of the final states). The set of strings accepted by automaton M constitutes a language represented as $L(M)$. Figure 2(a) represents an automaton M that accepts any binary string that contains 00 or 11 as a substring. Figure 2(b) represents an automaton M' that accepts any binary string that ends in 00.

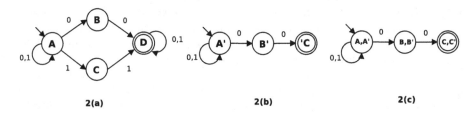

2(a)   **2(b)**   **2(c)**

Fig. 2. 2(a) Automaton M that accepts any binary string that contains 00 or 11 as a substring. 2(b) Automaton M' that accepts any binary string that end in 00 and 2(c) Intersection of M and M'

3.2   Intersection Model of Non-deterministic Finite Automaton

Suppose, we have 2 NFA's, M and M' with the following specifications: $M = (Q, \Sigma, \triangle, q_o, F)$ and $M' = (Q', \Sigma', \triangle', q'_o, F')$.

The intersection of M and M' is given as $T = M \cap M'$. The specification of T is defined as:

$T = (Q^T, \Sigma^T, \triangle^T, q_o^T, F^T)$ where,
$Q^T = \{(q, q')|q \in Q \text{ and } q' \in Q'\}$,
$\Sigma^T = \{\Sigma \cup \Sigma'\}$,
$\triangle^T = \{Q^T \times \Sigma^T \longrightarrow Q^T\}$,
$q_o^T = \{(q_o, q_o')\}$ and
$F^T = \{(q, q')|q \in F \text{ and } q' \in F'\}$

For an alphabet b in Σ^T, the transition function defined as $\triangle^T((q_1, q_1'), b) = (q_2, q_2')$ should fulfill the following conditions (1) $(q_1, q_2) \in Q$, (2) $(q_1', q_2') \in Q'$, (3) $\triangle(q_1, b) = q_2$ and (4) $\triangle'(q_1', b) = q_2'$). Figure 2(c) is an intersected NFA of Fig. 2(a) and (b).

4   APPLADroid

APPLADroid is an extension of novel static analysis technique named Sniff-Droid [3] to detect the inter-app privacy leaks in Android. Similar to SniffDroid, APPLADroid also models the ICC as Application Automaton, policies explaining ICC leakage rules as Policy Automaton and applies intersection property of NFA to detect the leakage paths from source in one app to sink in another app. However, APPLADroid is an improved version of SniffDroid in the following ways:

- SniffDroid could only detect malicious paths between two apps through the medium of shared preferences. However, APPLADroid can identify sensitive information flow across the chain of apps through all ICC mediums.
- SniffDroid represents component view of an app and highlights the flows of sensitive information across components in the intersection automaton (*size of automaton = number of components in the apps*), whereas APPLADroid constructs a more high-level representation of flows i.e. through apps (*size of automaton = number of apps*). It initially constructs ICC level automaton and further reduces it to app-level. In this way, we reduce the number of states in intersection automaton. Thus, APPLADroid is scalable and works in linear time w.r.t number of apps.
- SniffDroid does not store the ICC flows of an app. However, APPLADroid constructs a database of malicious ICC flows of an app. We have created an analysis engine and use already existing tools for capturing the flows. Thus, APPLADroid support reusability and saves time.
- SniffDroid does not perform the flow analysis of apps. However, APPLADroid conducts control flow, data flow and taint analysis to capture the malicious flow of sensitive information.

5   Design and Implementation

APPLADroid operates in two phases - *Intra-app* and *Inter-app*. In the first phase, APPLADroid identifies the flow of sensitive information from source to sink in a single app and creates a database of sensitive flows. Subsequently, in the second phase, APPLADroid models the inter-app malicious flows as Application Automaton, policies as Policy Automaton and perform an intersection to identify inter-app privacy leaks.

5.1   Intra-app

APPLADroid takes a sequence of apps as input and processes each app individually and parallelly by creating multiple instances; one for each app. Figure 3 shows the Intra-app sensitive flow detection. APPLADroid uses Droidsafe [4] and IC3 [5] to detect the malicious flows, and the respective ICC mediums and permissions responsible for the flows. However, Droidsafe can only detect the flows through source API (Application Program Interface) to sink API, source to intent, source to content provider and source to shared preferences. It misses the flows across ICC mediums, i.e. from intent to content providers, intent to shared preferences, shared preferences to intent, etc. To capture these flows, we created an analysis engine using Soot [9], which converts an apk into an intermediate representation named jimple, and performs control and data flow analysis to identify the sensitive flows across the ICC mediums. Consequently, APPLADroid stores all the malicious flows in the database.

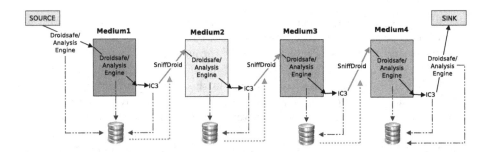

Fig. 3. Workflow for detection of intra-app sensitive flows

5.2   Inter-app

The inter-app privacy leakage detection by APPLADroid is shown in Fig. 4.

Graph Generator. This step extracts the information related to sensitive flows for each app from the database and generates separate graphs for the apps. An app is represented as a graph $G(V, E)$, where

- $V =$ vertex set of graph
- $E =$ edge set of graph.

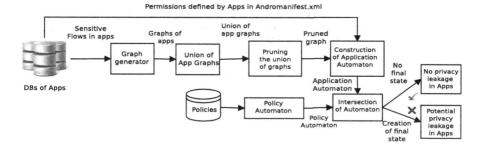

Fig. 4. Workflow for detection of inter-app privacy leaks

Vertex set V is defined as:

$$V = \eta \cup \delta \cup \lambda \cup \kappa \cup \{Package\ name\ of\ the\ app\} \cup \varepsilon \qquad (1)$$

where,

- η = Name of the app
- δ = The set of sensitive intents sent/received by an app
- λ = The set of sensitive shared preferences created/read by an app
- κ = The set of sensitive content URIs created/read by an app

The edges in an app graph represent the accessing and transmission of sensitive information through ICC mediums. The Edge set E is represented as (x, y) where x = source and y = target. The edges are constructed in the following way:

- If an app sends an intent carrying sensitive information, then x = app and y = intent.
- If an app receives an intent carrying sensitive information, then x = intent and y = app.
- If an app stores sensitive information in shared preferences created by the app itself, then x = app and y = shared preferences.
- If an app reads information from shared preferences of other apps, then x = shared preferences and y = app.
- If an app creates a content provider and stores sensitive information in it, then x = app and y = content URI of the provider.
- If an app reads a content provider carrying sensitive information in it, then x = content URI of the provider and y = app.
- If an app reads sensitive information from a source, then x = Source and y = app.
- If an app writes sensitive information to sink, then x = app and y = Sink.

An Example to Demonstrate the Generation of App Graphs

We describe the process of graph generation for the threat scenario described in Sect. 2.

- The app Medium1 accesses contact information from the contacts content provider of Android using URI *content* : *//com.android.contacts/phone* and, stores this information in a provider created by Medium1 named com.pro. Thus the app graph contains three vertices; one for the source (*contacts content provider*), one for the app (*Medium1*) and one for the sink (*com.pro/cte*). Figure 5(a) explains the graph generation process for Medium1.
- Medium2 app accesses information from the content provider *com.pro* of Medium1 and writes this information to an intent *com.demo.intent*. Thus, the app graph of Medium2 contains three vertices; source (*com.pro*), app (*Medium2*) and sink (*com.demo.intent*). Figure 5(b) highlights the graph generation process for Medium2.
- Medium3 app accesses information from *com.demo.intent* and, writes to a shared preferences named *myPref* created by the app itself. Thus, the app graph of Medium3 also contains 30 nodes; source (*com.demo.intent*), app (*Medium3*) and sink (*myPref*). Figure 5(c) describes the graph generation process for Medium3. An important observation is that the node for shared preferences contains the name of the app package. As shared preferences are

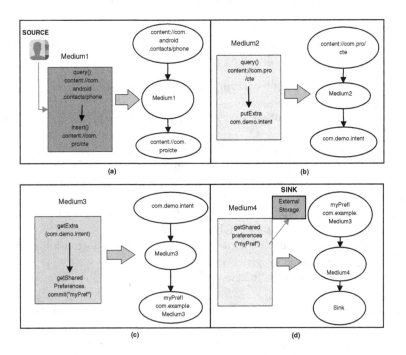

Fig. 5. Graph generation for the apps. (a) App graph for Medium1, (b) App graph for Medium2, (c) App graph for Medium3 and (d) App graph for Medium4

uniquely recognized by their name and package name [3], we append the name of the package in the vertex.

- Medium4 accesses the shared preferences of Medium3 *myPref* and writes this information in external storage. Therefore, app graph of Medium4 contains three nodes; source *myPref*, the app (*Medium4*) and *sink*. Figure 5(d) shows the graph generation process for Medium3.

Union of App Graphs. *Definition:* Suppose we have two apps - A_1 and A_2 modeled as app graphs - G_1 and G_2 with vertex set - V_1 and V_2, and edge set - E_1 and E_2, respectively. The union of app graphs A_U is computed as $A_U = G_1 \cup G_2$ with vertex set $V_U = V_1 \cup V_2$ and edge set $E_U = E_1 \cup E_2$.

This step detects the inter-app flow of sensitive information. For the example explained in the previous subsection, Fig. 6(a) shows the union of all the four app graphs. It can be observed that the union of app graphs captures the transmission of information from source to sink across the apps.

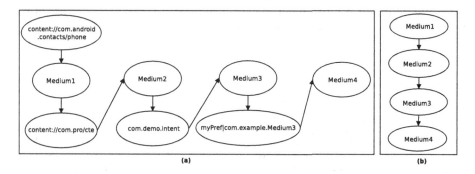

Fig. 6. (a) Union of app graphs and (b) Pruning the union of app graphs

Pruning the Union of App Graphs. *Definition:* Let the pruned graph for apps A_1 and A_2 with graphs G_1 and G_2 and union A_U, respectively, be represented as $A_P(V_P, E_P)$. The vertex set V_P is defined as:

$$V_P = A_1(\eta_1) \cup A_2(\eta_2) \tag{2}$$

The edge set E_P is defined as:

$$E_P = \{(x, y) | x \in A_1(\eta_1), y \in A_2(\eta_2) | if \ in \ A_U \ there \ exists \ a \ path \tag{3}$$
$$from \ x \rightarrow A_1(\delta) \rightarrow y \ or \ a \ path \ from \ x \rightarrow A_1(\lambda) \rightarrow y$$
$$or \ a \ path \ from \ x \rightarrow A_1(\kappa) \rightarrow y\}$$

Pruning removes the ICC nodes from the union of app graphs and simplifies the graph by clearly highlighting the inter-app malicious flow. *The size of the pruned graph = number of apps provided as an input to APPLADroid.* Figure 6(b) represents the pruned graph for the unioned graph shown in Fig. 6(a).

Construction of Application Automaton. *Definition*: Application Automaton is represented as $A(Q, \Sigma, \triangle, q_o, F)$ where,

Q = Android apps given as an input to APPLADroid ∪ {a dummy main state}.

Σ = Permissions used by the input apps to access sensitive information.

$\triangle$ = A transition function, $Q \times \Sigma \longrightarrow Q$. The transitions between states are labeled with sensitive permissions defined by the apps and associated with the stored malicious flows.

q_o = A dummy main state named as main.

F = set of final states given as $\{Q - q_o\}$.

The pruned graph is converted into Application Automaton by signifying a dummy state as an initial state and rest of the vertices as final states. As Android does not contain a single point of entry, therefore, we denote the initial state with a dummy entry point. Figure 7(a) shows the Application Automaton for the pruned graph shown in Fig. 6(b). The apps are labeled as final states and connected to an initial state through edges labeled with the permissions associated with the malicious flows present in the apps, as shown in Fig. 5.

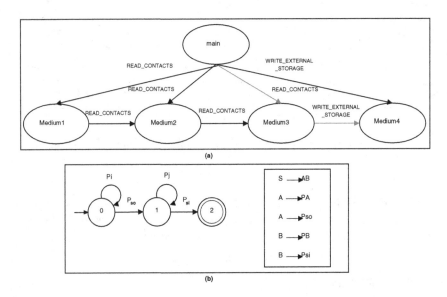

Fig. 7. (a) Application automaton and (b) Policy automaton and the grammar associated with it

Policies. If an app gets privileged to access sensitive information (not allowed to access by owned source permissions) through any of the ICC mediums of any other app, 0 and exfiltrates it to the outside world (by accessing sink), it is known as inter-app privacy leak. Thus, permissions act as the major evidence for the detection of inter-app privacy leak. APPLADroid creates policies by coupling source permissions with sink permissions. The policies are constructed in a way that if any source permission is accompanied by any sink permission, regardless of intermediate permissions, it leads to inter-app privacy leak. Example of a policy - $READ\_CONTACTS \rightarrow SET\_ALARM \rightarrow INTERNET$. The policies are modeled as Policy Automaton. Suppose P = set of permissions defined by Android framework, P_{so} = set of source permissions, and P_{si} = set of sink permissions, such that $P_i = P\backslash P_{so}$ and $P_j = P\backslash P_{si}$. The language for Policy Automaton is represented as:

$$L = P_i^* P_{so}(P_j)^* P_{si} \tag{4}$$

where $i \neq so$ and $j \neq si$.

Construction of Policy Automaton. *Definition:* Policy Automaton is defined as $R(Q, \Sigma, \triangle, q_o, F)$, where

Q = set of states: 0, 1 and 2.
Σ = permissions defined by the Android framework.
$\triangle$ = a transition function, $Q \times \Sigma \longrightarrow Q$. The edges between states are marked with permissions.
q_o = initial state 0.
F = Final state, 2.

Figure 7(b) represents the policy automaton on the basis of language specified in Eq. 4 and its associated grammar.

Intersection of Automaton: In this step, Application Automaton and Policy Automaton are intersected (as described in Sect. 3.2). If the intersected automaton possesses a final state, we can infer that privacy leakage exists in the apps. Figure 8 shows the intersected automaton for the application automaton shown in Fig. 7(a). The presence of the final state signifies that an inter-app privacy leakage exists among the apps.

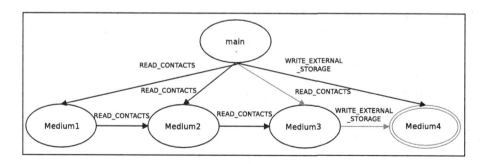

Fig. 8. Intersection of application automaton and policy automaton

6   Results and Discussion

APPLADroid accepts multiple apps as an input and provides intersected automaton as an output. If the output automaton contains a final state, we may conclude that the apps are involved in inter-app privacy leakage. To check the effectiveness and accuracy of APPLADroid, we tested it on Droibench samples, our self-made samples, and Google playstore apps.

Droidbench Samples. Droidbench is an extensive benchmark for analyzing the Android inter-app privacy leakage detection tools. APPLADroid has been analyzed on 9 inter-app privacy leakage test cases of *Droidbench 3.0* [10] branch and 6 test cases of IccTA branch [11]. APPLADroid successfully detected all the reported leakage paths. Table 2 shows the analysis results.

Self-made Samples. We created a dataset of 31 apps containing the inter-app privacy leakage. All the existing samples of droidbench possess leakage paths spanning across two apps. We created 10 samples containing leakage paths spanning through a chain of apps of length > 2. APPLADroid detected the paths with 100% precision and accuracy. Table 2 shows the analysis results.

Google Playstore Apps. We analyzed 2000 Google playstore apps using APPLADroid. We identified that real-world apps leak sensitive information through ICC mediums to other apps and sinks. Table 1 shows real-world intra-app and inter-app privacy leakage cases. Some of the apps such as *Aquamail, Microsoft Outlook* and *GoSMS* contain more than 100, 000 installs.

6.1   Comparison with Existing State-of-Art Approaches

We compared APPLADroid with existing open-source inter-app privacy leakage detection state-of-art analysis tools such as DIALDroid [7], IccTA [6] (IccTA performs inter-app analysis with APKCombiner [12]) and Covert [8]. Table 2 shows the results of comparison on Droidbench samples and self-made apps (we have compared the tools on the test cases where leakage path spans through a chain of apps of length > 2). APPLADroid outperforms the existing approaches as the recall and F-measure of APPLADroid is highest as compared to the existing state-of-art. One important observation is that none of the existing approaches could detect the leakage paths through different ICC mediums across a chain of apps (self-made apps). APPALDroid detects inter-app ICC leakage paths with the highest precision and accuracy.

7   Related Work

Inter-app analysis in Android has not received much attention from researchers and analysts. Limited approaches exist for inter-app analysis to detect privacy

Table 1. Analysis of real-world apps

S. no.	Source app	ICC medium	Sink app	Sink
1	moffice Outlook sync	Content provider	Mobisynapse	LOG/SQLite
2	GO SMS	Content provider	GO SMS Free message Plugin	SQLite
3	Aquamail	Content provider	Notify Pro	Logs
4	Aquamail	Content provider	Enhanced Call and SMS	Logs
5	Shake it Well	Intent	-	Internet
6	myLocation	Shared preferences	-	Readable shared preferences
7	Pansi SMS	Content provider	-	Public content provider
8	Maxthon Android Web Browser	Content provider	-	Public content provider
9	Droid Call Filter	Content provider	-	Public content provider
10	GO Twiwidget	Content provider	-	Public content provider
11	Beauty Plus	Shared preferences	-	Readable shared preferences

leakage. XManDroid [13] dynamically detects and prevents leakage by modifying the framework and enforcing policies to look for malicious ICC flows, but endures a lot of false positives. FUSE [14] conducts coarse-grained information flow analysis and thus, suffers from missed leaks. COVERT [8] applies formal model and model checking to symbolize apps and perform combination analysis, but fails to detect leaks, owing to its weak model and properties. IccTA [6] in combination with APKCombiner [12] detects inter-app privacy leaks by combining the apps and, further performing taint analysis. However, the technique is computationally expensive and does not work on most of the app pairs. DIAL-Droid [7] conducts large-scale app analysis by using SQLite databases. Hence, the technique is fast and scalable. However, it considers only intents and fails to detect leakage paths through content providers and shared preferences.

Table 2. Comparative analysis of inter-app privacy leakage detection techniques

Source App	Intermediate Apps	Destination App	DIALDroid	IccTA	Covert	APPLADroid
Droidbench 3.0						
SendSMS	-	Echoer	✓	✗	✗	✓
StartActivityForResult1	-	Echoer	✓	✗	✗	✓
Deviceld_Broadcast1	-	Collector	✓	✗	✗	✓
Deviceld_ContentProvider1	-	Collector	✓	✗	✗	✓
Deviceld_OrderedIntent1	-	Collector	✓	✗	✗	✓
Deviceld_Service1	-	Collector	✓	✗	✗	✓
Location1	-	Collector	✓	✗	✗	✓
Location_Broadcast1	-	Collector	✓	✗	✗	✓
Location_Service1	-	Collector	✗	✗	✗	✓
Erroneous App Pairings			-	-	172*	-
Droidbench IccTA Branch						
startActivity1_source	-	startActivity1_sink	✓	✓	✓	✓
startSevice1_source	-	startService1_sink	✓	✓	✓	✓
sendbroadcast1_source	-	sendbroadcast1_sink	✓	✓	✓	✓
Erroneous App Pairings			-	-	104*	-
Self-made Apps						
Medium1	Medium2, Medium3	Medium4	✗	✗	✗	✓
content_medium1	content_medium2	content_medium3	✗	✗	✗	✓
leak1	leak2	leak3	✗	✗	✗	✓
Erroneous App Pairings			-	-	-	-
Precision, Recall and F-Measure						
True Positive (✓) (Correctly detected)			11	3	3	15
False Positive (*) (Incorrectly detected)			0	0	276	0
False Negative (✗) (Missed)			4	12	12	0
Precision, p = ✓/(✓ + *)			100%	100%	1%	100%
Recall, r = ✓/(✓ + ✗)			73%	20%	20%	100%
F-Measure = 2pr/(p+r)			84.3	33.3	33.3	100

8   Conclusion

The access to the ICC mediums of an Android app by other apps may have dangerous ramifications such as privacy leak, privilege escalation, etc. APPLADroid captures privacy leaks maliciously executed through a chain of apps. It initially detects malicious flows in the apps through static analysis, and further models these flows as app graphs. Moreover, it resolves the sensitive information sharing between apps by performing the union of app graphs and creates Application automaton from the unioned graph. Subsequently, APPLADroid intersects Application Automaton with Policy automaton which signifies privacy leaking rules. If the intersected automaton contains a final state, we call the apps as potential privacy leaking partners. We have exhaustively analyzed APPLADroid on various apps from different sources. In future, we would work towards automatic exploit generation as a proof of concept for inter-app privacy leakage.

References

1. Barton, D.J.T.: Usable post-classification visualizations for Android collusion detection and inspection. Ph.D. thesis, Virginia Tech (2016)
2. Android Testing Cheat Sheet. https://www.owasp.org/index.php/Android_Testing_Cheat_Sheet. Accessed 18 June 2017

3. Jain, V., Bhandari, S., Laxmi, V., Gaur, M.S., Mosbah, M.: SniffDroid: detection of inter-app privacy leaks in Android. In: 2017 IEEE Trustcom/BigDataSE/ICESS, pp. 331–338. IEEE (2017)

4. Gordon, M.I., Kim, D., Perkins, J.H., Gilham, L., Nguyen, N., Rinard, M.C.: Information flow analysis of Android applications in DroidSafe. In: NDSS, vol. 15, p. 110 (2015)

5. Octeau, D., Luchaup, D., Dering, M., Jha, S., McDaniel, P.: Composite constant propagation: application to Android inter-component communication analysis. In: Proceedings of the 37th International Conference on Software Engineering, vol. 1, pp. 77–88. IEEE Press (2015)

6. Li, L., et al.: IccTA: detecting inter-component privacy leaks in Android apps. In: Proceedings of the 37th International Conference on Software Engineering, vol. 1, pp. 280–291. IEEE Press (2015)

7. Bosu, A., Liu, F., Yao, D.D., Wang, G.: Collusive data leak and more: large-scale threat analysis of inter-app communications. In: Proceedings of the 2017 ACM on Asia Conference on Computer and Communications Security, pp. 71–85. ACM (2017)

8. Bagheri, H., Sadeghi, A., Garcia, J., Malek, S.: COVERT: compositional analysis of Android inter-app permission leakage. IEEE Trans. Softw. Eng. **9**, 866–886 (2015)

9. Soot. https://github.com/secure-software-engineering/soot-infoflow-android. Accessed 08 Oct 2017

10. Droidbench 3.0. https://github.com/secure-software-engineering/DroidBench/tree/develop. Accessed 25 Aug 2017

11. Droidbench - IccTA Branch. https://github.com/secure-software-engineering/DroidBench/tree/iccta. Accessed 08 Aug 2017

12. Li, L., Bartel, A., Bissyandé, T.F., Klein, J., Traon, Y.L.: ApkCombiner: combining multiple Android apps to support inter-app analysis. In: Federrath, H., Gollmann, D. (eds.) SEC 2015. IAICT, vol. 455, pp. 513–527. Springer, Cham (2015). https://doi.org/10.1007/978-3-319-18467-8_34

13. Bugiel, S., Davi, L., Dmitrienko, A., Fischer, T., Sadeghi, A.-R.: XManDroid: a new Android evolution to mitigate privilege escalation attacks, Technische Universität Darmstadt, Technical Report TR-2011-04 (2011)

14. Ravitch, T., Creswick, E.R., Tomb, A., Foltzer, A., Elliott, T., Casburn, L.: Multi-app security analysis with fuse: statically detecting Android app collusion. In: Proceedings of the 4th Program Protection and Reverse Engineering Workshop, p. 4. ACM (2014)

Multiparty Evaluation of Finite State Machine

Dhaneshwar Mardi and Jaydeep Howlader[✉]

Department of Computer Science, National Institute of Technology Durgapur,
Durgapur, India
dhaneshwarmardi@gmail.com, jaydeep@cse.nitdgp.ac.in

Abstract. Finite State Machine (FSM) is a mathematical model of computation. FSM is often used to model the systems as a sequence of states and actions. The state captures the behavior of the system, and transition represents the action in the system. This paper presents a mechanism of privately evaluating FSM in the presence of the semi-honest adversary. We consider a set of mutually distrustful parties who want to evaluate a string on a FSM. Both the FSM and the input string are shared among the parties using a threshold secret sharing mechanism. Party individually does not know the FSM nor the input. Multiparty computation allows the parties to process the string on the FSM, collaboratively. During the execution, parties learn nothing more than the acceptance of the string.

1 Introduction

Formal language defines a set of strings together with a set of rules to define the memberships of the strings. The language $\mathcal{L}$ consists a set of alphabets, denoted as Σ and a grammar, denoted as G. Σ is a finite set of alphabets (alternatively called symbols or terminals). The language $\mathcal{L}$ is a subset of all possible strings over Σ, i.e. $\mathcal{L} \subset \Sigma^*$. The string $w \in \Sigma^*$ would be in $\mathcal{L}$ if w is derived by the grammar G. The grammar $G = \langle \Sigma, V_N, S, P \rangle$ is a four-tuples:

1. Σ is the finite set of alphabets.
2. V_N is the finite set of nonterminal such that $V_N \cap \Sigma = \Phi$
3. $S \in V_N$ is the start symbol
4. P is a finite set of productions in the form of $X \to \alpha$, where $X \in (\Sigma \cup V_N)^+$ and contains at least one nonterminal, and $\alpha \in (V_N \cup \Sigma)^*$.

The string $w_1 X w_3$ derives to $w_1 w_2 w_3$ (denoted as $w_1 X w_3 \Rightarrow w_1 w_2 w_3$) if there exists a production $X \to w_2$ in the grammar. The derivation operation is transitive and denoted as $\overset{*}{\Rightarrow}$. The string $w \in \mathcal{L}$, if $S \overset{*}{\Rightarrow} w$.

1.1 Regular Language and Finite State Automata

The language $\mathcal{L}_{\mathcal{R}}$ is regular if all the productions of the corresponding grammar are **type** 3. The **type** 3 productions are in the form of $A \to aB$ or $A \to a$, where

© Springer Nature Singapore Pte Ltd. 2019
S. Nandi et al. (Eds.): ISEA-ISAP 2018, CCIS 939, pp. 234–246, 2019.
https://doi.org/10.1007/978-981-13-7561-3_17

$A, B \in V_N$ and $a \in \Sigma$. Grammar basically defines the mechanism to generate strings of the language. On the other hand, given a string $w \in \Sigma^*$, whether $w \in \mathcal{L_R}$, is determined by the finite state machine (FSM). FSM is often called the recognizer as it accepts the string to be in $\mathcal{L_R}$ or rejects the string not to be in $\mathcal{L_R}$. The FSM $M = \langle Q, \Sigma, q_0, \delta, F \rangle$ is a five-tuples:

1. Q is a finite set of states.
2. Σ is the finite set of alphabets.
3. $q_0 \in Q$ is the initial (or start) state.
4. $F \subset Q$ is the set of final states.
5. δ is the set of transition functions. The transition function $\delta : Q \times \Sigma \to Q$ defines a move from one state to another on an alphabet.

Let q_i be the current state and $a_i a_{i+1} \ldots a_t$ be the current input string to the FSM. The FSM makes a **move** from state q_i to q_j if there exists a transition $\delta(q_i, a_i) \to q_j$ in the FSM. The **move** operation is denoted as $(a_i a_{i+1} \ldots a_t, q_i) \mapsto (a_{i+1} a_{i+2} \ldots a_t, \delta(q_i, a_i))$. The **move** operation is transitive and denoted as $\overset{*}{\mapsto}$. FSM accepts an input string $a_1 a_2 \ldots a_l$ if there exist **moves** $(a_1 a_2 \ldots a_t, q_0) \overset{*}{\mapsto} \delta(\delta(\delta(q_0, a_1), a_2), \ldots a_t) = q_f$ where $q_f \in F$. That is, FSM accepts the string if after executing all the **moves**, the FSM is in one of the final state.

An alternative representation of the transition function is in the form of transition matrix. Transition matrix, denoted as $\mathbb{T}$, is a $|Q| \times |\Sigma|$ matrix. The states are indexed to the rows and the alphabets are indexed to the columns. For every transition $\delta(q_i, a_j) \to q_j$, the $\mathbb{T}(i, j)$ contains the index of the state q_j. Alternatively the **move** is defined as $(a_j a_{j+1} \ldots a_t, q_i) \mapsto (a_{j+1} a_{j+2} \ldots a_t, \mathbb{T}(i, j))$.

1.2 Multiparty Computation

Multiparty Computation (MPC) protocol (introduced in [32] and [15]) allows a group of mutually distrustful parties $\{P_1, \ldots, P_n\}$ to compute a known function $f(x_1, \ldots, x_n)$ on their private inputs $x_1, x_2, \ldots, x_n$, respectively. It was shown in [15], that for every efficiently computable function f there exists an efficient MPC protocol $\mathcal{F}$, provided that a trapdoor-permutation exists. MPC protocols run in multiple *rounds*. The efficiency of the MPC is defined by the number of *rounds* and the *size* of the inputs.

We assume a linear secret sharing scheme (e.g., Shamir's Secret Sharing (SSS) [28]) that allows the parties to compute **addition** and **multiplication** of secret shares. The security properties of the MPC are inherited from the underline linear secret sharing scheme. Considering that SSS along with verifiable secret sharing (VSS) [14] is unconditionally secure against passive (or active) adversaries, implies that MPC is also secure against the passive (or active) adversaries.

We consider authenticated private channel between each peer of parties. There are two modes of communication(s):

- Parties perform secure computation over $\mathbb{F}_{p^k}$. Party learns nothing more than her input/output.

– Parties collaboratively reconstruct to reveal the secret. All parties learn the value simultaneously.

There are two type of adversaries in the system. The semi-honest adversary who follows the protocol correctly, but colludes to learn other's private values. In contrariety, malicious adversary who may deviate from the protocol in arbitrary ways. SSS is resilient upto $n/2$ semi-honest adversary [7] and $n/3$ malicious adversary [6] where n is the number of parties.

Threshold Secret Sharing Scheme. Let $\mathcal{P} = \{P_1, \ldots, P_n\}$ be the set of parties and S be a finite set of secrets, $|S| \geq 2$. A $(m\text{-}n)$ threshold secret sharing scheme is a two-tuples $\langle \mathcal{F}_S, \mathcal{F}_C \rangle$:

1. Function $\mathcal{F}_S : S \times R \to S^n$ is the sharing function. Dealer samples $r \in R$, uniformly and randomly from a uniform distribution R and computes the shares of the secret $s \in S$ as $\mathcal{F}_S(s, r) \to [s]$. The share $s_i \in [s]$ is privately communicated to party P_i.
2. Function $\mathcal{F}_C : S^m \to S$ is the reconstruction function. $\mathcal{F}_C$ defines an authorized set to reconstruction the secret. In SSS, any subset of at least m parties forms the authorized set. Here, m is the threshold.

SSS is a $(m\text{-}n)$ threshold secret sharing scheme over a prime field $\mathbb{F}_{p^k}$. To share a secret $s \in \mathbb{F}_{p^k}$, dealer chooses a random polynomial $\mathcal{F}_S(x) = s + \Sigma_{i=1}^{t-1} a_i x^i$ where $a_i \in \mathbb{F}_{p^k}$ and computes P_i's share as $(i, \mathcal{F}_S(i))$. Dealer privately communicates the share $(i, \mathcal{F}_S(i))$ to party P_i. Any subset of m parties can reconstruct the secret. Let $\mathcal{A} = \{P_{i_1}, P_{i_2}, \ldots, P_{i_m}\}$ be the authorized set, then the shares $\{(\mathcal{F}_S(i_1), \ldots, (\mathcal{F}_S(i_m))\}$ represent m points on the polynomial $\mathcal{F}_S(x)$. Applying Lagrange's interpolation, the polynomial is constructed and the secret $(s = \mathcal{F}_S(0))$ is computed:

$$\mathcal{F}_C(s_{i_1}, s_{i_2}, \ldots, s_{i_m}) = \Sigma_{l=i_1}^{i_m} s_l \left(\prod_{\substack{j=i_1,\ldots,i_m \\ j \neq l}} \frac{j}{j-l} \right)$$

$$= \mathcal{F}_S(0)$$

$$= s$$

1.3   Application of Multiparty FSM

FSM is often used as the basic modeling tool for many applications like digital circuit design, process chain management, Internet protocol parsing, string matching, etc. In those applications, FSM is publicly computable. That is, parties know the configuration of FSM as well as the input string. However, there are many applications where the FSM has to be evaluated privately.

Privacy in DNA String Searching and Matching: Assume Alice has found DNA sequences that contain sub-sequence close to a marker sequence[1]. Alice

---

[1] A genetic marker is a gene or DNA sequence with a known location on a chromosome that can be used to identify individuals or species.

would like to sell a service based on the marker sequence. But Alice would not like to disclose the marker. Similarly, Bob who wants to avail the service would not like to disclose his sequence. Privacy-preserving DNA string searching and matching demand a secure evaluation of FSM. In [13,30], authors present two-party computation on FSM where one holds the FSM, and the other can evaluate her sequence. The two-party computation guarantees that none of them would learn the others' private input.

Secure Smart Contract: A smart contract is a computer protocol intended to enforce the negotiation or performance of a contract without the involvement of third parties. The smart contracts are trackable and irreversible [9]. Smart contracts are usually deployed on the blockchain. The parties engage in the smart contract which maintains a FSM in the form of contract [19,20]. There are certain contracts (like auction [1,17], voting [18]) where privacy of data is important. For example: in voting, the contract would tally the votes without knowing 'who vote for whom' [21]. To enhance privacy in the smart contracts, certain FSMs have to be evaluated securely.

Secure Parsing of Internet Protocols: FSM is commonly used in the tokenization (lexical) and string matching applications [16]. The Internet protocols often include multiple entities. Some of the entities are considered to be a trusted third-party. The present trend is to replace the trusted third-parties with MPC. For example, Public Key Infrastructure (PKI) defines the trusted Certificate Authority (CA) as the repository of the certificates. The CA provides the certificate as on request. As and alternative of costly PKI certificate management a lightweight applications called identity-based public-key cryptography (ID-PKC) is proposed in [29]. The ID-PKC defines a trusted third-party called Private Key Generator (PKG) [2,3]. Recent technologies are attempting to replace the PKG with MPC. The protocol to model the PKG and subsequently, the ID-PKC requires the secure evaluation of FSMs.

Secure Computation of Markov Model: Hidden Markov model is a popular statistical tool in pattern recognition. Some applications, like speaker recognition, in particular, the computation involves personal data that can identify the individual and must be protected. Privacy-preserving techniques for hidden Markov model along with Gaussian mixture model is used in speaker recognition and other applications [4,5,24]. The Markov model is an extension of FSM (transition with probability). Therefore, privacy preserving speaker recognition intuitively implements the secure evaluation of FSM [5].

1.4   Related Work and Our Contribution

Secure evaluation of FSM has not been widely studied. There are some literatures where multiparty evaluation of FSMs are proposed as a computational tool. In [13,26,30], authors proposed a two-party evaluation of FSM. In those papers, one party holds the FSM, and the other party holds the input string. The protocol evaluates the input on the FSM where the parties learn nothing more than the output (acceptance or the input). The protocols are based on Boolean circuit [31,32], homomorphic encryption [26] and oblivious transfer [22,25,30].

In [5], authors proposed a MPC of hidden Markov model. The authors categorized the parties in two groups: (i) a set of parties collectively[2] possesses the hidden Markov model, (ii) another set of parties collectively possesses the input. The first group outsources the model, where the other group avails the service.

Our Contribution: In this paper, we present a general representation of FSM in the MPC setting. We consider a set of parties $\mathcal{P} = \{P_1, \ldots, P_n\}$. The FSM and the input is shared among the parties. Party individually does not know FSM transitions nor the input, but they can collaboratively compute the string on the machine.

Let the FSM be $M = \langle Q, \Sigma = \{0,1\}, q_0, \mathbb{T}, F \rangle$, where $\mathbb{T}$ is the transition matrix. Parties only know the number of state, the indices of the initial and final states, respectively. All other states are indistinguishable. The transition matrix is shared among the parties using a threshold secret sharing mechanism. The input string is also shared among the parties using threshold secret sharing mechanism. The proposed MPC obliviously[3] evaluates the input string on the FSM, where parties learn nothing more than the acceptance. Our computation is on the finite field $\mathbb{F}_{2^k}$ where k is the number of states. In the first proposal, we restrict the FSM with binary alphabet $\Sigma = \{0,1\}$ and then generalize the FSM for any arbitrary alphabet set with $|\Sigma| \leq 2^k$.

Organization of the Paper: The rest of this paper is organized as follows: in Sect. 2, we briefly discuss the construction of MPC over the finite field. In Sect. 3, we construct MPC of FSM and the mechanism to evaluate a string on the FSM. In Sect. 4, we generalize the FSM for any arbitrary alphabet set. Finally, we conclude the paper in Sect. 5.

2   Preliminary

SSS is one of the building blocks for MPC. In this section, we briefly discuss the construction of SSS over the finite field $\mathbb{F}_{2^k}$. Our protocol is based on the principle of Arithmetic Black Box (ABB). We present the basic ABB functions which are used in the construction of MPC of FSM.

2.1   Finite Field and Polynomials

Let $I(X) = a_0 + a_1 X + \cdots + a_k X^k$ be a polynomial of degree $k \geq 1$ where $a_i \in \mathbb{F}_p$ and p is prime. The polynomial $I(X)$ is irreducible if there does not exist any other polynomial $g(X)$ of degree lesser that k and divides $I(X)$. If $I(X)$ is an irreducible polynomial, then $\mathbb{F}_{p^k}$ is an extension of the field $\mathbb{F}_p$ with respective to the irreducible polynomial $I(X)$.

---

[2] Shares by a threshold secret sharing scheme.
[3] The sequence of states due to the transitions remain secret.

The elements of $\mathbb{F}_{2^k}$ are represented as $\alpha = b_0^{(\alpha)} + b_1^{(\alpha)}X + \ldots b_{k-1}^{(\alpha)}X^{k-1}$, where $b_i^{(\alpha)} \in \mathbb{F}_2$. Alternatively, the elements are represented as a k bit string. The arithmetic over $\mathbb{F}_{2^k}$ is as below:

Let $\alpha_1 = (b_{k-1}^{(\alpha_1)}, b_{k-2}^{(\alpha_1)}, \ldots, b_0^{(\alpha_1)})$ and $\alpha_2 = (b_{k-1}^{(\alpha_2)}, b_{k-2}^{(\alpha_2)}, \ldots, b_0^{(\alpha_2)})$ are two elements of $\mathbb{F}_{2^k}$. The addition is bit-by-bit XOR operation. That is, $\alpha_1 + \alpha_2 = (b_{k-1}^{(\alpha_1)} \oplus b_{k-1}^{(\alpha_2)}, \ldots, b_0^{(\alpha_1)} \oplus b_0^{(\alpha_2)})$. The multiplication involves two operations. Firstly, the two polynomial are multiplies in $\mathbb{F}_p[X]$. The result is a polynomial of degree $\leq 2(k-1)$. Subsequently, the polynomial is reduced by the modulo of the irreducible polynomial.

2.2   SSS over the Finite Field $\mathbb{F}_{2^k}$

Let dealer makes the secret shares of $s \in \mathbb{F}_{2^k}$ for n parties. Let the sharing is a $(m\text{-}n)$ threshold secret sharing. Dealer chooses $(m-1)$ random elements $\alpha_{i=1,\ldots,m-1} \in \mathbb{F}_{2^k}$ and forms the degree $(m-1)$ polynomial $f(X) = s + \sum_{i=1}^{m-1}\alpha_i X^i$. Dealer selects an irreducible polynomial $I(X)$ of degree m and defines $f(X) \in \mathbb{F}_{2^k}/I(X)$. A list of low-weight irreducible polynomials of degree $k \leq 10,000$ is present in [8,27].

Let the index of a party P_i be i. Dealer represents $x_i = \sum_{j=0}^{k-1} b^j X^j$, where $b_{j \neq i} = 0$ and $b_i = 1$. Thus, $x_i \in \mathbb{F}_{2^k}$ and represents the index of P_i. Dealer computes the share for P_i as $s_i = f(x_i) \mod I(X)$. Dealer privately communicates s_i to P_i. We denote the secret shares of s as $[s]$ and any share $s_i \in [s]$.

2.3   Secure Multiparty Computation and Arithmetic Black Box

Multiparty computation is often perceived to be impractical because all protocols are either require many rounds of interactions or expensive zero-knowledge proofs for verification. The basic model of circuit evaluation (e.g., Garble circuit [32] or Arithmetic circuit [10,23]) relies on the representation of the computation in the form of a circuit of ℓ inputs with basic operations (e.g. AND, XOR in Boolean circuit, and addition, multiplication in Arithmetic circuit). The circuit is encrypted as $E(C)$ and ℓ keys correspond to the inputs $\{i_1, i_2, \ldots, i_\ell\}$. One can efficiently compute the $E(C)$ in constant round. However, to setting up the circuit expensive zero-knowledge proofs are required.

An Arithmetic Black Box (ABB), on the other hand, is constant round and implements one primitive by using some other basic primitives as a random oracle. The primitive does not depend on the implementation of basic primitives. The security notion of *Universally Composability (UC)* defines that the implemented primitive intuitively inherits the security properties of the underlining basic primitives [11].

ABB over the $\mathbb{F}_{2^k}$: Based on SSS over $\mathbb{F}_{2^k}$, addition and constant multiplication can be done locally. Whereas, multiplication and reconstruction of the shared secret require one round of communication. We denote the secret sharing of $s \in \mathbb{F}_{2^k}$ as $[s]$. Let $[s_1], [s_2]$ are two shared secrets and c be a publicly known constant. We denote the addition as $[s_1 + s_2] \leftarrow [s_1] + [s_2]$, constant multiplication as $[cs_1] \leftarrow c[s_1]$ and multiplication as $[s_1 s_2] \leftarrow [s_1][s_2]$. The following ABB are realized using the above primitives [12]:

Pseudorandom Secret Sharing PSS(): A set of at least m parties participate in the computation. Without loss of generality, we assume that $\{P_1, \ldots, P_m\}$ participate in the computation of PSS. Each party P_i chooses her randomness $\alpha_i \in \mathbb{F}_{2^k}$ and makes share among the other parties $P_{j \neq i}$. Party P_j receives the share α_{ij} from party P_i. After all party does the sharing, P_j locally computes $\beta_j = \Sigma_{k=1}^m \alpha_{kj}$. The protocol intuitively shares a random element $\beta = \Sigma \alpha_i$, and party P_i possesses that share as $\beta_i \in [\beta]$.

The PSS incurs one round of operation.

Pseudorandom Bit Sharing PBS(): The PSS can be modified to share a pseudorandom bit. Let each party P_i chooses her randomness $\alpha_i = \{0, 1\} \in \mathbb{F}_{2^k}$ and executes the PBS. As the addition in $\mathbb{F}_{2^k}$ is bit-by-bit XOR, the shared secret results as $b = \oplus_{i=1}^m \alpha_i$, where $\alpha_i = \{0, 1\}$.

Bit Decomposition BD(): For a shares secret $[s]$ the protocol returns the shared secrets of the bits $[b_i^s], i=0,\ldots,k-1$ where $b_i^s \in \{0, 1\}$ and $s = \Sigma_{i=0}^k 2^i b_i^s$. The bit decomposition of the secret share $[s]$ is denoted as $[\![s]\!]$. A set of at least m computes the BD as below:

- Parties compute PBS for k times in parallel, and generates $\{[\alpha_{k-1}], [\alpha_{k-2}], \ldots, [\alpha_0]\}$ where $\alpha_i = \{0, 1\} \in \mathbb{F}_2^k$.
- Parties compute $[\alpha] = \Sigma_{i=0}^{k-1} [\alpha_i] X^i$ locally.
- Parties compute $[\alpha + s]$ locally and **reconstruct** $R = (\alpha + s)$. Let $(b_{k-1}^{(R)}, b_{k-2}^{(R)}, \ldots, b_0^{(R)})$ be the bit representation of R.
- Parties compute $[b_i^s], i=0,\ldots,k-1 = [b_i^{(R)} + \alpha_i]$ locally.

The BD incurs two round of operations.

3   Multiparty Evaluation of FSM

Let $M = \langle Q, \Sigma = \{0, 1\}, q_0, \mathbb{T}, F \rangle$ be a complete[4] deterministic FSM. Let k be the number of states. We define an encoding of states as $\mathcal{C} : Q \to \mathbb{F}_{2^k}$ as:

$$\mathcal{C}(q_i) = \begin{cases} 1 \in \mathbb{F}_{2^k} & \text{if } i = 0 \\ X^{i-1} \in \mathbb{F}_{2^k} & \text{otherwise} \end{cases}$$

The transition matrix is subsequently encoded as $\mathcal{C}(\mathbb{T})$. Below we present an example of the encoding of the transition matrix:

---

[4] For every state $q_i \in Q$ and $a \in \Sigma$, there is a transition in the FSM. If the FSM is not complete, one can add a sink state q_s and define transitions towards the q_s state.

Table 1. FSM Transition Matrix over the $\mathbb{F}_{2^k}$

	0	1			0	1
q_0	q_1	q_2		1	X	X^2
q_1	q_2	q_1	$\Rightarrow$	X	X^2	X
q_2	q_2	q_0		X^2	X^2	1

Transition Matrix $\mathbb{T}$ Encoded Transition Matrix $\mathcal{C}(\mathbb{T})$

3.1   Secret Sharing of FSM

Let there are n parties. The transition matrix is shared among the parties using SSS scheme over the $\mathbb{F}_{2^k}$. We represent the shared transition matrix as:

$$[\mathcal{C}(\mathbb{T})] = \begin{matrix} [\mathcal{C}(\mathbb{T}_{0,0})] & , & [\mathcal{C}(\mathbb{T}_{0,1})] \\ \vdots & ,_{,} & \vdots \\ [\mathcal{C}(\mathbb{T}_{k-1,0})], & [\mathcal{C}(\mathbb{T}_{k-1,1})] \end{matrix}$$

The parties only know the number of states, whereas the transitions are private. The first row index represents the initial state.

Multiparty FSM Transition: If the current state of the FSM is q_i and the current input to the FSM is b, then FSM makes a move to the state $\delta(q_i, b) \rightarrow q_j$. The transitions in MPC is realizes by the following Algorithm 1.

Algorithm 1. MPTrans($[\alpha], [b]$)

Input : $[x_i]$, the representation of the current state by $[\mathcal{C}(q_i)]$
            $[b]$, the shared value of the input alphabet. Here, $b = \{0, 1\}$
Output: $[x_j]$, the representation of the transited state. That is, x_j is
            the representation of $\mathcal{C}(\delta(q_i, b))$

1 Parties compute BD($[x_i]$) $\rightarrow ([b_{k-1}^{(x_i)}][b_{k-2}^{(x_i)}] \ldots [b_0^{(x_i)}])$
2 Parties compute $[x_j] = \Sigma_{i=0}^{k-1} \left([b_i^{(x_i)}] ([\mathcal{C}(\mathbb{T}_{i,0})][1 - b] + [\mathcal{C}(\mathbb{T}_{i,1})][b]) \right)$
   // Explained in Equation 1
3 **return** $[x_j]$

Multiparty FSM Evaluation: Consider that the input string is $w = (b_{l-1}^{(w)} b_{l-2}^{(w)} \ldots b_0^{(w)})$ where $b_i^{(w)} = \{0, 1\}$. The input to the FSM is the bit-wise secret share of the string. Therefore, parties possess the input as $[\![w]\!] = ([b_{l-1}^{(w)}][b_{l-2}^{(w)}] \ldots [b_0^{(w)}])$. The evaluation of the input is realized by the Algorithm 2.

Algorithm 2. MPEval($[\mathcal{C}(\mathbb{T})], [\![w]\!]$)

Input : $[\![w]\!] = ([b_{l-1}^{(w)}][b_{l-2}^{(w)}] \ldots [b_0^{(w)}])$, the input string
$[\mathcal{C}(\mathbb{T})]$, the transition matrix

Output: $[x]$, the state reached at the end of the string.

1 Parties compute the initial move as
$[x_1] = [\mathcal{C}(\mathbb{T}_{0,0})][1 - b_0^{(w)}] + [\mathcal{C}(\mathbb{T}_{0,1})][b_0^{(w)}]$

2 **for** $i = 1$ *to* $l - 1$ **do**

3 $\quad \lfloor$ Parties computes $[x_{i+1}] = \texttt{MPTrans}([x_i], [b_i^{(w)}])$

4 **return** $[x_l]$

Complexity of Multiparty FSM: The complexity of MPC is measured by the number of rounds and the number of basic operations[5]. Let the input string is l bits, and the FSM consists of k states. The complexity of multiparty FSM is derived from the ABB functions. Table 2 shows the complexity of the individual ABB functions.

Table 2. Functions and their complexities

Operation	ABB function	Number of rounds
PSS, PBS	1. Invocation of at least m secret sharing in parallel	One round
BD	1. Invocation of k PBS in parallel	One round
	2. Invocation of one revealing operation	One round
MPTrans	1. Invocation of BD	One round
	2. Invocation of $3k$ multiplications	Two rounds
MPEval	1. Invocation of l number of MPTrans	$3l$ rounds

Privacy of Multiparty FSM: SSS is information-theoretically secure against passive adversary with honest majority. The sharing function $\mathcal{F}_s(\cdot)$ includes randomness, thereby every share is computationally indistinguishable from other. In other words, given the two secret shares of the same secret $s \in \mathbb{F}_{2^k}$ ($\mathcal{F}_s(\alpha, r_2)$ and $\mathcal{F}_s(\alpha, r_2)$) no probabilistic polynomial algorithm exists to tell them 'apart'. Applying the security notion of UC, the output of any ABB function that includes the basic function $\mathcal{F}_s()$ is also computationally indistinguishable. Therefore, share addition, constant multiplication and multiplication are computationally indistinguishable.

In MPC of FSM, the transition matrix is shared among the parties. The rows of the matrix are indexing to the states, the columns are indexing to the alphabets. However, the cells of the matrix are private and indistinguishable. Given

---

[5] The basic operation includes either PSS, PBS, sharing secret, multiplication or revealing secret. Multiple basic operations are often performed in parallel and considered as one round.

an alphabet $[b] = \{[0], [1]\}$, the function MPTrans invokes the multiplication function obliviously. Therefore, the sequence of states traversed by the multiparty FSM are indistinguishable and reveal no information. Following, we show the obliviousness of the access to the state transition.

Consider the transition matrix shown in Table 1. Let q_1 be the current state and $b = 1$ be the current input alphabet. The state is encoded as $X \in \mathbb{F}_{2^3}$. Then BD(X) in public computes $(b_2^{(X)} = 0, b_1^{(X)} = 1, b_0^{(X)} = 0)$. The next state is derived as:

$$
\begin{aligned}
& b_0^{(X)}\big((\mathbb{T}_{0,0})(1-b) + (\mathbb{T}_{0,1})b\big) \\
+& b_1^{(X)}\big((\mathbb{T}_{1,0})(1-b) + (\mathbb{T}_{1,1})b\big) \\
+& b_2^{(X)}\big((\mathbb{T}_{2,0})(1-b) + (\mathbb{T}_{2,1})b\big)
\end{aligned} \tag{1}
$$

Equation 1 is data-oblivious. That is, access to the transition matrix is independent to the row and column indices.

4 Generalization of Multiparty FSM with Any Alphabet Set

In the previous section we restrict the FSM with binary alphabet. Here, we present the general form of MPC of FSM with arbitrary alphabet set. Firstly we define two functions:

Indexing Function: The index of an alphabet is a mapping that uniquely corresponds to a column of the transition matrix. Let the alphabet set contains z alphabets, and $\varphi = \lceil \log z \rceil$. The indexing function is one-to-one mapping $\# : \Sigma \to \{0,1\}^\varphi$. The simplest form of indexing function is the binary representation i.e., $\#(a_i) = \big(b_{\varphi-1}^{(a_i)} b_{\varphi-2}^{(a_i)} \ldots b_0^{(a_i)}\big)$ where $i = \Sigma_{j=0}^{\varphi-1} 2^j b_j^{(a_i)}$, and $b_j^{(a_i)} = \{0,1\}$. Subsequently, the alphabet set is indexed to an ordered sequence as $\#\Sigma = \{a_0, a_1, \ldots, a_{z-1}\}$.

Decoding Function: A decoder is a mapping $\mathcal{D} : \#\Sigma \to \{0,1\}^z$ where $\mathcal{D}(\#(a_i))$ is z bit binary string all '0's, except the ith bit is set to '1'. The decoder can be realize from the indexing function. Let the index of an alphabet be $\#(a_i) \to \big(b_{\varphi-1}^{(a_i)} b_{\varphi-2}^{(a_i)} \ldots b_0^{(a_i)}\big)$, then decoder outputs a bits stream of z bits as $\mathcal{D}(\#(a_i)) \to \big(\bar{b}_{z-1}^{(a_i)} \bar{b}_{z-2}^{(a_i)} \ldots \bar{b}_0^{(a_i)}\big)$ where:

$$
\bar{b}_0^{(a_i)} = (1 - b_{\varphi-1}^{(a_i)})(1 - b_{\varphi-2}^{(a_i)}) \ldots (1 - b_1^{(a_i)})(1 - b_0^{(a_i)})
$$

$$
\bar{b}_1^{(a_i)} = (1 - b_{\varphi-1}^{(a_i)})(1 - b_{\varphi-2}^{(a_i)}) \ldots (1 - b_1^{(a_i)})(b_0^{(a_i)})
$$

$$
\bar{b}_2^{(a_i)} = (1 - b_{\varphi-1}^{(a_i)})(1 - b_{\varphi-2}^{(a_i)}) \ldots (b_1^{(a_i)})(1 - b_0^{(a_i)})
$$

$$
\vdots
$$

$$
\bar{b}_{z-1}^{(a_i)} = (b_{\varphi-1}^{(a_i)})(b_{\varphi-2}^{(a_i)}) \ldots (b_1^{(a_i)})(b_0^{(a_i)})
$$

4.1 Generalized Multiparty FSM Transition

Consider the FSM with $k = |Q|$ states and $z = |\Sigma|$ alphabets. The order of the transition matrix is $k \times z$. The states are indexed to the rows, and the alphabets are indexed to the columns. The transition matrix is shared among n parties. Below we describe the transition of the FSM on input $[a]$ (where $a \in \Sigma$) and state $[X^i]$:

- Parties compute bit decomposition of the input alphabet as $\mathtt{BD}([a]) \rightarrow (b_{z-1}^{(a)}$ $b_{z-2}^{(a)} \ldots b_0^{(a)})$.
  Parties compute bit decomposition of the current state as $\mathtt{BD}([X^i]) \rightarrow (\bar{b}_{k-1}^{(x_i)}$ $\bar{b}_{k-2}^{(x_i)} \ldots b_0^{(\alpha)})$. BDs are invoked in parallel and incurs one round operation.
- Parties compute the decoder function $\mathcal{D}(BD([a])) \rightarrow ([\bar{b}_{z-1}^a][\bar{b}_{z-2}^a] \ldots [\bar{b}_0^a])$. This is a one round operation and incurs $\varphi \times z$ $\mathtt{multiplication}$ in parallel.
- Parties compute the transition as:

$$\mathtt{MPTrans}(\mathtt{BD}([X^i]), \mathtt{BD}([a])) := \Sigma_{u=0}^{k-1}\Big([b_u^{(x_i)}]\big(\Sigma_{v=0}^{z-1}[\mathcal{C}(\mathbb{T}_{u,v})][\bar{b}_v^{(a)}]\big)\Big)$$

This is two round operation. In the first round, there are $z \times k$ parallel $\mathtt{multiplication}$ operations. In the second round there are k $\mathtt{multiplication}$ operations.

4.2 Implement and Analysis

Let the FSM has k number of states. The alphabet set contains z distinct symbols. Also let $\varphi = \lceil \log z \rceil$. We set the finite field as $\mathbb{F}_{2^{max(k,\varphi)}}$.

In our implementation, the alphabets are represented by φ bits, whereas the states are represented by k bits. A decoder function is used to map an alphabet to a z bit string.

We apply the decoder only on the alphabets and not on the states because the inputs are generally available to the FSM beforehand. The input alphabets are independent and remain unchanged during the execution of the FSM. On the other hand, states are not independent. The present state is a function of the last encountered state and alphabet. So, introducing decoder will increase the latency and computation.

5 Conclusion

We have presented a MPC protocol with the honest majority for evaluating an input string on a FSM. There are two aspects of privacy. Firstly, the party individually does not know the FSM, nor the input string. Secondly, the proposed protocol is oblivious. That is the computation is independent of the input string. Therefore, the party learns nothing about the sequence of the states traversed by the FSM.

References

1. Abe, M., Suzuki, K.: Receipt-free sealed-bid auction. In: Chan, A.H., Gligor, V. (eds.) ISC 2002. LNCS, vol. 2433, pp. 191–199. Springer, Heidelberg (2002). https://doi.org/10.1007/3-540-45811-5_14

2. Al-Riyami, S.S.: Cryptographic schemes based on elliptic curve pairings. Ph.D. thesis, Royal Holloway, University of London, UK (2004)

3. Al-Riyami, S.S., Paterson, K.G.: Certificateless public key cryptography. In: Laih, C.-S. (ed.) ASIACRYPT 2003. LNCS, vol. 2894, pp. 452–473. Springer, Heidelberg (2003). https://doi.org/10.1007/978-3-540-40061-5_29

4. Aliasgari, M., Blanton, M.: Secure computation of hidden Markov models. In: 10th International Conference on Security and Cryptography SECRYPT 2013, pp. 242–253. SciTePress (2013)

5. Aliasgari, M., Blanton, M., Bayatbabolghani, F.: Secure computation of hidden Markov models and secure floating-point arithmetic in the malicious model. Int. J. Inf. Secur. **16**(6), 577–601 (2017)

6. Asharov, G., Lindell, Y., Rabin, T.: Perfectly-secure multiplication for any $t<n/3$. In: Rogaway, P. (ed.) CRYPTO 2011. LNCS, vol. 6841. Springer, Heidelberg (2011). https://doi.org/10.1007/978-3-642-22792-9_14

7. Ben-Or, M., Goldwasser, S., Wigderson, A.: Completeness theorems for non-cryptographic fault-tolerant distributed computation (extended abstract). In: 20th Annual ACM Symposium on Theory of Computing, pp. 1–10. ACM (1988)

8. Blake, I.F., Gao, S., Lambert, R.: Constructive problems for irreducible polynomials over finite fields. In: Gulliver, T.A., Secord, N.P. (eds.) ITA 1993. LNCS, vol. 793, pp. 1–23. Springer, Heidelberg (1994). https://doi.org/10.1007/3-540-57936-2_27

9. blockgeeks.com: A beginner's guide to smart contacts. https://blockgeeks.com/guides/smart-contract/

10. Bogetoft, P., et al.: Secure multiparty computation goes live. In: Dingledine, R., Golle, P. (eds.) FC 2009. LNCS, vol. 5628, pp. 325–343. Springer, Heidelberg (2009). https://doi.org/10.1007/978-3-642-03549-4_20

11. Canetti, R.: Universally composable security: a new paradigm for cryptographic protocols. In: 42nd Annual Symposium on Foundations of Computer Science, FOCS 2001, pp. 136–145. IEEE Computer Society (2001)

12. Damgård, I., Keller, M.: Secure multiparty AES (full paper). IACR Cryptology ePrint Archive, 2009/614 (2009)

13. Frikken, K.B.: Practical private DNA string searching and matching through efficient oblivious automata evaluation. In: Gudes, E., Vaidya, J. (eds.) DBSec 2009. LNCS, vol. 5645, pp. 81–94. Springer, Heidelberg (2009). https://doi.org/10.1007/978-3-642-03007-9_6

14. Gennaro, R., Rabin, M.O., Rabin, T.: Simplified VSS and fact-track multiparty computations with applications to threshold cryptography. In: 17th Annual ACM Symposium on Principles of Distributed Computing, PODC 1998, pp. 101–111. ACM (1998)

15. Goldreich, O., Micali, S., Wigderson, A.: How to play any mental game or a completeness theorem for protocols with honest majority. In: 19th Annual ACM Symposium on Theory of Computing, pp. 218–229. ACM (1987)

16. Graham, R.D., Johnson, P.C.: Finite state machine parsing for internet protocols: faster than you think. In: IEEE Security and Privacy Workshops, SPW 2014, pp. 185–190. IEEE Computer Society (2014)

17. Harkavy, M., Tygar, J.D., Kikuchi, H.: Electronic auctions with private bids. In: 3rd USENIX Workshop on Electronic Commerce. USENIX Association (1998)
18. Liaw, H.-T.: A secure electronic voting protocol for general elections. Comput. Secur. **23**(2), 107–119 (2004)
19. Mavridou, A., Laszka, A.: Designing secure ethereum smart contracts: a finite state machine based approach. CoRR, abs/1711.09327 (2017)
20. Mavridou, A., Laszka, A.: Tool demonstration: FSolidM for designing secure ethereum smart contracts. In: Bauer, L., Küsters, R. (eds.) POST 2018. LNCS, vol. 10804, pp. 270–277. Springer, Cham (2018). https://doi.org/10.1007/978-3-319-89722-6_11
21. Mitrou, L., Gritzalis, D., Katsikas, S.K.: Revisiting legal and regulatory requirements for secure E-Voting. In: International Conference on Information Security (SEC 2002), pp. 469–480. Kluwer (2002)
22. Naor, M., Pinkas, B.: Efficient oblivious transfer protocols. In: 12th Annual ACM-SIAM Symposium on Discrete Algorithms, SODA 2001, pp. 448–457. Society for Industrial and Applied Mathematics (2001)
23. Nargis, I., Mohassel, P., Eberly, W.: Efficient multiparty computation for arithmetic circuits against a covert majority. In: Youssef, A., Nitaj, A., Hassanien, A.E. (eds.) AFRICACRYPT 2013. LNCS, vol. 7918, pp. 260–278. Springer, Heidelberg (2013). https://doi.org/10.1007/978-3-642-38553-7_15
24. Nguyen, H.X., Roughan, M.: Multi-observer privacy-preserving hidden Markov models. IEEE Trans. Signal Process. **61**(23), 6010–6019 (2013)
25. Rabin, M.O.: How to exchange secrets with oblivious transfer (2005). http://eprint.iacr.org/2005/187
26. Sasakawa, H., Harada, H., duVerle, D., Arimura, H., Tsuda, K., Sakuma, J.: Oblivious evaluation of non-deterministic finite automata with application to privacy-preserving virus genome detection. In: 13th Workshop on Privacy in the Electronic Society, WPES 2014, pp. 21–30. ACM, New York (2014)
27. Seroussi, G.: Table of low-weight binary irreducible polynomials. Computer Systems Laboratory, Hewlett-Packard Company, August 1998
28. Shamir, A.: How to share a secret. Commun. ACM **22**(11), 612–613 (1979)
29. Shamir, A.: Identity-based cryptosystems and signature schemes. In: Blakley, G.R., Chaum, D. (eds.) CRYPTO 1984. LNCS, vol. 196, pp. 47–53. Springer, Heidelberg (1985). https://doi.org/10.1007/3-540-39568-7_5
30. Troncoso-Pastoriza, J.R., Katzenbeisser, S., Celik, M.: Privacy preserving error resilient DNA searching through oblivious automata. In: 14th ACM Conference on Computer and Communications Security, CCS 2007, pp. 519–528. ACM (2007)
31. Yao, A.C.C.: Protocols for secure computations (extended abstract). In: 23rd Annual Symposium on Foundations of Computer Science, pp. 160–164. IEEE Computer Society (1982)
32. Yao, A.C.C.: How to generate and exchange secrets (extended abstract). In: 27th Annual Symposium on Foundations of Computer Science, pp. 162–167. IEEE Computer Society (1986)

An Enhanced Privacy-Preserving Recommender System

Pranav Verma$^{(\boxtimes)}$, Harshul Vaishnav, Anish Mathuria, and Sourish Dasgupta

Dhirubhai Ambani Institute of Information and Communication Technology,
Gandhinagar, India
{201621017,anish_mathuria,sourish_dasgupta}@daiict.ac.in,
va.hv.02@gmail.com

Abstract. A recommender system stores historical data collected over a long period from various users, these are used to predict how new and existing users would rate an item. As user data is stored by the system, this poses threat to user's privacy. The goal of a privacy preserving recommender system is to hide user ratings from system and yet allow to make recommendations.

A recent example is the privacy-preserving recommender scheme proposed by Badsha, Yi and Khalil. Their scheme assumes that the server is semi-honest. However, when the server is malicious an attack is possible, as shown by Mu, Shao and Miglani. In this paper, we propose a simple modification to their scheme, which preserves the privacy of ratings against a malicious server. We demonstrate that the computation and communication costs of modified protocol are reasonable in comparison to original protocol.

Keywords: Recommender system · Privacy · Collaborative Filtering · Content Based Filtering · Homomorphic encryption

1 Introduction

Online services and users of such services are growing significantly in number. Recommender systems apply data mining techniques to predict users' interest on information, products and services among available items [16]. Many well known service providers, for example Amazon, YouTube, use recommender systems. These systems create user's profile by implicit feedback like clicking, downloading, time spent on a page; and explicit feedback like five star rating, upvote-downvote, like-dislike etc. Since it is difficult for a user to rate all items, a recommender system predicts those missing ratings based on user's behavior. To compute the missing ratings of user, recommender system utilize rating prediction techniques, such as: Collaborative Filtering and Content Based Filtering.

To make recommendations, a system needs information such as user's preferences, liking-disliking which imposes privacy concerns. Users give their personal information to the service provider in exchange of better recommendations. This

© Springer Nature Singapore Pte Ltd. 2019
S. Nandi et al. (Eds.): ISEA-ISAP 2018, CCIS 939, pp. 247–260, 2019.
https://doi.org/10.1007/978-981-13-7561-3_18

information can be sensitive and a user may want to hide these from recommender system as well as from other users. For example, an investor may like to keep his interest in particular stock hidden from others, while he will expect a recommender system to show him more relevant stocks as per his interests. Privacy-preserving recommender systems are helpful in such cases. The goal of a privacy-preserving recommender system is to preserve user's privacy by hiding their ratings from server and other users. Such approaches can be divided into three categories: perturbation, differential privacy and encryption based techniques. In perturbation and differential privacy based approaches, noise is added to hide the actual values, this noise can be derived from any distribution like Gaussian, Laplacian etc. This added noise reduces prediction accuracy and leak information sometimes [11]. Although encryption based approaches are comparatively costly in terms of required computations, they provide better privacy. In this paper we consider encryption based privacy preserving techniques based on homomorphic encryption (HE) schemes (like [5,7,13]) that allow operations to be performed directly on encrypted data.

Canny [3] showed that homomorphic encryption can be used in recommender systems, since there were only addition and multiplication operations are required to compute aggregate values. In [19] authors have proposed a recommender system *Cryptorec* which uses matrix factorization technique [10] for rating prediction. To provide privacy they employ HE, users send ratings in encrypted form and system with a trained model performs prediction. Bachrach et al. proposed to convert a trained neural network to *CryptoNets*, which works on encrypted data [8]. They used *Simple Encrypted Arithmetic Library (SEAL)* for homomorphic encryption. As high degree polynomial functions need large parameters it slows down the computation process. In cryptonet authors approximated sigmoid and rectified linear activation functions using square function which is lowest degree non-linear function. Badsha, Yi and Khalil (hereafter BYK) [1] utilize ElGamal homomorphic encryption scheme to compute cosine similarity between items and generate recommendation by collaborative and content based filtering techniques. Shmueli and Tassa [17] proposed a secure multiparty protocol, which is useful to generate recommendations using data from more than one vendor. They introduced a mediator that helps the involved parties to generate recommendations more accurately by sharing data with each other while preserving privacy of users. Yakut and Polat [20] proposed a similar system which involves multiple vendors, where they have added random noise into rating matrix to preserve user privacy.

Privacy Goals: To preserve user's privacy by hiding their ratings from other users as well as from server. A malicious server should not be able to read ratings in plaintext. The recommendations generated for an intended user should be available only to that user, server should not learn about predicted ratings of any item for the specific user.

Our Contributions: In this paper we revisit the BYK scheme proposed in [1]. A potential drawback of this scheme was pointed out by Mu, Shao and Miglani [6]. They proposed an attack that allows a malicious server to read a target user's ratings in plaintext. They also suggested a solution to this problem based on a public ledger visible to all users, but their solution is computationally costly for users. We propose a modification to BYK scheme that protect the user's private data against a dishonest server, meaning that even if server deviates from the protocol and behaves maliciously, it still cannot get ratings in plaintext. We argue that the modified scheme is secure against a malicious server and compare the performance with existing scheme. Our modification adds negligible costs for generating recommendation while protecting privacy against stronger adversary.

In the following section, we provide background on ElGamal encryption scheme, similarity measures and rating prediction techniques. In Sect. 3 we describe the protocol proposed in [1] and how a malicious server can read ratings in plaintext, along with solution proposed in [6]. Section 4 provides details of our proposed modification, followed by privacy analysis of the proposed protocol in Sect. 5. Cost analysis are mentioned in Sect. 6. The details of experiments we performed and the results are given in Sect. 7. Section 8 contains our conclusions.

2 Background

In what follows and rest of this paper we use the notations shown in Table 1.

Table 1. Notations

$\alpha_{i,j}$	Random number used to encrypt rating $r_{i,j}$	$\beta_{i,j}$	Random number used to encrypt flag $f_{i,j}$
q	Large prime number	$r_{i,j}$	Rating for item j by user i
$E()$	Public key encryption function	$\bar{r}_j$	Average rating for item j
$f_{i,j}$	Flag for rating $r_{i,j}$	$s(i_j, i_k)$	Similarity between items j and k
G	Cyclic group	g	Generator of G
$t_{i,j}$	Random number used to mask rating $r_{i,j}$	$U_{j,k}$	Users who rated both items j and k
i_j	j^{th} item	u_i	i^{th} user
m	Total number of items	x_i	User i's private key
n	Total number of users	Y	Common public key
P	Predicted rating	y_i	User i's public key

2.1 Cosine Similarity

The cosine similarity [2] measures the angle between two item vectors; smaller angle means more similar items. Similarity between items i_j and i_k is given as:

$$s(i_j, i_k) = \frac{\sum_{a=1}^{n} r_{a,j} r_{a,k}}{\sqrt{\sum_{a=1}^{n} r_{a,j}^2} + \sqrt{\sum_{a=1}^{n} r_{a,k}^2}}$$

Pearson's correlation coefficient [15] is also commonly used for similarity measures.

2.2 Prediction Techniques

A recommender system predicts ratings for items that a user has not seen, typically the item with highest predicted ratings are recommended to user. To predict ratings system uses features of items and users like similarity between items, similarity between users. The prediction techniques can broadly be classified into the following two categories:

Content Based Filtering: Look at what a user **u** likes, and check if the item **i** is similar to his liking.

Collaborative Filtering: Look who likes item **i**, then check if user **u** is similar to those users. There are two different approaches to collaborative filtering: Memory based techniques and Model-based techniques discussed in [4] and [12].

2.3 Homomorphic Encryption

A homomorphic encryption scheme allows to perform some computations on encrypted data and produces encrypted output which is similar to encryption of result obtained by performing computations on respective plaintexts. ElGamal homomorphic encryption system is one such scheme. It satisfies IND-CPA which guarantees that the ciphertext reveals nothing about the message. The BYK scheme uses ElGamal encryption where the message is raised to the generator.

Let G be a cyclic group of large prime order q, with generator g.

- *Key Generation*: Choose a random x, $1 \leq x \leq q - 1$. The public key is calculated as $y = g^x$.
- *Encryption*: The ciphertext for m is calculated as

$$(C_1, C_2) = (g^r, g^m y^r)$$

where r is a random number.
- *Decryption*: The ciphertext is decrypted using the private key as follows:

$$\frac{C_2}{(C_1)^x} = \frac{g^m y^r}{g^{rx}} = g^m$$

Usually we assume that the discrete logarithm (DL) problem is hard but if the value of m is small then it can be efficiently computed.

Additive Homomorphic Property: Let m_1 and m_2 be two messages. The corresponding ciphertext pairs are:

$$(C_{11}, C_{21}) = (g^{r_1}, g^{m_1} y^{r_1}) \qquad (C_{12}, C_{22}) = (g^{r_2}, g^{m_2} y^{r_2})$$

By multiplying the components of the two ciphertexts we obtain the pair:

$$(C, C') = (g^{r_1 + r_2}, g^{m_1 + m_2} y^{r_1 + r_2})$$

which is equal to ciphertext of $(m_1 + m_2)$, with random $r_1 + r_2$.

3   Badsha-Yi-Khalil Recommender Scheme

The protocol of Badsha, Yi and Khalil proceeds in three phases: average computation, similarity computation and secure rating prediction. To perform rating prediction securely values computed in the first two phases are used. In this section we will review the protocol for privacy-preserving average computation, as this step is necessary for both CF and CBF based recommendation generation.

Each user i chooses at random a private key x_i, $1 \leq x_i \leq q-1$ and computes its public key $y_i = g^{x_i}$. All users use the common public key $Y = g^{x_1 + \cdots + x_n}$.

3.1   Private Computation of Average Rating

The server first collects encrypted ratings from all users, and computes average rating for each item. Note that not all users are required to rate every item, for an item some users may have rated it and others may not. A flag is used to show whether or not a user has rated an item, flag $f_{i,j} = 1$ if user i has rated item j, otherwise it is 0.

Stage-I: Every user u_i $(1 \leq i \leq n)$, encrypts the rating and flags for all items i_j $(1 \leq j \leq m)$ using Y and sends the encrypted values to the server.

u_1 for i_j $E(g^{r_{1,j}}) = (g^{\alpha_{1,j}}, g^{r_{1,j}} Y^{\alpha_{1,j}})$ $E(g^{f_{1,j}}) = (g^{\beta_{1,j}}, g^{f_{1,j}} Y^{\beta_{1,j}})$

u_2 for i_j $E(g^{r_{2,j}}) = (g^{\alpha_{2,j}}, g^{r_{2,j}} Y^{\alpha_{2,j}})$ $E(g^{f_{2,j}}) = (g^{\beta_{2,j}}, g^{f_{2,j}} Y^{\beta_{2,j}})$

$$\vdots \qquad\qquad\qquad\qquad \vdots$$

u_n for i_j $E(g^{r_{n,j}}) = (g^{\alpha_{n,j}}, g^{r_{n,j}} Y^{\alpha_{n,j}})$ $E(g^{f_{n,j}}) = (g^{\beta_{n,j}}, g^{f_{n,j}} Y^{\beta_{n,j}})$

Stage-II: Once all user's ratings and flags are received, server multiplies them for each item, to homomorphically compute sum of ratings and sum of flags. for i_j:

$$(C_j, C_j') = \left(\prod_{i=1}^{n} g^{\alpha_{i,j}}, \prod_{i=1}^{n} g^{r_{i,j}} Y^{\alpha_{i,j}} \right) \qquad (D_j, D_j') = \left(\prod_{i=1}^{n} g^{\beta_{i,j}}, \prod_{i=1}^{n} g^{f_{i,j}} Y^{\beta_{i,j}} \right)$$

Server broadcasts C_j, D_j values to all users.

Stage-III: Every user u_i replies to server with $C_j^{x_i}$ and $D_j^{x_i}$.

Stage-IV: Server multiplies all received values and computes $\bar{r}_j$ as follows:

$$\frac{\prod_{i=1}^{n} g^{r_{i,j}} Y^{\alpha_{i,j}}}{\prod_{i=1}^{n} (C_j^{x_i})} = g^{\sum_{i=1}^{n} r_{i,j}} \qquad \frac{\prod_{i=1}^{n} g^{f_{i,j}} Y^{\beta_{i,j}}}{\prod_{i=1}^{n} (D_j^{x_i})} = g^{\sum_{i=1}^{n} f_{i,j}}$$

Now, to obtain $\sum_{i=1}^{n} r_{i,j}$ and $\sum_{i=1}^{n} f_{i,j}$, server has to solve discrete logarithm, brute-force technique to solve DL is computationally costly. Following the authors of [21], when x in g^x lies within a known interval, we can efficiently solve the DL using Pollard's lambda algorithm. A recommender system can compute this interval, as the total number of items, users and maximum possible rating is known. After solving DL server computes $\bar{r}_j$.

3.2 Mu-Shao-Miglani Attack

The assumption made in the previous protocol is that the server is semi-honest, which in practical applications may not always be true. Mu et al. [6] showed that a malicious server can obtain any rating given by any user. Suppose server wants to know user u_k's rating for item i_j. The encrypted rating sent by u_k to server in stage-I is:

$$(g^{\alpha_{k,j}}, g^{r_{k,j}} Y^{\alpha_{k,j}})$$

In place of C_j, server sends the value $\hat{C}_j = g^{r_{k,j}}$ to all users in stage-II. Then each user u_i will reply with the value $\hat{C}_j^{x_i}$ to server in stage-III. Now server can compute $r_{k,j}$ as follows:

$$\frac{g^{r_{k,j}} Y^{\alpha_{k,j}}}{(g^{\alpha_{k,j}})^{\sum_{i=1}^n x_i}}$$

Finally, server can solve for $r_{k,j}$.

3.3 Fix

Mu et al. proposed a solution using a public ledger which is visible to all users.

Each user before sending encrypted rating to server computes hash of the encryption and send that hash to server. This hash is used for commitment, that a user after sending the hash cannot change the encryption of ratings, server publishes all hashes on the public ledger. Once all hashes are published, users send their encrypted ratings to server, which again are published on the ledger. Server now computes sum of ratings and sum of flags on encrypted data (similar to original BYK protocol) and broadcasts one part of ciphertexts to all users. Each user using their private key computes $(C_j)^{x_i}$ and $(D_j)^{x_i}$. But before sending it to server, they verify the following:

- Check that the hashes published on ledger are correct or not, by computing hashes of encrypted ratings published in the ledger
- The values C_j and D_j can be verified by each user, as all the encrypted ratings are available to each user from ledger.

Now if the server acts maliciously and tries to send doctored value to any user, the user can verify it from ledger. Suppose server tries to read rating $r_{k,j}$, then in stage-II it will send $\hat{C}_j = g^{r_{k,j}}$ to all users. In stage-III each user before sending its reply, verifies the value from ledger. All users will find out that server is not sending the correct value, so they will abort the protocol.

The above proposal helps to preserve privacy of users from malicious server, but it is computationally very costly. They have to check if the hashes are correct for all users, and for all items. Each user also has to compute the sum of ratings and sum of flags, to verify the received value from server. The solution approach also increases communication overhead on users, as hashes are sent before encrypted ratings.

4   Modified Protocol

In the previous scheme we saw that a malicious server can obtain a rating assigned by any user. The reason is that the server is able to trick the user into sending the ephemeral key used to encrypt a private rating. We propose a modification to the previous protocol, where an additional ephemeral key is used to mask the rating value. In this section we will discuss first phase and see how our modification helps prevent the attack described earlier. Similar can be applied to remaining two phases of the BYK protocol. The modified encryption and decryption steps are shown below:

Encryption: The rating $r_{i,j}$ and flag $f_{i,j}$ are encrypted by user i as follows:

$$E(g^{r_{i,j}}) = (g^{\alpha_{i,j}}, g^{r_{i,j}} + t_{i,j} y^{\alpha_{i,j}}) \qquad E(g^{f_{i,j}}) = (g^{\beta_{i,j}}, g^{f_{i,j}} + t'_{i,j} y^{\beta_{i,j}})$$

where $t_{i,j}$ and $t'_{i,j}$ are random numbers chosen by i to mask the values of $r_{i,j}$ and $f_{i,j}$.

Decryption: An encrypted rating can be decrypted with private key x_i and $t_{i,j}$ as:

$$\frac{(g^{r_{i,j}} + t_{i,j} y^{\alpha_{i,j}})}{(g^{\alpha_{i,j}})^{x_i} g^{t_{i,j}}} = g^{r_{i,j}}$$

In our modified protocol (Table 2), stage-I and stage-II are similar to BYK protocol mentioned in Sect. 3.1, except the users here are encrypting ratings and flags after masking them. All users encrypt their rating and flags with key Y before sending it to server. Server then computes sum of rating and sum of flags on encrypted data for every item i_j, and broadcasts C_j, D_j to all users. In stage-III each user i replies with $C_j^{x_i} g^{t_{i,j}}, D_j^{x_i} g^{t'_{i,j}}$. Then server computes average as it does in previous approach.

Protection Against Malicious Server Attack
Now we will see what happens in the modified protocol, if a malicious server acts as mentioned in [6], server is acting malicious and want to get rating $r_{1,1}$. After all users have sent their ratings and flags in encrypted form, sever broadcasts $C_1 = g^{\alpha_{1,1}}$ to all users, and they respond with $C_1^{x_i} g^{t_{i,1}}$. Now server homomorphically adds these values and tries to retrieve $r_{1,1}$, for this server requires $g^{t_{1,1}}$ which server does not have. Thus server cannot obtain the rating $r_{1,1}$ in plaintext.

$$\frac{g^{r_{1,1}} g^{t_{1,1}} Y^{\alpha_{1,1}}}{(g^{\alpha_{1,1}})^{\sum_{i=1}^{n} x_{i,1}} g^{\sum_{i=1}^{n} t_{i,1}}} = \frac{g^{r_{1,1}}}{g^{\sum_{i=2}^{n} t_{i,1}}}$$

5   Privacy Analysis

Our modified protocol works on the assumption that server is malicious and will try to obtain user's ratings anyhow but will follow the protocol such that

Table 2. Modified protocol: average rating computation for item i_j

Users	Server
Stage-I:	
Each user i encrypts its rating and flag using Y	
for$(1 \leq i \leq n)$:	
$E(g^{r_{i,j}}) = (g^{\alpha_{i,j}}, g^{r_{i,j} + t_{i,j}} Y^{\alpha_{i,j}})$,	
$E(g^{f_{i,j}}) = (g^{\beta_{i,j}}, g^{f_{i,j} + t'_{i,j}} Y^{\beta_{i,j}})$	

$$\xrightarrow{E(g^{r_{1,j}}), E(g^{f_{1,j}}),...,E(g^{r_{n,j}}), E(g^{f_{n,j}})}$$

| **Stage-II:** | Compute C_j and D_j as follows: |

$$C_j = \prod_{i=1}^{n} g^{\alpha_{i,j}}, \ D_j = \prod_{i=1}^{n} g^{\beta_{i,j}}$$

$$\xleftarrow[broadcast]{C_j, D_j}$$

Stage-III
Reply as:
$$\left(C_j^{x_i} g^{t_{i,j}}, D_j^{x_i} g^{t_{i,j}} \right)$$

$$\xrightarrow{(C_1^{x_i} g^{t_{i,j}}, D_1^{x_i} g^{t_{i,j}},...,C_m^{x_i} g^{t_{i,j}}, D_m^{x_i} g^{t_{i,j}})}$$

| **Stage-IV:** | Compute |

$$\frac{\prod_{i=1}^{n} g^{r_{i,j} + t_{i,j}} Y^{\alpha_{i,j}}}{\prod_{i=1}^{n}(C_j^{x_i} g^{t_{i,j}})} = g^{\sum_{i=1}^{n} r_{i,j}}$$

$$\frac{\prod_{i=1}^{n} g^{f_{i,j} + t'_{i,j}} Y^{\alpha_{i,j}}}{\prod_{i=1}^{n}(D_j^{x_i} g^{t'_{i,j}})} = g^{\sum_{i=1}^{n} f_{i,j}}$$

Solve for $\sum_{i=1}^{n} r_{i,j}$ and $\sum_{i=1}^{n} f_{i,j}$, and compute $\bar{r}_j$

prediction scores are not altered. Users are assumed semi-honest, aka *honest-but-curious*, who will try obtain details of other users or server but will not disobey the protocol. It is also assumed that entities communicate over a secure channel and message (data or cipher) is shared only between involved entities, meaning message of one user is not shared to any other user unless required by the protocol.

We have used ElGamal Cryptosystem with minor modification which still has all properties and same security as of original ElGamal Cryptosystem which is a probabilistic scheme and satisfies IND-CPA property.

Privacy Goals

- Other users and server should not learn rating of a user.
- Server should not learn if a user has rated a particular item or not.
- Prediction values should be known only to the intended user.
- Server should not learn predictions of any user.
- User should not learn any information about server's data.

User Privacy

Initially, in stage-I, user's data (ratings and flags) are encrypted under common public key Y which cannot be decrypted without user's private key contribution as shown in stage-III and stage IV of protocol, even if all other users collude with each other (collusion of users is beyond our assumption). And after decryption, server only gets the aggregate values of ratings and flags which doesn't reveal any information about a particular user's data. Thus, a user's rating and flag cannot be obtained in plaintext by any other user or server. Similarly, without the knowledge of values of ratings and flags, server cannot determine whether an item is rated or not. Therefore, a user's ratings and flags remains unknown to all other parties involved in the protocol.

In recommendation generation process shown in [1], computation over prediction is done on ciphertext and which can only be decrypted by the user. As mentioned earlier, server cannot obtain any information from the ciphertext alone. However, server can maliciously alter the data of the prediction such that server will send high prediction values of the item(s) which server wants to promote/recommend for its own profit. For example, if server colludes with some third party company such that server will promote/recommend that company's product to the user in exchange of money. In our protocol, server never learns the item for which user needs prediction scores so it cannot obtain any information about the product category. And if server maliciously provide its own prediction then there is very small probability that server's item matches the user's category. In this way server can act maliciously to alter the prediction results but may provide poor services to users and users privacy is still maintained. Hence, we assume that server is malicious such that it'll try to obtain information but will not alter the prediction data.

Apart from this, with the modification over ElGamal cryptosystem the attack mentioned in [6] is also prevented, proved in previous section. Hence all the privacy goals are maintained in our modified protocol.

Server Privacy

In average and similarity computation, the result of decryption of aggregate values in stage-IV is only known to server. And in recommendation generation process, client only gets the aggregate values which doesn't reveal any information about server's or other user's data.

User Unlinkability

It means that server cannot relate any two instances of protocol. Therefore, server cannot tell that the user has used the same rating again. As the homomorphic scheme is probabilistic, different ciphertexts are generated even if the same message is encrypted twice. Thus, server cannot learn anything about ratings, flags and predictions with ciphertexts.

6   Cost Analysis

We compute the communication and computation cost to generate one recommendation, for server and a user. In both BYK and modified protocols, different rounds of communication happen in different phases (average, similarity and recommendation computation).

6.1   Communication Cost

We consider the amount of data transferred between two parties. This includes data transmitted by users while sending their preferences to server and by server to transmit recommendations to user. There can be intermediate communication between server and users to help server improve prediction.

We analyze the communication cost at each phase for n users and m items, we assume that the ciphertext C_1 and C_2 are of l bits. Since in the modified protocol there are no changes in rounds of communication in any phase, communication cost remains same for both protocols.

Table 3. Communication costs in modified protocol

Operation	User	Server
Average	$6m(l)$	$2mn(l)$
Similarity	$\dfrac{9m(m-1)}{2}(l)$	$\dfrac{3mn(m-1)}{2}(l)$
CBF	$2m(l)$	$4m(l)$
CF	$2m(l)$	$4m(l)$

Average Computation

- *User:* For one item each user will send 2 encrypted messages each for rating $(r_{i,j})$ and flag $(f_{i,j})$ in *stage-i*, and 2 encrypted messages in *stage-iii*. Thus, total communication cost for one item of every user is $6(l)$, so for m items $6m(l)$ bits.
- *Server:* For one item server sends n encrypted values for ratings, and n for flags. So for m items total communication cost for server is $2mn(l)$ bits

Similar communication cost analysis is done for remaining phases and results are tabulated in Table 3.

6.2   Computation Cost

To evaluate computation cost, we assume that each encryption takes one modular exponentiation operation (e), and homomorphic addition which is computed by multiplying the encrypted values takes mul time. The comparison is given in Table 4. The cost for server after modification is same as mentioned in [1].

Average Computation

- *User*: In *stage-i* each user performs 2 encryptions (one for both rating and flag) and in *stage-iii* it computes 2 modular exp. for one item. So, total computation cost for m items of every user is: $4m(e)$.
- *Server*: For each item and n users, server does $(n-1)$ multiplication operations for rating, and flag resulting in $2(n-1)$ computation per item. So total computation done by server for m items is: $2m(n-1)(mul)$.
- In modified protocol: Every user in *stage-iii* does 2 additional multiplication operations, so total computation by each user for m items: $4m(e)+2m(mul)$. The server's computation remains same as in the original protocol.

Computation cost for the remaining two phases viz. similarity and recommendation generation is computed the same way.

Table 4. Computation cost comparison

Operation	User		Server
	BYK protocol	Modified protocol	
Average	$4m\ (e)$	$4m\ (e)+2m\ (mul)$	$2m(n-1)\ (mul)$
Similarity	$3m(m-1)\ (e)$	$3m(m-1)\ (e)+2m(m-1)\ (mul)$	$3(n-1)\left(\frac{m(m-1)}{2}\right)\ (mul)$
CBF	$(m+2)\ (e)$	$(m+2)\ (e)+2\ (mul)$	$(m-2)\ (mul)+1\ (e)$
CF	$(m+2)\ (e)$	$(m+2)\ (e)+2\ (mul)$	$m\ (mul)+2\ (e)$

Observing Table 4, we can say that order of magnitude of BYK and modified protocols is same, hence it can be inferred that the graphs between number of items and computation cost have the similar shaped curve.

7   Experiment and Results

We have implemented the modified protocol in python on a machine having a clock speed of 2.0 GHz with 8 GB RAM and Linux environment. For computing discrete log and other mathematical computations we use the SageMath library. We took the same dataset used in [1], MovieLens dataset [15] which is publicly available. It includes 100,000 ratings (in range 1–5) collected from 943 users on 1982 items. In our implementation, we took 1000 items randomly from the dataset for our experiment while keeping all users. Using the SageMath library

functions, average time for one modular exponentiation (e) is 1.3×10^{-4} s, and
for multiplication (mul) is 1.9×10^{-6} s.

In our results we have computed the actual computation time required to
generate a recommendation including the time required for solving discrete logarithm (DL) problem. In [1] authors have compared their results with [14,18]
and [9] but they have not included the time taken to solve DL problem in their
results. In Table 5 we have shown the run-time for each phase on our machine
for 1000 items and 943 users.

Table 5. Computation costs in modified protocol

Operation	Time for user (in sec)	Time for server (in sec)
Average	2.69	52.88
Similarity	1999.64	40899.95
CBF	0.31	0.032
CF	0.31	0.366

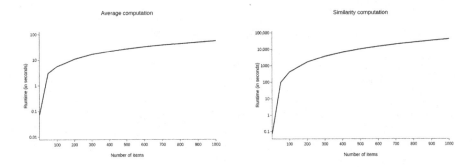

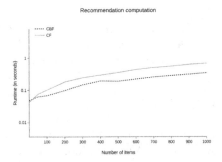

Fig. 1. Runtimes for all phases

Figure 1 shows runtimes for average, similarity and recommendation computation for modified protocol. Average and recommendation generation times are

fairly small, which is feasible for users, for servers though the time will reduce more as they usually have more computation power. Similarity computation is the most costly phase as it takes a lot of time to compute similarity between every pair of items, in our case 1000 items. These similarity values are stored in similarity matrix by server, so once the matrix is complete, it is not required to compute similarity for each request. The similarity matrix can be updated periodically, this will reduce overall rating prediction time. Our results show that modified protocol has competitive running time as compared to BYK protocol.

8 Conclusions and Future Work

Encryption-based privacy preserving recommender systems can preserve user privacy, as the rating data never leaves users without encryption. Any adversary or malicious server can try to read the ratings but cannot do so without knowing the secret key, known only to user. In this paper we analyzed and enhanced privacy of the scheme proposed by Badsha, Yi and Khalil in [1]. The modified scheme has communication cost equivalent to the previous one, without compromising the recommendation accuracy. It compares well with original scheme in terms of computation cost, so it can be used in real time recommender systems. In future we aim to design system where malicious users with fake ratings can be neutralized.

References

1. Badsha, S., Yi, X., Khalil, I.: A practical privacy-preserving recommender system. Data Sci. Eng. **1**(3), 161–177 (2016)
2. Breese, J.S., Heckerman, D., Kadie, C.: Empirical analysis of predictive algorithms for collaborative filtering. In: Proceedings of the Fourteenth Conference on Uncertainty in Artificial Intelligence, pp. 43–52. Morgan Kaufmann Publishers Inc. (1998)
3. Canny, J.: Collaborative filtering with privacy. In: 2002 Proceedings of the IEEE Symposium on Security and Privacy, pp. 45–57. IEEE (2002)
4. Desrosiers, C., Karypis, G.: A comprehensive survey of neighborhood-based recommendation methods. In: Ricci, F., Rokach, L., Shapira, B., Kantor, P.B. (eds.) Recommender Systems Handbook, pp. 107–144. Springer, Boston (2011). https://doi.org/10.1007/978-0-387-85820-3_4
5. ElGamal, T.: A public key cryptosystem and a signature scheme based on discrete logarithms. IEEE Trans. Inf. Theory **31**(4), 469–472 (1985)
6. Mu, E., Shao, C., Miglani, V.: Privacy preserving collaborative filtering (2017). https://courses.csail.mit.edu/6.857/2017/project/12.pdf
7. Gentry, C., Boneh, D.: A fully homomorphic encryption scheme, vol. 20. Stanford University, Stanford (2009)
8. Gilad-Bachrach, R., Dowlin, N., Laine, K., Lauter, K., Naehrig, M., Wernsing, J.: CryptoNets: applying neural networks to encrypted data with high throughput and accuracy. In: International Conference on Machine Learning, pp. 201–210 (2016)

9. Kikuchi, H., Kizawa, H., Tada, M.: Privacy-preserving collaborative filtering schemes. In: 2009 International Conference on Availability, Reliability and Security, ARES 2009, pp. 911–916. IEEE (2009)

10. Koren, Y., Bell, R., Volinsky, C.: Matrix factorization techniques for recommender systems. Computer (8), 30–37 (2009)

11. Machanavajjhala, A., Korolova, A., Sarma, A.D.: Personalized social recommendations: accurate or private. Proc. VLDB Endow. **4**(7), 440–450 (2011)

12. Marlin, B.: Collaborative filtering: a machine learning perspective. University of Toronto (2004)

13. Paillier, P.: Public-key cryptosystems based on composite degree residuosity classes. In: Stern, J. (ed.) EUROCRYPT 1999. LNCS, vol. 1592, pp. 223–238. Springer, Heidelberg (1999). https://doi.org/10.1007/3-540-48910-X_16

14. Polat, H., Du, W.: Privacy-preserving collaborative filtering using randomized perturbation techniques. In: 2003 Third IEEE International Conference on Data Mining, ICDM 2003, pp. 625–628. IEEE (2003)

15. Resnick, P., Iacovou, N., Suchak, M., Bergstrom, P., Riedl, J.: GroupLens: an open architecture for collaborative filtering of netnews. In: Proceedings of the 1994 ACM Conference on Computer Supported Cooperative Work, pp. 175–186. ACM (1994)

16. Ricci, F., Rokach, L., Shapira, B.: Recommender systems: introduction and challenges. In: Ricci, F., Rokach, L., Shapira, B. (eds.) Recommender Systems Handbook, pp. 1–34. Springer, Boston (2015). https://doi.org/10.1007/978-1-4899-7637-6_1

17. Shmueli, E., Tassa, T.: Secure multi-party protocols for item-based collaborative filtering. In: Proceedings of the Eleventh ACM Conference on Recommender Systems, pp. 89–97. ACM (2017)

18. Tada, M., Kikuchi, H., Puntheeranurak, S.: Privacy-preserving collaborative filtering protocol based on similarity between items. In: 2010 24th IEEE International Conference on Advanced Information Networking and Applications (AINA), pp. 573–578. IEEE (2010)

19. Wang, J., Arriaga, A., Tang, Q., Ryan, P.Y.A.: CryptoRec: secure recommendations as a service. CoRR abs/1802.02432 (2018). http://arxiv.org/abs/1802.02432

20. Yakut, I., Polat, H.: Arbitrarily distributed data-based recommendations with privacy. Data Knowl. Eng. **72**, 239–256 (2012)

21. Zhong, G., Goldberg, I., Hengartner, U.: Louis, lester and pierre: three protocols for location privacy. In: Borisov, N., Golle, P. (eds.) PET 2007. LNCS, vol. 4776, pp. 62–76. Springer, Heidelberg (2007). https://doi.org/10.1007/978-3-540-75551-7_5

Threshold Ring Signature with Message Block Sharing

Swati Rawal$^{(\boxtimes)}$ and Sahadeo Padhye$^{(\boxtimes)}$

Department of Mathematics,
Motilal Nehru National Institute of Technology Allahabad, Prayagraj 211004, India
swati.rawal25@gmail.com, sahadeomathrsu@gmail.com

Abstract. Lattices have attracted a great attention during recent years and many signature schemes have emerged based on lattices. In this paper we have proposed Threshold-Ring Signature K–out–of–$N scheme$, here signature is generated by a subset of K signers from the N signers while maintaining the anonymity of these K signers using the Ring Signature by Wang et al. The scheme uses message block sharing between members and is proved to be unforgeable as well as anonymous.

Keywords: Lattice-based cryptography · Threshold signature · Ring signature

1 Introduction

With the recent development in cryptography, need for resistance of quantum attacks, developed a new area of research, *Post Quantum Cryptography*. This area leads to the enhancement in our schemes so that they can run on classical computers and are quantum computer resistant. Post-Quantum cryptography has four main divisions *hash–based* signatures, *code–based* schemes, *multivariate* schemes and *lattice–based* schemes.

Lattice-based schemes gained a lot of attention during this time and many recent developments are also proposed. These schemes have two main advantages over others, first is their conceptual simplicity as they require linear operation over small integers unlike modular exponentiation in RSA, ElGamal and second, these schemes are supported by strong worst-case security assumption. This area became a new ground for researchers after the breakthrough of Ajtai [1] in 1996 who bridged the lattice problems with different complexities i.e. average-case complexity worst-case complexity.

In addition to encryption schemes, many signature schemes over lattices have been developed by the distinguish cryptographer. Ajtai [2] introduced trapdoor sampling algorithm to sample a random lattice along with the trapdoor basis. Using this algorithm Gentry et al. [9] developed pre-image sampleable function and introduced lattice based signature based on this one-way function. Gordon et al. [10] proposed group signature using trapdoor sampling. Wang and Sun [16]

© Springer Nature Singapore Pte Ltd. 2019
S. Nandi et al. (Eds.): ISEA-ISAP 2018, CCIS 939, pp. 261–271, 2019.
https://doi.org/10.1007/978-981-13-7561-3_19

also constructed ring signatures using this trapdoor sampling algorithm. Many signatures with different functionalities are also developed, like proxy signature [11], blind signature [14], short signature [8], ID-Proxy [17] and many more. Unlike these signature Lyubashevsky [12] gave a insight on how to generate signatures without trapdoor.

After the development of ring signature by Rivest, Shamir and Taumann [13], a variant or an extension was proposed by Bresson et al. [4] called as Threshold Ring signature which reduced the power of the signer. In a K–out of $-N$ threshold setting atleast K members are required to produce a valid signature. So that even if $K-1$ members are corrupt, they can't produce a valid signature. In the classical signature, Shamir secret scheme [15] was used to share a secret among the signers, but various other methods are introduced in lattice cryptography to develop threshold signature.

Cayrel et al. [5] gave a lattice-based threshold ring signature scheme, where at least t members are required to create a signature. In this scheme, every participant has their own public key thus verification time grows linearly with the number of participants. Also, Bendlin et al. [3] gave a variation of Gentry et al.'s signature scheme [9] in threshold setting by trapdoor sharing.

In this paper we use the message block sharing introduced by Choi and Kim from [6] to construct a threshold ring signature. There scheme used the concept of group signature from [10] thus the anonymity participant who signed is compromised. Here in this paper, we use the ring setting so that signer anonymity is maintained with advantage of threshold signature.

1.1 Organization of Paper

Section 2, introduces the preliminaries on lattices to get into this paper, the message block sharing and preimage sampling for extended lattices and ring signature scheme that we are using in our construction. In Sect. 3 we present our scheme followed with a toy example in Sect. 4. Section 5 analyse the security of the proposed scheme. Last section gives the conclusion.

2 Preliminaries

2.1 Notations

We denote the set of positive integers by $\mathbb{Z}_{>0}$. For any integer m, we denote $[m] = \{1, 2 \ldots, m\}$. For any $n \times m$ matrix $\mathbf{B}$, we denote $\mathbf{B} = [\mathbf{b}_1, \ldots \mathbf{b}_m]$ where $\mathbf{b}_i$'s are the column vectors of the matrix $\mathbf{B}$. For any $\mathbf{b} \in \mathbb{R}^n$, $\|\mathbf{b}\|$ denote the euclidean norm of vector and $\|\mathbf{B}\| = max_{i \in [m]} \|\mathbf{b}_i\|$. For a set $\mathbf{S} = \{\mathbf{s}_1, \ldots \mathbf{s}_m\}$ of linearly independent vectors $\overline{\mathbf{S}} = \{\overline{\mathbf{s}}_1, \ldots \overline{\mathbf{s}}_m\}$ denote *Gram-Schmidt Orthogonalization* of $\mathbf{S}$.

2.2   Lattices

Definition 1. *For* $\{\mathbf{b}_1, \ldots \mathbf{b}_n\}$, *n linearly independent vectors in* $\mathbb{R}^m$ *then lattice* $\mathcal{L}$ *is defined as*
$\mathcal{L}(\mathbf{B}) = \{\Sigma_{i=1}^n \mathbf{b}_i \mathbf{x}_i | \mathbf{x}_i \in \mathbb{Z}\}$.
The matrix $\mathbf{B} = [\mathbf{b}_1, \ldots \mathbf{b}_n] \in \mathbb{R}^{m \times n}$ *is known as a basis of the lattice* $\mathcal{L}$.

Next we define certain families of lattices introduced by Ajtai [2].

Definition 2. *For given a matrix* $\mathbf{A} \in \mathbb{Z}_q^{n \times m}$, *for some* $q, n, m \in \mathbb{Z}$ *we define*

1. $\mathcal{L}^{\perp}(\mathbf{A}) = \{\mathbf{x} \in \mathbb{Z}^m | \mathbf{A}\mathbf{x} = 0 \mod q\}$
2. $\mathcal{L}_y^{\perp}(\mathbf{A}) = \{\mathbf{x} \in \mathbb{Z}^m | \mathbf{A}\mathbf{x} = y \mod q\}$

Note that $\mathcal{L}_y^{\perp}(\mathbf{A})$ is coset of $\mathcal{L}^{\perp}(\mathbf{A})$ as $\mathcal{L}_y^{\perp}(\mathbf{A}) = t + \mathcal{L}^{\perp}(\mathbf{A})$ where t is an arbitrary solution (over $\mathbb{Z}^m$) of the equation $At = y \mod q$.

Definition 3. *For any* $\sigma > 0$, *the Gaussian function on* $\mathbb{R}^n$ *centred at c with standard deviation* σ *is defined as* $\rho_{c,\sigma}(\mathbf{x}) = \exp(-\pi \dfrac{\|\mathbf{x} - c\|}{\sigma})$, $\mathbf{x} \in \mathbb{R}^\mathbf{n}$.

We define the discrete gaussian function over any n-dimensional lattice $\mathcal{L}$ as
$D_{\mathcal{L}_{c,\sigma}}(\mathbf{x}) = \dfrac{\rho_{c,\sigma}(\mathbf{x})}{\rho_{c,\sigma}(\mathcal{L})}$, $\forall x \in \mathcal{L}$. Where $\rho_{c,\sigma}(\mathcal{L}) = \sum_{\mathbf{x} \in \mathcal{L}} \rho_{c,\sigma}(\mathbf{x})$.
Now we define the hard-on-average problem introduced by Ajtai [1] on which our scheme is based.

Definition 4. *(Shortest Integer Solution Problem (SIS))* *For a given positive integer* q, *a matrix* $\mathbf{A} \in \mathbb{Z}_q^{n \times m}$ *and a real* β, *find a non-zero integer* $\mathbf{x}$ *such that* $\mathbf{A}\mathbf{x} = 0 \mod q$ *and* $\|\mathbf{x}\| \leq \beta$.

Definition 5. *(Inhomogeneous Shortest Integer Solution (ISIS))* *For a given positive integer* q, *a matrix* $\mathbf{A} \in \mathbb{Z}_q^{n \times m}$, *a syndrome y and a real* β, *find a non-zero integer* $\mathbf{x}$ *such that* $\mathbf{A}\mathbf{x} = y \mod q$ *and* $\|\mathbf{x}\| \leq \beta$.

2.3   Message Block Sharing

This idea was introduced in [6] where we divide the original message into blocks of random size between the participants so that no block remain meaningful. Then we circulate uniform number of blocks among the participants keeping in mind that no block is shared by all participants. We give a brief description of the *k-out-of-N* message block sharing.

As the requirement is that no message block is shared by all participants, suppose m_i is any block of message then atleast one participant doesn't have it. Now for *k-out-of-N* sharing it is sufficient that $k - 1$ participant doesn't have it. Next condition for sharing is that each participant have same number of message blocks. To fulfil these condition we use binomial coefficients. We first divide the message into $^N C_{k-1}$ blocks and each participant obtain $^{N-1} C_{k-1}$ number of blocks.

We can consider a toy example to illustrate this. Consider *2-out-of-3* message block sharing. Let m be the message. We first divide the message into $3(= {}^3C_{2-1})$ blocks, say, $m_1\, m_2\, m_3$ and each participant gets $2(= {}^{3-1}C_{2-1})$ blocks. Hence, shared blocks are $\{m_1, m_2\}$, $\{m_1, m_3\}$, $\{m_2, m_3\}$.

Remark 1. To divide the message into ${}^N C_{k-1}$ blocks we need it to be sufficiently large. Thus here the security parameter is determined by the size of the original message.

2.4   Pre Image Sampling for Extended Lattice [16]

For some $k, k_1, k_2, k_3, k_4 \in \mathbb{Z}_{>0}$ with $k = k_1 + k_2 + k_3 + k_4$, let $\mathbf{A}_k = [\mathbf{A}_{k_1}, \mathbf{A}_{k_2}, \mathbf{A}_{k_3}, \mathbf{A}_{k_4}] \in \mathbb{Z}_q^{n \times km}$, where $\mathbf{A}_{k_i} \in \mathbb{Z}_q^{n \times k_i m}$, $i \in [4]$. Consider $\mathbf{A}_{k_1+k_3} = [\mathbf{A}_{k_1} \| \mathbf{A}_{k_3}] \in \mathbb{Z}_q^{n \times (k_1+k_3)m}$. Let us suppose we have short basis $\mathbf{B}_{k_1+k_3}$ of the lattice $\mathcal{L}^\perp(\mathbf{A}_{k_1+k_3})$ and given an integer $r \geq \|\overline{\mathbf{B}}_{k_1+k_3}\|.\omega(\sqrt{\log n})$, the *GenSamplePre* algorithm samples a preimage of the function $f_{\mathbf{A}_k}(\mathbf{e}) = \mathbf{A}_k\mathbf{e}$ mod q. $GenSamplePre(\mathbf{A}_k, \mathbf{A}_{k_1+k_3}, \mathbf{B}_{k_1+k_3}, \mathbf{y}, r)$ runs as follows:

1. Using distributions $D_{\mathbb{Z}^{k_2 m},r}$ and $D_{\mathbb{Z}^{k_4 m},r}$, sample[1] $\mathbf{e}_{(k_2)} \in \mathbb{Z}^{k_2 m}$ and $\mathbf{e}_{(k_4)} \in \mathbb{Z}^{k_4 m}$. Writing $\mathbf{e}_{(k_2)}$ as $[\mathbf{e}_{k_1+1}, \ldots, \mathbf{e}_{k_1+k_2}] \in \mathbb{Z}^{k_2 m}$ and $\mathbf{e}_{(k_4)}$ as $[\mathbf{e}_{k-k_4+1}, \ldots, \mathbf{e}_k] \in \mathbb{Z}^{k_4 m}$.

2. Define $\mathbf{z} = \mathbf{y} - \mathbf{A}_{k_2}\mathbf{e}_{(k_2)} - \mathbf{A}_{k_4}\mathbf{e}_{(k_4)}$ mod q. Run $SamplePre(\mathbf{A}_{k_1+k_3}, \mathbf{B}_{k_1+k_3}, \mathbf{z}, r)$ (from [9]) to sample a vector $\mathbf{e}_{(k_1+k_3)} \in \mathbb{Z}^{(k_1+k_3)m}$ from the distribution $D_{\mathcal{L}_{\mathbf{y}}^\perp(\mathbf{A}_k),r}$. Parse $\mathbf{e}_{(k_1+k_3)} = [\mathbf{e}_1, \ldots, \mathbf{e}_{k_1}, \mathbf{e}_{k_1+k_2+1}, \ldots, \mathbf{e}_{k-k_4}] \in \mathbb{Z}^{(k_1+k_3)m}$ and let $\mathbf{e}_{(k_1)} = [\mathbf{e}_1, \ldots, \mathbf{e}_{k_1}] \in \mathbb{Z}^{k_1 m}$, $\mathbf{e}_{(k_3)} = [\mathbf{e}_{k_1+k_2+1}, \ldots, \mathbf{e}_{k-k_4}] \in \mathbb{Z}^{k_3 m}$.

3. Output $\mathbf{e} = \{\mathbf{e}_{(k_1)}, \mathbf{e}_{(k_2)}, \mathbf{e}_{(k_3)}, \mathbf{e}_{(k_4)}\} = [\mathbf{e}_1, \ldots \mathbf{e}_k] \in \mathbb{Z}^{km}$.

Remark 2. According to construction, we have $\mathbf{A}_{k_1}\mathbf{e}_{(k_1)} + \mathbf{A}_{k_3}\mathbf{e}_{(k_3)} = \mathbf{A}_{k_1+k_3}\mathbf{e}_{(k_1+k_3)} = \mathbf{z}$ mod q. Therefore, $\mathbf{A}_k\mathbf{e} = \Sigma_{i=1}^4 \mathbf{A}_i\mathbf{e}_{(k_i)} = \mathbf{y}$ mod q, and the output $\mathbf{e}$ belong to $\mathcal{L}_{\mathbf{y}}^\perp(\mathbf{A}_k)$. From theorem 3.4 in [19], $\mathbf{e}$ is within negligible statistical distance of $D_{\mathcal{L}_{\mathbf{y}}^\perp(\mathbf{A}_k),r}$.

2.5   Ring Signature Scheme

We give brief description of Wang and Sun's [16] signature scheme. Consider the positive integers l, m, n, q, t, where $q \geq 2$ and $m \geq 5n \log q$. Let $\overline{L}, r$ be the parameters of the scheme defined as follows:

- $\overline{L} \geq O(\sqrt{n \log q})$, an upper bound on the Gram-Schmidt size of an participant's secret basis.
- $r \geq \overline{L}\omega(\sqrt{\log q})$ is the Gaussian parameter used to generate the required secret basis and short vectors (Fig. 1).

---

[1] We are using $\mathbf{e}_{(k_i)}$'s just to differentiate them from $\mathbf{e}_{k_i}$, as both of them are different. $\mathbf{e}_{(k_i)}$ belongs to $\mathbb{Z}^{k_i m}$ and $\mathbf{e}_{k_i} \in \mathbb{Z}^m$ is a k_ith vector of $\mathbf{e}_{(k_i)}$.

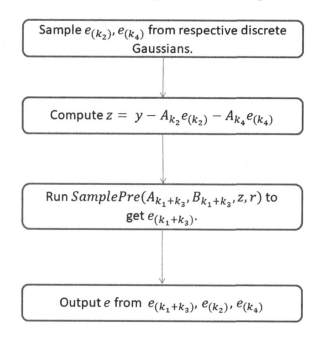

Fig. 1. *GenSamplePre* algorithm

We also define an hash function $H_1 : \{0,1\}^* \longrightarrow \mathbb{Z}_q^n$ viewed as random oracle.

$KeyGen(\lambda)$: Each participant using the input λ runs $TrapGen(1^\lambda)$ [9] to generate $\mathbf{A}_i \in \mathbb{Z}_q^{n \times m}$ with a basis $\mathbf{B}_i \in \mathbb{Z}^{m \times m}$ for lattice $\mathcal{L}^\perp(\mathbf{A}_i)$. We have $\|\mathbf{B}_i\| \leq \overline{\mathbf{L}}$ (theorem 3.2 [18]). $KeyGen$ outputs keys $(pk_i = \mathbf{A}_i, sk_i = \mathbf{B}_i)$ for each participant i.

$RingSign(R, sk_i, M)$: For a ring of l members with public keys $R = \{\mathbf{A}_1, \ldots, \mathbf{A}_l\} \in \mathbb{Z}_q^{n \times m}$, for $i \in [l]$ to generate the signature on message $M \in \{0,1\}^*$ participant proceed in the following manner:

- Let $\mathbf{A}_R = [\mathbf{A}_1 \| \ldots \| \mathbf{A}_l] \in \mathbb{Z}_q^{n \times lm}$ and $\mathbf{y} = H_1(M) \in \mathbb{Z}_q^n$ and define a label lab_R that describes how $\mathbf{A}_R$ is associated with ring members $\{1, \ldots, l\}$.
- Generate $\mathbf{e} \leftarrow GenSamplePre(\mathbf{A}_R, \mathbf{A}_i, \mathbf{B}_i, \mathbf{y}, r) \in \mathbb{Z}^{lm}$ distributed according to $D_{\mathcal{L}_\mathbf{y}^\perp(\mathbf{A}_R), r}$.
- $RingSign$ outputs the signature $\sigma = <\sigma, lab_R>$.

$RingVerify(R, M, \sigma)$: The verifier accepts the signature σ on message M if $0 \leq \|\mathbf{e}\| \leq r\sqrt{lm}$ and $\mathbf{A}_R \mathbf{e} \mod q = H_1(M)$ else he rejects it.

3   The Proposed Threshold Ring Signature Scheme

In this section, we first define the $K - out - of - N$ threshold ring signature scheme and it's properties. Then we describe our proposed scheme.

Definition 6. *Threshold Ring Signature (TRS)* - *A TRS working with a security parameter* λ, *a group of* N *users, and a number* K *which refer to the minimum number of user require to generate a valid signature, consist of following four algorithms.*

- **SetUp**: *Corresponding to the security parameter it generate the public parameters.*
- **KeyGen**: *Output the key pair* (sk, pk) *secret key and public key respectively for each member of the ring.*
- **SignGen**: *Generate the* σ *required signature on the message* m *using the keys generated by* $KeyGen$.
- **Verify**: *Output* 1 *if it is a valid signature else output* 0.

The threshold ring signature scheme should satisfy *anonymity* and *unforgeability* in order to meet its security requirements.

Definition 7. *Existentially Unforgeability* - *A TRS with parameters* (λ, N, K) *is said to be existentially unforgeable, if a probabilistic polynomial time adversary* $\mathcal{A}$ *accessing the* N *public keys,* $K - 1$ *secret keys and valid message-signature pairs* (m', σ) *can generate a valid signature for any message* m *where* $m \neq m'$ *with negligible probability.*

Definition 8. *Anonymity* - *A threshold Signature Scheme is said to have a anonymity property if it is not possible to tell which set of* K *members generated the signature.*

3.1   Proposed Scheme

Similar to Wang's scheme [16] we choose positive integers l, m, n, q, t, where $q \geq 2$ and $m \geq 5n \log q$ and $\overline{L}$ (the Gram-Schmidt upper bound), r (Gaussian parameter). Let $H_1 : \{0,1\}^\star \longrightarrow \mathbb{Z}_q^n$ be the hash function.

- *Setup* – Compute the bit length of the message M and output (n, N, K), the system parameters.
- *KeyGen*$(1^n, 1^N)$ – A member with index i generate $(\mathbf{A}_i, \mathbf{B}_i) \leftarrow TrapGen(1^n)$ [9], where $\mathbf{A}_i \in \mathbb{Z}_q^{n \times m}$ and $\mathbf{B}_i \in \mathbb{Z}^{m \times m}$ is a basis for $\mathcal{L}^\perp(\mathbf{A}_i)$. Then for each $i \in [N]$ we output the key pairs $(pk = \mathbf{A}_i, sk = \mathbf{B}_i)$. We set $R = \{\mathbf{A}_1, \dots \mathbf{A}_N\} \in \mathbb{Z}_q^{n \times m}$.

  Before proceeding towards signature generation algorithm we first do *message block sharing*. We distribute the corresponding message blocks $\Gamma_i = \{m_{i_1} \dots m_{i_t}\}$ for each member i, where $t = {}^{N-1}C_{k-1}$ and total number of such blocks are ${}^N C_{k-1}$.
- *SignGen*$(R, (\Gamma_i)_{i=1}^N), m)$ – Let S be the set of K members who want to sign on message m. Compute $\mathbf{A}_R = [\mathbf{A}_1, \dots, \mathbf{A}_N]$ and lab_R which contains the order of the N members associated with $\mathbf{A}_R$.
  Now each signer $i \in S$ we does the following:

1. Compute $M[i] = m_{i_1} \| \dots \| m_{i_t}$ and $y_i = H(M[i])$.
2. Now generate $\mathbf{e}_i \leftarrow GenSamplePre(\mathbf{A}_R, \mathbf{A}_i, \mathbf{B}_i, \mathbf{y}_i, r) \in \mathbb{Z}^{Nm}$ such that each $\mathbf{e}_i \sim D_{\mathcal{L}_\mathbf{y}^\perp(\mathbf{A}_R), r}$.

Output the signature $\sigma = (\mathbf{e}, \mathbf{y}, lab_R)$, where $\mathbf{e} = \Sigma_{i=1}^K \mathbf{e}_i$ and $\mathbf{y} = \Sigma_{i=1}^K \mathbf{y}_i$.
- $Verify(\sigma)$ – This algorithm outputs 1 if $\|\mathbf{e}\| \le Kr\sqrt{Nm}$ and $\mathbf{A}_R\mathbf{e} \bmod q = \mathbf{y}$ otherwise it return 0.

Correctness: Since each $\mathbf{e}_i$ is the output of $GenSamplePre$ algorithm thus each $\mathbf{e}_i$ satisfies $\mathbf{A}_R\mathbf{e}_i = \mathbf{y}_i \bmod q$ and $\|\mathbf{e}_i\| \le r\sqrt{Nm}$.
Now,
$$\|\mathbf{e}\| = \|\mathbf{e}_1 + \dots + \mathbf{e}_K\|$$
$$\le r\sqrt{Nm} + \dots + r\sqrt{Nm}(K \text{ times}) \le Kr\sqrt{Nm}.$$
and
$$\mathbf{A}_R\mathbf{e} \bmod q = (\mathbf{A}_R\mathbf{e}_1 + \dots + \mathbf{A}_R\mathbf{e}_k) \bmod q$$
$$= \mathbf{y}_1 + \dots + \mathbf{y}_K = \mathbf{y}.$$
Thus both verification conditions are justified, hence our signature scheme is correct.

4   Toy Example for the Signature Scheme

To better understand the scheme, we describe a toy example for *2-out-of-3* threshold scheme, with following system parameters $q = 2$, $n = 2$ and $m = 4$, these parameter satisfy the condition i.e. $m \ge 5n \log q$. Let the three public keys for the signers be $A_1 = \begin{bmatrix} 1 & 0 & 0 & 1 \\ 0 & 1 & 0 & 0 \end{bmatrix}$, $A_2 = \begin{bmatrix} 1 & 1 & 0 & 1 \\ 1 & 0 & 1 & 1 \end{bmatrix}$, $A_3 = \begin{bmatrix} 0 & 0 & 0 & 1 \\ 0 & 0 & 1 & 1 \end{bmatrix} \in \mathbb{Z}_q^{2 \times 4}$.

Corresponding secret key i.e. the basis $B_i's$ of the lattices $\mathcal{L}^\perp(A_i)'s$ are $B_1 = \begin{bmatrix} 0 & 1 & 0 & 0 \\ 0 & 0 & 2 & 0 \\ 1 & 0 & 0 & 0 \\ 0 & 1 & 0 & 2 \end{bmatrix}$, $B_2 = \begin{bmatrix} 1 & 0 & 0 & 0 \\ 0 & 1 & 0 & 0 \\ 0 & 1 & 0 & 2 \\ 0 & 0 & 1 & 0 \end{bmatrix}$, $B_3 = \begin{bmatrix} 1 & 0 & 0 & 0 \\ 0 & 0 & 1 & 0 \\ 0 & 2 & 0 & 0 \\ 0 & 0 & 0 & 2 \end{bmatrix} \in \mathbb{Z}^{4 \times 4}$.

Then, $A_R = [A_1, A_2, A_3] = \begin{bmatrix} 1 & 0 & 0 & 1 & 1 & 1 & 0 & 1 & 0 & 0 & 0 & 1 \\ 0 & 1 & 0 & 0 & 1 & 0 & 1 & 1 & 0 & 0 & 1 & 1 \end{bmatrix}$. Consider, the message $m = 110100111$, we use a toy hash function $H : \{0,1\} \longrightarrow \mathbb{Z}_2^2$ which divides the input into two equal parts and then XOR each part and gives resultant as output so that it belongs to $\mathbb{Z}_2^2$.

For message block sharing, we divide the message m as $m = m_1\|m_2\|m_3$ where $m_1 = 110$, $m_2 = 100$ and $m_3 = 111$. Thus the first ring member have the blocks (m_1, m_2), second member have blocks (m_2, m_3) and third member have blocks (m_3, m_1). Now, for signature generation, suppose the first and the third member agreed for signature generation, they proceed $SignGen$ algorithm accordingly. We demonstrate for first signer

1. He compute $M[1] = m_1\|m_2 = 110\|100$ and then its hash image is $y_1 = 01$ ($1 \oplus 1 \oplus 0 = 0$ and $1 \oplus 0 \oplus 0 = 1$).

2. He run $GenSamplePre(A_R, A_1, B_1, y_1, r)$ (say $r = 3$). $GenSamplePre$ works in the following manner with $k_1 = k_2 = k_3 = 1$, $k = 3$ and $A_{k_i} = A_i, i \in [3]$, $A_k = A_R$ and $B_{k_1} = B_1$.

(i) Sample $e_{(k_2)}$ and $e_{(k_3)}$ from distributions $D_{\mathbb{Z}^4, r}$ say, $e_{(k_2)} = \begin{bmatrix} 1 \\ 2 \\ 0 \\ 0 \end{bmatrix}$, $e_{(k_3)} = \begin{bmatrix} 1 \\ 0 \\ 1 \\ 0 \end{bmatrix}$, (where we can check $\|e_{(k_2)}\| \leq r.\sqrt{m}$ and $\|e_{(k_3)}\| \leq r.\sqrt{m}$)

(ii) Now, compute $z = y_1 - A_{k_2} e_{(k_2)} - A_{k_3} e_{(k_3)} \mod 2 = \begin{bmatrix} 1 \\ 1 \end{bmatrix}$

(iii) Next, he run $SamplePre(A_{k_1}, B_{k_1}, z, r)$ and output a sample $e_{(k_1)} = \begin{bmatrix} 0 \\ 1 \\ 2 \\ 1 \end{bmatrix}$

such that $A_{k_1} e_{(k_1)} = 0 \mod 2$. (check $\|e_{(k_1)}\| \leq r.\sqrt{m}$).

(iv) $GenSamplePre$ returns $e_1 = [e_{(k_1)}, e_{(k_2)}, e_{(k_3)}]^T = [0\ 1\ 2\ 1\ 1\ 2\ 0\ 0\ 1\ 0\ 1\ 0]^T$, where $\mathbf{x}^\mathbf{T}$ represents the transpose of the vector $\mathbf{x}$.

In the similar manner third user also proceed with $M[3] = 111\|110$, here $y_3 = 10$. He also runs the $GenSamplePre(A_R, A_3, B_3, y_3, r)$ and obtain the output $e_3 = [0\ 0\ 1\ 1\ 1\ 1\ 0\ 1\ 1\ 0\ 1\ 1]^T$. Finally the algorithm $SignGen$ outputs signature $\sigma = (e, y)$, where $e = e_1 + e_3 = [0\ 1\ 3\ 2\ 2\ 3\ 0\ 1\ 2\ 0\ 2\ 1]^T$ and $y = y_1 + y_3 = [1\ 1]^T$. Now the Verification algorithm $Verify$ checks whether $A_R e = y$ and $\|e\| \leq K.r\sqrt{Nm}$.

(i) $\|e\| = \sqrt{1 + 9 + 4 + 4 + 9 + 1 + 4 + 4 + 1} = \sqrt{37} \leq K.r\sqrt{Nm} = 2.3.\sqrt{12}$ and

(ii) $A_{R}e = \begin{bmatrix} 1\ 0\ 0\ 1\ 1\ 1\ 0\ 1\ 0\ 0\ 0\ 1 \\ 0\ 1\ 0\ 0\ 1\ 0\ 1\ 1\ 0\ 0\ 1\ 1 \end{bmatrix} \begin{bmatrix} 0 \\ 1 \\ 3 \\ 2 \\ 2 \\ 3 \\ 0 \\ 1 \\ 2 \\ 0 \\ 2 \\ 1 \end{bmatrix} = \begin{bmatrix} 2+2+3+1+1 \\ 1+2+1+2+1 \end{bmatrix} = \begin{bmatrix} 1 \\ 1 \end{bmatrix} \mod 2$

Thus, this is an valid signature on the message.

5 Security Analysis

We now discuss the anonymity and unforgeability of our threshold ring signature scheme according to the definitions in Sect. 3.

Theorem 1. *The proposed TRS satisfy anonymity i.e. if $ISIS_{q,Nm,r}$ is hard, we can't distinguish between two signatures σ_1, σ_2 issued by two different sets of signers on the same message m.*

Proof. Recall the signature generation algorithm $SignGen$, σ_1, σ_2 are sum of vectors from $\mathbb{Z}^{Nm}$. Thus their distinguishability depend on these vectors. These vectors have same distribution of domain in $f_{(\mathbf{A}_R)}$ and are within negligible statistical distance from $D_{\mathcal{L}_\mathbf{y}^\perp(\mathbf{A}_R),r}$, thus, are computationally indistinguishable. Hence, σ_1, σ_2 follows the same.

Theorem 2. *The Proposed TRS is existentially unforgeable.*

Proof. If we assume that there are $K-1$ corrupt members then the problem of unforgeability reduces to unforgeability of e_i generated during signing process. That can be guaranteed from the hardness of $ISIS_{q,Nm,r}$ and the collision resistance of the hash function. Hence, we can say that our construction is unforgeable.

Our scheme is based on ISIS problem which have no known attacks and simpler to grasp as we are just dividing the message. Here, we decide the ring size after getting the message which can be inefficient in some situations. So, developing more efficient variant of threshold signature with better implementation is always encouraged. If we compare with other schemes, Feng et al.'s [7] threshold signature is based on sequential signing which doesn't allow each signer to generate their own signatures and moreover, its hardness is based on NTRU lattice and closest vector problem which is not secure. Cayrel et al.'s [5] and Bendlin et al.'s [3] schemes are based on syndrome decoding and lattice trapdoor sharing respectively are efficient enough but a bit complicated.

6 Conclusion

In this paper, we propose a threshold ring signature scheme with a simpler tool of message block sharing. Here the ISIS problem with suitable parameters is used as a hardness assumption as the base of our security, which give us a strong security notions. Both unforgeability and anonymity are taken care in the signature generation.

References

1. Ajtai, M.: Generating hard instances of lattice problems (extended abstract). In: ACM Symposium on the Theory of Computing, pp. 1–32 (1996)
2. Ajtai, M.: Generating hard instances of the short basis problem. In: Wiedermann, J., van Emde Boas, P., Nielsen, M. (eds.) ICALP 1999. LNCS, vol. 1644, pp. 1–9. Springer, Heidelberg (1999). https://doi.org/10.1007/3-540-48523-6_1
3. Bendlin, R., Krehbiel, S., Peikert, C.: How to share a lattice trapdoor: threshold protocols for signatures and (H)IBE. In: Jacobson, M., Locasto, M., Mohassel, P., Safavi-Naini, R. (eds.) ACNS 2013. LNCS, vol. 7954, pp. 218–236. Springer, Heidelberg (2013). https://doi.org/10.1007/978-3-642-38980-1_14
4. Bresson, E., Stern, J., Szydlo, M.: Threshold ring signatures and applications to ad-hoc groups. In: Yung, M. (ed.) CRYPTO 2002. LNCS, vol. 2442, pp. 465–480. Springer, Heidelberg (2002). https://doi.org/10.1007/3-540-45708-9_30
5. Cayrel, P.-L., Lindner, R., Rückert, M., Silva, R.: A lattice-based threshold ring signature scheme. In: Abdalla, M., Barreto, P.S.L.M. (eds.) LATINCRYPT 2010. LNCS, vol. 6212, pp. 255–272. Springer, Heidelberg (2010). https://doi.org/10.1007/978-3-642-14712-8_16
6. Choi, R., Kim, K.: Lattice-based threshold signature with message block sharing. In: Proceedings of Symposium on Cryptography and Information Security (2014)
7. Feng, T., Gao, Y., Ma, J.: Changeable threshold signature scheme based on lattice theory. In: Proceedings of International Conference on E-Business and E-Government(ICEE), pp. 1311–1315 (2010)
8. Fenghe, W., Zhenhua, L.: Short and provable secure lattice-based signature scheme in the standard model. Secur. Commun. Netw. 9, 3627–3632 (2016)
9. Gentry, C., Peikert, C., Vaikuntanathan, V.: Trapdoors for hard lattices and new cryptographic constructions. In: Proceedings of ACM Symposium on Theory of Computing, pp. 197–206 (2008)
10. Gordon, S.D., Katz, J., Vaikuntanathan, V.: A group signature scheme from lattice assumptions. In: Abe, M. (ed.) ASIACRYPT 2010. LNCS, vol. 6477, pp. 395–412. Springer, Heidelberg (2010). https://doi.org/10.1007/978-3-642-17373-8_23
11. Jiang, Y., Kong, F., Ju, X.: Lattice-based proxy signature. In: Proceedings of International Conference on Computational Intelligence and Security, pp. 382–385 (2010)
12. Lyubashevsky, V.: Lattice signatures without trapdoors. In: Pointcheval, D., Johansson, T. (eds.) EUROCRYPT 2012. LNCS, vol. 7237, pp. 738–755. Springer, Heidelberg (2012). https://doi.org/10.1007/978-3-642-29011-4_43
13. Rivest, R.L., Shamir, A., Tauman, Y.: How to leak a secret. In: Boyd, C. (ed.) ASIACRYPT 2001. LNCS, vol. 2248, pp. 552–565. Springer, Heidelberg (2001). https://doi.org/10.1007/3-540-45682-1_32
14. Rückert, M.: Lattice-based blind signatures. In: Abe, M. (ed.) ASIACRYPT 2010. LNCS, vol. 6477, pp. 413–430. Springer, Heidelberg (2010). https://doi.org/10.1007/978-3-642-17373-8_24
15. Shamir, A.: How to share a secret. In: Proceedings of ACM, pp. 612–613 (1979)
16. Wang, J., Sun, B.: Ring signature schemes from lattice basis delegation. In: Qing, S., Susilo, W., Wang, G., Liu, D. (eds.) ICICS 2011. LNCS, vol. 7043, pp. 15–28. Springer, Heidelberg (2011). https://doi.org/10.1007/978-3-642-25243-3_2
17. Zhang, L., Sang, Y.: A lattice-based identity-based proxy signature from bonsai trees. Int. J. Adv. Comput. Technol. 4, 99–144 (2012)

18. Alwen, J., Peikert, C.: Generating shorter bases for hard random lattices. In: Proceedings of STACS 2009, pp. 75–86 (2009)
19. Cash, D., Hofheinz, D., Kiltz, E.: How to delegate a lattice basis. Cryptology ePrint Archive, Report 2009/351 (2009)

Secure Software Systems

Testing Program Crash Based on Search Based Testing and Exception Injection

Faisal Anwer[1]([✉]), Mohd. Nazir[2], and Khurram Mustafa[2]

[1] Department of Computer Science, Aligarh Muslim University, Aligarh, India
`faisalanwer.cs@amu.ac.in`
[2] Department of Computer Science, Jamia Millia Islamia (A Central University),
New Delhi, India
`{mnazir,kmustafa}@jmi.ac.in`

Abstract. Program crash has always been one of the serious issues, especially in modern applications. It poses severe security concern to the applications and may pose a life threatening concern. Several such instances of program crash have been observed in popular software such as Hadoop, Eclipse and others. It is very much desirable that a program should be tested for crash well before the deployment. A method has been proposed in this paper using search based algorithm and exception injection in order to test program for crash that may caused mainly due to abnormality of external resources. The proposed method facilitates tester to locate the program location, where any such crash may happen. Moreover, it can protect program from such threats well in advance.

Keywords: Search based technique · Program crash ·
Exception injection · Unhandled exception

1 Introduction

Application crash is a serious concern in any application. It abruptly terminates the application and in worst case may lead to total denial of services for valid users. The application needs to restart in the case of crash, which obviously takes time. If an attacker is able to crash an application the service will suffer from prolonged outage. This will lead to financial, brand image, and other losses [1]. Crashes also provides valuable information to attackers about the system and its internal details. An attacker may try to find the code path from starting to the point where crash happened. This will help them to formulate an attack.

For an instance, recently Facebook has faced worst shutdown and restricted around 135 million people to log-in and the reason was improper error handling [2]. In an another incident of same nature, SQL Server Management Studio was found crashing due to unhandled exceptions [3]. Also a high impact severe bug has been discovered in SAP application server for JAVA that can lead to application crash [4]. Significant cases of program crashes in popular applications such as Hadoop and Eclipse under different releases have been observed.

© Springer Nature Singapore Pte Ltd. 2019
S. Nandi et al. (Eds.): ISEA-ISAP 2018, CCIS 939, pp. 275–285, 2019.
https://doi.org/10.1007/978-981-13-7561-3_20

Application crash happens if the exceptions are not handled properly. Exceptions may be responsible for application crash besides program inconsistency [5,6], resource leakage [7] and information leakage [8]. The exceptions may be raised due to input parameters such as *divide-by-zero-exception* or failures of external resources. These failures may lead to uninitialized object and subsequently calling any member will lead to *Null-pointer-dereference*. This type of vulnerabilities would allow remote attacker to crash the system. One of the special case of external resource failure is intermittent failure of external resources. Application interacts with several external resources in general that may be noisy and unreliable. External resources may exhibit unpredictable and transient failures, which if not handled may lead to sudden application crash. Several cases of program crash due to intermittent and transient failures have been observed in the literature.

Testing of these exceptions need special attention since identification of statements that may raise exceptions and generating those need proper setting. Also path coverage of those exception prone locations and generating sequence or pattern of exceptions to model intermittent failure of external resources show significant challenges due to complex branching conditions. Complete path testing is an essential activity to uncover error prone locations, which are not very feasible by merely running the application with a set of input parameters. Researchers and practitioners propose several techniques for testing the program automatically and to tackle these issues.

Random testing [9–11], symbolic testing [12–15] and Search based testing [16–19] are widely used automatic testing techniques that have shown promising path coverage. Pure Random testing technique does not need internals of programs and are easy to follow but fails to explore search space in a structured way. It may fail to explore important paths (i.e., path to which special cases of input data can lead to an execution) and it may also explore the same program path repeatedly. Now a days researchers are using grammar based random testing to make the technique more affective.

Symbolic testing is a promising technique that thoroughly executes the program symbolically taking into consideration each and every path. This approach automatically detects corner cases, where programmer fails to allocate memory or manipulate buffers, which may lead to security vulnerabilities [15]. Although, a number of security testing methods based on symbolic execution have been proposed in the literature such as [13–15,20] but it also suffers from limitations notably includes dealing with native calls, floating point computations and dealing with complex constraints. These limitations are the noteworthy challenges before research community and several solutions are proposed in this direction [21]. Search based testing has shown exciting result in security testing research. Several methods have been developed using search based testing such as [16–19]. This technique has shown very promising results in solving branching conditions and generating test cases for them. In the presented framework, we use advantage of search based testing to traverse each and every path to execute different pattern of exceptions that are added as aspects.

2   External Resource Abnormality

An application may interact with several external resources. These resources may show unpredictable failure or may fail intermittently. These intermittent failure of resources may generate a pattern of exceptions that may finally lead to program crash. Suppose a program's control graph is given as depicted in the Fig. 1. Each path of this graph may have several external resource call that may return normal or exception control such as *(fcall(),exception/normal)*. Exception pattern graph of a particular path can be depicted as given in Fig. 2, where each node is a call to external resource. We can observe from this exception pattern graph that for a single path several patterns may exist and some of them may crash the program. For example following could be the different patterns:

1. (fcall(),exception),(fcall(),exception),(fcall(),exception)
2. (fcall(),normal),(fcall(),exception),(fcall(),exception)
3. (fcall(),normal),(fcall(),normal),(fcall(),exception)
4. (fcall(),normal),(fcall(),normal),(fcall(),normal)
5. (fcall(),normal),(fcall(),exception),(fcall(),normal), and others

So for an effective testing of program crash, the main task includes generation and execution of the patterns. Testing a program where external resources are participating is not straight forward, one way is to mock the external resources to throw exceptions. Simply covering exceptional edges may not be enough as some failures occur due to specific patterns.

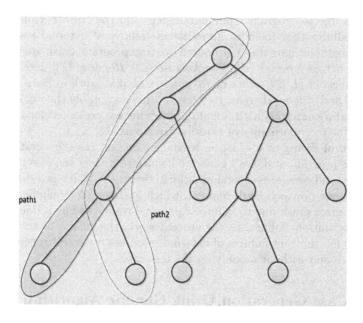

Fig. 1. Program control path

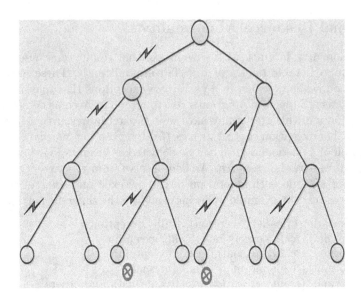

Fig. 2. Exception patterns

3 Related Study

Previous work on testing of program crash can be divided on two broad categories, crash due to program input parameters and the crash because of environmental failures that includes intermittent failures of external resources. A number of methods have been proposed to test program crash due to input parameters such as *jcrasher* [10], *Checkncrash* [22], *Randoop* [23], Exe [13], work of *Bhattacharya et al.* [24], work of *Romano et al.* [25], work of Barr et al. [26], *evosuite* [27] and others. whereas, very few techniques notably the work of Zhang et al. [28] and *Symexc* [21] with certain limitations are presented for testing the exceptions due to abnormality of external resources.

The work of Zhang et al. [28] is dependent on test cases generated by the author of the program, it doesn't generate its own test cases and also it amplifies the test cases and generates several additional test cases, which is a cumbersome task. While, our previous work *Symexc*, which is based on symbolic execution tests the program crash due to failure of external resources but it does not consider the intermittent failure. In the current work, the goal is to test program crash due to intermittent failures of external resources using self generated optimal test cases and without amplifying the test cases.

4 Test Case Generation Using Genetic Algorithm

GA is a meta-heuristic optimizing search based technique. It is widely applied to automate testing task by automatically generating test data according to a test adequacy criterion, known as fitness function. Goal of this technique is to maximize the satisfiability of fitness function through continuous refining of inputs. A good test case obtained through search based testing can expose defects and system vulnerabilities. Figure 3 presents an overview of main tasks of Genetic algorithm. *Initially* random set of inputs are selected and then refined on the basis of *fitness function* until a solution is found or maximum number of iteration is reached. On each iteration a subset of population is *selected* of those that have more chances of generating the final solution. Selected population are paired and *crossed over* with their chromosomes to generate offspring. They are further *mutated* to generate better solutions.

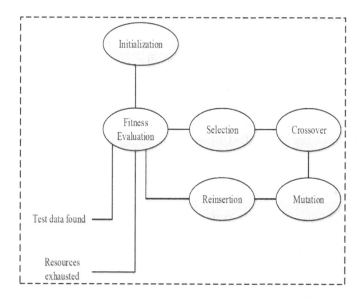

Fig. 3. Main tasks of a Genetic Algorithm

Search based testing specially genetic algorithm is widely applied to test vulnerabilities such as BoF, SQli, XSS and others [16–19]. Among these, Grosso et al. [16] have proposed a method using genetic algorithms, linear programming, and static and dynamic information to detect BoF. Antoniol [17], have examined the possibility of applying search based software testing for detecting the software vulnerabilities such as BoF, SQLi and others. Avancini and Ceccato [18] have proposed genetic algorithm based method to test XSS vulnerability.

Genetic algorithm has also been applied for code coverage [27,29] so that no untested path remain in the program and faults such as unchecked exceptions may be raised in program paths. Evosuite [27] can cover several coverage criterion such as branch, statement, method etc and especially exception coverage criteria. Although it handles undeclared exception effectively but it can not test undeclared exceptions raised due to intermittent failures of external resources such as *RemoteException* or others as discussed in the work of Zhang and Elbaum [30].

5   The Framework

The framework is proposed to test program for security vulnerabilities that arise due to abnormality of external resources. The framework creates dummy environment that can generate pattern of exceptions to represent external resource abnormality. These vulnerabilities may be exploited by the attackers to crash the application.

5.1   Problem Description

A program may interact with several resources, where some of them could be external. These resources may behave abnormal at some moment of time and consequently may throw exceptions, which shows the function is not able to handle a particular situation. Although, these exceptions are generally handled at compile time but due to improper exception handling, program may generate unhandled exceptions. Program should be tested for these type of cases, which are not very efficiently handled in any tool or method. These scenario may abruptly terminate whole application or part of it.

5.2   Architecture

The framework has three main components *exception generator, aspect creator* and *test case generator*. Exception generator generates patterns of exceptions in each program path. Aspect creator creates aspects for generated exceptions and weave these to the program. Test case generator uses genetic algorithm to generate optimal test cases to traverse each and every path. The proposed framework is expected to provide the following benefits for program security:

1. It tests programs for vulnerabilities where merely traversing a program doesn't generate any error. Full path traversing may be applied to hit a particular target.
2. It tests programs for program crash in case of abnormality of external resources. Previous methods concentrate program crash mainly due to input parameters.

The framework depicted in the Fig. 4 works as follow: Firstly, the PUT pass through exception generator to generate set of exceptions in every path that a program may generate due to abnormality of external resources. Secondly, for all possible generated exceptions, aspects are created through aspect generator. These aspects generate actual exceptions at proper location during run time. Next test cases are generated to cover each and every path of the program. PUT with the aspects are executed through test cases to generate patterns of exceptions. At last these patterns are executed to hit those injected exceptions and a log is maintained to store program crash cases.

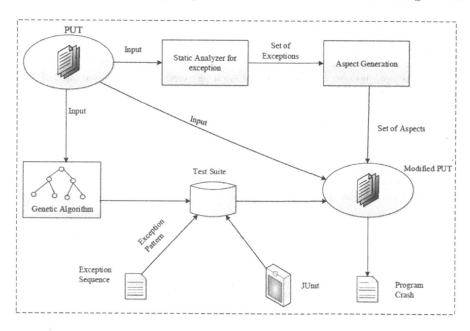

Fig. 4. A Framework for detecting vulnerabilities due to external resource abnormalities

5.3   Algorithm

This section briefly demonstrates Algorithms designed for the framework as given in Algorithm 1. First of all optimal test suits are generated to cover unique paths of the program. This means each test case will cover a unique path in the program. Each test case is used to identify sequence of external functions and their exception patterns in each path. Finally, test cases are executed that invokes the generated exception patterns at each path. Exceptions are invoked using aspects in the program.

5.4   Implementation

Although the framework is implemented using java based platform, it is generic in nature and can be implemented using other OOP languages such as C++. Implementation is based on concept of static exception analysis, aspect oriented programming (AOP) and Genetic Algorithm. The framework is actually hybridization of these important concepts, which are explained below.

– Static exception analysis, statically analyse program for various activities such as to identify set of exceptions the program may throw, whether thrown exceptions can be caught or not etc. Several methods based on static analysis were presented in the literature such as [31–33]. Among these methods, Robillard and Murphy [31] presented a tool that list down all exceptions that

---

Algorithm 1: Testing the abnormality of external resources

Data: Program P

Result: Instances of Program crash

1 Generate optimal test suits T such that each test case covers a unique path of P;

2 **for** *each test case t of T* **do**

3 | Identify external function sequence;

4 | Generate sequence of exceptions SEt;

5 | Generate set of patterns Pt for SEt;

6 **end**

7 **for** *each test case t of T* **do**

8 | **for** *each patter p of Pt* **do**

9 | | Execute test case t;

10 | **end**

11 **end**

---

might throw at different points. *Javadoc*, which is a tool to generate API documentation can also be used to list down all the exceptions a program may generate.

– AOP is a easy to understand and efficient programming technique for modularising concerns that cross cut the basic functionality of programs [34]. It separates these cross cutting concerns such as security, safety, logging and so on into aspects. AOP includes several elements including the following:

  • *Join Points:* It is the point where one can include crosscutting code. The points may be like calling a method, executing a method, executing exception handling and so on.

  • *Point Cut:* It specifies where and when one can add the crosscutting code.

  • *Advice:* It indicates that when we want to execute our code with respect to join points like before, after or around.

– Genetic Algorithm is recognized as one of the most effective testing techniques for uncovering code vulnerabilities. It automatically detects corner faults where programmer generally fails to allocate memory or manipulate buffers, which leads to security loop holes. The framework apply Evosuite [27] to generate optimal test cases of the PUT.

The framework, which is based on above said components is implemented as below:

1. Exception Generation: PUT is statically executed through Javadoc, which is a tool to generate API documentation in HTML format using a structured comments mentioned in source code. This tool finds out all exceptions that a function may throw.

2. Aspects Creation: For all those generated exceptions, aspects are created through Aspectj [35], which is an aspect oriented programming tool for Java. AspectJ Development Tools (ADT) can be easily plugin to the prominent java editor such as eclipse. The framework uses Aspectj to weave generated

exceptions to the program. These aspects are combined with the program so that it becomes part of PUT.

3. Test Case Generator: Test cases for each path are generated using genetic algorithm. Our aim is to generate unique test case for each path. We have applied Evosuite, a GA based testing method to generate test cases for each path. Its special feature is that it generates unique test case for each path.

4. Exception Sequence Generation: The test cases are executed to generate exception sequence at each path. The test cases that do not encounter any exceptions are discarded in this step.

5. Exception Patter Generation: On the basis of exception sequence, exception patterns at each path are generated by systematically switching on and off of exceptions. Suppose a particular path may generates two exceptions, then in this case there would be $2^2 = 4$ patterns.

6. Updated Test Case Execution: Finally, each test case is executed for the exception patterns in a particular path. A single test case handles all the exception patterns in a particular path and program crash instances are logged.

6   Conclusion and Future Work

Application crash abruptly terminates the application and in worst case, it leads to total denial of services for valid users. One of the reason of the crash is abnormality of external resources that is rarely addressed till now. This work has concentrated on testing this abnormal condition using different patterns of exceptions in each path. Each pattern contains sequence of normal and exception return of external function call. The proposed framework is a hybridization of three important concepts namely, static exception analysis, AOP and genetic algorithm. The future work includes validation of the proposed framework on some open source java programs having significant interaction with external resources.

References

1. Anwer, F., Nazir, M., Mustafa, K.: Security testing. In: Mohanty, H., Mohanty, J.R., Balakrishnan, A. (eds.) Trends in Software Testing, pp. 35–66. Springer, Singapore (2017). https://doi.org/10.1007/978-981-10-1415-4_3
2. Facebook crash is 'worst in four years'. http://www.bbc.co.uk/newsbeat/article/11403897/facebook-crash-is-worst-in-four-years. Accessed 05 Jan 2017
3. SQL Server Management Studio 2012/2014 crashes when closing (2013). https://connect.microsoft.com/SQLServer/feedback/details/774317/sql-server-management-studio-2012-2014-crashes-when-closing. Accessed 25 Dec 2016
4. SAP NetWeaver Enqueue Server DoS vulnerability (2015). https://erpscan.com/advisories/erpscan-16-019-sap-netweaver-enqueue-server-dos-vulnerability. Accessed 25 Dec 2016

5. Anwer, F., Nazir, M., Mustafa, K.: Automatic testing of inconsistency caused by improper error handling: a safety and security perspective. In: Proceedings of the 2014 International Conference on Information and Communication Technology for Competitive Strategies, p. 43. ACM (2014)

6. Anwer, F., Nazir, M., Mustafa, K.: Safety and security framework for exception handling in concurrent programming. In: 2013 Third International Conference on Advances in Computing and Communications (ICACC), pp. 308–311. IEEE (2013)

7. Natarajan, M.: Automated source code analysis to identify and remove software security vulnerabilities: case studies on Java programs. Int. J. Softw. Eng. 06(01), 3–32 (2013). http://www.ijse.org.eg/2013.asp?txtLoginUser=&txtLoginPasswd=

8. Siedersleben, J.: Errors and exceptions – rights and obligations. In: Dony, C., Knudsen, J.L., Romanovsky, A., Tripathi, A. (eds.) Advanced Topics in Exception Handling Techniques. LNCS, vol. 4119, pp. 275–287. Springer, Heidelberg (2006). https://doi.org/10.1007/11818502_15

9. Forrester, J.E., Miller, B.P.: An empirical study of the robustness of windows NT applications using random testing. In: Proceedings of the 4th USENIX Windows System Symposium, Seattle, pp. 59–68 (2000)

10. Csallner, C., Smaragdakis, Y.: JCrasher: an automatic robustness tester for Java. Softw.: Pract. Experience 34(11), 1025–1050 (2004)

11. Claessen, K., Hughes, J.: Quickcheck: a lightweight tool for random testing of haskell programs. In: ACM Sigplan Notices, vol. 46, no. 4, pp. 53–64 (2011)

12. Cadar, C., Engler, D.: Execution generated test cases: how to make systems code crash itself. In: Godefroid, P. (ed.) SPIN 2005. LNCS, vol. 3639, pp. 2–23. Springer, Heidelberg (2005). https://doi.org/10.1007/11537328_2

13. Cadar, C., Ganesh, V., Pawlowski, P.M., Dill, D.L., Engler, D.R.: EXE: automatically generating inputs of death. ACM Trans. Inf. Syst. Secur. (TISSEC) 12(2), 10 (2008)

14. Godefroid, P., Klarlund, N., Sen, K.: DART: directed automated random testing. In: ACM Sigplan Notices, vol. 40, no. 6, pp. 213–223. ACM (2005)

15. Godefroid, P., Levin, M.Y., Molnar, D.A., et al.: Automated whitebox fuzz testing. In: NDSS, vol. 8, pp. 151–166 (2008)

16. Grosso, C.D., Antoniol, G., Merlo, E., Galinier, P.: Detecting buffer overflow via automatic test input data generation. Comput. Oper. Res. 35(10), 3125–3143 (2008). http://www.sciencedirect.com/science/article/pii/S0305054807000305. Part Special Issue: Search-based Software Engineering

17. Antoniol, G.: Keynote paper: search based software testing for software security: breaking code to make it safer. In: International Conference on Software Testing, Verification and Validation Workshops, ICSTW 2009, pp. 87–100. IEEE (2009)

18. Avancini, A., Ceccato, M.: Towards security testing with taint analysis and genetic algorithms. In: Proceedings of the 2010 ICSE Workshop on Software Engineering for Secure Systems, pp. 65–71. ACM (2010)

19. Avancini, A., Ceccato, M.: Comparison and integration of genetic algorithms and dynamic symbolic execution for security testing of cross-site scripting vulnerabilities. Inf. Softw. Technol. 55(12), 2209–2222 (2013)

20. Cadar, C., Dunbar, D., Engler, D.R.: KLEE: unassisted and automatic generation of high-coverage tests for complex systems programs. In: OSDI, vol. 8, pp. 209–224 (2008)

21. Anwer, F., Nazir, M., Mustafa, K.: Testing program for security using symbolic execution and exception injection. Indian J. Sci. Technol. 9(19) (2016)

22. Csalner, C., Smaragdakis, Y.: Check'n'crash: combining static checking and testing. In: Proceedings of the 27th International Conference on Software Engineering, pp. 422–431. ACM (2005)
23. Pacheco, C., Ernst, M.D.: Randoop: feedback-directed random testing for Java. In: Companion to the 22nd ACM SIGPLAN Conference on Object-Oriented Programming Systems and Applications Companion, pp. 815–816. ACM (2007)
24. Bhattacharya, N., Sakti, A., Antoniol, G., Guéhéneuc, Y.-G., Pesant, G.: Divide-by-zero exception raising via branch coverage. In: Cohen, M.B., Ó Cinnéide, M. (eds.) SSBSE 2011. LNCS, vol. 6956, pp. 204–218. Springer, Heidelberg (2011). https://doi.org/10.1007/978-3-642-23716-4_19
25. Romano, D., Di Penta, M., Antoniol, G.: An approach for search based testing of null pointer exceptions. In: 2011 IEEE Fourth International Conference on Software Testing, Verification and Validation (ICST), pp. 160–169. IEEE (2011)
26. Barr, E.T., Vo, T., Le, V., Su, Z.: Automatic detection of floating-point exceptions. In: ACM SIGPLAN Notices, vol. 48, no. 1, pp. 549–560 (2013)
27. Fraser, G., Arcuri, A.: 1600 faults in 100 projects: automatically finding faults while achieving high coverage with evosuite. Empirical Softw. Eng. **20**(3), 611–639 (2015)
28. Zhang, P., Elbaum, S.: Amplifying tests to validate exception handling code. In: Proceedings of the 34th International Conference on Software Engineering, pp. 595–605. IEEE Press (2012)
29. Tonella, P.: Evolutionary testing of classes. In: ACM SIGSOFT Software Engineering Notes, vol. 29, no. 4, pp. 119–128. ACM (2004)
30. Zhang, P., Elbaum, S.: Amplifying tests to validate exception handling code: an extended study in the mobile application domain. ACM Trans. Softw. Eng. Methodol. (TOSEM) **23**(4), 32 (2014)
31. Robillard, M.P., Murphy, G.C.: Static analysis to support the evolution of exception structure in object-oriented systems. ACM Trans. Softw. Eng. Methodol. (TOSEM) **12**(2), 191–221 (2003)
32. Fu, C., Ryder, B.G.: Navigating error recovery code in Java applications. In: Proceedings of the 2005 OOPSLA workshop on Eclipse technology eXchange, pp. 40–44. ACM (2005)
33. Wu, X., Xu, Z., Wei, J.: Static detection of bugs caused by incorrect exception handling in Java programs. In: 2011 11th International Conference on Quality Software, pp. 61–66. IEEE (2011)
34. Kiczales, G., Mezini, M.: Aspect-oriented programming and modular reasoning. In: Proceedings of the 27th International Conference on Software Engineering, pp. 49–58. ACM (2005)
35. Laddad, R.: AspectJ in action: enterprise AOP with spring applications. Manning Publications Co., Shelter Island (2009)

Social Network Analytics

Fuzzy String Matching Algorithm for Spam Detection in Twitter

Alok Kumar[1]([✉]), Maninder Singh[2], and Alwyn Roshan Pais[1]

[1] Information Security Research Lab,
Department of Computer Science and Engineering,
National Institute of Technology Karnataka, Surathkal, Karnataka, India
alok_21@outlook.com, alwyn.pais@gmail.com
[2] Department of Computer Science and Engineering, Thapar University,
Patiala, Punjab, India

Abstract. In recent times one of the most popular Internet activity around the world is visiting online social websites. The number of users and time spent by users on these social networks is increasing exponentially. Moreover, users tend to rely on the trustworthiness of data present on these networks. But in wrong hands this trustworthiness can easily be exploited and used to spread spams. Users can easily be harassed by spam messages which waste time and can fool users to click on malicious links. Spam effects many different type of electronic communications including instant messaging, email and social networks. But due to open nature, huge user base and reliance on users for data, social networks are worst hit because of spams. To detect spams from the social networks it is desirable to find new unsupervised techniques which can save the training cost which is required in supervised techniques.

In this article we present an unsupervised, distributed and decentralized technique to detect and remove spams from social networks. We present a new technique which uses fuzzy based method to detect spams, which can detect spams even from a single message stream. To handle huge data in networks, we implement our technique to work on MapReduce platform.

1 Introduction

In the last decade, social networks have become important means of communication where users connect with other users and exchange information. Microblogging platforms like twitter are very popular in recent times, serving more than 335 million monthly active users who send more than 500 million tweets daily [1]. As the social networks like Twitter continue to grow, so will be the problem of spams in these networks. In Twitter, limit on the length of a message (140 characters) has made many spam detection tools less effective [2]. The use of URL shortening further hide the spam links and thus making more difficult for URL blacklisting to catch malicious links [3,4]. Finally, detection of spam has become more complicated because of non-symmetric nature of social links.

© Springer Nature Singapore Pte Ltd. 2019
S. Nandi et al. (Eds.): ISEA-ISAP 2018, CCIS 939, pp. 289–301, 2019.
https://doi.org/10.1007/978-981-13-7561-3_21

Figure 1 show an example of spam messages over twitter. It can be seen in the figure that spam messages include famous hash tags which helps in wide spread of the spam content and whenever any victim searches for same hashtag, s/he can be exposed to the spam messages. Each spam message also include external URL which re-directs the victim to malicious pages. Moreover, spammers also use URL shorteners which helps to hide malicious URL. For reaching out to more users and to maximize the effect, spammers use multiple content-sharing platforms to circulate same malicious content. Spammers target trust based social networks which enable them to connect to novice users who are more likely to read and click on malicious contents. Spams in online social networks spread quickly because of viral and wide distribution of information. A study [5] also tells that the email spams have dropped by half and spammers are now targeting social networks for spreading spams. A survey [6] also estimated that about 67% of users on social networks have been spammed one time or the other.

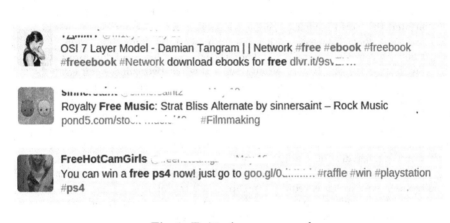

Fig. 1. Twitter's spam example

Successful defending from these spams is need of the hour which can improve the overall experience of users over social networks. Further, it decreases the overall load from the system which is wasted in handling these unwanted contents. But the problem is little knowledge about spammers and techniques adopted by them to spread spams. This is the main reason why till date efficient techniques are not available which can detect and remove spammers and malicious content from the social networks.

In this article, we propose a new technique which automatically scans the messages for the spam content. The technique is based on fuzzy string matching, which can detect spams which are obfuscated by spammers. Usually, spammers tend to alter spam content to bypass the filters, but with the proposed technique these altered spam messages can also be detected. Further, the technique is implemented over MapReduce platform which enables the proposed technique to handle large bulk of messages from the network without creating a bottleneck. Major contributions of the article are–

- A fuzzy string based spam detection technique is proposed which can detect spams using content of messages.
- To handle large networks like twitter, the proposed technique is implemented on MapReduce platform which is first of a kind work.

The remaining article is organized as follows: Sect. 2 provides the related work for schemes proposed for spam and spammers detection. The proposed scheme is presented in Sect. 3. Evaluation of the proposed scheme is provided in Sect. 4. Finally, we conclude our article in Sect. 5.

2 Related Work

Due to world wide problem of spams, many supervised and unsupervised techniques have been proposed in literature to detect spam content and spammers.

Lee et al. [7] deployed honeypots in social networks and used machine learning algorithm to detect spam messages. Benevento et al. [8] gave technique which used the user-based social-network and video-based features to detect spam messages in video social networks. The above two techniques used supervised machine learning techniques which has some inherited drawbacks, when these are applied to large social networks. Further, labeling of training set is required for machine learning algorithms which requires human intervention. Moreover, labeling is needed again and again to maintain the effectiveness of such techniques.

[9–11] are techniques which are based on linked based detections. These all used human based trust relationship for detection of spam messages. Further, such techniques use network graph, where nodes represent the users and links between nodes represents the relationship between any two users. All these techniques assume that social networks are fast mixing, which is not true in each case. More over the detection is based on assumption where each node knows the remaining network.

Perez et al. [12] used the content based and behavioral based algorithms, where on the bases of similarity score, cloned profiles can be identified in social networks. But such techniques cannot detect spams from compromised accounts.

Lin et al. [13] proposed an exact string matching technique which scans each message for spam. Author extracted features from the messages and these features are fed to machine learning algorithm to identify spams. But spammer can easily bypass the technique with minor changes in the spam message content.

Rahman et al. [14] proposed a technique which protects the users from spams. It uses the URL content of messages to detect the spams. Various features are extracted from messages which contain URL, which are then fed to machine learning algorithm to identify spams. The technique fails if the spammer uses URL shortener. Finally, technique can only catch spams which contain URL's.

Our technique in many expects is different from all the above discussed techniques. The proposed technique is an unsupervised one, thus it has no overhead for labeling of training set in machine learning algorithms. Proposed technique is distributed and decentralized and thus there is no need for central data collection. Thus, do not create bottleneck for the network. The proposed technique uses fuzzy based method to detect spams, thus it can catch normal as well as altered spam messages. Finally, the proposed technique is implemented over MapReduce platform thus can handle large networks easily without becoming bottleneck.

3   Approach

In this section, we present the proposed technique. Work flow for the proposed technique is given in Fig. 2. The proposed scheme has two main modules, *feature extraction* where features (lexical and status) are extracted from messages. Next module is *fuzzy string matching*, which facilitates us to perform approximate string matching. Further, to incorporate large data sets, the *fuzzy string matching* module is implemented over MapReduce platform. Each module is discussed separately in next subsections. Prior to that we provide the problem classification.

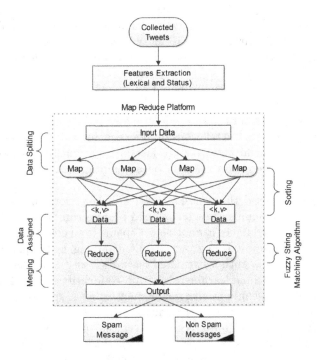

Fig. 2. Work flow

3.1   Problem Classification

The spam detection can be treated as a binary classification problem where either a message is spam or is genuine. Each spam message is assigned a positive value '1' and a non-spam message is assigned a value '0'.

3.2   Features Extraction

To detect spams from the message stream, content features are extracted from the messages. Content features include the status and lexical features. Status features include the Length of message, presence of URL and presence of hot topics. The spam message are generally large in length, contains a URL to mislead the victim and include hot topic to increase the presence over the network. Thus, scanning for these features helps in filtering of the spam messages. Lexical features include the breaking of the messages into unigram, bigram, trigram tokens which excludes all the punctuations and any meaningless words.

3.3   Fuzzy String Matching Algorithm over MapReduce Platform

The features extracted from the previous module are then fed to fuzzy string matching algorithm. Fuzzy string matching algorithm is inspired from the work of Grier et al. [3]. They presented a first in-depth analysis of spam on twitter and further analyzed click-through rate for spams on twitter. They identified the diversity of spam messages and found that all the spam messages contain words like free eBooks, music, games, books, downloads, etc. Table 1 shows the findings of Grier et al. with the percentage of spam content in the spam messages. But in their work they did not provide any methods to filter spam messages. Taking this as ground reality for our proposed technique, fuzzy string based algorithm is designed which detects these words in the tokens of messages. For the same, a small dictionary of spam words is created and this is compared with tokens of the message to find whether a message is spam or not.

Twitter is a very large online social network which accumulates around 6000 tweets per second, which add up to around 350,000 per minutes [15]. If this huge number of messages is fed to a simple fuzzy string algorithm running on a single machine, this will result in a bottleneck and a normal system will not be able to handle such large load. To improve the efficiency, to distribute the load, to handle large number of messages, to decrease the response rate, and to improve detection rate we implemented our algorithm code with *Map Reduce*.

MapReduce [16] is a model (programming) for processing big data sets with distributed and parallel algorithms running on a cluster. Usually, MapReduce consists of two sub modules namely, mapper and reducer. *Mapper* performs the initial data processing, where it splits the input, then it scrambles and sort it. The sorted data is then fed to the *Reducers*, which do further processing of the data and produces output. Such model can be thought of as a specialization of *split − apply − combine* strategy [17] for data processing. MapReduce facilitates distributed and parallel processing of mapping and reducing operations, provided

Table 1. Percentage of spam content [10]

Category	Fraction of spams
Free music, Games, Books, Downloads	29.82%
Jewelery, Electronics, Vehicles	22.22%
Contest, Gambling, Prizes	15.72%
Finance, Loans, Reality	13.07%
Increase Twitter following	11.18%
Diet	3.10%
Adult	2.83%
Charity, Donation scams	1.65%
Pharmaceuticals	0.27%
Anti virus	0.14%

the mapping and reducing operation are independent. The number of mapper and reducer can vary according to need. There can be either one mapper and one reducer which represents implementation of MapReduce over single machine which is generally known as *Single Node MapReduce*, or we can have multiple mappers and reducers which shows MapReduce implementation over multiple machine which is generally known as *Multi Node MapReduce*. So depending on the need, nodes (slaves) can be varied in MapReduce implementation.

In our case, the dataset includes messages from twitter, where all messages are independent. Further, as discussed earlier, the size of data handled by twitter is also huge. Thus, MapReduce is a viable option for our technique, where multiple mappers and reducers can work in parallel to identify spams from the messages. The main two modules of the MapReduce, *Mapper* and *Reducer* are discussed in details below -

Mapper- As the name suggests, mapper maps the input for the reducer. Mapper reads the input files and splits the input uniformly and writes this data over temporary storage. This temporary data is scattered uniformly and is sorted. Then, the sorted input is fed to the reducer. Algorithm 1 presents the mapper algorithm which helps in the preliminary filtering of spam messages. Here the messages are scanned for URL and if they have URL and are greater than a threshold length, they are affixed a value '0' else they are discarded. All the messages with affixed '0' are sorted and they are then fed to the reducer.

Reducer- As the name suggests, reducer reduces the input fed by mapper and gives the output. It is the place where the actual processing is done and here the fuzzy string matching algorithm is implemented. The output from all the reducers is merged to give the final output. Algorithm 2 presents the reducer algorithm which is applied to each message one at a time. Firstly punctuations are removed from the tweet message and the message is converted into token. These set of tokens are compared with the spam word dictionary using the fuzzy

---

Algorithm 1. Mapper Algo

    Input   : Twitter messages Msg, i = 1,2,3,...n, Length threshold Len
    Output: Msg1:0, Msg2:0, Msg3:0,...
1 Initialization;
2 **for** *all i* **do**
3 | **if** *Msg contains url and length(Msg) > Len* **then**
4 | | Return msg : 0
5 | **else**
6 | | Return NULL
7 | **end**
8 **end**

Algorithm 2. Reducer Algo

    Input   : Msg1:0,Msg2:0,Msg3:0,...¿, Array of spam words Spam[n], variable x=0
    Output: Msg1:0 or Msg1:1, Msg2:0 or Msg2:1, Msg3:0 or Msg3:1,...
1 Initialization;
2 **for** *all msg* **do**
3 | msg $\leftarrow$ lowercase(msg)
4 | Words[] $\leftarrow$ split(Msg)
5 | **for** *all Words[]* **do**
6 | | **for** *all Spam[]* **do**
7 | | | **if** *fuzzy_matching(Words[],Spam[]==True)* **then**
8 | | | | x=1
9 | | | **end**
10 | | **end**
11 | **end**
12 | **if** *x == 1* **then**
13 | | Return msg:1
14 | **else**
15 | | Return msg:0
16 | **end**
17 **end**

---

string matching algorithm. If there is a match the message is spam and the affixed value '0' of the message is changed to '1', else if there is no match the affixed value remain unchanged. The output of all the reducers is merged together to get the final output where all the spam messages have affixed value '1' and all the non-spam messages have affixed value '0'.

4 Evaluation

In this section, we identify how effective the proposed technique is in catching spams from the message stream. For the same, we initially decide the metrics. Then we create the required dataset. Finally, we test the proposed scheme against the dataset to test its efficiency.

4.1 Metrics

For evaluation of the proposed technique, we find the accuracy, true positive, false positive rate (FP), true negative and false negative rate (FN). Table 2 shows the confusion matrix, where a represents the number of spam messages which are classified correctly, *b* represents the spam messages which are not caught by the proposed technique, *c* represents the number of non-spam messages which are misclassified as spam messages and *d* represent the number of non-spam messages classified correctly. The accuracy is the fraction of correct classification which is $(a + d)/(a + b + c + d)$. FP is denoted by $c/(c + d)$ and FN is denoted by $b/(a + b)$. The effectiveness of the spam detection can be evaluated by finding the total spam detected and comparing with total spam present in the dataset.

Table 2. Confusion matrix

		Predicted	
		Spam	Non spam
Actual	Spam	a	b
	Non spam	c	d

4.2 Machine Setup

We implement the proposed technique on the machine with Core - i7 processor, with 12 GB ram (master) and 6 GB ram (slaves). The operating system used was Ubuntu 14.04, JDK version used was 1.8.0_45 and the hadoop version was 1.2.1 (Table 3). Master machine running applications - NameNode, TaskTracker, DataNode, Jobtracker, Secondary-NameNode. Slave machines running applications - DataNode and TaskTracker.

Table 3. Machine details

Processor	Intel core 3rd generation i7-3770S processor
Ram (Master/Slave)	(12 GB/6 GB) DDR3 1600 MHz
Operating system	Ubuntu 14.04
Java JDK	JDK 1.8.0_45
Hadoop	1.2.1

4.3 Dataset

The dataset is created using the Twitter stream during May'18 with the help of Twitter API which is used for getting the tweet messages from the twitter. The messages with out a URL are filtered out and all non-English tweet are also removed from them as the proposed technique is based on English language only. This leaves us with 31,000 messages which have both spam and non-spam messages.

Dataset Ground Truth- The dataset is fed directly to exact string matching technique to find the existing spams in the dataset and the technique filtered

1829 spam messages. Same dataset was also fed to fuzzy based string matching technique to find any existing altered spam in the dataset but no such spam message was found and thus the dataset of 31,000 tweets have 1829 spam messages and no altered spam (Table 4). Additional 5000 alter spams are added to the dataset which include known number of one alphabet, two alphabets and three alphabets altered spams. Finally the dataset have 36,000 tweets in total with 1829 non altered spams and 5000 altered spams.

Table 4. Dataset

Total messages	Spam messages	Non-spam messages
31,000	1829	29171

4.4   Performance Measure

Initially the proposed technique was setup without MapReduce over a single machine and the fuzzy based matching was set to catch spams with similarity of (.80). The above setup identified 4205 spam messages which includes the spam messages with no alteration and spam messages with 1 alphabet alteration and some false positive and false negative (Table 5).

Table 5. Results of the proposed technique

Fuzzy string matching variation	Total messages	Total spams	Spam detected	False positive	False negative
Similarity (0.80)	36000	6829	4205	374	2998
Similarity (0.70)	36000	6829	5903	558	1484

To further improve the detection rate, the fuzzy based technique was set to catch spams with similarity of (.70) which identified 5903 spams. This significantly improved the detection of spam messages, as now the technique was able to catch spam messages with no alteration, 1 alphabet alteration and 2 alphabets alteration, but this also increased the false positive rate (Table 5). But still the updated setup was not able to catch the 3 alphabets altered spams. If we further try to improve the detection rate by reducing the similarity, it exponentially increased the false positive rate of the technique. Thus we limit our experimental results only till (.07) similarity in fuzzy string matching. The accuracy for the proposed scheme when the similarity is set to (.80) is 90.6% which increases to 94.3% when the similarity is lowered to (.70). The FP and FN for the similarity (0.80) is 0.12 and 0.439 respectively. Whereas, FP and FN for the similarity (.70) is 0.19 and 0.217 respectively. It can be observed that when we tried to decrease the false negative rate, the false positive rate increased. The variation of True positive and False positive can be seen in Fig. 3 and in figure we can see that the value of True positive increase significantly when we decreased the similarity to (.70).

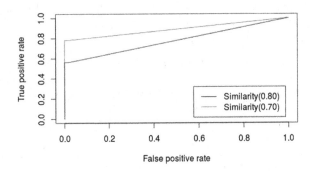

Fig. 3. True positive vs false positive

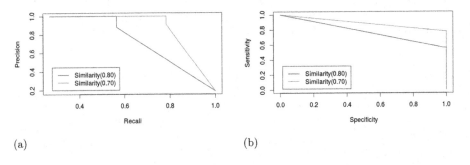

(a)   (b)

Fig. 4. Graphical results for the proposed scheme (a) precision vs recall, (b) sensitivity vs specificity.

Figure 4(a) shows the result of precision and recall for the proposed technique. It shows the results for both the variations and it can be observed that the technique achieves high recall and precision when similarity is set to (.70).

The Fig. 4(b) shows the sensitivity and specificity variation for the proposed technique and it can be seen in the figure that similarity (0.70) outperforms similarity (0.80). It can be noted that the value of sensitivity increases for the same specificity when we lower the similarity to (.70).

Now the proposed technique is migrated to be implemented on MapReduce. Table 6 shows the results of running the proposed technique with increasing the number of nodes (slaves). The original dataset used in previous evaluation is very small, to see the advantages of the MapReduce, multiple instances of same dataset is used which can mimic a large dataset. Here x10 means that 10

Table 6. MapReduce and dataset variation results

Nodes ↓ /Dataset →	x10	x20	x30	x40	x50	x100	x150	x200	x250	x300	x350	x400	x450
Master	**0:14**	0:24	0:32	0:36	0:43	1:18	1:44	2:29	2:54	3:33	4:03	4:40	5:22
Master + 1Node	0:16	**0:19**	**0:21**	**0:24**	**0:28**	1:05	1:11	1:53	1:57	2:35	2:45	3:05	3:35
Master + 2Node	0:17	0:20	0:23	0:27	0:31	**0:49**	**1:07**	**1:27**	**1:45**	2:25	2:45	3:01	3:27
Master + 3Node	0:18	0:20	0:25	0:27	0:31	0:53	1:11	1:32	2:00	**2:21**	2:40	3:01	3:28
Master + 4Node	0:18	0:21	0:26	0:30	0:36	0:54	1:13	1:34	2:03	2:24	2:39	3:03	3:31
Master + 5Node	0:18	0:21	0:25	0:27	0:35	0:56	1:15	1:36	2:00	2:23	**2:36**	**2:56**	**3:24**
Master + 6Node	0:19	0:21	0:26	0:30	0:34	0:56	1:15	1:37	2:01	2:25	2:47	3:04	3:34
Master + 7Node	0:19	0:22	0:26	0:30	0:34	0:55	1:16	1:37	2:03	2:25	2:45	3:05	3:33

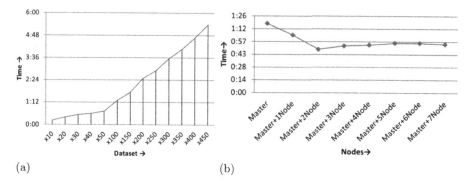

(a)   (b)

Fig. 5. Graphical results for MapReduce setup of the proposed scheme (a) MapReduce time vs dataset variation results, (b) MapReduce time vs nodes (slaves) variation results for a 100x dataset.

instances of same dataset are fed to the technique and so on. In the Table 6 we can see that if we increase the size of dataset the time increases linearly which is very much needed, if we want to handle large databases.

In Fig. 5(a) we can see the linear growth of time when we increase the dataset in case of master with 0 nodes (slaves), Same nature is also shown by all the other variations too. The time required by the proposed technique also decreases significantly if the number of nodes (slaves) are increased, as same work can be parallely divided onto many machine. But it can be seen that after this decreasing time phase the time required tend to increase again as overhead of dividing the same work to more machines increases and thus the time required also increases (Fig. 5(b)).

Various finding of running the technique over MapReduce platform, varying the nodes (slaves) and dataset are-

- If the size of dataset increases, the time required for a MapReduce variation to run the technique also increases linearly.
- If the number of nodes (slaves) is increased, the time required to handle the same dataset decreases significantly.
- But if we further increase the nodes (slaves), the time required tend to increase because of increased overhead to handle more machines for same piece of work.

– Many times it is also observed that the time required for a variation tend to fluctuate enormously, main reason for such fluctuation can be ir-responsive node (slave) or if node (slave) cannot reply in fixed time or if the data is lost over the network. In such scenarios, master cannot obtain results on time and Master either returns an error or processes the work on its own. Either of the cases results in extra time for processing same data, resulting in abnormal fluctuations in some rare cases.

5   Conclusion and Future Scope

The proposed article discusses the problem of spams in online social networks like twitter and how spammers can evade the existing techniques by just simple obfuscation of spam content. We proposed a new technique which is based on fuzzy string matching which can even catch the obfuscated spams and more importantly spams from the compromised accounts. As the majority of spams originate from compromised accounts, the technique proposed is a major breakthrough for spam catching in online social networks. The technique uses MapReduce platform for implementation, which enables the technique to handle large datasets easily without becoming a bottleneck for the network. The FP and FN for the technique was very low and the variation in number of the nodes (slaves) also showed that the time required to handle a dataset also decrease when we increase the number of nodes (slaves).

As future work, the technique can be altered to use machine learning at place of using static dictionary for catching spams. Moreover, the technique can also be implemented using GPU which can speed up the process and further improve the efficiency of the technique.

References

1. Twitter: number of monthly active users 2010–2018, August 2018. https://www.statista.com/statistics/282087/number-of-monthly-active-twitter-users/
2. Gao, H., Chen, Y., Lee, K., Palsetia, D., Choudhary, A.N.: Towards online spam filtering in social networks. In: NDSS (2012)
3. Grier, C., Thomas, K., Paxson, V., Zhang, M.: @ spam: the underground on 140 characters or less. In: Proceedings of the 17th ACM Conference on Computer and Communications Security, pp. 27–37. ACM (2010)
4. Thomas, K., Grier, C., Song, D., Paxson, V.: Suspended accounts in retrospect: an analysis of twitter spam. In: Proceedings of the 2011 ACM SIGCOMM Conference on Internet Measurement Conference, pp. 243–258. ACM (2011)
5. Barracuda labs 2010 annual security report. http://www.barracudalabs.com/research%5Fresources.html
6. http://nakedsecurity.sophos.com/2011/01/19/sophos-security-threat/-report-2011-social-networking/
7. Lee, K., Caverlee, J., Webb, S.: Uncovering social spammers: social honeypots+ machine learning. In: Proceedings of the 33rd International ACM SIGIR Conference on Research and Development in Information Retrieval, pp. 435–442. ACM (2010)

8. Benevenuto, F., Rodrigues, T., Almeida, V., Almeida, J., Gonçalves, M.: Detecting spammers and content promoters in online video social networks. In: Proceedings of the 32nd International ACM SIGIR Conference on Research and Development in Information Retrieval, pp. 620–627. ACM (2009)

9. Yu, H., Kaminsky, M., Gibbons, P.B., Flaxman, A.: Sybilguard: defending against sybil attacks via social networks. In: ACM SIGCOMM Computer Communication Review, vol. 36, pp. 267–278. ACM (2006)

10. Yu, H., Gibbons, P.B., Kaminsky, M., Xiao, F.: Sybillimit: a near-optimal social network defense against sybil attacks. In: IEEE Symposium on Security and Privacy, SP 2008, pp. 3–17. IEEE (2008)

11. Danezis, G., Mittal, P.: Sybilinfer: detecting sybil nodes using social networks. In: NDSS (2009)

12. Perez, C., Birregah, B., Layton, R., Lemercier, M., Watters, P.: REPLOT: retrieving profile links on twitter for suspicious networks detection. In: 2013 IEEE/ACM International Conference on Advances in Social Networks Analysis and Mining (ASONAM), pp. 1307–1314. IEEE (2013)

13. Liu, L., Jia, K.: Detecting spam in chinese microblogs-a study on sina weibo. In: 2012 Eighth International Conference on Computational Intelligence and Security (CIS), pp. 578–581. IEEE (2012)

14. Rahman, M.S., Huang, T.K., Madhyastha, H.V., Faloutsos, M.: Efficient and scalable socware detection in online social networks. In: USENIX Security Symposium, pp. 663–678 (2012)

15. Twitter usage statistics (2018). http://www.internetlivestats.com/twitter-statistics/

16. Dean, J., Ghemawat, S.: MapReduce: simplified data processing on large clusters. Commun. ACM **51**(1), 107–113 (2008)

17. Wickham, H., et al.: The split-apply-combine strategy for data analysis. J. Stat. Softw. **40**(1), 1–29 (2011)

Author Index

Printed in the United States
By Bookmasters